Month-By-Month
GARDENING
IN
MINNESOTA

Month-By-Month GARDENING *IN* MINNESOTA

Melinda Myers

edited by Chuck Levine

COOL
SPRINGS
PRESS

Nashville, Tennessee

Dedication

I dedicate this book to all the northern gardeners who have so generously shared their insights and innovations for gardening in the always challenging northern garden environment.
—Melinda Myers

I dedicate my portion of this book to my wife Tarri and my children Rachel, Jacob, and Noah who have allowed me the time to be the gardener I want to be. To my parents, Sherwin and Gloria for encouraging me to be whatever I wanted to be; to the folks at the Minnesota State Horticultural Society who have given me this opportunity; and lastly to the many students, teachers and friends who have inspired me.
—Chuck Levine

Acknowledgments

Thanks to Marjee Righeimer and the Minnesota State Horticulture Society for their enthusiastic cooperation in this endeavor. I look forward to a long and productive partnership with all the Northern Gardeners. I also want to thank the University of Wisconsin and Minnesota Extension specialists, staff and master gardeners, botanical garden and arboretum staff throughout the upper midwest, horticulture professionals (you know who you are), teaching colleagues, various plant society members, avid gardeners, and friends in the media for your enthusiasm and wealth of knowledge. A special thanks to my family and friends for their patience and tolerance during the process. My daughter Nevada, who keeps me focused on what is important in life despite looming deadlines; and husband Wes, for tolerating the process that consumed every surface in our home. Thanks to my friends for fueling me with food, enthusiasm, faith, and laughter throughout the long year. And finally, a special thanks to all my friends at Cool Springs Press. Angela, my editor, found the way to get and keep me moving when the process seemed overwhelming. Cindy, my fellow northerner, kept me motivated, laughing, and out of trouble. And Roger, thanks for believing in me.
—Melinda Myers

Copyright © 2001 Melinda Myers

Myers, Melinda.
    [Month-by-month gardening in Minnesota]
    Minnesota horticultural society's month-by-month gardening in Minnesota / Melinda Myers ; edited by Chuck Levine.
        p. cm.
    Includes bibliographical references (p.   ).
    ISBN 1-888608-96-X (paperback. : alk. paper)
    1. Gardening--Minnesota.   I. Title: Month-by-month gardening in Minnesota. II. Levine, Chuck.   III. Title.
SB453.2.M6 M94 2001
635.9'51776--dc21

                                       2001004055

Published by Cool Springs Press,
a division of Thomas Nelson, Inc.,
P.O. Box 141000, Nashville, Tennessee 37214.
www.ThomasNelson.com

First printing 2001

Printed in the United States of America
10 9 8 7 6 5 4 3 2 1

Horticultural Nomenclature Editor: Lee Hansen
Cover photo by: Alan and Linda Detrick
        (©1998 Alan and Linda Detrick)

Contents

Contents

Benefits of Gardening Month by Month

Whether you are hoping for a big harvest, a beautiful landscape, or a little stress relief, knowing the when and how of gardening will help you be a success. Use this book to eliminate some of the guesswork. It is a guide to help, not restrict, your gardening efforts and experimentation.

1 Make a landscape plan. Put your gardening and landscape plans on paper to help you grow and develop a beautiful landscape and productive garden. And don't worry—a landscape plan is meant to change, not remain stagnant, over time. Make needed and desired changes along the way to achieve your landscaping goals.

2 Start or continue a garden journal. It can be as simple as a spiral notebook, as complex as a computer spreadsheet, or as fancy as a beautiful journal with advice, pictures, and inspirational quotes. Use this to record planting information, growing records, and pest management strategies.

Refer to your garden plan, journal information, and this book to help you get the most enjoyment from your Minnesota garden. These tools can help you repeat successes and avoid making the same mistakes.

3 Refer to *Month-By-Month Gardening in Minnesota* throughout the year. Each chapter features a different group of plants and the care needed to grow them in Minnesota. Check out the monthly entries for guidance on the time to plant, water, prune, fertilize, and manage pests. These are general guidelines to use as a starting point.

4 Consult with local experts—I always do—to fine-tune these recommendations to fit your backyard growing conditions and gardening style.

GARDENING IN MINNESOTA

I have been lucky enough to call the northland my home for over 20 years. In that time, there have been no two years or growing seasons exactly the same. This is part of the challenge and fun of northern gardening. The changing seasons and changeable weather put you and your gardening skills to the test each year.

Weather Conditions

Northern gardeners have the extreme cold and shorter season to make their gardening a challenge. And all of us face untimely snowstorms, flooding, and drought.

Benefits of Gardening Month by Month

Wherever you live, select the hardiest plant available. Locate your community on the hardiness map. These ratings reflect the plant's ability to survive the average minimum winter temperature. Select plants rated for this or colder (lower number) climates. Remember, hardiness is just a cold-tolerance rating. You must also match the plant to the growing conditions. Increase the chance of survival by providing the proper growing conditions and care. A healthy plant has a better chance of surviving normal and unexpected weather extremes.

Use the average frost dates to help with planting dates. The maps give you the average dates for the last spring frosts and first fall frosts in Minnesota. These averages are based on a hundred years of data. This does not take into account the late spring and early fall frosts that commonly fall outside these dates.

Consider the air and soil temperatures when planting. Areas near Lake Superior are frost-free earlier, but the soil and air stay cooler later into spring and early summer. Planting too soon can delay growth and harvest. Wait to plant tropical plants, such as **Tuberous Begonias** and **Tomatoes**, until after all danger of frost has past and both the air (day and night) and soil temperatures have warmed. **Pansies**, **Lettuce**, and dormant perennials can be moved outdoors almost as soon as the snow melts and the soil is workable.

Use the weather information, the month-by-month planting guides, and your own experience to time planting and care.

Soil Conditions

Soil, like the weather, presents challenges to gardeners. The southeastern part of the state has limestone bedrock. The western part of the state has soils that developed from limestone rocks. This results in alkaline (high pH) soils that can make it difficult to grow **Rhododendron**, **Blueberries**, and other acid-loving plants. The northeastern part of Minnesota has granite and bedrock. This results in acid soils that make it difficult to grow many silver-leafed plants such as **Lavender** and **Dianthus** that prefer more alkaline soils.

It is difficult to change the soil pH and takes years to repair the damage caused by misapplication of lime (makes soil more alkaline) and other pH altering materials. Test your soil and follow the recommendations whenever you attemp to change the soil pH.

Minnesota soils are of two basic types: forest and prairie. Glacially deposited ten to twenty thousand years ago, soil particle size ranges from silt to gravel with boulders scattered throughout. The agriculturally rich prairie soil is found in the Red River Valley of south central Minnesota with forest soils dominant in the north and isolated pockets throughout the entire state. These soils support the deciduous and coniferous forests of Minnesota.

Most urban sites have poor soil due to construction, excavation of topsoil, and years of misuses. Proper preparation and care of all these soils will help improve your gardening results. Adjust watering and fertilization to fit the soil and plant requirements.

Planning and Improving Your Minnesota Garden

An attractive, healthy landscape starts with a plan. Draw a base map of your existing landscape. Locate the house, trees, shrubs, gardens, and other elements on the plan. Use this as a basis to make future additions, deletions, and changes to your landscape.

Gather ideas from friends, neighbors, and professionals. Take a walk through a nearby botanical garden, participate in a garden tour, or visit a home and garden show for ideas and inspiration.

Benefits of Gardening Month by Month

Use trees as the long-term framework of your landscape. They provide structure, screen views, shade the house, and add year-round beauty. Place large shade trees on the east and west side of the house. They will shade the windows from the summer sun and reduce cooling costs. Avoid growing large shade trees on the south side of your home. They will block the winter sun, reduce solar heating, and increase winter fuel costs. Include shrubs to screen views, highlight focal points, and attract wildlife. Look for hardy plants with attractive bark, colorful flowers, and bird-attracting fruit for winter interest. Select plants that fit the available growing space. Keeping a 10-foot shrub down to 3 feet is a lot of work and hard on the plant.

Include flowers, vines, and groundcovers for splashes of color, focal points, and wildlife attraction. They can be planted in beds, grown in containers, or mixed with your trees and shrubs. Use them as short-term accents or long-term additions to your plan.

Take your time. Part of the joy of gardening is watching your efforts over time. I believe that a landscape is always a work in progress for most gardeners. Take pictures and videotape your progress. It will be fun and helpful to see where your landscape started and the changes you have made along the way.

Stuck or overwhelmed? Consider hiring a professional for some help. Some of the best landscapes I find come from a cooperative effort between a landscape designer and an avid gardener. The designer can give you guidance on plant and bed placement. They may be able to save you some time and money by helping you avoid some mistakes. Take advantage of their expertise and combine it with your desire to get the most from your landscape.

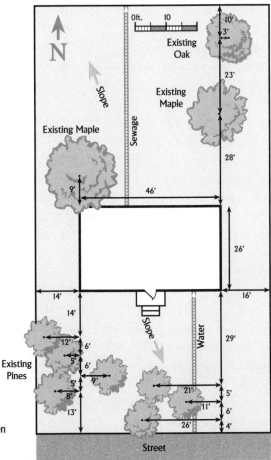

Base Layout Map of Garden

General Horticultural Practices

Soil Preparation

Soil is the foundation of your gardening success. Time and effort spent preparing and managing your soil will be rewarded with years of gardening success.

Start with a soil test to find out what your soil has and needs. The results will help you determine how much and what type of fertilizer to add for the plants you are growing. Contact your local University of Minnesota Extension Service for soil test information.

Take a soil test anytime the ground is not frozen and has not been recently fertilized. Collect separate samples for each gardening area. You will want one report for the lawn areas, a separate one for flowers, and so on. Start with new areas and those experiencing problems. Stagger testing to spread out the cost and time involved.

Remove 4- to 6-inch-long plugs of soil from five or more scattered spots within the garden you are testing. Mix these together to create a representative sample of the garden soil. Send 1 cup of soil to the University of Minnesota Extension Service or other state certified soil testing lab. Allow two weeks for the results.

Incorporate the recommended fertilizer and organic matter at the rate and time recommended on the soil test report. See each chapter for fertilizer information on the specific type of plant you are growing. Like water, too much or not enough fertilizer can influence the health and vigor of your plants. Over-fertilizing, fertilizing at the wrong time, or using the wrong product can injure plants, harm the environment, and waste time and money.

Add compost, well-rotted manure, or peat moss into the soil. Organic matter is an amazing additive that improves drainage in clay soils and the water-holding capacity in sandy soils. Incorporate a 2- to 4-inch layer into the top 6 to 12 inches of the garden soil.

Do not add sand unless you are prepared to truck it in by the semi. You must add 1 inch of sand for every 1 inch of soil you plan to amend. This is a large expense and a lot of work. Adding less than this will give you concrete, not a well-drained soil.

Work the soil when it is moist, but not wet. Grab a handful of soil and gently squeeze it into a ball. Tap the ball with your finger. If it breaks into smaller pieces, it is ready to work. Otherwise, go back inside and wait for the soil to dry. Patience now will eliminate clods, cracking, and the frustration caused by dealing with damaged soil.

Planting

Proper planting is important to establishing a healthy, long-lived plant. There is more to it than making sure the green side points up. Preparing the site, digging the hole, and planting at the proper depth and time will increase your transplanting and gardening success. Follow the planting guidelines in each chapter to learn how and when to plant trees, shrubs, flowers, and all the other plants in your landscape.

Watering

Summer droughts and spring floods remind us of the value of water and watering properly. The garden hose can be a great help or a detriment to landscape plants. Consider the plant, soils, and weather when watering the landscape. Each chapter focuses on watering needs and strategies for that group of plants throughout the year. Use these guidelines to help conserve our valuable resource and reduce the risk of over- and under-watering our plants.

Adjust watering to fit the weather, soil, and plant. Water more frequently during the hot, dry days of July and August. Decrease watering during the cool days of spring and summer. And always consider rainfall when calculating water needs. Nature often provides regular—sometimes too regular—irrigation for our planting.

Water gardens growing in clay soil thoroughly but less frequently than those growing in sandy and rock soils. Clay soil holds the moisture longer. Wait until the top few inches start to dry, about every seven to ten days, before watering again. Water thoroughly, wetting the total root zone. Apply needed water to sandy soils in two applications. Water thoroughly so that the root zone is moist. Wait three to five days and water again if the top few inches have begun to dry.

New plants need more frequent watering to get established. Check them several times a week, and water often enough to keep their roots moist. Gradually decrease watering frequency to encourage deep, drought-tolerant roots. Give established plants a helping hand during extended dry periods. Their extensive root system allows them to find and use water from a large area for most of the season. Help maintain growth, improve productivity, and minimize pest problems through proper watering.

Water plants early in the morning to reduce the risk of disease and foliar burn. Keeping leaves dry at night helps prevent the development and spread of fungal leaf spots and blight. Allowing leaves to dry before the heat of midday reduces water lost to evaporation and damage caused by the bright sun shining on wet leaves.

Use shredded leaves, cocoa bean shells, and woodchips as a mulch to reduce watering needs. A thin layer of these materials over the soil surface will conserve moisture, reduce weeds, and gradually improve the soil.

Fertilization

A trip to the garden center and down the fertilizer aisle can be very overwhelming. There seems to be a bag and formulation for every plant you can imagine. It is difficult to decide which product is best for your garden situation.

Start by reading the front label. Look at the three numbers on the bag. These represent the amount of nitrogen, phosphorus, and potas-sium in the fertilizer. The first number on the left is nitrogen. It is essential to plant growth and is used to grow leaves and stems. The middle number is the percentage of phosphorus in the fertilizer. This nutrient encourages root, flower, and fruit development. The last of the three numbers is the percentage of potassium. Plants use this to help fight disease and increase hardiness.

Most soils have high to excessive levels of phosphorus and potassium. Avoid complete fertilizers, such as 10-10-10, and those with high percentages of phosphorus and potassium. Adding more can interfere with the uptake of other essential nutrients and pollute our groundwater.

Select the fertilizer formulation recommended by your soil test. Or check the fertilizer recommendations in each chapter for the plant you are trying to grow. These are based on general plant needs for Minnesota.

Now decide on liquid or dry fertilizers. Liquid fertilizers can be applied with a sprinkling can, garden hose, or spray tank. Dry fertilizers are spread on the soil surface. Apply dry fertilizers to the soil using a small shaker, hand-held spreader, or push-type spreader.

Look for the words *slow-release* or *fast-release* on the bag. Use slow-release fertilizers to provide a

General Horticultural Practices

constant supply of nutrients over a long period of time. Try fast-release fertilizers when you want a quick fix. These need to be applied several times throughout the garden season.

Choose between an organic or inorganic form of fertilizer. Inorganic fertilizers come in a variety of formulations and are in a form ready for the plants to use. Use organic fertilizers to improve the soil, while providing small amounts of nutrients over a long period of time.

Select the fertilizer that best suits the plants, soil, and your gardening style. Use the fertilizer recommended by your soil test report. Or try a low-nitrogen, slow-release fertilizer to reduce the risk of burn and overfertilization.

Composting

Make your own organic matter (compost) by recycling all your pest-free plant debris. It is as simple as putting it into a heap and letting it rot. The more effort you put into the process, the sooner you get compost.

Start with green debris. Shred fallen leaves, add herbicide-free grass clippings, and include other plant debris. Do not add meat and animal products that can attract rodents. Do add soil and enough water to moisten the pile. Make it at least 3 feet tall and wide for quicker results.

Turn the pile occasionally to speed up decomposition.

Start a holding pile. Use the second pile to store plant debris until you have enough to make a new pile. The first pile will decompose faster if fresh materials are not continually being added.

Use finished compost to amend new and existing gardens. Try mixing it with topsoil to create a well-drained potting mix for container gardens. Or topdress, by spreading a thin layer of compost over the soil surface in lawns, perennial gardens, and groundcover plantings.

Pruning

Keep your plants healthy and attractive with proper pruning. Train young plants, develop a strong framework, encourage flowers and fruiting, or repair damage. Know why you are pruning before you make the first cut. A plan will help you achieve your goals and maintain the health of the plant.

Pruning also includes deadheading, pinching back, and other related grooming techniques. Pinch back leggy plants to encourage fuller, more compact growth. Deadhead faded flowers to encourage rebloom and discourage reseeding. Prune some young perennials to control height and bloom time.

Check the pruning section in each month to find out when and what to prune for the results you desire.

Pest Management

Author's Caution

Insects, disease, wildlife, and weeds all add to the challenge of growing a healthy landscape. Some are essential to the health of our landscape, while others need to be managed to minimize the damage they cause.

Use a Plant Health Care approach (the horticulturist's version of IPM, Integrated Pest Management) to manage your landscape. It starts with proper plant selection and care and ends by managing pest problems using a variety of the most environmentally sound techniques, with chemicals as a last resort.

Select the most pest-resistant varieties available and grow them in the proper location. This helps you avoid many pest problems, eliminating the need for control. Provide proper care, such as watering, fertilizing, and pruning, based upon the plant's needs.

Monitor the garden throughout the growing season. Finding pests early can mean the difference between picking off a few sick leaves and spraying a plant throughout the season. Look under the leaves, along the stems, and on the ground for signs of insects, disease, and wildlife.

General Horticultural Practices

Remove weeds as soon as they appear. Not only do they compete with your garden plants for water and nutrients, but they also harbor insects and disease. Remove them before they have a chance to set seed and infect the soil for next season. Mulch to prevent weeds.

Follow the planting and care guidelines in this book to keep your plants healthy and more resistant to pests. Cover the plants, hand pick, or trap insects to minimize the negative attack on the good insects, fungi, and wildlife in our environment. Properly identify all pests before reaching for a pesticide. Sometimes the pest we see is not causing the damage. Other times the damage is done, the pest is gone, and there is no need to treat. Always find out what is causing the damage and if control is needed to maintain the health of the plant. Consult your local county office of the University of Minnesota Extension office or garden center for advice. It is important to use the right product or technique at the right time to maximize effectiveness and minimize the negative impact on the environment.

Consider all control options and their impact on the plant, your health, and the environment. Select the most environmentally friendly method that fits your gardening style and the plant's needs. Always read and follow all label directions before using any product in your landscape. Make sure it is labeled to control the pest on the plant you want to treat. Wear any protective clothing recommended or required by the label. Consider wearing long sleeves, pants, goggles, and gloves as a regular part of your pesticide application gear.

Evaluate the success of control measures used and record this in your journal. Mark next year's calendar and review this book's monthly pest management sections to help reduce and control problems next season.

Winter Care

Some plants need a little help surviving our winters. Snow is the best mulch, but it often arrives too late, melts too soon, or comes and goes throughout the winter.

Apply winter mulches of evergreen boughs, straw, or marsh hay to the ground after it freezes. The goal is to keep the soil constantly cold throughout the winter. Fluctuating soil temperatures cause early sprouting and frost heaving. Early sprouting results in damaged leaves and flowers when the normal cold temperatures return. Frost heaving causes the soil to shift, damaging roots and often pushing perennials and bulbs right out of the ground.

Use discarded holiday trees, decorative fencing, burlap, or other items to create windbreaks and shade for tender plants and broadleaf evergreens. Place them on the windward and sunny sides of the plant. The screening reduces the wind and sun that reaches the plants and dries the leaves.

See fall and winter entries for more ideas on winter protection. A little preventative action in the fall can save a lot of time repairing damage and money spent replacing damaged plants.

For More Information

Use the *Minnesota Gardener's Guide* as a companion to this book. It features more details on individual plants and additional gardening techniques suited for Minnesota.

Contact your local county office of the University of Minnesota Extension Service. They have excellent publications and master gardeners to help with your garden and landscape.

Visit the library and check out the many garden books and magazines. It is a great place to spend your spare time in January, dreaming and planning for the upcoming season.

General Overview

Month-By-Month Gardening in Minnesota focuses on individual elements that make up your landscape. Each chapter focuses on a different group of plants and the major tasks and timing involved with keeping them healthy and attractive.

Annuals have been a traditional favorite of Minnesota gardeners. They add lots of color throughout the short growing season. Learn how to start them indoors, plant them outdoors, manage pests, and keep them looking beautiful throughout the growing season.

Bulbs are little packets of energy and surprise. Some add color early in the season before other plants dare to show their leaves. Summer bulbs can brighten the shade and provide a tropical feel to your landscape. Learn how to use and care for them in the landscape to get the most out of these plants.

Fruits can turn an attractive landscape into an edible paradise. Consider adding just a few of your family favorites to small yards. Use edible plants for hedges, groundcovers, and shade. Or create your own fruit farm if space is unlimited. Explore the possibilities and learn the essentials of planting, fertilizing, harvesting, and caring for fruits in your landscape.

Herbs and *Vegetables* can grow alone or coexist with other plants in the garden. Use their texture and color to brighten up the landscape and feed your family. Include fun and flavorful plants that the whole family can enjoy. Find out how to plan, plant, and maintain a garden that the whole family can harvest and eat.

Houseplants keep dirt under a gardener's fingernails all year round. Their foliage livens up the house, improves the environment, and provides some green relief for the housebound gardener. Learn how to take the frustration out of indoor gardening with proper care and pest management.

Lawns create a green palate for the other landscape plants. Whether it is your pride and joy or just something to keep your feet from getting muddy when it rains, proper care will keep your lawn green and growing. Learn when and how to plant, fertilize, control weeds, and manage other problems to maintain an attractive green carpet in your landscape.

Perennials have exploded in popularity. Their seasonal interest and potential years of service make them a good addition for most landscapes. Perennials, like all living things, require some maintenance. Selecting the right plant for the location and giving proper care can result in a beautiful garden with minimal effort on your part. Learn how to transplant, when to deadhead, and how to mix perennials for maximum enjoyment.

General Overview

Roses have long been a garden favorite providing fragrance, beauty, and sometimes frustration for gardeners. Find out how to get all the benefits, reduce the work, and increase your rose growing success. Learn how to plant, care for, and winter-protect roses for long-term beauty and survival.

Shrubs are often relegated to the lot line or shoved against the foundation of our homes. Explore other uses for shrubs in both small and large landscapes. Use them to create privacy, attract wildlife, and add four seasons of interest to your landscape. Keep them looking beautiful by following this chapter's tips on proper selection, planting, and care.

Trees create a framework upon which to build the rest of your landscape. Their longevity depends on proper selection, care, and management of the surrounding landscape. Find out how to plant, prune, manage pests, and grow attractive trees for your landscape and future generations.

Vines and **Groundcovers** complete the outdoor living space. They soften structures, unify plantings, and add texture and color throughout the landscape. Learn how to select the best plants for your specific needs, manage them for health and beauty, and minimize problems.

Now let's get started gardening month by month!

USDA Cold Hardiness Map

Avg Annual Min. Temp.		Zone
-40°F	to -45°F	2b
-35°F	to -40°F	3a
-30°F	to -35°F	3b
-25°F	to -30°F	4a
-20°F	to -25°F	4b

Annuals

Splashes of red **Geraniums**, white **Alyssums**, and purple **Petunias** brighten up many Minnesota gardens. The season-long color has earned these and many other annuals a spot in almost every landscape. Annuals are plants that grow from a seed, flower, produce seeds, and die within one year. They may be changed seasonally and yearly for added interest.

Annuals have traditionally been used in both front and backyard gardens. They can be found in pots or growing in the soil. Often restricted to small gardens just outside the door, they create a colorful and friendly entrance for family and friends. *Consider expanding your use of annuals throughout the landscape, using some of the following suggestions:*

- *Mix* annuals with perennials. Use them to provide continuous bloom and to fill in empty spaces reserved for expanding perennials. Select informal and subtler annuals that have the look and feel of perennials.

- *Add* annuals to bulb plantings. A groundcover of **Pansies** will make a nice backdrop of color for spring-flowering bulbs. Or use **Impatiens** to mask the declining foliage of late-blooming **Daffodils**. Plant annuals in between spring-flowering bulbs. They will help cover the fading bulb foliage.

- *Use* annuals in containers to brighten areas that lack planting space. Combine upright and trailing annuals to balance and complement the container. Select a mixture of plants with similar growing requirements and foliage and flowers that combine well.

- *Tuck* a few annuals in tree and shrub planting beds. Never add soil or do extensive digging around the base of trees and shrubs. Instead, dig several holes throughout the planting bed. Sink 8- to 12-inch nursery pots in these holes. Plant a few annuals in slightly smaller containers. Set the potted annuals inside the sunken pots. It will look as if they were always there. This technique will save you a lot of digging while also reducing the damage to the all-important tree and shrub roots.

Planning the Annual Flower Garden

A good design starts with a good plan.

- Place the garden in an area where it can be viewed without creating a maintenance nightmare. Avoid building flowerbeds in areas that are hard to reach, require hand trimming of the surrounding grass, or are beyond the reach of the garden hose.

- Start small and build on your gardening success. Create a garden that can be managed in the time and with the effort you want to expend. We all get excited at planting time, but interest and energy may wane once mid-July and the weeds arrive.

- Make the garden wide enough for visual impact. A 3-foot by 6-foot garden will have greater impact than a 1-foot-wide planting that encircles the yard. Try making the garden width two-thirds the height of the background. For example, if planting your garden next to a 6-foot fence, then the garden should be at least 4 feet wide.

Annuals

- Add pathways or stepping-stones to any gardens over 6 feet wide. You will then be able to reach all the plants in the garden for easy care and maintenance.

- Leave at least 1 foot of space between the last row of annuals and the backdrop. This provides access to the backside of the garden. The extra space also increases air circulation that helps decrease disease.

Once you decide on the size of your garden, it is time to decide on the style. Use your landscape design as a starting point. Place flowers in straight lines or geometric designs for a more formal look. Try massing flowers and creating sweeps of color for a more informal feel.

Use flower color to create mood and interest in the landscape.

- Add warm colors of orange, red, and yellow to attract attention, warm the location, and make large spaces appear smaller. Remember, it only takes a few warm-colored annuals to steal the show.

- Consider using cool colors of green, blue, and violet to make a small area appear larger or to make hot spots feel cooler. A basket of blue **Pansies** or a planter filled with green foliage plants can make a small, south-facing patio feel cool and roomy.

- Use contrasting colors—warm with cool—for an attractive, eye-catching blend. Yellow and blue or red and green are just two of the many attractive combinations.

- Combine similar, complementary colors for a different look. The common tones help hold the design together. Mix bold colors of red, orange, and yellow. These strong colors provide equal weight and interest in the flower garden. Mixing cool colors creates a subtle yet attractive blend.

- Use color echoing—repetition of a color from one plant to another—to provide a sense of unity in your flower gardens. Repeat the color from one flower to the next plant's flower, flower part, or foliage. Using this type of repetition is subtle, but it is as effective as repeating the same plant throughout the design.

- Design a monochromatic garden by using the same color flowers throughout. This style can be quite dramatic. Some gardeners find this style boring, while others like the elegant, more formal appearance.

- Consider the plant's texture in your design. Use fine-textured plants—those with spiky flowers and grass-like leaves—as filler and background. Add bold-textured plants—those with large, round flowers and wide leaves—for focal points and accents.

Select plants suitable for your growing conditions and gardening style as well as the design features.

- For healthier plants that need much less care from you, match plants to the available sunlight and soil type. Plants that are poorly matched to the available sunlight and soil type not only look bad, but they are more susceptible to insects and disease.

- Avoid annuals that require deadheading, pinching, and staking if you do not like to fuss over your garden. Look for varieties of low maintenance plants that may be more free-flowering or dwarf.

- Allow some time to locate some of the more hard-to-find annuals. You may need to start these annuals from seed indoors. You will need to invest a little time, space, and dedication for success. Look at it as an early start to the growing season or as a fun activity for your whole family to enjoy. See January and February "Planting"

Annuals

for tips on starting annuals from seeds.

Invest some time in soil preparation before planting. Your effort will pay off with less work during the remainder of the season. Start the preceding fall or in spring as soon as the soil is workable.

1 *Start by outlining* the border of new gardens. Use a garden hose or rope to help visualize and mark the boundaries. Once you have the desired size and shape, then the hard work begins. *Edge* the bed with a sharp edger or spade.

2 *Remove* the grass with a sod cutter, or use a total vegetation killer such as Roundup® or Finale® to kill the existing grass. This also works on existing beds filled with Quackgrass, Ground Ivy, and other perennial weeds. Wait the required time listed on the label, usually 7 to 14 days, to start preparing the soil.

3 *Take a soil test* to find out what type of fertilizers and amendments should be added. Contact your local extension office for directions on how to take a soil test. A 2- to 3-inch layer of compost, shredded leaves, or other organic matter can be worked into the top 6 to 12 inches of the soil. These materials help improve the drainage of heavy clay soils and increase the water-holding capacity of sandy soils.

4 *Add* the type and amount of fertilizer recommended by the soil test report provided by the Extension service. If soil test recommendations are not available, add 1 to 3 pounds per 100 square feet of a low nitrogen fertilizer. Use the higher amount of a slow release formulation if you plan on fertilizing just once during the growing season. Check the label for specific recommendations.

5 Wait until the soil is slightly moist before *spading* or *tilling* in the fertilizer and amendments. Test the moisture content by grabbing a handful of soil. Gently squeeze the soil into a ball, and then tap it. If it stays in a ball, it is too wet and you need to wait a few days. If it breaks into smaller pieces, it is ready to work.

6 *Work* the fertilizers and amendments into the top 6 to 12 inches of soil. Sprinkle the garden with water long enough to moisten the top 2 to 3 inches of soil or wait a few days for the soil to settle.

Planting

Do not be too anxious to start planting. The air may be warm, but the soil stays cool for a long time. *Harden off* plants by gradually preparing them for their move outdoors. Stop fertilizing, reduce watering, and gradually expose them to the cool temperatures and direct sunlight. After two weeks, they will be ready for their outdoor location. Seeds need warm soil to germinate as well. Check package directions for planting times.

Plant hardened-off, frost-tolerant (hardy) plants such as **Snapdragons** and **Pansies**, in mid- to late April. Young plants will need protection from hard frosts.

Wait until after the danger of frost has passed (late May to early June) to plant half-hardy annuals such as **Ageratum, Cleome**, and **Lobelia**. Plant **Impatiens**, **Coleus**, and other frost-sensitive (tender) plants once air and soil have warmed. Check planting tags for more specific information on timing, spacing, and care.

Make sure the roots of transplants are moist when planting outdoors. Carefully remove the transplants from their containers. Squeeze the planting pack and slide out the transplant. Gently massage the roots of potbound plants. This encourages the roots to grow beyond the rootball and into the surrounding soil.

Water deeply, moistening the top 6 inches of soil. Check new plantings every few days. Water when the top few inches of soil just start to dry. As the roots expand, water thoroughly but less frequently.

Remove the flowers and pinch back leggy transplants. This encourages root development and branching for fuller plants. Remove the flowers on every other plant or every other row if you cannot sacrifice all the blooms at one time. Remove the remaining flowers as the others start to form new blooms.

Care

Established annual gardens need some regular care. The amount of care depends on individual plant needs and the weather, but the following are some general care tips:

- Provide established annuals with about 1 inch of water each week. *Water* established plants growing in clay soils in one application each week and those growing in sandy soils in two applications of $^1/_2$ to $^3/_4$ inch each week. Let soil moisture, not the calendar, be your guide. See the "Watering" sections for more tips.

- *Spread* a thin layer of cocoa bean shells, shredded leaves, or herbicide-free grass clippings over the soil surface. These mulches will help conserve moisture, reduce weeds, and improve the soil.

- *Fertilize* annual gardens based on soil test results. Make one application of a slow-release, low-nitrogen fertilizer at planting. Use 3 pounds per 100 square feet to take care of your fertilizer needs for the season. Or use 1 pound (2 cups) per 100 square feet, or 4 tablespoons per 10 square feet, of a low-nitrogen fertilizer once a month for the first three months of the growing season.

- *Avoid* fertilizers high in phosphorus and potassium unless recommended by soil test results. Most garden soils have high to excessive levels of both these nutrients. Adding more can interfere with the uptake of other nutrients.

- *Remove* faded flowers to encourage continual bloom. Some flowers, such as **Impatiens** and the **Wave Petunia**, need little if any deadheading.

Pests

You cannot control the environment, but you can work with nature to keep pest problems under control. *Keep plants healthy to minimize the damage caused by insects and disease.*

- Use pest-resistant varieties of annuals whenever possible. Check plants frequently for signs of pests. Pick off infected leaves and insects as soon as they appear.

- Remove weeds whenever they appear. It is much easier to pull and cultivate young weeds with shallow roots before they become established. Be careful not to damage desirable plants when removing the weeds. I have accidentally weeded out a few of my flowers in an overzealous attempt to control the weeds!

Minnesota Annuals

Common Name (Botanical Name)	Hardiness*	Light	Size	Space Between Plants	When to Start Seeds Indoors**
Ageratum (*Ageratum houstonianum*)	Half-hardy	Full to part sun	6 to 24 inches by 6 to 12 inches	6 to 9 inches apart	6 to 8
Alyssum (*Lobularia maritima*)	Hardy	Full to part sun	4 to 8 inches by 10 to 15 inches	6 to 8 inches	4 to 6
Begonia (*Begonia semperflorens-cultorum*)	Tender	Sun to shade	6 to 12 inches tall and wide	6 to 12 inches	12
Cleome (*Cleome hasselrana*)	Half-hardy	Full to part sun	36 to 48 inches by 18 to 24 inches	24 inches	6 to 8
Cockscomb (*Celosia argentea*)	Half-hardy	Full sun	6 to 36 inches by 8 to 20 inches	6 to 15 inches	4 to 6
Coleus (*Solenostemon scutellarioides*)	Tender	Full to part shade	6 to 24 inches by 12 inches	10 to 12 inches	8
Cosmos (*Cosmos* species)	Half-hardy	Full sun	12 to 72 inches by 12 to 24 inches	12 inches	6 to 8
Dusty Miller (*Senecio cineraria*)	Hardy	Full sun	6 to 15inches by 8 to 12 inches	8 to 12 inches	8 to 10
Flowering Tobacco (*Nicotiana alata*)	Half-hardy	Full to part sun	8 to 60 inches by 6 to 24 inches	8 to 12 inches	6 to 8
Fuchsia (*Fuchsia × hybrida*)	Tender	Full to part shade	Trailing or 12 to 24 inches tall	12 inches apart or 3 plants per 8-inch pot	12+
Geranium (*Pelargonium × hortorum*)	Tender	Full sun	12 to 20 inches by 12 inches	8 to 12 inches	12
Impatiens (*Impatiens wallerana*)	Tender	Full to part shade	6 to 18 inches by 12 to 24 inches	8 to 12 inches	12 to 14
Lisianthus (*Eustoma grandiflorum*)	Half-hardy	Full to part sun	6 to 30 inches by 6 to 12 inches	6 to 10 inches	20
Lobelia (*Lobelia erinus*)	Half-hardy	Full to part sun	4 to 8 inches by 6 to 16 inches	6 to 8 inches	10 to 12
Marigold (*Tagetes* species)	Tender	Full sun	6 to 36 inches by 6 to 15 inches	6 to 15 inches	4 to 6
Moss Rose (*Portulaca grandiflora*)	Tender	Full sun	4 to 8 inches by 6 to 12 inches	6 inches	6 to 8
Nasturium (*Tropaeolum majus*)	Half-hardy	Full sun	8 to 12 inches by 12 to 14 inches	8 to 12 inches	6 to 8
Pansy (*Viola × wittrockiana*)	Hardy	Full to part sun	4 to 8 inches by 9 to 12 inches	6 inches	10 to 12
Petunia (*Petunia × hybrida*)	Half-hardy	Full to part sun	6 to 18 inches by 6 to 36 inches	6 to 24 inches	10 to 12
Pinks (*Dianthus chinensis*)	Hardy	Full to part sun	6 to 12 inches by 12 inches	6 to 12 inches	10
Salvia (*Salvia splendens*)	Tender	Full sun	8 to 30 inches by 8 to 12 inches	8 to 12 inches	6 to 8
Snapdragon (*Antirrhinum majus*)	Hardy	Full to part sun	6 to 48 inches by 6 to 12 inches	6, 8, or 12 inches	6 to 8
Spike (*Cordyline* species)	Half-hardy	Full to part sun	24 inches by 15 inches	12 to 15 inches	12
Sunflower (*Helianthus annuus*)	Half-hardy	Full sun	24 to 120+ inches by 12 to 24 inches	24 inches	3 to 4
Treasure Flower (*Gazania rigens*)	Half-hardy	Full sun	6 to 12 inches tall and wide	6 to 10 inches apart	4 to 6
Verbena (*Verbena* species)	Half-hardy	Full sun	6 to 15 inches by 8 to 24 inches	6 to 12 inches	12 to 14
Vinca (*Catharanthus roseus*)	Tender	Full to part sun	8 to 18 inches by 8 to 12 inches	8 to 12 inches	12
Zinnia (*Zinnia elegans*)	Half-hardy	Full sun	3 to 36 inches by 15 to 24 inches	6 to 15 inches	4

*See "Planting" in Introduction   **Prior to last spring frost (in weeks)

Planning

The catalogs are pouring in and the wish list keeps growing. *Develop a plan for this season's garden before placing your order.*

- *List* the flower seeds you have and want to use this season. Then compare it to the list of seeds you plan to order.

- *Review* your garden journal and pictures of last year's landscape. Plan to expand or reduce planting space based on last year's experience.

- *Consider* increasing space by expanding existing gardens or adding new planting areas. Remember more planting space means an increase in maintenance as well.

- *Decrease* maintenance by selecting low-maintenance annuals, mulching, sharing the workload, or by decreasing the planting space. Reduce the size of the garden or convert it to a perennial, shrub, groundcover, or turf area.

- *Draw* a sketch of the proposed changes. Put it aside for a few days to consider the impact on the appearance and maintenance of the landscape.

- *Develop* a plant list. Make sure the plants are best suited to the growing conditions and will give you the desired look. See "Planning the Annual Flower Garden" in the introduction to this chapter for more detailed information.

- *Order* any seeds that you plan on starting indoors. It will soon be time to start planting them.

Planting

Although it is too early to plant outside, it is never too early to prepare for the season ahead. *Now is the time to prepare your light setup for starting annuals indoors.*

1. *Select* an out-of-the-way area that will not be forgotten. You will need a nearby power source and enough room for all the seedlings you plan to start.

2. You can purchase a seed starting system from a garden supply catalog or build your own. All you need are cool, fluorescent lights, a light fixture to hold them, and a system for keeping the lights 6 inches above the tops of the seedlings.

3. *Build* your own system by mounting the light fixtures on shelves, creating tabletop supports for the lights, or designing a stand-alone system. (See the illustration for one possibility.) Note that the pulley system allows the lights to be lowered and raised over the growing seedlings.

Pulleys

Timer

Fluorescent Lights

Weights

Light Stand

4. *Paint* the shelving white or *use* reflective surfaces under and around the unit to increase the light reaching the young seedlings.

Once the light system is in place, you are ready to start planting seeds. For the best chance of success, give seeds warm temperatures to germinate and light as soon as sprouting occurs. Many gardeners germinate seeds in a warm location and then move the seedlings under light after sprouting. Others use bottom heat or a warm location along with the lights to germinate seeds and grow seedlings. (See February "Planting" for tips on starting seeds and care.)

Start **Pansies** at the end of the month to have large transplants ready for your early spring garden.

Care

Check on **Geraniums** that you are storing in the basement or other cool, dark location for the winter. Plant any that have started growing. Move them to a warm, sunny location and treat them as you would your other houseplants.

Watering

Adjust your watering schedule to match the needs of **Coleus**, **Geraniums**, **Fuchsias**, and other annuals overwintered as houseplants. The shorter days, less intense sunlight, and low humidity of winter changes the plants' needs. Water the soil thoroughly and wait until the soil is slightly dry before watering again.

Water seedlings often enough to keep the soil moist but not wet. Overwatering can cause root rot and seedling failure. Allowing the soil to dry stresses seedlings, resulting in poor growth, or even seedling death.

Fertilizing

Do not be overanxious to fertilize **Fuchsias**, **Geraniums**, and other annuals you are growing as houseplants for the winter. The poor growing conditions of indoors during the winter results in slow plant growth that requires very little if any fertilizer. Only fertilize plants with stunted growth, yellow leaves, or other signs of nutrient deficiencies.

Seedlings will need to be fertilized once sprouted and actively growing. Use a diluted solution of houseplant fertilizer according to label directions.

Pests

Monitor plants for fungus gnats, mites, aphids, and whiteflies.

- Fungus gnats do not hurt the plants, but they are a nuisance. Often mistaken for fruit flies, they can be found flitting throughout the house. These insects feed on the organic matter in the soil, such as dead plant roots and peat moss. Keep the soil slightly drier than normal to reduce the populations.

- Aphids, mites, and whiteflies suck out plant juices, causing leaves to yellow and brown. Look for poor growth and a clear sticky substance called honeydew on the leaves. See November "Pests" for details on managing these insects.

Pruning

Keep pinching back leggy **Geraniums**, **Coleus**, **Impatiens**, and other annuals that you are overwintering as houseplants. Remove the growing tips or pinch stems back to just above a set of healthy leaves. This encourages branching and stouter stems.

Planning

Make your final wish list and order your seeds as soon as possible, especially those you need to start indoors. *Gather your planting materials while waiting for your seed order to arrive.*

• Finish assembling your light setup and seed starting area. See January "Planting" for ideas on creating your own system.

• Purchase a sterile potting or seed starter mix. These mixes increase your success by retaining moisture, providing good drainage, and allowing you to start disease-free.

• Gather and clean your planting containers. Use flats and pots purchased at the garden center or recycled from last year's garden. Disinfect used pots in a solution of one part bleach to nine parts water. Or gather emptied yogurt containers or used coffee cups for seed starting. Rinse these containers and punch holes in the bottom.

• Buy or make plant labels. Use them to label flats and pots with the name of the seeds you are growing. Try adapting Popsicle sticks, discarded plastic spoons, or similar items into labels. Be sure to use a permanent marker.

• Create a seeding chart for recording plant names, starting dates, and other important information. Use your garden journal or other notebook to record and save this valuable information for next year. Consider investing in a journal if you do not already own one.

Planting

Seeds can be started in one of two ways. Sow them in a flat and then transplant young seedlings into individual containers. Or sow one to two seeds directly into the individual pots. *To start seeds:*

1 *Fill* flats or containers with a sterile starter mix. Moisten the mixture prior to seeding. *Sprinkle* fine seeds on the soil surface and water them in. Larger seeds need to be planted a little deeper. Use a chopstick, pencil, or similar item to dig a shallow furrow or punch a planting hole into the mix. Plant seeds at a depth that is about twice their diameter.

2 *Sprinkle* seeds in the furrow or drop one or two in each hole. Cover with soil and water in with a fine mist. Avoid a strong stream of water that can dislodge the seeds.

3 *Keep* the soil warm and moist to ensure germination. Use commercially available heating cables or place the flats in a warm location. I have seen flats on top of refrigerators, heating ducts, or other warm places to keep the starting mix warm. *Cover* the containers with a sheet of plastic to help conserve moisture. Check daily and water often enough to keep the soil surface moist, but not wet.

4 *Remove* the plastic and move the container to a sunny window as soon as the seedlings appear. Place lights 6 inches above the plants and keep them on for 16 hours a day. Lighting them longer will not help the plants, but will needlessly increase your electric bill.

5 *Transplant* seedlings growing in flats as soon as they form two sets of leaves (seed and true). The seed leaves are nondescript, while the true leaves look like the particular plant's leaves.

Transplanting Seedlings

Check the planting dates on the seed packets and in catalogs. Sow seeds according to the label directions. February is the time to start many of the spring-blooming and long-season annuals.

- Start **Impatiens**, **Petunias**, **Wax Begonias**, **Pansies**, and **Gerbera Daisies** in early February in southern Minnesota and two weeks later in northern Minnesota. Use pelleted (coated) **Petunia** and **Begonia** seeds to make the planting of these small seeds easier. Or mix these and other small seeds with sand. This helps you spread the seeds more evenly over the soil surface.

- Sow **Ageratum**, **Lobelia**, and **Love-in-a-Mist** seeds in mid- or late-February (for those in the north).

Care

Continue monitoring annuals that are stored in the basement. Pot up any that start to grow and move them to a sunny window. Water the soil thoroughly whenever the top few inches start to dry.

Check annuals that are growing indoors as houseplants. Pinch back the stems that grow and stretch for the light. These cuttings can be rooted and used to start new plants for this year's garden.

Watering

Check seeded flats and seedlings every day. Keep the soil moist until the seeds germinate. Once germinated, continue to check seedlings every day. Water often enough to keep the soil moist but not wet.

Continue watering annuals that you are growing as houseplants. Water thoroughly until the excess runs out the bottom. Allow the top few inches of soil to dry before watering again.

Fertilizing

Fertilize seedlings once they begin to grow. Use a diluted solution of a complete water-soluble fertilizer every other week. Follow mixing directions on the label.

Pests

Check seedlings for sudden wilting and rotted stems caused by damping off. This fungus disease causes young seedlings to collapse. Remove infected plants as soon as they are discovered. Drench the soil with a fungicide labeled for this use. Prevent this disease by using a sterile starter mix and clean containers.

Ignore fungus gnats. These pests do not harm the plants. Decrease populations by keeping potting mix slightly drier than normal.

Look under the leaves and along the stem of annual plants for signs of mites, aphids, and whiteflies. Get out the hand lens and check for speckling, a clear sticky substance, and the insects themselves. See November "Pests" for specific suggestions.

Pruning

Pinch back indoor plantings to keep them compact. Remove the stem tip or a portion of the stem just above a healthy leaf. *Start new plants from stem and leaf pieces that are 4 to 6 inches long.*

1 *Remove* the lowest set of leaves and dip the stem in a rooting compound. This material contains a fungicide to prevent rot and hormones to encourage rooting.

2 *Place* cuttings in moist vermiculite, perlite, or a well-drained potting mix. Roots should form in one to two weeks.

3 *Transplant* rooted cuttings into a small container of potting mix. Water frequently enough to keep the soil slightly moist, but not wet.

Planning

Continue to monitor and record seed starting results in your journal. This information will make next season even more successful.

Take advantage of the few sunny, snow-free days. Measure the length and width of flowerbeds. Multiply these two dimensions to calculate the square footage of the bed. Use this information to calculate the number of plants you will need. See May "Helpful Hints" for exact details.

This is also a good time to locate areas for new planting beds. Mark beds and begin preparation as soon as the soil can be worked. See April "Helpful Hints" for more details.

Planting

Continue seeding annuals. Plant seeds in flats or individual containers filled with moist sterile starting mix.

- Plant **Coleus, Dusty Miller, Nicotiana, Pinks, Melampodium, Snapdragons**, and **Verbenas** in early March. Northern gardeners can wait till the middle of the month.

- Seed **Alyssum, Moss Rose**, (**Portulaca**) and **Salvia** in mid- to late March.

- Keep the soil warm and moist until the seeds germinate. Move them under lights as soon as they sprout.

- Transplant seedlings from flats into individual containers as soon as the first set of true leaves appear. The first leaves to appear are seed leaves. The next to appear are true leaves, and it is then time to transplant.

Plant or *repot* **Geraniums** that were stored in a cool, dark location for winter. Use a well-drained potting mix and a clean container with a drainage hole. Cut plants back to 4 to 6 inches above the container. Water the soil thoroughly, allowing the excess to run out the bottom of the pot.

Care

Move **Pansies** started indoors in January to your cold frame to harden off. The cold frame will protect them from frost but will allow them to adjust to the cooler, harsher outdoor conditions. Reduce watering and stop fertilizing until they are planted in their permanent location.

Vent your cold frame on sunny days to prevent heat damage. Automatic venting systems are available from some garden centers and through many garden catalogs.

Watering

Check seedlings every day. Water whenever the soil surface begins to dry. Apply enough water to thoroughly moisten the soil. Avoid overwatering which can lead to root rot and damping-off disease.

Water potted annuals whenever the top few inches of soil start to dry. Apply enough water so that some runs out the drainage holes. Pour off any excess water that collects in the saucer. Leaving water in the saucer can lead to root rot.

Take a walk out to the cold frame. Check soil moisture and water as needed. Plants growing in the cold frame will need less frequent watering during this hardening off process.

Fertilizing

Start fertilizing recently potted annuals when new growth appears. Use a dilute solution of any flowering houseplant fertilizer on these and other annual plants.

Fertilize seedlings every other week with a dilute solution of any complete water-soluble fertilizer. Check the label for mixing rates.

Pests

Continue monitoring for whiteflies, fungus gnats, aphids, and mites.

- Use yellow sticky traps to capture the whiteflies. High populations causing plant damage can be controlled with insecticides. Use a product labeled for controlling whiteflies on indoor plants. Make three applications, every five days, in a well-ventilated location. Start the process over if you miss one application.

- Control aphids and mites with insecticidal soap. Spray the upper and lower surface of the leaves and stems. Repeated applications may be needed to control large populations.

Monitor seedlings for damping-off. See February "Pests" for more information.

Pruning

Pinch out the growing tips of leggy annuals to encourage branching. Pinched plants will develop stouter stems and more branches.

Take 4- to 6-inch cuttings from annuals you want to propagate. Root cuttings in moist vermiculite, perlite, or well-drained potting mix.

Helpful Hints

Spring never seems to arrive early enough for gardeners. Get a jump on the growing season by using cold frames and row covers. These systems allow you to move plants outdoors earlier in spring. Use them to harden off indoor grown seedlings or to start annuals from seed.

Purchase or make your own cold frame from plywood and old window sashes or plastic. Most cold frames are 3×6 feet or made to fit the size of the window sashes or other material used for the cover. *To build your own cold frame:*

1 Make the back wall 18 to 30 inches tall and the front slightly lower, about 12 to 24 inches. Cut side walls 3 feet long and with a slanted top to match the height of the front and back walls. The cold frame cover can be a wood frame covered with plastic or discarded windows.

2 Use 2×2s for the corners. Make the posts longer than the sides if you want to use them to anchor the frame in place.

3 Face the front of the cold frame toward the south for maximum light and heat. Face the back of the cold frame north or against a building. Placing the cold frame next to the house will provide screening from the wind and a little additional heat from the foundation.

Cold Frame

Row covers of polypropylene fabrics can also be used to extend the season. The row cover fabrics help trap heat around the plants while allowing air, water, and light through to the plants. Loosely drape fabric over the plants. Anchor on the sides, leaving enough slack in the fabric to allow for plant growth. See the illustration in the "Herbs and Vegetables" chapter on page 112.

Transplant rooted cuttings (usually ready in one to two weeks) into small containers filled with moist, well-drained potting mix.

Planning

Visit local garden centers and greenhouse growers for new ideas. Find a vacant space in the landscape or add a few planters to accommodate these late additions to your plan.

Make sure your journal is current. Record weather conditions, seed starting dates, and other helpful garden information. Compare the current season with last year's garden records. Make needed adjustments in planting time based on current weather and past experience.

The changeable weather is hard on gardens and anxious gardeners. Make sure both the air and soil are warm before planting. Only the seeds of hardy plants can tolerate the cold soils of April.

Planting

Take a soil test if this has not already been done. A soil test will tell you how much and what type of fertilizer you need.

Prepare annual gardens for planting. Use the soil test information as your guide.

1 *Start* by checking the soil moisture. Grab a handful of soil and gently squeeze it into a ball.

Lightly tap the soil ball. If it breaks into smaller pieces, it is ready to work. If it stays in a wet ball, the soil is too wet to work. Wait a few days and try again.

2 Once the soil is dry enough, *work* 2 inches of aged manure, compost, or peat moss into the top 6 to 12 inches of garden soil. The organic matter will improve the drainage of heavy clay soils and increase the water-holding capacity of sandy soils.

3 *Rake* the garden smooth, sloping the soil away from building or center of island beds. Lightly sprinkle with water or wait a week to allow the soil to settle.

Plant hardened-off hardy annuals, such as **Pansies** and **Dusty Miller**, outdoors in mid- to late April. Let the weather and soil temperature be your guides. Keep mulch or row covers handy to protect transplants from unexpected drops in temperature.

Start **Zinnias, Marigolds, Calendula, Celosia (Cockscomb), and Gaillardias (Blanket Flowers)** indoors in early April.

Transplant seedlings as needed. Move seedlings from flats to individual containers as soon as the first set of true leaves appear.

Care

Adjust lights over seedlings. The lights should be about 6 inches above the tops of the young plants. Lower the lights if seedlings are long and leggy. Raise the lights as seedlings grow.

Fluorescent Lights

Seed-Starter Tray in 10×20" Flat Tray

Check seedlings and transplants growing in cold frames. Open the lid on sunny days to prevent heat buildup. Lower the lid in late afternoon to protect cold-sensitive plants from cold nights. Consider purchasing an automatic ventilation system to make your job easier.

Harden off indoor-grown transplants before moving them into the garden.

- Move transplants to a cold frame or protected location two weeks prior to planting.

- Cut back on watering and stop fertilizing.

- Gradually introduce plants to full sun conditions. Start by placing them in a partially shaded location. Give them direct sun for a few hours. Increase the amount of sun the plants receive each day.

- Cover the transplants or move them into the garage when there is a danger of frost. By the end of two weeks, the plants are ready to plant in the garden.

Watering

Do not stop now. Keep potted annuals, seedlings, and transplants growing and thriving with proper watering. Check seedlings and young transplants daily. Water potted annuals thoroughly every time the top few inches of soil start to dry.

Check plants growing outdoors in the cold frame and garden. Water only when the soil is slightly dry. Overwatering can lead to root rot.

Fertilizing

Incorporate fertilizer into the soil prior to planting. Follow soil test recommendations. If these are not available, apply 3 pounds (2 cups equals 1 pound) of a slow-release, low-nitrogen fertilizer per 100 square feet or 1 pound of a quick-release formulation.

Continue fertilizing indoor plants and transplants every two weeks. Use a diluted solution of any complete water-soluble fertilizer.

Pests

Continue monitoring and controlling mites, aphids, and whiteflies. Spray the upper and lower surface of leaves and stems with insecticidal soap to control high populations of aphids and mites. Repeat as needed. Try trapping whiteflies with commercial or homemade yellow sticky traps. See December "Pests" for additional details.

Avoid damping-off with proper germination, watering, and care of seedlings. Use a fungicide soil drench to treat infected flats.

Remove weeds as soon as they appear. Pull or lightly hoe annual weeds. Quackgrass, Ground Ivy, and Bindweed should be pulled and destroyed to prevent rerooting. Consider treating badly infested gardens with a total vegetation killer prior to planting. Begin preparing the soil for your annuals 4 to 14 days after treatment. Be sure to read and follow all label directions carefully.

Pruning

Prune back leggy annuals as needed. Use the cuttings to start additional plants for this summer's garden.

Planning

Hopefully you made a plan before you started planting and plant shopping. Or maybe you had a plan but the labels and pictures of other plants were too tempting to resist. Join the club! Now is the time to take inventory and reevaluate planting space and garden locations.

See this month's "Helpful Hints" for tips on calculating the number of plants you will need for the available planting space.

Planting

Continue planting hardy annuals. Plant half-hardy annuals in the garden after the danger of a hard frost has passed. This is early to mid-May in southern Minnesota and late May to early June in the northern areas. Wait until both the air and the soil are warm to plant tender annuals. This is usually late May in southern parts of the state and early June in northern Minnesota.

Proper soil preparation is critical in planting success. Add organic matter and fertilizer to the top 6 to 12 inches of garden soil. Rake smooth and allow the soil to settle.

Harden off indoor-grown transplants prior to placing in the garden.

- Start two weeks prior to planting. *Cut back* on water and *stop* fertilizing. Move transplants outdoors to a protected location. Give plants several hours of direct sun. Increase the amount each day. Cover or move transplants into the garage in case of frost.

- Carefully *remove* transplants from their containers. Squeeze the container and slide the plant out of the container. Do not pull it out by the stem.

- Gently and ever so slightly *loosen* the roots of root-bound transplants. Place annuals in the soil at the same depth they were growing in the pot. Cover with soil and gently tamp to remove air pockets.

- *Space* plants according to the "Planting Chart" in the chapter introduction or the directions on the plant tag. Do not crowd the annuals. Overplanting reduces air circulation and increases the risk of disease problems. Use excess plants for container gardens, herb gardens, shrub beds, or to fill bare spots in perennial gardens. Or share them with a friend or neighbor. I have a wonderful neighbor who adopts my spares—this way we both get to enjoy them!

Remove flowers and *cut back* leggy annuals at the time of planting. This encourages root development, branching, and better looking, healthier plants in the long run. Can't stand to remove those beautiful flowers? How about a compromise? Remove the flowers on every other plant or every other row at planting. Remove the remaining flowers the following week. Then it will not seem so long before the new flowers appear.

Plant seeds of **Cleome**, **Cosmos**, **Four-o'-clocks**, **Globe Amaranth**, **Gloriosa Daisies**, **Morning Glories**, **Moss Roses**, and **Snapdragons**.

Care

Thin or *transplant* annuals directly seeded into the garden. Leave the healthiest seedlings properly spaced in their permanent garden location. Move extra transplants to other planting beds and gardens with extra planting space.

Place stakes next to tall annuals that need staking. Early stake placement prevents root and plant damage caused by staking established annuals that are already flopping over.

Watering

Water transplants and potted annuals growing indoors as needed. Keep the soil moist but not wet. Cut back on watering as you prepare the plants to move outdoors. See "Planting" for more details on hardening off transplants.

Check new transplants every few days. Water deep enough to moisten the rootball and surrounding soil. Apply water when the top few inches of soil start to dry. Reduce watering frequency as the transplants become established.

Fertilizing

Stop fertilizing indoor- and greenhouse-grown transplants two weeks prior to planting outdoors. Use a starter solution of fertilizer at the time of planting. Check the label for mixing directions.

Mix fertilizer and organic matter into the soil prior to planting. Follow soil test recommendations or use 3 pounds of a slow-release, or 1 pound of a quick-release low-nitrogen fertilizer per 100 square feet.

Incorporate a slow-release granular or pelletized fertilizer into the potting mix of container gardens. A small amount of the fertilizer will be released every time you water over the next several months. This constant feeding is good for the plants and the gardener, as it saves you some work.

Pests

Protect new plantings from cutworm damage. These insects chew through the stems of young transplants. They are most common in planting beds recently converted from lawn. Use cutworm collars made of cardboard or plastic. Recycle paper towel and toilet paper holders, plastic margarine tubs, or yogurt containers. Remove the bottom of the plastic containers and cut the paper rolls into 3- to 4-inch lengths. Slice the containers down the sides. Place collars around the new transplants and sink the bottoms several inches into the soil.

Start watching for aphids, mites, spittlebugs, plantbugs, slugs, and earwig damage. See June "Pests" for details on these insects. *Pull* or *cultivate* weeds as soon as they appear. Be careful not to damage the tender roots of transplants while weeding.

Watch for signs of deer, rabbits, and woodchucks. These animals appreciate a few fresh greens—your new transplants—in their diets. Repellents applied before they start feeding may give you control. Fencing small garden areas may help keep out deer, as they do not seem to like to feed in small, fenced-in areas. A 4-foot high fence anchored in the ground will help keep rabbits out. Fencing may not be the most attractive remedy, but it beats having no flowers at all.

Protect hanging baskets from birds and chipmunks. Cover baskets with bird netting. Secure the netting above and below the container. Do this at the first signs of a problem. Quick action will encourage the birds and animals to go elsewhere. Remove netting once wildlife is no longer a threat.

Pruning

Remove flowers at planting time to encourage root development. Pinch back spindly transplants above a set of healthy leaves. Pruning will encourage branching and will ultimately result in more flowers.

Planning

Take a walk around the yard. Look for bare or drab areas that would benefit from a little annual color. Use annuals to mask declining spring bulbs and early blooming perennials. Consider adding a pot of annuals to the patio, deck, or entranceway. You will be amazed at the difference a few plants can make.

Planting

Get busy planting. Early June is peak planting time for gardeners in the northern part of the state. The air and soil have finally warmed. Even gardeners in southern Minnesota benefit from the delay. The transplants quickly adjust to these warmer outdoor conditions.

Finish planting tender annuals early in the month for the best and longest possible flower display. Check out your local garden center for larger transplants. Use these for a quicker show or for later plantings.

Reduce transplant shock by planting in early morning or late afternoon. Proper planting and post-planting care will help the transplants adjust to their new location. See May "Planting" for tips on hardening off, planting, and care.

Care

Now is the time to mulch. Use cocoa bean shells, pine needles, shredded leaves, and other organic material as mulch. A thin layer (1 to 2 inches) of mulch helps conserve moisture, moderate soil temperature, and reduce weeds.

Finish staking tall annuals that need a little added support. Stake early in the season to reduce the risk of damaging taller, more established plants.

Watering

Check new plantings several times per week. Water whenever the top few inches of soil begin to dry.

Water established annuals thoroughly, but only when needed. Adjust the watering schedule to fit the plant's needs and growing conditions. Water when the top few inches of soil start to dry. In general, apply 1 inch of water once a week to plants growing in clay soils. Apply $1/2$ to $3/4$ inch of water twice a week in sandy soils.

Apply water in early morning to reduce disease caused by wet foliage at night, leaf burn due to wet leaves in midday, and moisture loss due to evaporation.

Consider using a watering wand or drip irrigation system to water the soil without wetting the foliage. This puts the water where it is needed and helps reduce the risk of disease.

Do not be fooled by wilting plants. Drooping leaves can indicate drought stress. It is also one way that some plants conserve moisture. Wait until the temperature cools and see if the plants recover. Always check the soil moisture before reaching for the hose.

Fertilizing

Use a starter solution of fertilizer at planting. This diluted solution will help get the transplants off to a good start. Check the label for mixing directions.

Incorporate a slow-release, complete fertilizer in the potting mix for your containers. Every time you water, you will be fertilizing. Or use a flowering plant fertilizer every two weeks. Mix the fertilizer with water according to the package directions.

Pests

Remove spotted, blotchy, and discolored leaves as soon as they are discovered. Several fungal diseases can damage annuals. Sanitation is the best way to control and reduce the spread of disease.

Monitor the garden for insects. *Minimize your use of pesticides.* The fewer pesticides used, the greater number of beneficial insects you will find. Look for ladybugs, lacewings, praying mantises, and other insects that eat aphids and other troublesome pests. Also watch for bees, butterflies, and hummingbirds that come to visit your garden. Protect and encourage these visitors by mini- mizing your use of pesticides. See December "Helpful Hints" and July "Pests" for ideas on controlling unwelcome insect pests.

Continue pulling weeds as they appear. It is much easier to keep up with a few weeds than it is to reclaim an annual garden gone bad. Pull and destroy Quackgrass, Creeping Charlie, and other perennial weeds that invade the annual garden.

Watch for signs of deer, rabbits, and woodchucks. Spray plantings with repellents or use scare tactics to keep the animals away. Reapply repellents after bad weather and vary the scare tactics to increase success.

Protect containers and new plant- ings from birds and chipmunks. Cover new plantings and containers with bird netting. This discourages the animals, and hopefully they will find another place to nest and dig. Remove netting once plants are established and the threat of wildlife is passed.

Pruning

Remove flowers—*deadhead*—as they fade. Pinch or cut the flowering stem back to the first set of leaves or flower buds. Use a knife or garden shears to make a clean cut. This improves the plant's appearance and encourages continual bloom.

Annual
Deadheading

- **Ageratums, Cleomes, Gom- phrenas, Impatiens, Narrow- leaf Zinnias, New Guinea Impatiens, Wax Begonias,** and **Pentas** are self-cleaning. These drop their dead blooms and do not need deadheading.

- Remove **Begonia** and **Agera- tum** flowers during wet weather to reduce disease problems.

- Remove flowers on **Coleus** as soon as they appear. This keeps plants full and compact.

- Pinch back leggy **Petunias** to encourage branching all along the stem. Cut stems back above a set of leaves.

Annual
Pinching Back

Planning

This is actually my favorite time to plan. Everyone's gardens are looking good, and it is a great time to get some new ideas.

Visit botanical gardens, participate in community garden tours, and take a walk through the neighborhood. Be sure to bring your garden journal, camera, or sketchpad to record planting schemes and combinations that you want to try.

Evaluate your own landscape. Make notes on what is working and what needs to be redesigned for next year. Jot down a few possible solutions based on your recent tour of gardens.

Planting

There is still time to plant. Stop by your favorite garden center. Many offer late-season transplants for replacements or late additions. You might even find a bargain or two worth adding to the garden.

Care

Continue staking tall plants that tend to flop. Loosely tie plant stems to the stake. Use twine or cushioned twist ties to secure the plants to the stake.

Mulch the soil in your annual garden. Shredded leaves, cocoa bean shells, and pine needles make attractive mulches. Apply a thin layer to help conserve moisture, moderate soil temperature, and reduce weeds.

Harvest flowers for fresh indoor enjoyment. Cut the flowers early in the morning for the best quality. Use a sharp knife or garden shears to cut the stem above a set of healthy leaves. Recut the stems just prior to placing the flowers in the vase. Harvest a few extras to share with friends and neighbors.

Wait until midday to harvest flowers for drying. Pick flowers at their peak. *Remove* the leaves and gather a few stems into a bundle. Secure with a rubber band. Then use a

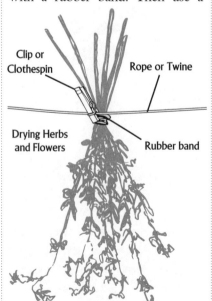

Clip or Clothespin

Rope or Twine

Drying Herbs and Flowers

Rubber band

spring-type clothespin to hang the bundle from a line, rack, or other structure in a dry, dark location.

Watering

Water established plantings when the top few inches of soil are slightly dry. See June "Watering" for more information.

Fertilizing

Do not fertilize annuals where you used a slow-release fertilizer. That fertilizer is still providing your annuals with the nutrients they need.

Apply a low-nitrogen, quick-release fertilizer if this is your method of choice. Apply these fertilizers once each month (per label directions) throughout the growing season.

Be careful not to overfertilize **Cosmos** and **Nasturtiums**. Too much nitrogen can prevent bloom and encourage floppy growth of **Cosmos** plants.

JULY

Pests

Continue monitoring for pests.

- Japanese beetles are now starting to appear in scattered parts of the state. These small, shiny beetles eat holes in plant leaves. Lacy leaves are often the first clue that the beetles are present. Remove and destroy the beetles. Insecticides can be used, but they are harmful to other beneficial insects. Do not use commercially available traps. These tend to bring more Japanese beetles into your garden.

- Keep watching for plantbugs. These insects suck out plant juices. Their feeding causes spotting, yellowing, and browning of the leaves. Repeated applications of insecticidal soap will help reduce the damage.

- Check plantings for signs of leafhoppers. These wedge-shaped insects hop off the plant when disturbed. Their feeding can cause stunting and tip burn on the leaves. These insects also carry the aster yellow disease that causes a sudden wilting, yellowing, and death of susceptible plants. Prevent the spread of this disease by controlling the leafhoppers. Treat problem leafhoppers with insecticidal soap. Several applications may be needed for control.

Helpful Hints

July and early August are usually the hottest part of our growing season. Extreme heat can cause annuals to stop blooming, decline, and even die. **Reduce the stress to your plant with a little preventative care.**

- *Mulch* soil with shredded leaves, cocoa bean shells, pine needles, or other organic mulch. A thin layer of mulch helps keep the soil and plant roots cool and moist.
- *Water* plants thoroughly but less frequently. This encourages deep roots that are more drought tolerant.
- *Stop fertilizing* during extremely hot, dry weather. This can damage already stressed plants.
- Use heat and drought-tolerant plants, such as **Zinnia, Moss Rose, Gazania, Dusty Miller, Sunflower,** and **Cleome,** for the hotspots in your landscape.

- See December "Helpful Hints" for details on controlling aphids, mites, slugs, and earwigs.

Sanitation is usually sufficient to keep flower diseases under control. Pick off spotted leaves as soon as they appear. Deadhead flowers during rainy periods to reduce the risk of botrytis blight. Thin out plantings infected with powdery mildew. This increases air circulation and light penetration to help slow the spread of the disease.

Continue pulling and cultivating weeds. Mulched gardens will need much less attention.

Keep applying repellents to discourage troublesome deer, rabbits, and woodchucks. Make sure fencing is secure and still doing its job.

Pruning

Deadhead flowers for continual bloom and beauty. Pinch back leggy plants to encourage branching and more flowers.

Cut back **Lobelia** and heat-stressed **Alyssum**. Cut plants back halfway, continue to water, and wait for the weather to cool.

Stagger pinching and pruning within each flowerbed. This will keep you in flowers all season long.

Compost trimmings to get a second benefit from the plants. As these stems break down, they turn into compost that can be used to prepare future planting beds.

AUGUST

Planning

Keep visiting botanical and public gardens. Participate in their educational events and garden tours. This is a great way to find out if those annuals do as well in our area as the catalogs claim.

Planting

Replace weatherworn annuals with fall bedding plants. Purchase **Pansies**, **Flowering Kale**, and other cool-weather annuals to spruce up the garden for fall. You may have to wait until late August when transplants are available.

Care

The heat usually continues and often peaks this month. *Protect your plants and yourself from heat stress.*

- Mulch annuals to keep the roots cool and moist. Place a thin layer of shredded leaves, cocoa bean shells, or other organic material on exposed soil around the plants.

- Watch for heat stall in the garden. **Purple Alyssum**, **Lobelia**, **Snapdragons**, **Garden Pinks**, and **French Marigolds** are a few annuals that stop flowering during extremely hot weather. Wait for the weather to cool for these plants to start flowering. If this is a yearly problem, find a cooler location for these plants. Next year, replace them with **Zinnia**, **Gazania**, **Moss Rose**, and other more heat-tolerant plants.

- Wear a hat and long sleeves to protect eyes and skin from the sun's rays. Try gardening in early morning or evening to avoid the extreme heat. Just watch out for the mosquitoes!

Watering

Let the weather and your plants determine your watering schedule. Water annuals whenever the top few inches of soil start to dry. Mulched and shaded gardens need less frequent watering. Check plantings several times a week during extremely hot, dry weather.

Fertilizing

Do not fertilize gardens that received a slow-release (season-long) treatment in the spring.

Make your monthly application (if a quick-release fertilizer was your choice) as the weather conditions allow. Avoid fertilizing gardens during hot, dry periods. Adding fertilizer when water is limited can damage plant roots.

Continue fertilizing container gardens. Use a quick-release fertilizer according to label directions.

Check the fertilizer needs of the containers that received a slow-release fertilizer mixed into the soil at planting. If the plants appear less vigorous and foliage is pale, you may need to fertilize. Use a quick-release fertilizer according to label directions.

Pests

Continue monitoring plants for insects and disease. Mites and aphids are big problems during hot, dry weather. Watch for slugs and earwigs in shaded locations and during cool, wet weather. See December "Helpful Hints" for more details.

Japanese beetles are just finishing their aboveground feed. They will soon enter the soil and lay their eggs. Their young larvae, grubs, will begin feeding on grass roots. Treat the adults now to reduce future problems.

Check **Zinnias**, **Begonias**, and other annuals for powdery mildew. This fungal disease looks as if someone has sprinkled baby powder on the leaves. Make a note in your journal to use mildew-resistant plants and to correct growing conditions next year. Proper spacing for improved air circulation and sufficient sunlight will help reduce the risk of this disease.

Remove leaves with spots and discolored flowers. Sanitation is often the most effective treatment for fungal diseases in the garden. Discard infected plant parts to reduce the spread of disease.

Continue pulling weeds before they set seed. One plant can leave behind hundreds of seeds for next season. Spend a little time pulling weeds now and save yourself a lot of time next year.

Watch for signs of deer, rabbits, and woodchucks. Apply repellents, vary scare tactics, and check fencing in plantings that have been constantly plagued by these animals.

Pruning

Continue to deadhead faded flowers. Cut back to the first set of leaves or flowering offshoots. Pinch back leggy plants for a fresher look. Use a sharp knife or hand pruners to prune

Helpful Hints

It is never too soon to start preparing for winter. ***Start taking cuttings from annuals you want to overwinter indoors.*** Your garden plants are healthier and will root faster now than they will later in the season.

1 Coleus, Geraniums, Wax Begonias, Browallia, Impatiens, Fuchsia, Annual Vinca, and **Herbs** are commonly saved this way.

2 Take a 4- to 6-inch cutting from the tip of a healthy stem. Remove any flowers and the lowest set of leaves.

3 Dip the cut end in a rooting hormone to encourage rooting and discourage rot. Place the cutting in moist vermiculite, perlite, or a well-drained potting mix.

4 Place in a bright location away from direct sun. Keep the rooting mix moist.

5 Plant rooted cuttings—usually ready in two weeks—in small containers filled with a well-drained potting mix. Move to a sunny window and care for them as you would your other houseplants.

the plant one-fourth to halfway back. Cut just above a bud or set of healthy leaves. The remaining plant looks better and heals faster.

Take cuttings now to start new plants for overwintering annuals. See "Helpful Hints" for details.

Enjoy the fruits—or should I say flowers—of your labor:

• Harvest fresh flowers in the morning when the plants are full of moisture. Take a bucket of water out to the garden to

keep the cut flowers fresh. Once inside, recut the stems and place in clean water.

• Wait until midday, when flowers have less moisture, to harvest them for drying. Pick flowers when they have just reached maturity. Harvest strawflowers when the blossoms are half open. Remove foliage, tie in a bundle, and hang the flowers upside down to dry.

Planning

Your garden has filled in and is starting to reach its peak. It always seems to happen just before the first killing frost. So get out the camera and start taking pictures. This visual record of your garden will make it easier to plan future gardens. Plus, it may help you through those long, dark winter months.

Continue to record successes, challenges, and new ideas in your journal. These notes and your pictures will help make winter planning easier. Or join other gardeners who use their video cameras for this task. Walk around your yard filming and critiquing your landscape. Use this "home movie" when planning landscape and garden improvements.

Planting

Garden centers are filling with **Pansies**, **Ornamental Kale**, and other fall annuals. These plants tolerate the cool fall temperatures and extend your garden enjoyment even after frost.

Try planting **Second Season Pansies** and other cold-hardy **Pansies**. Plant them now for two seasons of enjoyment. These will bloom in fall, survive the winter, and provide another floral display in spring. Plant them in bulb gardens as groundcover around **Tulips**, **Daffodils**, and **Hyacinths**. Their colorful flowers make a nice addition to blooming bulbs and help mask the declining foliage.

Care

Get out the row covers, blankets, and other frost protection. September frosts are common in the northern and even southern parts of the state. Protect the plants from the first frosty days of fall, and then you often have an additional week or two of warm weather. Those few extra days of flowers mean a lot when the snow begins to fall.

- *Apply* frost protection in late afternoon when the danger of frost is forecast. Cover plants with row covers (season extending fabrics) or blankets.

- *Remove* blankets in the morning once the temperature is warm. Recover plants each night there is a danger of frost. Row covers can remain on the plants day and night during threatening weather. These products let air, light, and water through while trapping heat near the plants.

- *Move* containers into the house, porch, or garage when there is a danger of frost. Move them back outdoors during the day or when warmer weather returns.

Extending
the Season

- *Move* **Hibiscus** and other tropical plants to their indoor locations. These plants need bright light for the winter. Place them in a south-facing window or under artificial light for best results.

Watering

Keep watering container gardens. Check them daily and water as needed.

Check soil moisture before watering flower gardens. Only water when the top few inches of soil begin to dry. Continue to water thoroughly, but you will probably need to water less frequently. Cooler fall temperatures and rain showers usually take care of this job for you.

Fertilizing

Keep fertilizing container plants as needed. Follow label directions on the container. Most gardens do not need to be fertilized this late in the season.

Pests

The season is winding down and so are some of the pest problems. *Remove all diseased and insect-infested plant material during fall cleanup.* This reduces the potential for problems next season.

Powdery mildew often peaks in fall. Make a note to replace susceptible plants or use slightly shorter plants in front to mask the discolored foliage.

Remove weeds as they appear and before they have a chance to set seed.

Watch for squirrels digging in the garden. They love to store their nuts in gardens where the digging is easy. Tolerate the disturbance or discourage them with scare tactics and repellents.

Helpful Hints

The cooler weather reminds us that winter is on its way. Many gardeners like to bring their annuals indoors and keep them for next year's garden. I prefer to let most of my annuals die a quick death at the hands of Jack Frost. But there are always a few plants I just cannot part with each year. *Here are a few ways to keep plants for the winter. Pick the method that works best for the type of plant and the time and space you have available.*

- *Take cuttings* from your favorite plants. This method, described in August "Helpful Hints", takes up less space and minimizes the risk of bringing insects and diseases inside.
- *Transplant* flowers from the garden into a container. Or bring outdoor planters inside. Isolate these plants for several weeks before introducing them to your indoor plant collection. Unwanted insects often move inside with the plants. Place plants under lights or in a sunny window. Water and care for them as you would your other houseplants. Do not be alarmed if the leaves begin to yellow. These leaves often drop and are replaced by new, more shade-tolerant leaves. Some gardeners cut back the plants; I prefer to leave them intact. The more leaves on the plant, the more energy will be produced to help it through the transition.
- *Dig up* your **Geraniums** and store them in the basement in a cool, dark area. This method worked for most of our parents and grandparents. Unfortunately, we do not always have the cool basements and root cellars they possessed. It is very difficult to keep these plants from growing or drying out while in storage. This is the least successful method. If it is your only option, it is worth a try. We know they will die if left outside.

Pruning

Take cuttings of **Browallia, Coleus, Fuchsia, Geraniums, Impatiens, Wax Begonias, Annual Vinca**, and **Herbs** you plan to overwinter indoors. See August "Helpful Hints" for details.

Continue to harvest flowers for fresh arrangements and drying. Collect extra flowers to dry and use later for holiday decorations and gifts.

Planning

Take one last look at the garden. Make your final evaluations, being sure to include both successes and failures. Write down all those new plants and great ideas you want to try next season.

All America Selection® winners have been tested and judged at trial gardens across the United States. They are selected for their superior performance in garden situations. There have been over 300 AAS® winning annuals since the program started in 1933. See www.all-americaselections.org for a list of current and past winners.

Proven Winners® are selected by an international group of growers and propagators. They develop and test new hybrids for growers and home gardeners. Proven Winners® are more colorful, vigorous, and versatile than existing varieties. For more information see www.provenwinners.com.

Note which plants are frost tolerant. **Pansies**, **Snapdragons**, **Ornamental Kale**, **Alyssums**, and **Pinks** are a few annuals that tolerate frost. Plan to include these in future fall gardens.

Record the locations and flowers that are first to freeze. **Coleus**, **Impatiens**, and **Begonias** are killed by the first frost and often leave a big hole in the garden. Use these in areas where their early demise will not be a problem. Or plant them under trees, near the south side of the house, or in other areas that are the last to freeze.

Planting

Nature is busy planting your garden for next year. **Flowering Tobacco**, **Cosmos**, **Alyssum**, **Cleome**, and **Snapdragons** are a few of the annuals that may reseed in the garden. Most are lost to fall cleanup and soil preparation. I count on these volunteers to fill in empty spaces in my mixed (annual, perennial, and shrub) garden. Pull out plants, but do not cultivate the soil. Sprinkle any remaining seeds over the soil surface. Next spring, wait for the surprise. You may want to turn only a few small spaces over to nature and save the rest for spring planting.

Care

Hopefully the weather has been mild and the gardens are in their glory. *Here are some tips for getting your garden ready for winter:*

- Keep frost protection nearby. Cover plants in late afternoon when there is a danger of frost.

Remove the coverings when temperatures warm. Recover as needed.

Cold Weather Protection

- Move containers into the garage, porch, or house when there is a danger of frost. Move them back outdoors when warm weather returns.

- Call it quits when you are tired of gardening or the meteorologist says cold weather is here to stay.

- But wait, you're not done yet! Shred fallen leaves with your mower and work them into the top 6 to 12 inches of garden soil. The leaf pieces decompose over the winter, improving the drainage of heavy clay soils and the water-holding capacity of sandy soils.

- Do not till areas where you are trying to let annuals reseed.

Watering

Keep watering container gardens. It is almost time to pack away the garden hose and water wand.

Water annuals moved indoors whenever the top few inches of soil start to dry. Water thoroughly. Empty any excess water that collects in the saucer.

Fertilizing

Take a soil test if you have not already. See the introduction to this chapter or contact your local University of Minnesota Extension Service for soil test information. Send the sample in now so that you will have the results for winter planning and spring soil preparation.

Pests

The killing frost signals the end of the growing season and the start of fall cleanup. Remove all insect- and disease-infested plants. Discard or bury—do not compost—these plants. *Fall cleanup is the best way to reduce the risk of insects and disease in next year's garden.*

Helpful Hints

Hibiscus, Bougainvillea, Oleander, and other tropicals need to move indoors for winter.

1 *Start* by bringing them into the garage, screened-in porch, or indoor room away from your houseplants. Keep them isolated for several weeks. Check for insects. Use insecticidal soap to treat any mites and aphids you discover. Handpick and destroy larger caterpillars, slugs, earwigs, and beetles.

2 *Move* the plants indoors to a warm, sunny location. A south-facing window, Florida room, or atrium would work fine. Or add an artificial light to improve the light conditions found in most of our homes.

3 Continue to *water* thoroughly whenever the top few inches of soil start to dry. Do not fertilize until the plant adjusts to its new location and shows signs of growth.

4 *Prune* only enough to fit the plant into its winter location. Do not worry about the falling leaves. The plant will replace the fallen leaves as soon as it adjusts to its new location.

5 *Continue* to watch for pests and water as needed. Enjoy the added greenery and occasional flowers.

6 *Prune* overgrown plants in late February.

Record pest problems, control methods used, and successes and failures. These records will help you anticipate and reduce future pest problems through proper planning and plant selection.

Pruning

Remove faded flowers as well as dried up leaves and stems on plants moved inside for winter. Allow them to adjust to their new location before cutting back severely.

Planning

It is never too soon to start planning for next season. Take inventory of all your tools, seeds, and gardening equipment as you pack them away for winter storage. Start a list of replacement tools and supplies that you will need for next year. Do not forget to include those items you have always wanted but keep forgetting to buy. Remember, the gift-giving season is not too far away.

Planting

Finish soil preparation as the last few leaves drop and before the ground freezes. Take a soil test now if you did not get around to it last month. Test soil every three to five years, or whenever soil conditions change or plant problems develop.

Store leftover seeds in their original packets. These contain all the plant and planting information you need. Store these in an airtight jar in the refrigerator. The consistent storage conditions help preserve the seeds' viability.

Care

Clean garden tools before storing them for winter. See this month's "Helpful Hints" for details.

Move all fertilizers and pesticides to a secure location. Liquid materials should be stored out of direct light in a frost-free location. Granules must be kept dry. All pesticides should be kept in a locked location away from children and pets.

Check on **Geraniums** and other annuals in dormant storage. Move plants to a cooler, darker location if they begin to grow. If growth continues, pot them up and move them to a sunny window or under artificial lights.

Watering

Water annuals being grown indoors for the winter. Apply enough water so that the excess runs out the drainage hole. Pour off any water that collects in the saucer. Repeat whenever the top few inches start to dry.

Fertilizing

Indoor plants, including annuals grown indoors, need very little fertilizer. Use a dilute solution of flowering houseplant fertilizer if plants are actively growing and showing signs of nutrient deficiency. Otherwise, wait until plants adjust to their new location and begin to grow.

Pests

Watch for whiteflies, aphids, mites, and any other insects that may have moved indoors on the plants. These pests suck out plant juices, causing the leaves to yellow and eventually brown.

- High populations of aphids and mites can be controlled using insecticidal soap. Check the label before mixing and applying this or any other chemical.

- Whiteflies can also stress and stunt plants. These insects multiply quickly and are much harder to control. Try trapping whiteflies with commercial or homemade yellow sticky traps. Check your local garden center to purchase ready-to-use traps. Or make your own using yellow cardboard and tanglefoot, a sticky pine resin. The whiteflies will be attracted to the yellow, stick to the trap, and die. This will not eliminate the whiteflies but may reduce the populations enough to minimize stress to plants. Whiteflies are difficult to control with pesticides. Use three applications, five days apart, of an insecticide labeled for controlling whiteflies. If you miss one application, you will need to start the whole treatment process over. Apply in a well-ventilated location.

Constructing Whitefly Traps

- Fungus gnats are small insects that are often found flitting across the room. They do not hurt the plants; they just annoy us. These insects feed on the organic matter in the soil, such as dead plant roots and peat moss. Keep the soil slightly drier than normal to reduce their populations.

Helpful Hints

Clean hand tools, shovels, rakes, and hoes before putting them in storage for the winter. It is easier to do the job now than to wait until spring when the rust and hardened soil are harder to remove.

1 ***Wash*** or ***wipe off*** excess soil. Use a narrow putty knife to remove hardened soil. Or soak soil-encrusted tools in water and scrub with a wire brush.

2 ***Remove*** rust with a coarse grade of steel wool or medium-grit sanding paper or cloth. Add a few drops of oil to each side of the tool surface. Use a small cloth to spread it over the metal. This will help protect the surface against rust.

3 ***Sharpen*** the soil-cutting edges of shovels, hoes, and trowels to make digging easier. Use an 8- or 10-inch mill file to sharpen or restore the cutting angle. Visit your local hardware store for all the necessary equipment.

Press down and forward when filing. The file only cuts on the forward stroke. Lift the file, replace it to the original spot and push down and forward on the file again. Repeat until the desired edge is formed. File into or away from the cutting edge. It is safer to file away from the cutting edge. The edge will not be as sharp, but there is less risk of hurting yourself.

4 Check the handles for splinters and rough spots. Use 80-grit sandpaper on rough, wooden-handled tools. Coat with linseed oil.

5 Make sure the handles are tightly fastened to the shovel, hoe, or rake. You may need to replace or reinstall missing pins, screws, and nails. It is cheaper to replace a problem tool than to pay the doctor bills when the shovel flies off the handle!

Pruning

Prune and shape as needed. Most of the plants are spending their energy adjusting to their new location. They are trying to survive and very little new growth appears. Things will improve as the days lengthen and light intensity increases.

DECEMBER

Planning

Garden planning often gets lost in the chaos of the holiday preparations. Take advantage of the coming holidays to extend your garden season and share it with others. Frame your best garden and flower photos and give them as gifts to friends and relatives. Use dried flowers from your garden to decorate gift packages and cards. A bouquet of dried flowers makes a great gift for any housebound person—gardener or not.

Score points with the family and start cleaning out the basement. (They don't need to know that you are making room for a new or expanded seed starting setup!) See January "Planting" for more details.

Planting

Make a wish list of materials needed for your new seed starting endeavor. Be sure to include seeds, flats, containers, and other supplies that you will need. Your family will now be on to you and your recent cleaning frenzy—but you can solve their gift buying dilemmas. Consider giving the same type of gift or gardening gift certificate to your favorite gardeners.

Care

Check on plants stored in the basement. The stems should be firm but dormant. Move them to a cooler, darker location if they start to grow. If growth continues, pot them up and move them to a sunny window or under artificial lights.

Continue to care for annuals and tropicals (**Hibiscus** and such) that are growing indoors for the winter. Keep them out of drafts and in the brightest possible location.

Watering

Water indoor plants whenever the top few inches of soil start to dry. Apply enough water so that the excess runs out the bottom. Pour off any water that collects in the saucer.

Fertilizing

Plants are still struggling to adjust to their indoor location. The poor light and low humidity result in poor growth. Wait until plants start to grow before adding any fertilizer. Apply a dilute solution of any flowering houseplant fertilizer to plants that are actively growing and showing signs of nutrient deficiencies.

Pests

Continue to check plants for signs of whiteflies, mites, and aphids.

- Try trapping whiteflies with commercial or homemade yellow sticky traps. Coat a piece of yellow cardboard with tanglefoot. Place them in and near the infested plants. This will not kill all the whiteflies, but it is often enough to reduce the damage to a tolerable level. Use insecticides as your last resort. Select one labeled for controlling whiteflies on indoor plants. Spray three times, five days apart in a well-ventilated location. If you miss an application, you must start over.

- Control mites and aphids with a strong blast of water followed by a treatment of insecticidal soap. This product is a soap that is effective at killing insects, but it is safe for people and the environment. Repeated applications may be necessary.

Pruning

Pinch and clip as needed. Keep pruning to a minimum by removing only dead leaves and dead stems.

Helpful Hints

Some insects can become pests in the garden. Proper identification and early intervention are the best way to control these pests and minimize the negative impact on the environment.

- *Check* the upper and lower leaf surfaces and stems for aphids, mites, and plantbugs. These pests suck out plant juices, causing leaves to yellow and brown. Spray plants with a strong blast of water to dislodge these insects. Use insecticidal soap to treat damaging populations. This is a soap formulated to kill soft-bodied insects, but it will not harm the plant or environment.
- *Ignore* frothy masses (they look like spit) that appear on the stems of various plants. This is the hideout for spittlebug—not the work of neighborhood children. These insects feed on plants but rarely cause damage. Use insecticidal soap to control high populations if they at are damaging the plants.
- *Watch* for holes in the leaves. See the hole but not the pest? The culprits are probably earwigs or slugs. Both pests prefer cool, dark, and damp conditions. They feed at night, leaving holes in leaves and flowers.
- Earwigs are slender insects with pinchers at their rear. They do not crawl into your brains, but they are known to give many gardeners the willies! Trap them with a bamboo tube or crumpled paper under an overturned pot. European gardeners move their earwigs to the orchard. These insects eat codling moths and other harmful pests. If this is not your choice, drop them into a bucket of soapy water and destroy. As a last resort, use an insecticide labeled for controlling earwigs on annuals.
- Slugs are snails without shells. Use beer traps to control these pests. Place a shallow tin filled with beer in the soil. The slugs crawl in and drown. Or empty half a bottle of beer and lay it on its side. The bottle acts as shelter, keeping rain from diluting the beer. The slugs crawl in the hole and drown in the beer. Tuck bottles under the plants for a neater appearance.

Helpful Hints

Help small children handle the anticipation of the holidays by starting their own indoor annual gardens. Give them fancy pots or—better yet—the materials to decorate their own. Help them fill the pots with a sterile potting mix. Let them plant a few **Coleus** seeds or transplant one of your small annual plants into their container. Help them water and find the perfect growing location at home. Follow up and see how the plant and your young gardener are doing. Who knows? You may just end up with a helper or two next season!

Bulbs

Close your eyes and picture a beautiful snow-covered landscape. A nice thought in January, but by March you are probably ready for a little color other than white. Bulbs can give you that first glimpse of color that signals spring is on its way. Their beauty comes with little input from you. Plant them, provide basic care, and enjoy. Plus, the enjoyment of spring-flowering bulbs, comes when you are busy with other landscape and planting projects. **True bulbs** include things such as **Flowering Onions**, **Tulips**, **Daffodils**, and **Hyacinths**. Gardeners often use the term *bulb* to include **true bulbs**, **corms**, **rhizomes**, **tubers**, and **tuberous roots**. All of these are underground storage structures that provide the plant with everything it needs to sprout and flower. Once up and growing, the leaves manufacture the food that is stored in the bulb for the next growing period.

Daffodil Bulb

Bulbs are also classified by bloom time and hardiness. Knowing the type, bloom time, and hardiness will help you know when and how to plant and propagate your bulbs. *Spring-flowering and early summer-flowering bulbs are planted in the fall, bloom in the spring or early summer, and are generally hardy.* They include **Tulips**, **Daffodils**, **Iris**, and **Squills**. These bulbs need a cold period to flower.

Summer-flowering bulbs include **Lilies**, **Tuberous Begonias**, and **Cannas**. Some are hardy and need a cold period to bloom, while most are non-hardy (tender) and must be brought indoors for winter.

Planning

Walk through your garden, review your garden journal, or look at pictures of past springs. Where can your landscape use a splash of color? *Some ideas for where to plant bulbs include:*

- Add a large bed of hardy bulbs for a dynamic spring display.

Follow with **Annuals** to mask declining plants and provide color through the fall.

- Plant small groups of hardy bulbs throughout your perennial gardens. As the bulbs fade, the Perennials will hide the declining bulb foliage and provide additional bloom.

- Dress up shrub beds and groundcovers with hardy and tender bulbs. They will add an element of surprise as well as color.

- Naturalize bulbs in wooded areas and use short bulbs, such as **Crocus** or **Squills**, in the lawn. Select bulbs suitable for naturalizing. When used in the lawn, the bulbs should be tough enough to tolerate mowing—or you will need to tolerate a little long grass in the spring

Keep the bulbs blooming and healthy by planting them in the right location. Most bulbs require well-drained soils with 6 to 8 hours of direct sun. To prepare the soil, work 2 inches of organic matter

Bulbs

into the top 8 to 12 inches of soil. This improves drainage in clay soils and increases the water-holding capacity in sandy or rocky soils. Use shade-tolerant plants like **Daffodils** and **Tuberous Begonias** where sunlight is limited. Remember that spring-flowering bulbs growing near deciduous trees (those that lose their leaves in winter) get the needed sunlight before the trees leaf out.

Avoid planting bulbs next to your home's foundation or near any source of artificial heat, such as the dryer vent. Bulbs planted in these locations are more likely to sprout during a winter thaw.

Buying Bulbs

Most people think about buying bulbs in the spring when they are blooming, not in the fall when we should be planting. Many bulb catalogs are taking advantage of this. You can now order your bulbs in the spring, and they will be shipped to you in fall in time for planting. Just remember not to get carried away by the beauty of spring—all those bulbs will need to be planted! I have spent many a cold November day planting bulbs before the first major snowstorm.

Shop early at the garden center for greater variety and better quality bulbs. Purchase full-size bulbs that are firm and are free from soft, dry, or discolored spots and pests. Store your bulbs in a cool, dark place until planting. Always select the bulb best suited to the growing location. They should fit the light, soil, and other growing conditions of the planting site.

Planting

Soil preparation is the first step in planting. Add 2 inches of organic matter and 1 pound per 100 square feet of a low-nitrogen (the first of three numbers on the fertilizer bag), slow-release fertilizer to the soil. Work these into the top 8 to 12 inches of the soil. Bonemeal is a traditional favorite that is generally not needed. Most of our soils already have the phosphorus that bonemeal provides. Select a fertilizer with little or no phosphorus and potassium (the second and third numbers on the fertilizer bag).

Plant hardy spring- and summer-flowering bulbs in fall. Wait until late September (in the northern part of the state) or early October (in the southern part of the state) to plant these bulbs. Planting earlier increases the risk of bulbs sprouting prematurely during a warm fall. You can keep planting these bulbs until the ground freezes. There are even some tricks that can be used after the ground freezes. See November "Planting" for some ideas.

Summer- and fall-blooming tender bulbs are planted outdoors in spring after the danger of frost. Consider starting them indoors in mid- to late March for earlier flowering in the garden. Plant the transplants outdoors after the danger of frost.

Autumn Crocus (*Colchicum*) should be planted by late August or early September. These fall-blooming corms will flower soon after planting. Watch for their leaves the following spring. You can also plant or transplant them in late spring or summer if the bulbs or transplants are available.

To plant bulbs once the soil is prepared:

1 *Arrange* and properly space the bulbs on the soil surface. Use a bulb planter or trowel to set bulbs at the proper depth and spacing.

2 For larger beds, *excavate* the entire bed to the proper planting depth. Arrange and properly space the bulbs in the bottom of the planting hole. Fill the hole with amended soil and water. To make the process easier, prepare as much of the planting area as possible when adding bulbs to existing plantings.

Bulbs

3 Bulbs should be planted at a depth of two to three times the height of the bulb. For example, a 1-inch-tall bulb should be planted 2 to 3 inches deep. See the chart in this chapter for spacing recommendations for particular bulbs.

4 Do not plant bulbs deeper than 6 inches in poorly drained and clay soils where they can rot. You can plant deeper in well-drained and sandy soils.

5 Lightly *tamp* the soil surface to remove air pockets. Water thoroughly to the settle the soil and get the bulbs off to a good start.

See the May and June "Planting" sections for details on planting non-hardy bulbs.

Care

Even though the spring-flowering bulbs are in the ground, your work is not quite over. *Here are some tips for getting the most out of your bulbs:*

- *Mulch* borderline hardy, late planted, or expensive (more for your sake than for the plant) bulbs in the fall after the ground freezes. Winter mulch insulates the soil, preventing fluctuating temperatures that lead to untimely sprouting and frost heaving.

- Snow is the best mulch. Evergreen branches, straw, or weed-free hay work well for those in southern Minnesota with less reliable snow cover.

- *Remove* the mulch in spring after the severe weather has passed or the plants begin to grow.

- *Remove* **Tulip** and **Hyacinth** flowers as they fade. This will allow more energy to go into the bulb rather than seed production. *Deadhead* other bulb flowers if they appear unsightly.

- *Leave* the leaves intact until they yellow or dry naturally. Removing the leaves prematurely can result in a lack of flowers and poor growth next season.

At some point, your bulbs will probably need to be divided. Here are some tips for when and how to divide:

- Most bulbs grow and produce offsets such as bulblets, cormels, or additional tubers and longer rhizomes. When they become overcrowded, this will lead to poor growth, failure to bloom, and the need to divide. Quick spreaders need division every two to four years, while others can remain intact for many years.

- *Divide* spring-flowering bulbs when the plants become overcrowded and the plants decline or fail to bloom.

- *Dig*, *separate*, and *replant* the bulbs in late spring or early summer, as the leaves begin to wither. Or mark the location and do it in the fall during bulb planting season.

- Tender bulbs such as **Tuberous Begonias**, **Dahlias**, and **Cannas** can be divided in fall after they are dug or in spring before planting. I prefer spring division. The plants will be growing and can recover quickly from the dividing.

- *Each division must have at least one eye.* These swollen buds appear on the stem of the **Dahlia**, the rhizomes of the **Iris** and **Canna**, and the corm of the **Caladium**. This eye will sprout and grow into a new plant.

Watering

Spring-flowering bulbs usually receive sufficient water from normal rainfall and irrigation. Water new bulb plantings several times during a dry fall and as needed in spring. Soak the top 6 to 12 inches of soil whenever it is dry.

Bulbs

Summer-flowering, tender bulbs need 1 inch of water each week. Water deeply to soak the top 6 to 8 inches of soil. Container plantings must be checked and usually watered once a day.

Cover the soil with shredded leaves, cocoa bean shells, finely shredded bark, or some other material. A 1- to 2-inch layer will conserve moisture and reduce weed problems.

Fertilization

Fertilize only if needed. Pale leaves and poor growth are signs that the bulbs need fertilizing. Healthy flowering bulb plants are probably receiving enough fertilizer from the surrounding plantings. As you fertilize the **Annuals** and **Perennials** in the planting bed, you are enriching the soil for the bulbs as well.

You can add fertilizer to improve bloom and increase offset production. Apply a slow-release, low-nitrogen fertilizer in spring as the leaves begin to peak through the soil.

Incorporate fertilizer in the soil prior to planting tender bulbs. You may need additional fertilizer mid-season. Check the directions for the fertilizer used.

Pests

Well-sited bulbs are fairly pest free. Proper soil preparation and care will prevent most disease problems. The few insects that appear are usually easy to control.

Animals are the biggest problem. Squirrels love to dig freshly planted bulbs, voles like to eat the bulbs in winter, while rabbits and deer wait till spring to munch on the flowers and leaves. *Try these tactics to minimize the damage from animals:*

- Commercial and homemade repellents may provide some relief. Apply them as soon as there is potential for damage. Hot pepper, mothballs (keep away from children and pets), human hair, and highly scented soaps are just a few of the home remedies. TreeGuard®, Ropel®, and Hot Pepper Wax™ spray are a few of the commonly found commercial repellents.

- Scare tactics including white bags and balloons on sticks, clanging pans, and radios may provide some relief. Vary the tactics used for better results. However, I have found that urban animals are so accustomed to the noise and smell of people that these tactics do not work.

- Create a barrier with chicken wire. Dig the planting hole to the proper depth. Place and properly space bulbs in the planting hole. Cover bulbs with 1 inch of soil. Cover with chicken wire and fill the hole with the remaining soil. The wire screening will keep out voles, chipmunks, and squirrels. I like to bend the screening over the sides to further discourage wildlife.

- Plant **Daffodils**, **Hyacinths**, **Snowdrops**, and **Winter Aconites** that tend to be resistant to animal damage.

Minnesota Bulbs

Common Name (Botanical Name)	Plant in Garden	Depth	Spacing	Blooms	Hardiness
Autumn Crocus (*Colchicum*)	June to early September	4 inches	6 to 8 inches	September	Hardy
Caladium (*Caladium × bicolor*)	late May to early June outdoors; Mid- to late March indoors	1 inch	12 inches	Foliage all season	Tender
Calla Lily (*Zantedeschia aethiopica*)	late May to early June outdoors; mid- to late March indoors	3 to 4 inches	12 to 18 inches	June to July	Tender
Canna (*Canna generalis*)	late May or early June outdoors; mid- to late March indoors	4 to 6 inches	12 to 24 inches	Summer to Fall	Tender
Crocus (*Crocus vernus*)	October until ground freezes	3 inches	3 to 4 inches	March to April	Hardy
Daffodil (*Narcissus*)	October until ground freezes	5 to 6 inches	6 to 9 inches	April to May	Hardy
Dahlia (*Dahlia*)	late May to early June outdoors; mid- to late March indoors	4 inches	12 to 24 inches	July to October	Tender
Gladiolus (*Gladiolus × hortulanus*)	May to June	3 to 6 inches	6 to 9 inches	Summer to Frost	Tender
Glory-of-the-Snow (*Chionodoxa luciliae*)	October until ground freezes	3 inches	4 inches	April	Hardy
Grape Hyacinth (*Muscari botryoides*)	October until ground freezes	3 inches	4 inches	April to May	Hardy

Minnesota Bulbs

Common Name (Botanical Name)	Plant in Garden	Depth	Spacing	Blooms	Hardiness
Hyacinth (*Hyacinthus orientalis*)	October until ground freezes	6 inches	6 to 9 inches	May	Hardy
Iris (Bearded) (*Iris* hybrids)	mid-July to September	At soil surface	5 to 9 inches	May to mid-June	Hardy
Lily (*Lilium*)	October until ground freezes	3 to 6 inches	12 to 20 inches	Summer	Hardy (varies with species and cultivar)
Ornamental Onion (*Allium*)	October until ground freezes	2 to 6 inches	4 to 8 inches	May to September	Hardy (zone hardiness varies with species)
Siberian Squill (*Scilla siberica*)	October until ground freezes	3 inches	4 to 6 inches	April to May	Hardy
Snowdrops (*Galanthus nivalis*)	October until ground freezes	3 inches	4 inches	March to April	Hardy in zone 4
Tuberous Begonia (*Begonia × tuberhybrida*)	late May to early June outdoors; mid- to late March indoors	1 inch	12 inches	Summer to Frost	Tender
Tulip (*Tulipa*)	October until ground freezes	5 to 6 inches	6 to 9 inches	April to May	Hardy
Winter Aconite (*Eranthus hyemalis*)	October until ground freezes	3 inches	3 inches	March to April	Hardy

Planning

Break out the catalogs, surf the Internet (www.bulb.com is a great site), and start a wish list of new, non-hardy bulbs that you want to try this summer. Review your landscape plan, journal, and garden photos to find suitable locations for the new additions. Keep in mind that last year's plants have grown and multiplied, so you will need to find additional space or new homes for some of them as well.

Keep your resolution to faithfully write in your garden journal. Record details on planting times, bulb forcing techniques, successes, and challenges encountered this season. Make a list of your favorites and those that need to be replaced.

Planting

You may have received an **Amaryllis** as a gift or have one stored in the basement. Now is the time to pot it up and get it growing.

1 *Plant* the **Amaryllis** in a pot slightly larger than the bulb.

2 *Place* the bulb so that the pointed half is above the soil.

3 *Fill* the pot with any sterile, well-drained potting mix.

4 *Water* and *move* the pot to a cool, bright location, such as a sunny window in a cool room with temperatures around 60 to 65 degrees Fahrenheit. Keep the soil moist, but not wet. Soon new growth will appear as either flowers or leaves. Be patient; after one appears, the other should soon follow.

5 *Remove* the flower stem when the plant has finished flowering to direct the energy to rejuvenating the bulb not producing seeds.

6 *Move* the plant to a sunny window, continue to water and fertilize with any dilute solution of a flowering houseplant fertilizer.

7 *Harden off* the plant and move it outdoors after the danger of frost. Water and fertilize as needed. Bring it back indoors, before the first fall frost, for winter and a chance to rebloom. Allow the plants to go dormant. Do not water for 8 to 10 weeks. Then topdress or repot. It will take 4 to 8 weeks to rebloom.

Plant any leftover spring bulbs. There is still time to force them for spring bloom. See October "Helpful Hints" for tips on forcing bulbs.

Care

Things are pretty quiet outdoors. You can still add winter mulch if the ground is not covered with snow. I collect and recycle my neighbors' Christmas trees. The branches make an attractive winter mulch. Cover bulb plantings with evergreen branches for insulation. This keeps the ground cold and helps prevent sprouting during winter thaws.

Check on non-hardy bulbs tucked away for winter storage. Discard any soft, discolored, or rotting bulbs. Move sprouting bulbs to a cooler (45 to 50 degrees Fahrenheit), dark location. If they continue to grow, you may end up with a few extra houseplants for spring.

Start bringing forced bulbs planted in October out of cold storage. Stagger forcing times to extend your indoor bloom. Move bulbs to a cool, bright location. Water thoroughly as the soil below the surface just begins to feel dry and wait for a glorious display. Remove spent flowers, continue to water, and fertilize with a diluted solution of any flowering houseplant fertilizer.

Check on the remaining bulbs you have in cold storage. The soil should remain slightly moist and the temperatures between 35 and 45 degrees Fahrenheit. Gradually reduce the storage temperature or move bulbs to a cooler location if they begin to sprout.

Watering

Water **Amaryllis** and any other flowering bulbs, keeping the soil moist but not wet.

Fertilizing

Fertilize **Amaryllis** and forced bulbs when they have finished blooming. This will help restore some of the spent energy. Use a dilute solution of any flowering houseplant fertilizer.

Pruning

Remove spent flowers on **Amaryllis** and other forced bulbs. Leave the leaves intact if you plan on reblooming them in the future.

Pests

Insects: Fungus gnats and aphids may become a problem. Fungus gnats are the little fruit fly–like insects that can be seen flitting around your plants. Keep the soil slightly drier to reduce their populations. These are not harmful to the plants—just a nuisance to you. Aphids, which are small, teardrop-shaped insects, can weaken plants. Treat outbreaks with insecticidal soap. You may need several applications.

Helpful Hints

Many garden magazines and books talk about reblooming **Amaryllis** as if it were as easy as growing **Impatiens** in the shade. Don't be discouraged if that has not been your experience. You are in the majority. I have met many frustrated gardeners who grow a great crop of leaves but no flowers. ***Here are a few techniques that you may want to try for reblooming Amaryllis:***

- ***The traditional approach:*** Keep the **Amaryllis** growing indoors throughout the spring. Move the plant outdoors for summer. Some gardeners sink the pot in the ground to reduce the need for water. Stop fertilizing midsummer and cut back on water in late August. Move the pot indoors. Cut back or allow the leaves to dry naturally. Store it in a cool, dark place for 3 months. Move the pot to a sunny window, water as needed and wait. With some luck you should have flowers in a month.
- ***Bare-root storage:*** Keep the plant growing indoors throughout the spring. Plant the bulb directly in the garden for the summer. Dig it up and move it indoors prior to the first fall frost. Allow the leaves to dry and store the bare root in a cool, dark location. Plant the bulbs in January and grow in a sunny location.
- ***Continual care:*** Keep your **Amaryllis** plant growing year round. Leave it in the container. Move it outdoors for summer and indoors in a well-lit location for winter. I used this method and was rewarded with flowers in summer and winter.

Diseases: Check stored bulbs and discard any that are showing signs of mold and bulb rot.

Aphid

Planning

Pull out the wish list and finalize your order for tender bulbs. You will need to start these bulbs in mid-March for earlier summer bloom. Watch for hardy bulb catalogs in the spring. Many catalogs include their spring-flowering bulbs as well. Place the order now and the hardy bulbs will be delivered in fall. This allows you to take care of both orders at once. Update your landscape plans and identify potential planting areas for new and stored bulbs.

Monitor your outdoor plantings. Use your journal to record any observations and any needed actions. Note any areas with standing water or ice. These conditions can lead to bulb rot and even death. Note the location of any bulbs that sprout during one of our winter thaws. Plan on moving them this year or mulching them next fall after the ground freezes.

Hybrid **Tulips** and **Hyacinths** are generally not long lived in Wisconsin. Increase their longevity by mulching the bulbs in summer, removing flower stems after the flower fades, and using species or perennializing **Tulips** such as **Triumph Tulips, Darwin Tulips,** or **Species Tulips.**

Planting

If you can find them, you can plant them—**Paper-white Narcissus**, that is. Check garden centers and catalogs for availability. *Here are some tips for forcing your* **Paper-whites**:

1 *Fill* a shallow container with sterile pea gravel, pebbles, or marbles. Add enough water to reach the top of the gravel. *Place* the bulbs on the gravel and cover with just enough gravel to hold them in place.

2 Or *plant* them in a container of any well-drained potting mix. Leave the tops of the bulbs exposed. Keep the planting mix moist, but not wet.

3 *Move* the potted bulbs to a cool (45 to 60 degrees Fahrenheit) location for rooting.

4 *Place* them in a bright location as soon as the leaves start to grow. It takes just a few weeks to get flowers. This is a great project for kids or any anxious gardener.

You can still purchase, plant, and force **Amaryllis** into bloom. See January "Planting" for details.

Once the **Amaryllis** *flowers have faded, repot any plants that were held over from last year.*

1 *Remove* any bulblets that formed in the past year. Plant these in separate small pots.

2 *Plant* Amaryllis in a pot slightly larger than the bulb. Fill the pot with any sterile, well-drained potting mix. Place the bulb so that the pointed half is above the soil.

3 *Water* and *move* the potted bulb to a sunny location. Allow the soil to dry slightly between watering.

4 *Fertilize* with any dilute solution of a flowering houseplant fertilizer.

5 *Harden off* and move outdoors after the danger of frost.

6 Bring it back indoors for winter and a chance to rebloom.

You can still pot up spring-flowering bulbs for indoor forcing. They need about twelve to fifteen weeks of 35- to 45-degree Fahrenheit temperatures. They will be flowering about the time your outdoor gardens begin to bloom. This makes them perfect to use outdoors in flowerboxes and containers. The forced bulbs can add color in areas where bulbs will not usually grow.

Care

Remove several more pots of forced bulbs from storage. Stagger removal times by two weeks to extend the bloom period. Move the bulbs to a cool, sunny window where they can be enjoyed. Water thoroughly whenever the soil below the surface just starts to dry and wait for the colorful show. Remove spent flowers, continue to water, and fertilize with a diluted solution of any flowering houseplant fertilizer.

Check on the remaining bulbs you have in cold storage. The soil should remain slightly moist and the temperatures between 35 and 45 degrees Fahrenheit. Gradually reduce the storage temperature or move bulbs to a cooler location if they begin to sprout.

Now take a look outside. February often means a winter thaw and hundreds of calls from anxious gardeners—"My bulbs have sprouted! What do I do?" The answer: "Nothing, now." Fortunately bulbs are tough. The exposed leaves may be damaged by the subsequent cold, but the flower buds are usually still buried in the soil.

Early blooming **Tulips** and **Daffodils** may suffer if we have an extended thaw followed by a cold snap. The plants will survive, though the flowers may be lost for this year. Next fall, mulch areas prone to early sprouting. Wait until the ground lightly freezes and cover these areas with straw, marsh hay, or evergreen branches. Or move the bulbs to a location that is less affected by the fluctuating temperatures.

Watering

Keep the soil moist on potted bulbs that you are trying to force. Continue to water forced bulbs if you plan on reblooming them in the future.

Fertilizing

Apply a diluted solution of any flowering plant fertilizer to **Amaryllis** and forced bulbs once they stop blooming.

Pruning

Remove spent blooms and drying leaves on forced bulbs.

Pests

Fungus gnats are often mistaken for fruit flies. They can be seen flitting across a room, usually in front of a guest. These gnats feed on the organic matter in the soil and are not harmful, just annoying. *To control fungus gnats:*

- Try living with them. The populations will rise and fall and eventually disappear (or maybe I just get used to them).

- Allow the soil to dry slightly between watering. Fungus gnats thrive in moist, organic soils. Keeping it dry helps reduce their population.

- Try an environmentally friendly product sold as Gnatrol®. The active ingredient is *Bacillus thuringiensis israelensis*. This particular bacteria only kills the larvae of fungus gnats and mosquitoes. Check garden catalogs if you cannot find it in your local garden center.

Planning

Get out your garden journal and start recording bloom times. Your camera is another good way to record the seasonal progressions in your garden. Watch for small, early bulbs such as **Snowdrops** and **Winter Aconites** that will start appearing as the snow recedes. Recording bloom times helps you identify slow periods of few blooms in the garden.

Start a wish list of those bulbs you want to add to your garden. Consider adding some of the early blooming minor bulbs. Though small in stature, they add a touch of color when you are starved for a little glimpse of spring. My spring garden is probably my favorite. Every day is a surprise, with plants breaking through the soil and forgotten bulbs starting to bloom. And then, of course, the weather adds an element of excitement and challenge.

Planting

Start planting tender bulbs indoors in mid- to late-March through early April. **Cannas**, **Dahlias**, **Tuberous Begonias**, and **Caladiums** started indoors will bloom earlier in the garden. If indoor growing space is limited, wait and plant them directly outdoors in late spring.

- Clean and divide bulbs if this was not done in fall. Make sure there is at least one eye for every division. Without this eye, the division will not grow and develop into a plant.

- Fill flats with a mixture of half peat and half perlite or vermiculite, or use any well-drained potting mix.

- Set **Begonia** tubers hollow side up in the mix. Plant so that the top of the tuber is even with the soil surface.

- Place **Canna** rhizomes, eyes facing up, in the mix. Bury these so the upper half of the rhizome is just above the soil surface.

- Plant **Dahlia** tuberous roots in small pots so that the tuberous root is covered and the eye is 1 inch below the soil surface.

- Plant **Caladium** tubers with knobby side up in small pots. Cover tubers with 1 to 2 inches of soil.

- Water and move plants to a warm location.

- Place planted bulbs under artificial lights or near a sunny window as soon as they sprout.

- **Cannas** and **Tuberous Begonias** can be transplanted into individual containers as soon as several leaves develop.

Care

Check for frost heaving. Unmulched gardens or those with inconsistent snow cover are subject to freezing and thawing temperatures. The fluctuating temperatures cause the soil to shift, pushing bulbs and other plants right out of the soil. Gently tamp heaved plants back in place.

Take a look under the winter mulch. Remove the mulch only if the bulbs start to grow and temperatures are hovering near freezing. Keep some mulch handy to cover bulbs during extreme cold snaps. Fortunately, bulbs are tough and can tolerate pretty cold temperatures and even a blanket of snow. In fact, snow makes the best mulch.

Remove forced bulbs from cold treatment. Those bulbs planted in November are ready to come out of cold storage.

Keep the foliage of **Amaryllis** and other forced bulbs growing in a sunny window. These can be rebloomed with a little care from you. See January and December "Helpful Hints."

Watering

Keep the soil moist for newly planted tender bulbs and

MARCH

flowering bulbs. Allow the top few inches of soil of forced bulbs that are finished blooming to dry slightly before watering again.

Usually there is no need to water outdoors. The northern part of the state may still be blanketed in snow, and the rest of the state experiences spring one day and blizzards the next.

Helpful Hints

Many florists are selling hardy **Oriental** and **Asiatic Lilies** as well as the traditional **White Lily** for Easter. *Keep your Lilies looking healthy by:*

* Placing them in a cool, bright location in your home. Avoid heat ducts and warm rooms.
* Keep the soil moist, but not wet. Perforate or remove the decorative foil and place the pot on a saucer. Make sure that the water does not collect in the saucer, decorative pots, or baskets. This can lead to root rot. See April "Helpful Hints" for moving them into the garden.

Fertilizing

Hardy bulbs need little fertilization. Fertilize now through April if you want to increase vigor and if you did not fertilize in the fall. For best results, apply a low-nitrogen, slow-release fertilizer to bulbs as they begin to sprout outdoors.

Fertilize **Amaryllis** and other forced bulbs that you want to keep. Use a dilute solution of any flowering houseplant fertilizer. Apply it after they are through flowering.

Pruning

Leave bulb foliage intact. The green leaves produce energy that is needed for the plants to grow and flower next year. Deadhead the flowers as needed.

Pests

Disappearing bulbs is a common complaint. They were fine last spring, but they never showed up this year. *Here are some possible solutions for your disappearing bulbs:*

* Check soil drainage. Poorly drained soils and those covered with ice or standing water can cause bulbs to rot and seem to disappear.

* Review maintenance practices. Removing bulb leaves right after flowering reduces the energy available for continued growth. These bulbs may produce a few undersized leaves with no flowers or they may disappear completely.

* Squirrels may be digging and moving bulbs. Every year I discover a few **Tulips** that have been moved to different parts of my yard or into the adjacent park. It adds an extra element of surprise to my spring garden.

* Other animals may be eating the bulbs as fast as they grow.

Animals are the biggest—not only in terms of size but also in the amount of damage—pest of bulbs. If you were able to save the bulbs from the marauding squirrels in the fall, you will now need to fend off the hungry rabbits and deer. It can be frustrating watching your beautiful flowers disappear before your eyes. See "Pests" in the introduction to this chapter for tips on reducing animal damage.

APRIL

Planning

Keep recording bloom times. Photograph or videotape your spring garden. I find pictures make future planning much easier.

Record significant weather information in your journal. These events often impact plants later in the growing season. Refer to these records when the weather patterns reoccur in the future. Experience is the best way to improve your gardening skills. Writing them down ensures that you will remember them.

This is also a good time to update your existing plans and labels. Mark bulb locations for future plantings and transplanting. Use large, colorful golf tees to mark bulb locations. Draw the locations, and record plant names on your garden map. Color code and number the golf tees to correspond to the map.

Planting

Finish planting tender bulbs indoors, if you want earlier flowering outdoors this summer. See March "Planting" for directions.

Purchase pre-cooled Lily bulbs and plant them outdoors as soon as the soil is workable. Hardy **Lilies** need at least 6 to 8 hours of sun and well-drained soils for best results. Work several inches of organic matter into the top 8 to 12 inches of soil. The organic matter improves the drainage of clay soils and the water-holding capacity of sandy soils. Store these bulbs in a cool, dark place until planting. An extra refrigerator or the coolest corner of your basement would work well as areas for chilling your spring-flowering bulbs. Leave the bulbs packed in peat moss or sawdust in the perforated plastic bag.

Care

Remove forced bulbs from storage. Use some for indoor enjoyment. Move a few of the potted bulbs from cold storage directly outdoors to planters and window boxes. This is a great way to brighten up drab areas and create a surprise in the spring landscape.

Remove winter mulch as the bulbs begin to grow and the weather consistently hovers near freezing. Northern gardeners may want to keep a little mulch handy in case of sudden and extreme drops in temperature.

Replant or firm frost-heaved bulbs back into place. Frost heaving occurs in unmulched gardens or those with inconsistent snow cover. The fluctuating temperatures in the exposed soil cause the soil to shift, pushing bulbs and other plants right out of the soil.

Watering

Water indoor plants as needed. Keep the soil of newly planted tender bulbs and blooming plants moist. Continue to water forced bulbs thoroughly as the soil just starts to dry.

Outdoor bulb plantings may need to be watered in a dry spring. Water when the bulbs show signs of wilting. Soak planting beds with 1 inch or enough water to moisten the top 6 to 8 inches of soil.

Fertilizing

Most bulbs get sufficient nutrients from the soil. Fertilization can help increase flowering and vigor. Use a low-nitrogen fertilizer with little or no phosphorus and potassium. Fertilize bulbs once in spring as they begin to sprout. Do not fertilize if it was done last fall.

Pruning

Leave bulb leaves intact. They are manufacturing the energy needed for plants to grow and bloom next season.

Remove faded flowers. Deadheading **Tulip** hybrids and **Hyacinths** helps to lengthen their lifespan. Deadhead other bulbs for aesthetic reasons.

Pests

Frost damage can damage **Daffodil** buds and prevent them from fully developing. The emerging flower stalks of **Daffodils** are often overlooked in spring. Their flat appearance makes them blend in with the foliage. A cold snap can damage the tender buds. Plant later-blooming Daffodils or winter mulch the bulbs next fall to prevent early sprouting. There is always next year.

Bud blast results in brown, dry, and failed **Daffodil** *flower buds.* It appears to be more common on late-blooming and double-flowering cultivars. Extreme temperature fluctuations, inadequate water, and wet fall seasons have been blamed for this disorder. Adjust care and replace varieties that continually suffer from this disorder.

Helpful Hints

Do not compost that Easter Lily. Move it outdoors and start your own Easter-in-July garden. Both the traditional and hardy **Lilies** forced for Easter can be planted outdoors for years of added beauty. Northern gardeners may have limited success with the traditional **Easter Lily** and may want to consider one of the hardier species now being sold by florists.

1 Continue to grow and care for your **Lily** after the flowers fade.

2 *Remove* faded flowers and *fertilize* with a dilute solution of any flowering houseplant fertilizer.

3 *Prepare* a planting site in full sun with well-drained soils. Plan on using these tall plants as backdrops or vertical accents.

4 *Move* the bulbs outdoors in late May or early June. Transplant slightly deeper so that the bulb is about 3 to 5 inches deep. Leave the leaves intact and water as needed.

5 Be patient. The bulbs may not bloom until the second summer (mid- to late-July) after transplanting.

Continue to monitor and manage animal damage and disappearing bulbs. See March "Pests" for details.

Pull or cultivate weeds as they appear. They will be smaller and easier to remove from the moist soil common to spring. It is also less overwhelming to pull a few weeds every week than to spend hours digging out a weed-infested planting.

Prevent iris borer with proper sanitation in the fall. If this wasn't done, and borers have been a problem, you may decide to use an insecticide. Read and follow label directions; these are pesticides that should be handled carefully. Apply a systemic insecticide, labeled for use on iris borers, when the leaves are 4 to 6 inches tall. Later applications are not effective. By that time, the borers are safely inside and eating their way through the **Iris**. Not sure you have borers? Make a note in your journal to dig and divide declining **Iris**. Check the rhizomes, cut out the borers and the surrounding tissue before replanting. Monitor these for future problems.

Planning

Keep evaluating your garden and recording information in your journal. This is an excellent time to reflect on your early spring garden.

Identify possible planting locations for fall additions of spring-flowering bulbs. This will reduce your panic and improve your results during the fall scramble to get the bulbs into the ground.

As bulbs fade, plan to deal with the fading foliage. See this month's "Helpful Hints" for some ideas.

Finalize summer bulb garden plans. Consider using tender bulbs to fill voids left by early bloomers or winter-killed plants. Use them in containers to dress up the steps, patio, or other areas that lack planting space.

Planting

Prepare the soil before planting tender bulbs outdoors. Add organic matter to the top 8 to 12 inches of soil. Once the soil warms, you can begin planting the bulbs of **Gladiola**, **Cannas**, and **Dahlias**. Wait until late May or early June to plant the **Caladium** corms, **Begonia** tubers, and transplants of tender bulbs outdoors.

- Plant **Gladiolus** corms every two weeks from mid-May through June. This will extend the bloom time throughout the summer. Plant full-size, healthy corms 4 inches deep and 9 inches apart.

- Cut **Canna** rhizomes into smaller sections with at least one or two eyes per division. Plant them 4 to 6 inches deep and 12 to 20 inches apart.

- Divide **Dahlias** so that each tuberous root has a portion of the stem containing at least one eye. Plant 4 inches deep with the tuber laying on its side and the eye facing upward. Install the stakes for tall Dahlias at this time so you won't spear the buried tuber later. Fill the planting hole with soil and water.

- Plant **Tuberous Begonias** and **Caladiums** outdoors in late May or early June when the soils are warmer. Plant **Tuberous Begonias**, hollow side up, and **Caladiums** 1 inch deep and 12 inches apart. Both are good shade-tolerant plants.

In late May (early June for those in the north), plant forced bulbs outdoors. Move **Amaryllis** plants outside for summer. See January and December "Helpful Hints."

Care

Harden off tender bulb transplants that have been growing indoors. Start two weeks prior to planting. Stop fertilizing and reduce watering frequency. Move plants outdoors in a shaded area. Gradually increase the light until it is comparable to the final planting location. Cover or bring plants indoors during cold days and nights.

Watering

Water as needed. Newly installed transplants and containers need extra care. Check containers daily and water when the top few inches of soil begin to dry. Keep the soil around new transplants moist. Reduce the watering frequency as the plants become established.

Fertilizing

Incorporate a low-nitrogen, slow-release fertilizer into the soil prior to planting. Follow soil test recommendation or use 1 pound of fertilizer per 100 square feet. Or water in transplants with a starter solution of fertilizer. Follow mixing directions on the label.

Pruning

Deadhead faded flowers of **Tulips** and **Hyacinths** to promote more vigorous growth. Deadhead other bulbs for aesthetic reasons. You may want to remove the whole flower stem for a cleaner look.

Remove only diseased, yellow, or dried foliage. Leave the remaining leaves intact. These are producing the needed energy for next year's flower display. The same goes for bulbs naturalized in lawn areas. Keep the lawn as tall as possible to maintain bulb leaves. Mow around taller bulbs that have been grown in the lawn. You may consider replacing tall bulbs with **Squills** or **Grape Hyacinths**. These smaller bulbs are more tolerant of mowing.

Pests

Diseases: Continue to monitor for bulb rot. Remove infected plants and plan on improving soil drainage at the end of spring or next fall. Remove any spotted or disease infested leaves.

Helpful Hints

Nothing is prettier than a mass planting of Tulips or Daffodils—that is until the flowers fade and the big leaves sit there and slowly decline. Do not remove the leaves until they naturally decline; instead, consider ways to mask their untidy appearance.

- Plant **Annuals** between bulbs. **Pansies** are a nice choice for an early season display. Select a heat-tolerant variety or replace them with a summer annual. This gives you more variety in one planting bed.
- Mix bulbs with **Perennials**. As the bulb foliage declines, the perennials start growing and hide the leaves. You also avoid digging and disturbing bulbs with yearly planting.
- Tie foliage with string or rubber bands. This is not the best for the plant but may be an acceptable compromise between aesthetics and plant health.
- Treat them like **Annuals**. Remove the foliage and flowers right after bloom. Plant new bulbs each fall.

Insects: Sanitation is the best control for iris borer. Fall cleanup eliminates the egg laying sites for the adult moth. You may choose to use an insecticide on **Iris** with a history of borer problems or those that were not cleaned in fall. Treat the foliage when it is 4 to 6 inches tall. Use a systemic insecticide labeled for use on iris borer. Late treatments are not effective.

Monitor **Lilies** for stalk borer. Infested stems start to wilt, leaves yellow, and the stem can eventually die. Fall cleanup and a weed-free garden are the best defenses against this pest. Remove and destroy borer-infested stems as found.

Animals: Continue to monitor and control animal damage. A 4- to 5-foot-tall fence around a small garden will help keep deer at bay. Use decorative posts and a black or green mesh fence. It keeps deer away without being too obtrusive. See "Pests" in chapter introduction for more ideas.

Weeds: Continue to pull weeds as they appear. Early control reduces future problems and results in a more attractive bulb display.

Planning

Make sure all your bulbs are marked and mapped on your garden plan. This will be the last sign of many of them until next spring.

Planting

Always prepare the soil before planting hardy or tender bulbs and transplants. Work 2 inches of organic matter into the top 8 to 12 inches of soil. Good drainage is the key to growing bulbs. See "Planting" in the introduction for more details.

Plant tender bulb plants outside after the danger of frost. Gardeners in northern Minnesota may just be starting while those in the southern half of the state are finishing up.

Finish planting tender **Caladium** corms, **Canna** rhizomes, and **Begonia** tubers directly in the garden by early June. This will give them time to grow and flower before the snow flies.

Keep planting **Gladiolus** corms every two weeks through June. Continual planting gives you a long period of bloom to enjoy in the garden or as cut flowers.

Dig and divide overgrown **Siberian Iris** after they finish blooming. Keep the soil around the transplants moist, but not wet. It may take divisions more than a year to recover and bloom.

Dig and divide spring-flowering bulbs after the leaves fade. The plants have already stored their energy for the next season and the faded leaves make them easy to locate. Otherwise, mark the spot and move them in fall while you are planting your other bulbs.

Plant pre-cooled **Lily** bulbs or potted plants. They need well-drained soils and lots of sun. Try using a few in containers. They make a nice vertical accent for planters. Bulbs grown in containers will need to be planted in the garden in the fall to survive our cold Minnesota winter.

Plant **Annuals**, **Perennials**, or nonhardy bulbs among spring-flowering bulbs. The new plants will help mask the declining foliage of the bulbs.

Care

Don't worry if you accidentally dig up hardy bulbs while planting Perennials and Annuals. Just pop them back in the ground. If you divided them with the shovel, consider it propagated. Replant both halves. You may be lucky and get two bulbs from one.

Mulch tender bulbs with cocoa bean shells, shredded leaves, or twice-shredded bark. A 1- to 2-inch layer will help conserve moisture, reduce weeds, and eventually add organic matter to the soil.

Stake tall **Bearded Iris** flowers for a more attractive display. Many garden centers and catalogs sell stakes specifically for this purpose. Or try making your own with thin sturdy wire.

Stake tall **Dahlias** at planting to avoid spearing the buried tuberous root. Tall **Gladiola** benefit from staking. A gardener I know used a piece of lattice as a stake. She painted it white and elevated it on stakes, parallel to the ground. The **Gladiolus** flower stems grew through the holes in the lattice. The structure helped create a beautiful picture of blooms, complete with hummingbirds feeding at the flowers.

Watering

Keep the soil moist, but not wet around new plantings. Established plants need 1 inch of water per week. If it rains, you just need to make up the difference. Water clay soils in one application each week and sandy soils in two applications (of half the needed water) each week.

Fertilizing

Add 1 pound per 100 square feet of a low-nitrogen, slow-release fertilizer in the soil prior to planting. Or water transplants in with a starter solution of fertilizer.

Incorporate a slow-release fertilizer into the soil of container gardens prior to planting. These pots will not need to be fertilized for six to eight weeks or even more. Follow package directions. Or use a diluted solution of any flowering plant fertilizer every two weeks.

Pruning

Deadhead faded flowers to improve the appearance and reduce disease problems. Only remove half of the faded **Siberian Iris** blooms. This will increase flowering next season while allowing a few seedpods to develop for winter interest.

Pinch out the tips of **Dahlias** when they reach 15 inches. This encourages branching and results in more flowers on each plant. You can also pinch back leggy **Begonias** at this time.

Remove yellow and dry foliage on spring-flowering bulbs.

Helpful Hints

Utility work, home repair, or a move may mean an untimely move for garden plants. Bulbs do best if moved in spring after the leaves die or in fall during normal planting times. These bulbs can be dug and stored in a cool, dark area until the planting site is ready.

Growing plants can be dug, taking as much of the root system as possible, and transplanted to a new location. Heel in or plant them in containers if a permanent location is not available. Heeling in provides a temporary planting place for the bulbs until the permanent location is available. Dig a trench and set the plants close together in the trench and cover the roots with soil to heel in.

Pests

Diseases: Botrytis blight and powdery mildew may be problems on **Tuberous Begonias**. The blight causes brown spots on flowers and leaves. Powdery mildew starts as a white, powdery substance on the leaves and causes them to eventually yellow and brown. Remove faded flowers and infected leaves to control botrytis blight. Powdery mildew is most common in shade during periods of fluctuating humidity. You cannot change the weather, but you can reduce the occurrence of this disease. Properly space **Begonias** to ensure good air circulation and light penetration. If this is a yearly problem, find a more suitable location for these plants.

Leaf spot fungal disease is occasionally found on **Iris**. Remove infected leaves as soon as they are found. Sanitation and drier weather keep this disease in check.

Animals: Birds, chipmunks, and squirrels often pull out, nest in, or dig up potted plants. Spray with a repellent or temporarily cover new plantings with bird netting. Hopefully, they will find some other gardener to bother!

Weeds: Pull weeds as soon as they appear. Mulch the soil with a 1- to 2-inch layer of cocoa bean shells, shredded leaves, or twice-shredded bark.

Planning

Continue to look for opportunities for adding bulbs. That new perennial garden or shrub bed may benefit from some spring color. Keep recording bloom times, evaluating, and photographing the summer bulb garden.

Bulb catalogs may begin to arrive, or dig out those that offered bulbs last spring. Order spring-flowering bulbs now for fall delivery.

Planting

Lilies are potted, blooming, and available in many garden centers. Plant them in areas that receive at least 6 hours of direct sun with well-drained soil.

Plant **Autumn Crocus** as soon as they are available. They produce leaves in spring and will surprise you with flowers this fall.

Start digging and dividing Iris in mid- to late July, about six to eight weeks after bloom. Cut leaves in a fan shape back to 6 inches. This makes them easier to handle, reduces water loss, and improves their appearance. Dig rhizomes and check for borers. Kill borers and remove old and damaged rhizomes.

Plant the healthy rhizomes 5 inches apart in a properly prepared location. The rhizomes should be just below the soil surface or half buried with the leaves and buds facing upward.

Care

Stake and tie **Dahlias**, **Lilies**, and **Gladiola** as needed. Be careful not to spear the bulb while installing the stake. Allow enough space between the plant and stake to accommodate the bulb. Avoid this problem next year by staking tender bulbs at the time of planting. Or surround tall plants with slightly shorter and stiffer plants that will serve as a living support.

Watering

Water as needed. Established plantings need 1 inch of water each week. You may need to supplement natural rainfall. Provide needed water in one application on clay soils and in two applications on sandy soils.

Check container plantings, including **Amaryllis**, every day. Water thoroughly when the top few inches begin to dry.

Fertilizing

Container gardens need regular fertilizer applications. Plantings with a slow-release fertilizer incorporated into the soil at planting do not need additional fertilizer for one to three months. Check and follow label directions. Other container gardens benefit from regular fertilizer applications. Select a product good for flowering plants and follow the label directions.

Fertilize inground plantings as needed. Tender bulbs growing in the shade need less fertilizer than those in full sun. Sprinkle a low-nitrogen, slow-release fertilizer around the plants at a rate of 1 pound fertilizer per 100 square feet.

Pruning

Disbud **Dahlias** for fewer but larger flowers. Remove at least two pairs of side buds that develop below the terminal (tip) bud. Remove three pairs of buds if you want giant **Dahlias**.

Deadhead summer-flowering bulbs as needed. This increases flowering, reduces disease, and improves the overall appearance.

Remove discolored leaves and those with holes, brown spots, or soft areas. Cleanup is one of the most effective and environmentally friendly ways to control pests. Discard, do not compost, pest-infected foliage.

Pests

Insects: Check limp and pale **Irises** for borer. Dig up rhizomes, cut off soft and borer-infested portions of the rhizome, and replant. Make a note on your garden calendar to cut back and clean up **Iris** foliage in fall.

Stalk borers feed inside stems and cause them to wilt and die. Remove infested stems and kill the borers if they are still present (smashing or chopping in half works well). Mark your calendar and watch for this pest next season.

Earwigs, aphids, and mites are common pests found on a variety of plants, including bulbs. Earwigs often feed on flower petals. They can be trapped and killed or treated with an insecticide. Aphids and mites can be controlled with insecticidal soap.

Thrips cause a scratched appearance on the leaves and distorted flowers on **Gladiola** and occasionally on **Dahlias**. Repeated applications of insecticides can help minimize the damage. Badly infested **Gladiolus** corms should be treated or discarded prior to storage.

Helpful Hints

Spring and summer-flowering bulbs make great additions to any flower arrangement. Their beauty and fragrance (some, not all) extend your garden enjoyment to the indoors. ***Increase the vase life of cut flowers by:***

- Using a sharp knife or cutting scissors, *cut* the base of the stem on an angle.
- *Place* flowers in water right after cutting. Take a bucket of water along with you to the garden. This is better for the flowers and makes it easier for you to manage all those blooms.
- *Harvest* most flowers as the buds are just beginning to open. Harvest **Gladiola** when the flowers on the bottom $1/3$ just start to open, the middle $1/3$ are swollen, and the top $1/3$ are tight buds.
- Place freshly harvested **Gladiola** in a bucket of warm water in a cool location to harden. This should keep the flower stems straight.
- Give **Daffodils** a vase of their own. They excrete a gummy substance from the cut stem. This substance blocks the stems of other cut flowers, shortening their vase life.

Diseases: Powdery mildew, leaf spot, botrytis, and anthracnose are often seen in wet summers. These cause leaves to be spotted or discolored. Reduce powdery mildew problems in the future by growing susceptible plants in locations with sufficient light and air circulation. Fungicides can be used to prevent the spread. It is safe to save the bulbs of mildew-infected plants. Bulbs of diseased plants should only be saved if the bulb is firm and free from streaking and discoloration.

Remove infected leaves and faded flowers to reduce botrytis blight, leaf spot, and anthracnose disease.

Sanitation and improved weather are usually sufficient control.

Animals: **Lilies** are a favorite of rabbits and deer. Homemade and commercial repellents may provide some relief. Start applying repellents early, vary the products used, and repeat applications after heavy rains. Scare tactics may be effective. Your creativity and tolerance of the scare tactics are the only limits.

Weeds: Continue to pull weeds as they appear. Mulch plants with a 1- to 2-inch layer of organic material. This will to reduce weeds and moisture needs.

AUGUST

Planning

Finish ordering bulbs from catalogs. Order early for the best selection. Consider growing some **Autumn Crocus** this year. Find a location that will tolerate their early spring leaf growth but not be subject to deep cultivation over summer. **Autumn Crocus** mixes well with groundcovers and low-growing Perennials.

Planting

Plant **Autumn Crocus** *now through early September.* These new additions will bloom for you this fall. Prepare the soil prior to planting. Mark the location so that you will not disturb the plant over summer.

Finish digging and dividing **Irises**. Cut leaves in a fan shape back to 6 inches. Dig rhizomes and check for borer. Kill borers and remove old and damaged rhizomes. Plant the healthy rhizomes 5 inches apart in a properly prepared location. The rhizomes should be just below the soil surface or half buried with the leaves and buds facing upward.

Care

Leave foliage on tender and summer bulbs as long as possible. Dig **Gladiola** only after foliage has yellowed and dried naturally.

Allow **Lily** foliage to yellow and die naturally. Cut, do not pull, the leaves.

Continue to disbud and tie tall **Dahlias** as needed. See July "Pruning" for details.

Watering

Water as needed. Established plants need 1 inch of water per week. If it rains, you will just need to make up the difference. Water clay soils in one application and sandy soils in two applications.

Check container plantings, including **Amaryllis**, every day. They usually need a thorough watering once a day.

Water the soil, not the foliage, to minimize disease problems and moisture lost to evaporation. Use a watering wand or other hose attachment that allows you to place the water where it is needed, on the soil. These tools also help extend your reach, making watering an easier and drier experience.

Fertilizing

Stop fertilizing inground plantings and reduce fertilization of container plantings. Late season fertilization encourages late season growth that will not prepare the plant for winter.

Pruning

Continue deadheading plants as needed. This helps reduce disease and improves their appearance.

Continue cutting **Gladiola** and **Dahlias** for indoor enjoyment.

Pests

Monitor plants for pest problems. Properly identify the cause and all control options before treating. Your local county office of the University Extension Service is a good source for help.

Diseases: Powdery mildew is a fungal disease that grows on the leaf surface. It looks as though someone sprinkled baby power on the leaves. Fall cleanup will help reduce the source of infection next season. Review the growing conditions and make needed adjustments in next year's design. Properly space and grow plants in their preferred light conditions to reduce mildew disease. Virus and aster yellows can cause poor flowering and distorted flower spikes on **Gladiola**. There are no chemical cures for these diseases. Remove infected plants as soon as they are found. This helps reduce the risk to nearby healthy plants. Control aphids and leafhoppers feeding on the plants. These insects carry the diseases from sick to healthy plants. Controlling the insects reduces the spread of these diseases. Discard corms of any diseased **Gladiola**.

Insects: Monitor plants for thrips, aphids, and mites. Thrips are tiny and difficult to control. Repeated applications of an insecticide may reduce problems. Treat or discard thrip-infested **Gladiolus** corms prior to winter storage. Damaging populations of aphids and mites can be controlled with insecticidal soap.

Weeds: Removing weeds now means fewer next season. Pull or cultivate weeds as soon as they appear and prior to seed set. There is still time to mulch the garden. A thin layer of cocoa bean shells, shredded leaves, or twice-shredded bark can help reduce weeds and conserve moisture. Extending a little effort now can save you two months of weeding.

Helpful Hints

Autumn Crocus (*Colchicum*) can add the "ah factor" to your garden. I like to design little surprises into my gardens to make people stop, take a second look, and say "Ah, what a great idea!" Seeing **Crocus** blooming in September can do just that.

Part of the surprise is how these plants grow. They produce leaves in early spring. The leaves persist for about six to eight weeks and then die back for the season. Then suddenly, in late August or September, the flowers (no leaves) appear. It truly was a surprise in my garden.

Here are some tips for growing success:

- Mix these bulbs with **Perennials** and groundcovers. **Autumn Crocus** planted in **Vinca** groundcover (**Periwinkle**) doubles your bloom time. The Vinca produces attractive flowers in spring followed by the leafless Autumn Crocus blooming in fall.
- Select a planting location where the early spring foliage will be hidden or a nice addition, not a distraction, in the garden.
- Plan and plant these fall-blooming beauties June through late August or early September when they are available.
- Dig and divide them (when necessary) as soon as the leaves die in spring. Plant divisions in other garden areas or share with friends.

Planning

Visit your favorite garden center and purchase your spring-flowering bulbs. Remember to factor in the bulb order you made last spring. Buy some extra bulbs for forcing.

Start your planting records when you purchase your bulbs. Record the name of the bulb and where and when you bought it. Some gardeners save the package cover or care tag for future reference.

Select healthy bulbs with a strong growing tip. They should be full size, firm, and free from signs of insects and disease. Shop early for a greater selection of varieties and healthier bulbs.

Store bulbs in a cool, dark place until it is time to plant. The basement, spare refrigerator, or similar location will work.

Planting

Always prepare the soil prior to planting. Bulbs need well-drained soil for best results. It is easier to prepare the soil correctly in the first place than to try to fix it after the bulbs are planted. See the chapter introduction for more information.

You can still dig, divide, and transplant **Bearded Iris.** The later you plant, however, the greater the risk of winter injury. Cut leaves in a fan shape back to 6 inches. Dig rhizomes and check for borers. Kill borers and remove old and damaged rhizomes. Plant the healthy rhizomes 5 inches apart in a properly prepared location. The rhizomes should be just below the soil surface or half buried with the leaves and buds facing upward. Start transplanting existing bulbs. This spreads out planting time and helps you with the final spacing and placement of your new additions.

Wait to plant spring-flowering bulbs. Bulbs planted early are more likely to sprout during a warm fall. Wait until late September in the northern part of the state and early October in the southern part of the state to start planting. You have plenty of time—until the ground freezes—to get these bulbs into the ground.

Care

Store new bulbs in a cool, dark place until they can be planted. The basement, spare refrigerator, or similar location will work. Avoid storing bulbs in a refrigerator that contains ripening fruit (this interferes with flower development) or can be accessed by children who might accidentally eat the bulbs.

Move **Amaryllis** indoors before the first fall frost. Store the bulb in a cool, dark location or continue to grow it indoors. See January "Helpful Hints" for information on reblooming.

Caladiums, **Calla Lilies**, and **Tuberous Begonias** can be grown indoors for the winter. Move container plants inside prior to the first killing frost. Dig up inground plants, pot up, and move indoors. Care for them as you would your other houseplants.

Yellowing foliage or the first fall frost means it is time to get busy. *Dig, cure, and store tender bulbs for winter.*

1   Carefully *dig up* tender bulbs. Allow plenty of digging room for the additional bulbs that have formed over summer.

2   *Prepare* (cure) bulbs for storage. Set them in a warm, dry place out of direct light. See the Storage Chart on page 69 for specific recommendations.

3   Gently *brush off* (do NOT scrub) excess soil and *trim off* dried foliage and stems.

4 **Place** cured bulbs in a box or flat filled with peat moss, sawdust, or other storage material. **Gladiola** prefer to be stored dry (uncovered).

5 **Label** the type and color of the bulb.

6 **Move** to a cool, dark location for the winter.

Specific Storage Requirements for Tender Bulbs

Bulb	Cure Time	Storage	Storage Temperature
Tuberous Begonias	several days	dry peat	45 to 50 degrees Fahrenheit
Caladium	several days	dry peat	65 to 70 degrees Fahrenheit
Calla	1 to 2 days	peat moss or perlite	50 degrees Fahrenheit
Canna	overnight	peat moss	45 to 50 degrees Fahrenheit
Dahlia	several hours	dry peat or sawdust	45 degrees Fahrenheit
Gladiola	3 to 4 weeks	dry/ uncovered	40 degrees Fahrenheit

Watering

Keep watering as needed. The cooler temperatures and fall rains usually mean less work for you. Continue to check container gardens daily. Water these when the top few inches of soil start to dry. **Amaryllis** is the exception. Reduce watering on Amaryllis that will be stored dormant during the fall.

Thoroughly water new plantings. They will benefit from additional irrigation during a dry fall.

Pruning

Fall cleanup improves the health and appearance of your bulbs. Remove and discard foliage. Leave **Siberian Iris** leaves and seedpods intact for fall and winter interest.

Pests

Insects: Prevent iris borer by removing old **Iris** leaves and debris. Fall sanitation eliminates the sites for iris borer adults to lay their eggs. Without eggs, there will be no borers next season.

Thrips overwinter on the corms of **Gladiola**. Discard thrip-infested corms or treat with an insecticidal dust prior to storage. Label the bulbs as treated with insecticide as a reminder to wear gloves when handling the corms next spring.

Diseases: Remove and discard disease-infested leaves. Do not store any tender bulbs that show signs of rot or disease. One bad apple—or in this case, bulb—can spoil the bunch.

Animals: Squirrels, voles, and chipmunks will be looking forward to the bulbs. See "Pests" in the introduction to this chapter for tips on preventing animal damage.

Fertilizing

Follow soil test recommendations or incorporate 1 pound of a low-nitrogen fertilizer per every 100 square feet at planting. Stop fertilizing container gardens.

Planning

Now is the time to put your plans in action. But like every good gardener, you are probably still making adjustments to that plan. And if you do not have a plan, here are a few ideas to keep in mind as you plant:

- Create impact in your landscape with bulbs. It may be a splash of color at your front door to welcome visitors or a mass of **Daffodils** visible from the den.

- Create pathways and rivers of bulbs through the landscape. A ribbon of color can add interest and help lead visitors through your landscape.

- Add some minor bulbs. These small stature, early blooming bulbs can add little glimpses of color in even the smallest yard. I like to use these along garden paths to catch visitors' attention and slow them down.

Planting

October marks the peak of fall planting in the bulb garden.

Always prepare the soil prior to planting. Only work the soil when it is slightly moist. Bulbs need well-drained soil to prevent rotting and get the best results. Follow your soil test recommendation or add at least 2 inches of organic matter and 1 pound of a low-nitrogen, slow-release fertilizer per 100 square feet. Dig the fertilizer and amendments into the top 8 to 12 inches of soil.

Start planting **Daffodils, Tulips, Crocus,** *and other spring-flowering bulbs.* These are generally planted at a depth of two to three times the vertical diameter. See the Planting Chart at the end of this chapter for specific details on common bulbs.

Continue transplanting existing bulbs as needed.

Plant last year's forced bulbs outdoors if this was not done in spring. Remember, they probably will not bloom until the second spring after planting.

Plant bulbs in pots for forcing. Store them in a cold, 35- to 45-degrees Fahrenheit storage area for thirteen to fifteen weeks. Plant bulbs in early October for January flowers, mid-October for February flowers, and early to mid-November for March and April flowers.

Care

Dig, cure, and store tender bulbs after a light frost. See September "Helpful Hints" for more specific details.

1 Carefully *dig up*, do not pull, tender bulbs. Allow plenty of digging room for the additional bulbs that have formed over summer.

2 *Prepare* (cure) bulbs for storage. Set them in a warm dry place out of direct light. See the Storage Chart on page 69 for specific recommendations.

3 Gently *brush off* (do NOT scrub) excess soil and *trim off* dried foliage and stems.

4 *Place* cured bulbs in a box or flat filled with peat moss, sawdust, or other storage material. **Gladiola** prefer to be stored dry (uncovered).

5 *Label* the type and color of the bulb.

6 *Move* to a cool, dark location for the winter.

Watering

Thoroughly water new bulb plantings. They may need additional water during a dry fall.

Water potted bulbs before placing them in cold storage. Check occasionally to make sure the soil remains moist.

Fertilizing

Follow soil test recommendations or add 1 pound of a low-nitrogen, slow-release fertilizer per 100 square feet of garden bed at planting.

Pruning

Fall cleanup improves the health and appearance of your bulbs. Remove and discard foliage. Leave **Siberian Iris** leaves and seedpods intact for fall and winter interest.

Pests

Fall cleanup is an important key to pest control. Remove diseased or pest-infected foliage. This reduces the source of insects and disease for next season.

Every month check on tender bulbs in storage. Remove and discard any soft, discolored, or rotting bulbs.

Insects: Treat or discard thrip-infested **Gladiola** prior to storage. These tiny insects overwinter on the corms.

Helpful Hints

Force spring-flowering bulbs for a touch of spring indoors. **Daffodils, Tulips,** and **Hyacinths** are often used for forcing. Select shorter cultivars or those specifically recommended for forcing. Plant several bulbs in a 4- to 6-inch container filled with a well-drained potting mix. Water thoroughly and move to a cold location (35 to 45 degrees Fahrenheit) for 13 to 15 weeks. *For cold treatment:*

- Store potted bulbs in a spare refrigerator. A colleague once told me, "Every gardener should have a spare refrigerator. Not for beer and soda, but for storing bulbs." Do not store fruit with the bulbs, and make sure the family knows this is not some new cooking trend.
- Store bulbs in a root cellar, attic, or other areas where the temperatures stay cold but above freezing.
- Bury the potted bulbs in a vacant garden area outdoors. Dig a trench the same depth as the containers. Place the containers in the trench and fill with soil. Cover the area with evergreen branches or straw once the ground begins to freeze.
- One gardener gets double duty from his pond. Once the pond is drained for winter, he fills it with potted bulbs. He covers the pots with dry leaves and the pond with a piece of plywood.
- A master gardener bought one of the Styrofoam cut-flower containers from a wholesale florist. He fills it with potted bulbs and stores it in his unheated garage for winter. The unheated garage gives the bulbs the cold they need and the insulated container prevents them from freezing in extremely cold weather.

Remove old **Iris** foliage and debris. This eliminates the egg-laying habitat for the adult moth. The moth (adult iris borer) will look for a more suitable patch to lay her eggs.

Animals: Monitor animal activity. Squirrels and chipmunks seem to appear from nowhere as soon as the bulbs go into the ground.

Naphthalene flakes (mothballs), cayenne pepper, thiram-based, or other repellents may provide some relief. See "Pests" in the introduction to this chapter for more ideas on managing wildlife damage.

Planning

So you bought too many bulbs or overestimated your planting space. Join the club. Here are some possible planting solutions:

- Heel in bulbs in a vacant or annual garden area. Dig a trench the proper planting depth. Fill the trench with bulbs spaced a few inches apart. This acts as a temporary holding location until space becomes available. Transplant these bulbs in spring once the foliage dies or in fall during the normal planting season.

- Force bulbs for indoor enjoyment or gifts.

- Scatter bulbs of **Daffodils**, **Crocus**, **Grape Hyacinths**, **Snowdrops**, or **Squills** and plant them where they fall. This creates a more informal or natural appearance.

- Plant bulbs along the woodland or shade garden's edge. These areas usually receive sufficient sunlight in spring before the trees leaf out.

- Plant **Squills**, **Grape Hyacinths**, or **Crocus** in the lawn. These can add a bit of color to the sea of green. Wait until after flowering to cut the grass. Then mow the grass as high as possible to allow the leaves to grow and replenish the bulb's energy.

Planting

Keep planting spring-flowering bulbs until the ground freezes. Plant bulbs at a depth two to three times the vertical diameter. See the Planting Chart in this chapter for more detailed information.

You can still plant spring-flowering bulbs once the ground lightly freezes. It just takes a little extra effort and creativity. One of my students shared this technique:

1 *Use* a shovel to break through the frost and outline small planting areas.

2 *Slide* the shovel under one edge of the outlined area and *pry* off the frozen soil. It will lift off just like a manhole cover.

3 *Plant* the bulbs at the proper depth and space.

4 *Water* the newly planted bulbs and replace the soil "lid."

Continue planting bulbs in pots for forcing. Store them in a cold, 35- to 45-degrees Fahrenheit storage area for thirteen to fifteen weeks. Plant bulbs in early to mid-November for March and April flowers.

Care

Check on tender bulbs and **Amaryllis** in winter storage. Look for signs of rot, mold, or softening. Discard any diseased bulbs. Throwing out one bulb will prevent the rest from going bad.

Check on bulbs in cold storage. Make sure the soil is still moist. You will need to move them to a cooler location if sprouting occurs.

Mulch after the ground lightly freezes. This is usually around Thanksgiving in the southern part of the state and a few weeks earlier in the north. I often wait until after Christmas to recycle holiday trees as my mulch. A layer of evergreen branches, straw, or hay works fine. Do not worry if it snows before you get the mulch in place. Snow is the best mulch available and it is free. Gardeners in the northern part of the state can usually count on this. Those in the southern areas need to keep the mulch handy for when the snow disappears.

Mulch insulates the soil, eliminating fluctuating soil temperatures caused by changeable winter weather. Keeping the soil temperature constant prevents early sprouting. Mulched soil stays frozen and the bulbs stay dormant even during a winter thaw. This layer of insulation also prevents frost heaving that is caused by the freezing and thawing of the soil. The shifting soil can dislodge and even push bulbs right out of the soil.

Watering

Thoroughly water new plantings. Do not water frozen soil.

Check on forced bulbs and water if the soil begins to dry.

Fertilizing

Follow soil test recommendations or add 1 pound of a slow-release, low-nitrogen fertilizer per 100 square feet at planting.

Established bulb plantings need little if any additional fertilizer. Fertilize to promote vigor and better bloom. Spring, as the bulbs sprout, or fall, before the ground freezes, are the best times to fertilize. Fertilize established bulb plantings now if it was not or will not be done in the spring. Do not fertilize after the ground freezes.

Helpful Hints

If your landscape has become a fine dining location for squirrels, deer, and rabbits you need to change your animal management strategy. ***Once you give up on repellents, scare tactics, and fencing you might want to try some of the more animal-resistant bulbs.*** **Daffodils** have been the long time favorite for gardeners plagued by animals. There are a few others you can add to the list. **Autumn Crocus (*Colchicum*), Hyacinth (*Hyacinthus*), Glory-of-the-Snow (*Chionodoxa*), Grape Hyacinth (*Muscari*), Ornamental Onions (*Allium*), Squills (*Scilla*), Snowdrops (*Galanthus*), Snowflake (*Lycoris*),** and **Winter Aconite (*Eranthis*)** are usually left undisturbed by animals. Keep in mind, however, that in years of high animal populations and limited food, they will eat almost anything.

Pests

Continue to monitor animal activity. Squirrels and chipmunks often dig up and move the bulbs as fast as we can plant. Naphthalene flakes (mothballs), cayenne pepper, thiram-based, or other repellents may provide some relief. See "Pests" in the introduction to this chapter for more ideas on managing wildlife damage.

Voles are also a problem. High populations can damage bulbs and other plantings. This rodent can be killed with a snap trap baited with peanut butter and oats. Place the trap in a PVC pipe or under cover to prevent accidental harm to songbirds. Poisonous baits are also available.

Keep these away from children, pets, and wildlife. Read and follow all label directions carefully.

Check tender bulbs in storage. Remove and discard any rotted, moldy, or diseased bulbs.

Pruning

Finish fall cleanup. Pest-free debris can be composted. Leaves from insect- and disease-infested plants should be discarded.

Planning

The holidays are approaching, and it is a good time to reflect on the recent garden season. Review your garden journal, make needed additions, and start planning for next season. No plan would be complete without a wish list of new bulbs, tools, books, and materials needed for next season. These all make great holiday gifts to give and receive.

Planting

Try forcing **Amaryllis** and **Paper-whites** for indoor bloom. These bulbs do not need a cold treatment and are readily available at most garden centers. See February "Planting" for tips on forcing **Paper-whites** (*Narcissus*) and for potting and growing **Amaryllis**.

Care

Plant any leftover bulbs for forcing. These won't be flowering until late March or April when many of our outdoor bulbs are blooming. I like to use these as accent plants or in containers and windowboxes in my landscape. Mulch bulbs with evergreen branches, straw, or marsh hay after ground freezes.

Helpful Hints

Whether you forced them yourself or bought them at a store, it is possible to rebloom forced bulbs. Crocus, **Daffodils,** and other hardy bulbs can be planted outdoors for future enjoyment.

1   **Remove** the faded flowers and **fertilize** with any dilute solution of flowering houseplant fertilizer.

2   **Move** the plant to a sunny window and water when the soil starts to dry. Keep the plants growing as long as possible. Remove foliage as it yellows and dries.

3   Once foliage dries, **store** bulbs in a cool, dark location in the basement, garage, or root cellar for the summer. Plant the bulbs outdoors in fall. Just remember where you stored the bulbs.

4   Or **plant** these forced bulbs outdoors when soil warms. The plants will produce leaves but no flowers the first spring. Watch for blossoms the following year.

Watering

Drain and store the hose for winter if it has not already been done. Check bulbs in cold storage for forcing. The soil should be moist (like a damp sponge), but not wet. Keep the soil around **Amaryllis** and **Paper-whites** moist as well. Check these plants every few days and water as needed.

Pests

Continue to monitor and control animal damage. Check stored bulbs monthly for signs of rot and disease. Discard infested bulbs immediately.

Pruning

Cleanup should be complete.

Fertilizing

Do not fertilize.

Fruits

You do not need a large yard or an orchard to raise fruit for your family. Use fruit trees in place of ornamental trees, **Raspberries** and **Currants** in place of hedges, **Strawberries** in place of groundcover, and **Grapes** instead of ornamental vines on your arbor. Soon you will find yourself living in an attractive and edible landscape.

Planning

All good landscapes, even the edible ones, start with a plan. Sit down with the family and friends who will share the work and harvest. Make a list of fruits that people like to eat. Check on the space and growing conditions required by each one. Most fruits need full sun and moist, well-drained soil for best growth and productivity.

Now look at your landscape plan. How much suitable growing space do you have available, and for what type of fruits? Consider using dwarf varieties for small locations. *Espalier* (pruning so they are flat) a fruit tree or two against a sunny wall. It can add interest to a bare wall, while producing fruit in a very small area. Or train **Apples** and **Pears** into living fences. This exten-

sive pruning system allows you to create a living and edible fence that also provides screening. Visit the Chicago Botanical Gardens to see many examples of this technique.

Check your list against the University of Minnesota Extension Service's recommendations. This is the most up-to-date source of information on fruit varieties suited to our climate. Eliminate fruit that is not hardy or suited to our area. Select the most pest-resistant varieties available.

Make note of any plants that need pollinators. This means you will need two different plants to ensure fruit production. Some fruits are particular and only accept pollen from certain varieties, while others are less particular. Make sure the two fruits bloom at the same time so they can lend each other a helping hand.

Once you have your list, start looking for sources for these plants. Very few garden centers carry a wide selection of fruit plants. Check out garden catalogs that carry or specialize in fruit plants. They offer the biggest selection and give you the best chance of finding the desired varieties.

Soil Preparation

A good harvest starts with proper soil preparation.

Small fruits, such as **Raspberries** *and* **Strawberries**, *grow in small beds or planting areas.*

1 Edge the bed with a shovel or edger.

2 Remove the existing grass and weeds with a shovel or sod cutter. Or kill the grass with a total vegetation killer such as Roundup® or Finale®. Wait four to seven days for the grass to die. Remove the dead sod or till it into the soil. Check the label for replanting information. Or use one of these non-chemical methods to eliminate existing grass.

- Cover the area with black plastic for one season to kill the weeds and grass. The soil will be ready to work in the spring.

- Cut the grass very short. Cover with several layers of newspaper and woodchips. Plant the **Raspberries** and **Strawberries** right through the mulch and buried turf.

Fruits

- Create a raised planting bed. Cover the short grass with newspaper and 6 to 8 inches of topsoil. You are ready to plant. The newspaper and grass eventually decompose.

3 Take a soil test to find out what if any lime, organic matter, or fertilizer you need to add. Most fruits prefer a soil pH of 6 to 6.5. Do not lime your soil unless the soil test recommends it. Gardeners in the southern part of the state have alkaline soil and should not add lime. Those in central and northern Minnesota have acidic soil. Follow soil test recommendations.

4 Follow soil test recommendations for fertilization. If these are not available follow the recommendations on page 81 in "Small Fruit Fertilization."

5 Almost all soils benefit from additional organic matter. A 2- to 4-inch layer of organic matter worked into the top 12 inches of soil will help improve drainage in clay soils and water retention in sandy soils.

Tree fruits, such as **Apples, Pears, Plums,** *and* **Cherries,** *should be planted in full sun and well-draining soil.* Place trees on a southeast-facing slope if at all possible. Avoid hilltop locations where the winds can be damaging and fireblight, a deadly bacterial disease, is more likely to invade. Do not plant in low spots that tend to be frost pockets in the spring and fall. A late spring frost can kill the flowers (needed for fruit to form) and an early fall frost can damage the harvest.

Only amend the soil (addition of organic matter) if you can prepare the total area where the roots will grow. This is usually not practical in a home landscape. Otherwise, plant the trees in the existing soil and let them adapt to their permanent growing conditions right away.

Planting

Plant fruit trees in the spring for best results. Purchase trees as bare-root or potted plants. Most catalogs and a few nurseries carry bare-root plants. These trees are cheaper, but require more care and have a greater risk of failure. Potted plants can be planted throughout the early part of the growing season. Plant early to allow the plants to establish themselves before cold winter temperatures set in.

Check bare-root plants as soon as they arrive at your home. Unwrap the roots and make sure they are moist. Wet the roots and cover with moist peat moss or sawdust. Store in a cool, frost-free, partially shaded location.

Store potted plants in a protected location out of the wind. Keep the soil moist, but not soggy. Water thoroughly so that the excess water runs out of the drainage holes. Water again when the top 3 to 4 inches begin to dry.

Begin planting when the soil is workable and plants are available.

Planting bare-root fruit trees:

1 Dig a hole at least two to three times wider than, but not deeper than, the container. Use your shovel to scrape and roughen the sides of the planting hole.

2 Soak the roots of bare-root trees for 2 to 4 hours if their roots dried in transport or storage.

3 Place the bare-root tree in the planting hole so that the graft is 2 to 3 inches above the soil line. Bury the graft union if non-hardy rootstocks are used. Check the plant label for specific guidelines.

Fruits

4 Position the tree so that the roots spread away from the trunk. Cut off any broken or extremely long roots.

5 Fill the hole with the original soil removed from the planting hole. Water to help settle the soil and remove air pockets.

6 Prune thin, unbranched stems (whips) back to 30 to 45 inches tall. Remove only broken and damaged limbs on branched trees. Leave four or five evenly spaced branches on the stem. See February "Helpful Hints" for more on pruning tree fruits.

7 Stake trees on dwarfing rootstocks at time of planting. Place a stake next to the tree trunk on the windward side. This way the wind will usually blow the tree away from, not into, the stake. Use fabric strips to secure the tree to the stake.

8 Mulch with a 2- to 3-inch layer of woodchips or shredded bark. Keep the mulch away from the trunk. Cover at least the planting area with the mulch.

Planting potted fruit trees:

1 Dig a planting hole the same depth as the container and at least two to three times bigger in diameter. Use your shovel to scrape and chop the sides.

Roughening the inside of the hole allows the roots to grow beyond the planting hole.

2 Cut the bottom off the pot. Set it in the hole so that the tree will be planted at the same depth it was growing in the pot. Plant deeper if the root graft is located above the pot and rootstock is not reliably hardy. Check the label for specific planting directions.

3 Slice through the side of the container and peel away the pot. Use this technique to avoid damaging young plants that have not yet formed a tight rootball.

4 Slice through roots that encircle the pot. This helps potbound plants develop roots that will grow into the surrounding soil.

5 Fill the planting hole with the soil removed for planting. Water to help remove air pockets and settle the soil.

6 Apply a 2- to 3-inch layer of woodchips or shredded bark over the planting hole. Pull the mulch away from the tree trunk and extend it to the edge of the planting area.

Currants, Gooseberries, and Elderberry:

Plant these fruits in cool, moist locations. Grow them in full sun or partial shade with good air circulation. Avoid hot, dry, and poorly drained locations. Plan to do a little hunting to find a source for these plants. Purchase one-year-old plants if possible. You may have to start your own plants from cuttings or layers.

1 Plant dormant plants in the garden as soon as they arrive. Remove any broken stems and roots. Soak the roots of bare-root plants for 2 to 4 hours before planting.

2 Dig a planting hole slightly deeper and two to three times wider than the rootball. Set the plant in the hole so that the roots point outward and the lowest branch is even with the soil line.

3 Fill the hole with the soil removed from the planting hole. Water to remove air pockets and settle the soil. Mulch the soil with woodchips or shredded bark to keep roots cool and moist.

4 Allow at least 3 to 4 feet per plant. Space **Currants** 3 to 4 feet apart within rows 6 to 8 feet apart.

5 Plant **Elderberries** 7 to 8 feet apart within rows 10 to 12 feet apart.

Blueberries:

Grow hardy **Blueberries** in full sun and moist, acidic soils. Avoid low areas or other frost pockets in the landscape. Grow **Blueberries** in an area where you can easily cover the plants to protect the buds from late spring frosts.

- Have your soil tested before amending the soil. Lower the pH of alkaline soils by adding sulfur or aluminum sulfate. Follow soil test recommendations before attempting to lower soil pH. See May "Planting" for details on amending the soil and planting **Blueberries**.

Grapes:

- Buy dormant bare-root plants from quality garden catalogs. Or check your local nursery for two-year-old bare-root or potted plants.

- Start your own **Grapes** from hardwood cuttings taken in late winter. Or try layering a one-year-old cane. See May Vines and Groundcovers "Helpful Hints" on page 331 for details on propagating Grapes and other small fruit by this method.

Handling bare-root Grapes:

1 Store bare-root plants in a cool (non freezing), shaded location until they can be planted. Cover them with moist sawdust or peat moss to prevent the plants from drying.

2 Soak roots in water for several hours (no longer) before planting.

3 Dig a hole larger than the roots. Roughen the sides of the planting hole. Cut any broken or extremely long roots. Spread the roots so that they extend away from the trunk. Plant at the same depth it was growing in the nursery. Fill with the soil removed from the planting hole. Water to help the soil settle and eliminate air pockets.

Handling potted Grape plants:

1 Dig the planting hole the same depth as, but two to three times wider than, the container. Use your shovel to roughen the sides of the planting hole.

2 Remove the bottom of the container and set the pot in the planting hole.

3 Slice the side of the pot and peel it away from the rootball. Use a knife to cut through any girdling roots.

4 Backfill with existing soil. Water to help settle the soil and remove air pockets.

Strawberries:

1 Plant **Strawberries** in early spring when the plants are available and the soil can be worked.

2 Store plants that arrive early in a cool, moist location. Either heel them in outdoors or store in a refrigerator until they can be planted in the garden.

- Remove the wrapping from plants to be heeled in. Dig a trench 6 to 8 inches deep in a cool, shaded location. Place plants 2 inches apart in the trench with the roots down. Fill the trench with soil and water. Plant the **Strawberries** within several weeks.

- Keep plants in the plastic shipping material if they are to be refrigerated. Do not moisten the plants prior to storage. Excess moisture causes disease and rot. Wrap dry roots with a moist paper towel if necessary. Store in the refrigerator, away from **Apple** and **Pear** fruit, for as long as six weeks. **Apple** and **Pear** fruit give off ethylene gas which reduces storage life and plant quality.

3 Remove dried leaves and dead runner stems prior to planting. Dig a hole deep enough for the roots to hang straight down without hitting the bottom. Spread out the roots and fill the hole with soil.

4 Make sure the roots and the base of the crown (the point where stems join the leaves) are covered with soil. Firm the soil around the planting and water.

5 Space **Strawberries** based on the training method you choose:

- Use the Matted Row System for lower maintenance and **June-bearing Strawberries**. Plant Strawberries 14 to 24 inches apart in rows 36 inches apart. Allow runners to develop and fill in, creating rows 12 to 15 inches wide.

- Use the Hill System to maximize the harvest in small spaces. Plant **Strawberries** in beds made of three rows. Space plants 12 inches apart within the bed. Leave 30 to 36 inches between each bed. Remove the runners as soon as they appear.

Raspberries:

1 Purchase disease-free plants from a reputable nursery or mail-order catalog. Store plants in a cool, moist location until planting. Check to make sure roots and the surrounding packing material stays moist.

2 Plant in spring as soon as the soil is workable and plants are available. Control weeds and prepare the soil by working several inches of organic matter into the top 6 to 12 inches of soil prior to planting.

3 Place the **Raspberry** plants slightly deeper in the planting furrow or hole than they were growing in the nursery. This will prevent root exposure as the ground settles. Gently firm the soil, and water.

4 Select a planting and training method that best suits you and your gardening location:

- Consider using the Narrow Hedgerow Planting System. Plant **Red Raspberry** plants 2 to 3 feet apart in rows that are at least 6 feet apart. Space **Black** and **Purple Raspberries** 4 feet apart in rows that are at least 8 feet apart. Confine new growth to 12- to 15-inch wide rows.

- Grow **Raspberries** in clusters instead of rows when using the Hill System. Space individual plants 4 to 5 feet apart. Allow new shoots to develop within 1 foot of the original planting.

Pruning

Many backyard fruits require special pruning and training systems to ensure a good harvest. Match the training system with the available space, landscape style, and your gardening goals.

Prune tree fruits every year to maintain the health and productivity of your trees. Maintain a strong, open framework that allows light to penetrate the canopy for flower and fruit production. Train young fruit trees to establish a strong framework. Prune so that the top of the tree is narrower than the bottom. This allows light to reach all parts of the tree. The more light, the greater the productivity.

Consider using a Central Leader Pruning System. It is good for the plant's health and productivity and is easy for you. See February "Helpful Hints" for details.

Fruits

Training Grapes:

- Grow **Grapes** on a fence, arbor, or a trellis constructed just for them. Select a support system strong enough to hold the weight of the plant and easy enough for you to prune and train the Grapes.

- Pruning and training **Grapes** is not for the weak at heart. You must be aggressive with the pruners and remove a large amount of growth each spring. Insufficient pruning will result in excessive, but less productive growth. See March "Helpful Hints" for details on training and pruning Grapes.

Blueberries:

- Prune **Blueberries** like all the other fruit in spring—before growth begins. The first two years, remove only broken and dead branches. Once the plants are established, by the third spring, you will need to do a little more aggressive pruning.

- Start by removing any damaged or broken branches. Remove some of the smaller, bushy growth and a few young shoots. Leave the most productive shoots. These are thick, hard, and 3 inches or longer. The more pruning you do, the smaller the crop will be, but the bigger the fruit.

- Change your pruning strategy after the fifth year. Remove the weakest and oldest canes to ground level. Leave five or six of the healthiest, heavily budded stems intact. Prune back extremely tall canes to the height of the other branches.

Currants and Gooseberries:

- Train **Currants** and **Gooseberries** the same way. Prune when the plants are dormant in late winter or early spring. You can remove winter damage and train the plant at the same time.

  - At Planting: Prune right after planting. Remove any broken or damaged stems. Prune remaining stems back to 8 to 10 inches.

  - 2nd year: Remove all but six to eight of the healthiest canes. Always remove any canes lying on the ground or shading out the center of the plant.

  - 3rd year: Leave three or four of last year's stems in place. Keep four or five of the new stems. Remove everything else.

  - 4th year and beyond: Keep three or four each of the two- and three-year-old canes. Repeat this each spring.

Elderberries:

- **Elderberries** are easy to prune and train. Remove any broken or damaged stems at the time of planting. Prune the remaining stems back to 8 to 10 inches. The following year, in late winter or early spring, remove any weak or broken branches. Prune out any shoots rubbing other stems or growing toward the center of the plant. Leave six to eight healthy canes for the coming season. Repeat this each year in late winter or early spring.

Raspberries:

- Train **Raspberries** to keep the plants healthy and productive while making it easier for you to harvest. Proper timing is critical for fruit production.

- The Hill System: Place a wooden or metal stake at the center of each hill. Allow canes to develop within 1 foot of the stake. Loosely tie the canes to the stake after pruning.

- The Narrow Hedgerow System: Use a trellis made of sturdy posts and wire to keep the **Raspberries** inbounds. Place posts every 20 to 30 feet for adequate support. Prune old and new growth to maintain narrow rows that are 12 to 15 inches wide.

Fruits

- **Summer-bearing Red Raspberries** produce their fruit on second-year growth (floricanes). **Fall-bearing Raspberries** produce the fall crop on new growth (primocanes) and the summer crop on these same canes the following summer.

- Consider planting both **Summer-** and **Fall-bearing Raspberries**. Sacrifice the summer crop on the Fall-bearing plants to reduce maintenance and increase fall production. You will still get two crops (summer and fall) of Raspberries, just from separate plantings.

- See February and July "Pruning" for more specifics on pruning **Raspberries**.

See Fruit "Helpful Hints" on page 356 for tips on ongoing care of **Strawberries**.

Watering

Young trees need regular watering to establish a healthy root system. *Give new plants 1 to 2 inches of water (3 to 5 gallons per tree) each week.* Water whenever the top 4 to 6 inches of soil start to dry. Water the planting hole and surrounding soil. This will encourage a larger, more drought-tolerant root system.

Give established plants the same amount of water, just less frequently. Their larger root system is able to seek out and find more available water. Apply 1 inch of water to the root zone. Water only when the top 6 inches throughout the area begin to dry.

Water more frequently in hot weather and less often in cooler periods. Check sandy soils twice a week and clay soils every seven to ten days. Water when the top 6 inches begin to dry.

Make sure small fruits receive sufficient moisture throughout the season. Water is necessary for flower bud development, fruit set, and fruit development on **Raspberries**, **Strawberries**, and other small fruits. Continue watering fruit during dry spells, even after the harvest. This will ensure a healthier, hardier, more productive plant for next season.

- Small fruits generally need 1 inch of water each week. Adjust watering based on rainfall. Water plants growing in clay soils once a week. Provide the needed water in two applications to plants growing in sandy soils.

- Mulch the soil to conserve moisture, reduce weeds, and moderate soil temperature. Use some type of organic mulch that will also help improve the soil as it decomposes.

- Use woodchips, shredded bark, or shredded leaves for tree fruits, **Raspberries**, and other shrub-type fruits. Use shredded leaves for **Strawberries**. These create fewer problems when renovating the plantings.

- Apply a thin layer (1 to 2 inches) of shredded leaves and other fine mulches. Use a thicker layer (3 to 4 inches) of woodchips and other coarse mulches.

Fertilization

Use your soil test as a guide. Provide fruit plants with needed fertilizer to improve health and increase fruit production. Overfertilization can lead to little or no fruit and increase the risk of fireblight disease. Follow these guidelines if soil test information is not available.

Small Fruit Fertilization

Blueberries: Sprinkle fertilizer on the ground in a 12- to 18-inch circle around each plant.

- Planting year: 2 tablespoons of ammonium sulfate (21-0-0) applied two to four weeks after planting.

Fruits

- 2nd year: $1/4$ cup of ammonium sulfate (21-0-0) per plant as growth begins or blooms appear.

- 3rd and 4th years: $3/8$ cup of ammonium sulfate per plant as growth begins.

- 5th year and beyond: $1/2$ cup of ammonium sulfate per plant as growth begins.

Currants, **Gooseberries**, **Elderberries**, and other bush fruits, such as **Viburnums** and **Juneberries**: Sprinkle fertilizer on the ground in an 18-inch circle around each plant.

- Planting year: 2 tablespoons of ammonium nitrate (33-0-0) per plant, applied three to four weeks after planting.

- 2nd year: $1/4$ cup ammonium nitrate per plant in the spring before new growth appears.

- 3rd year: $3/8$ cup of ammonium nitrate in the spring before new growth begins.

- 4th year: $1/2$ cup ammonium nitrate in the spring before new growth begins.

- 5th year and beyond: $2/3$ cup ammonium nitrate per plant in the spring before new growth begins.

- Or use well-rotted manure instead of the fertilizer. Spread 10 pounds of a well-rotted manure around each plant. Keep the manure 1 foot away from the plant.

Grapes: Sprinkle fertilizer on the ground in an 18-inch circle around each plant.

- Planting year: Apply 2 tablespoons ammonium nitrate two to three weeks after planting, or use 20 pounds of aged manure applied between 1 and 4 feet from the trunk.

- 2nd year: $1/4$ cup ammonium nitrate per plant before the buds swell.

- 3rd year: $1/4$ to $2/3$ cup ammonium nitrate plus 1 tablespoon of a high potassium fertilizer (0-0-60) or (0-0-50) per plant before the buds break.

- Reduce the amount of nitrogen fertilizer applied if you get excessive vine growth. Apply half the recommended rate before growth begins and the remainder in mid-June if the leaves sprout early and experience frost damage.

Raspberries: Apply fertilizer alongside all the plants in the row or sprinkled in an 18-inch circle around individual plants grown in the Hill System.

- Planting year: Apply 1 to $1^1/2$ pounds (2 to 3 cups) of ammonium nitrate (33-0-0) per 100 feet, or $1/4$ cup per plant in the Hill System, after the plants are established (mid- to late-June).

- Bearing years: Apply $3/4$ pound (1 cup) of ammonium nitrate (33-0-0) per 100 feet or $1/4$ cup per plant before growth begins and again in late May or early June.

- Or use 150 pounds of well-rotted cow manure per 100 feet before growth begins in spring. Spread the manure along the row, keeping it 1 foot away from the plants.

June-bearing Strawberries:

- Planting year: $3/4$ to $1^1/2$ pounds ($1/2$ to 1 cup) ammonium nitrate (33-0-0) per 100 feet of row, or 1 teaspoon of ammonium nitrate per plant, when runners begin to form (mid-June). Apply the same amount of fertilizer in early August.

- Bearing years: $3/4$ pound or 1 cup of 33-0-0 per 100 feet of row, after harvest and again in early August.

Everbearing Strawberries:

- Planting year: 1 teaspoon of ammonium nitrate per plant about 3 weeks after planting and again in mid-July.

- Bearing years: Fertilize every month they flower and fruit.

Fertilizer Tip

- You can substitute other nitrogen fertilizers for ammonium nitrate. You will need about $1/3$ more ammonium sulfate and 5 times more Milorganite® than the rate for ammonium nitrate.

- See Fertilizer Needs in Charts section of the Appendix on page 350 for more information.

Tree Fruit Fertilization

Apples, **Pears**, **Peaches**, **Plums**, and **Cherries** need a minimal amount of fertilizer to stay healthy and productive. Use the plant's yearly growth as your guide. Young fruit trees typically grow 10 to 20 inches each year. Bearing trees grow 8 to 12 inches. Do not fertilize in spring if the previous season's growth is longer than normal. Fertilize in spring before growth begins, only if growth is at or less than the normal rate.

- Apply 1 ounce of actual nitrogen per each year of tree age. This is equal to 3 ounces (6 tablespoons) of ammonium nitrate (34-0-0) or 10 ounces (about 1 cup) of a 10 percent commercial fertilizer. Multiply the age of the tree (years in the ground at this location) times the amount of fertilizer per year to get the total amount needed. Never exceed 1 pound of actual nitrogen per tree per year, no matter how old. Sprinkle the needed fertilizer over the soil under the tree canopy.

- Cut this rate in half for **Pear** and other fruit trees at high risk for fireblight disease. Spring fertilization encourages lush growth that is more susceptible to this disease.

Pests

Animals are by far the biggest pest problem. Birds, squirrels, deer, rabbits, and voles all want to share in the harvest, or at least nibble on the plant. Barriers, repellents, and fencing can help give you an edge over the wildlife. Start controls before you have to chase the animals out of their fine dining location—your backyard! Vary tactics to keep them guessing and leery of moving in. See August and October "Helpful Hints" for more details on keeping animals at bay.

- Does it seem like you did everything correctly, but still have no fruit? See the Fruit Helpful Hint on page 357.

Minnesota Fruits

Apples: (zones 3 to 4/needs pollinator)/Use Malling M26, M7, or M7A dwarf rootstock for shorter trees. 'Cortland' has good quality, tender flesh and ripens in late August. 'Empire' is a high-quality 'McIntosh' with firm flesh that ripens in early October. 'McIntosh' is the most popular apple in Wisconsin; it ripens in mid-September. Try disease-resistant types, such as 'Macfree' and 'Novamac'. 'NovaEasygro' is a new disease-resistant fall apple with good quality; it ripens in late September. 'Spartan' has good quality fruit on a medium-sized tree; it ripens late September to October.

Apricot: (zone 4 [winter hardy—the fruit is often lost to spring frost]/needs pollinator) The 'Harcot' has sweet, firm flesh and is self-fruitful; it ripens in mid-July. 'Moongold' has a tough skin; it is good for processing or desserts. It ripens in mid-July. 'Sungold' has tender skin and a sweet, mild flavor. It ripens in mid- to late July.

Blueberries: (zones 3 or 4 half-highs/self-fruitful cultivars need pollinator) 'Northcountry' (self-fruitful) has sky-blue fruit on a small plant. 'St. Cloud' (self-fruitful) is a Minnesota introduction; it is the least hardy but has superior fruit. 'Northbluedark' blue fruit has a good fall color, is self-fruitful, and ripens in July. 'North Sky' is a small, 10- to 20-inch plant with medium sky-blue fruit, a good fall color, and better winter hardiness. It is self-fruitful. 'Friendship' is a University of Wisconsin introduction with sky-blue fruit that ripens in July to August; it is self-fruitful.

Cherries, Sour: (zones 3 to 4/self-fruitful) 'Montmorency' is the standard tart cherry; it is moderate quality and ripens in mid-July. 'North Star' is the hardiest with good quality fruit and leaf spot resistance; it ripens in mid-July. 'Meteor' is very hardy, has large red fruit with yellow flesh, and resists leaf spot; harvest in late July.

Currants: (zones 3 to 4/self-fruitful) 'Wilder' is vigorous with red fruit; harvest begins in early July. 'Red Lake' is hardy and vigorous, producing large red fruit with mild flavor.

Elderberry: (zones 3 to 4/self-fruitful) 'Adams' has large fruit and vigorous growth; it ripens in early August. 'York' is more productive than 'Adams' and has large, sweet fruit and an attractive plant; it ripens in mid- to late August.

Gooseberries: (zones 3 to 4/self-fruitful) 'Downing' is hardy and productive with good quality, pale green fruit. 'Poorman' is hardy, less thorny, and produces red fruit. 'Pixwell' is hardy and moderately productive with pink, mild-flavored fruit.

Grapes: (zones 3 to 4/self-fruitful) 'Valiant' is a medium-sized, tart blue grape; it is hardy and ripens in mid-August. 'Beta' has small, blue, tart fruit; it also ripens in mid-August. 'Fredonia' is a good quality grape for fresh use or for preserves; it is hardy and productive and ripens in early September. 'Edelweiss' is a 'White Swenson' with good flavor for fresh use; it is ready in early September. 'Red Swenson' produces red, high-quality fruit; it ripens in mid- to late September.

Minnesota Fruits

Peaches: (zone 4b/self-fruitful) Peach crops are often lost to the spring frost, and the trees are short-lived, but nothing beats the sweet flavor of a peach picked right off the tree. Plant every three years to ensure a replacement for dying plants. **'Reliance'** is one of the hardiest.

Pears: (zones 3 to 4/needs pollinator) **'Parker'** is a good quality, but poor keeper; it ripens in mid-August. **'Gourmet'** is a very hardy dessert pear with crisp, juicy fruit; it ripens in mid-September. **'Luscious'** is sweeter than **'Bartlet'** and hardy; it ripens in late September.

Plums: (zones 3 to 4/some self-fruitful) **'Mount Royal'** is a good quality, blue plum for zones 4 and 5; it is self-fruitful and ripens in early September. **'Stanley'** is a late-blooming, heavy producer that is sweet and moderately hardy. It is self-fruitful; plant with 'Mount Royal' for a better yield. **'Underwood'** is a good quality, red, round plum; it is hardy, needs a pollinator, and ripens in mid-August. **'Pipestone'** is very large, red plum; it is very hardy, needs a pollinator, and ripens mid-August. **'Alderman'** is a new introduction from the University of Minnesota. It has burgundy-red fruit of excellent quality, needs a pollinator, and ripens in late August. **'Superior'** is an excellent quality red plum; it is moderately hardy, needs a pollinator, and ripens in late August. **'Kaga'** and **'Toka'** are red plum pollinators.

Red Raspberries, Summer-bearing: (zones 3 to 4/self-fruitful) **'Boyne'** is vigorous and hardy with good quality fruit; it ripens in late June. **'Reveille'** has a very good flavor, tolerates fluctuating spring temperatures, and is very winter hardy. **'Nordic'** fruit is superior to 'Boyne', has fewer thorns, and greater disease resistance. It is a cold hardy cultivar from Minnesota. **'Latham'** is hardy and productive with a mild flavor.

Red Raspberries, Fall-bearing: (best in zone 4/self-fruitful) **'Redwing'** is a newer variety from Minnesota; it ripens in mid-August. **'Fallgold'** is a yellow-fruited cultivar with good winter hardiness; it ripens in late August.

Strawberries, June-bearing: (zones 3 to 4/self-fruitful) **'Earliglow'** is an early season berry with good flavor and some disease resistance. **'Honeoye'** is very productive and very hardy. **'Kent'** produces a lot of large fruit with a mild flavor. **'Sparkle'** is a high-quality, tasty berry and very hardy.

Strawberries, Everbearing: (zones 3 to 4/self-fruitful) **'Ogallala'** produces large quantities of soft fruit on vigorous, hardy, and drought-tolerant plants. **'Ozark Beauty'** has good flavor, is winter hardy, and has some disease resistance.

Strawberry, Day-neutral (produces crops midsummer and fall): (zones 3 to 4/self-fruitful) **'Tribute'** has bright red, firm fruit and some disease resistance. **'Tristar'** has sweet, firm fruit and works well in hanging baskets.

Planning

The holidays are over, and our tight clothes signal that it is time to start eating healthy. What better way to make this prospect appealing than to grow your own healthy fruit?

Break out the landscape plan and start looking for areas to add some fruit trees, a row of **Raspberries**, or a patch of **Strawberries**. You do not need a lot of space, just some sunlight and creative planning.

Start gathering catalogs for planting ideas and potential plant sources. Check with the Minnesota State Horticultural Society your local botanical garden, or University of Minnesota Extension Service for addresses.

Planting

The ground is frozen and most likely covered with snow. *Get your planting tools ready for the season.* Find your shovel, trowels, and other tools. Make sure they are clean, oiled, and sharp. If not, now is the time to burn a few calories and get busy.

- Use a wire brush to knock off any soil. Follow this with steel wool or medium-grit sandpaper to remove any rust that may have collected.

- Sharpen the edges with a metal file. Sharp shovel, hoes, and trowels make digging and planting easier and less tiring. Rub in a few drops of oil to help prevent rust.

Care

Check winter mulches on **Strawberries**. Replace any that were dislodged in bad weather. Can't see the mulch for the snow? That's great. Snow is the best insulation available. No snow and no mulch? Get busy. Locate straw or evergreen branches. Cover plantings to protect the overwintering flower buds and prevent frost heaving.

Watering

Do not water. Check the landscape and fruit plantings for flooded areas and ice. Make a note of these problem areas in your journal and on your landscape plan. These areas are more likely to be damaged or die over the winter. Evaluate landscape changes you can make to fix these problems. It may be as easy as moving a downspout or sump pump discharge. Or you may need to move the plants or raise the planting beds if the water cannot be redirected.

Fertilizing

Check the yearly growth on tree fruits, such as **Apples**, **Pears**, **Plums**, and **Cherries**. Start at the tip of the branch and trace it back to the terminal bud scale scars. These ridges encircle the stem and mark one year's growth. Young fruit trees typically grow 10 to 20 inches each year. Bearing trees grow 8 to 12 inches. Stunted plants will benefit from a spring application of fertilizer. Make a note not to fertilize those that are growing more than normal. Overfertilization can stimulate stem and leaf growth, prevent fruiting, and increase the risk of disease.

Pests

Check stems of **Plums**, **Cherries**, and other stone fruits for black knot cankers. The mature canker is a black, bumpy growth on the stem. The immature canker looks like an abnormal swelling of the branch. Prune out any mature and immature cankers you see. Prune 9 inches below the canker and disinfect your tools between cuts. Use rubbing alcohol or a solution of one part bleach to nine parts water.

Look for tent caterpillar, gypsy moth, and other egg masses throughout the winter. Tent caterpillars eggs look like a glob of mud stuck on the branch. Prune out or smash the eggs. This will prevent feeding damage caused by these wormlike insects in May. Gypsy moth egg masses are yellow. Scrape these egg masses off the tree trunk and destroy.

Look for signs of animal damage. Droppings, tracks, and feeding damage are clues you need to get busy. Use repellents to keep deer and rabbits away. Reapply after bad weather or as recommended by the label directions.

Make sure all animal fencing is still in place and working. Add an extra section of hardware cloth to areas buried in snow. The 4-foot rabbit fencing will do no good if half of it is buried in snow. An extra section will help reduce rabbit damage.

Pruning

Remove hazardous or storm-damaged branches. Save major pruning for late winter. You can correct winter damage, adjust for animal feeding, and do structural pruning all at one time.

Helpful Hints

Consider some nontraditional fruit plants for the landscape. Many of the plants grown for their beauty also produce edible fruit.

- **Juneberry** or **Serviceberry** *(Amelanchier)* produces tasty fruit that birds and people enjoy. The berrylike fruit looks like **Blueberries.** Their nutty blueberry flavor is good fresh from the tree or baked in a pie. I will never forget Julie and Sarah, 4 and 6 at the time, climbing over my trash container to beat the birds to a handful of Juneberries. All Juneberries are edible, but some species and cultivars produce larger fruit. **Saskatoon Serviceberry *(Amelanchier alnifolia)*** and its cultivars for **'Honeywood'**, **'Smokey'**, **'Northline'**, **'Parkwood'**, **'Pembina'**, and **'Theissen'** produce large, tasty fruit and are hardy in zone 4. **Allegheny Serviceberry *(Amelanchier laevis)*,** another North American native, produces large ($^3/_8$-inch), sweet fruit on trees hardy to zone 4.

- **American Cranberrybush Viburnum *(Viburnum trilobum)*,** has long been used for preserves. Personally, I would need a lot of sugar to find this tasty. 'Andrews', 'Hahs', and 'Wentworth' were selected for their larger fruit. If, like me, you don't like the flavor, the fruit is attractive and provides good winter interest.

- **Hardy Kiwis *(Actinidia arguta)*** became popular soon after the tropical Kiwi fruits were a hit at the grocery stores. These Asian introductions produce small grape-size fruit, but are hardier than the tropical types. The small fruits are sweet and high in vitamin C. You need a male and female plant, with a few exceptions, to produce a crop of fruit. Rated hardy for zones 3 to 4, you will need to give them a little winter protection the first few years. Plant in a protected location and protect the trunks in zone 4. The whole plant may need protection in zone 3. Or try the more ornamental **Arctic Beauty Kiwi *(Actinidia kolomikta,* 'Arctic Beauty')*.** This plant produces beautiful green leaves with cream and pink blotches. The male is more colorful, but you will need a female as well to get fruit.

Planning

So you filled every possible planting location in your landscape. Consider growing **Strawberries** and **Dwarf Apples** in containers.

Planting

It is still too early to plant. Look through your potting supplies and locate suitable containers for planting **Strawberries** and **Dwarf Apples**. These plants can be ornamental as well as fun to eat. You will need to find a place (unheated garage or enclosed porch) to overwinter them.

Care

Check on any potted fruit plants you have stored for winter. Make sure the temperatures are cold enough to keep them dormant. Temperatures should be near freezing. Check on mulch or other insulation used to keep the roots from freezing. Adjust the location and winter protection as needed.

Watering

Water container plants overwintered in an unheated garage or porch. Water thoroughly any time the soil thaws and the top 4 to 6 inches are dry. No need to water outdoor plants.

Fertilizing

Do not fertilizer frozen soil. The plants cannot use the fertilizer and it washes off the soil, into the sewer, and pollutes our waterways.

Pests

Keep monitoring for animal damage. See October "Helpful Hints" for more control suggestions.

Apply dormant oil, such as Volck, All Seasons®, or lime sulfur, to control mites, scales, and other overwintering insects. Only apply dormant oils when the temperatures are 40 degrees Fahrenheit at application and for the following 12 hours. The February thaw is a good time to make this application.

Watch for cankers (sunken, discolored areas) on stems. Prune 9 to 12 inches below the canker. Discard or destroy the infected branch. Disinfect tools between cuts to prevent spreading the disease to healthy tissue. Use rubbing alcohol or a solution of one part bleach to nine parts water.

Continue checking for egg masses of tent caterpillar and gypsy moths. See January "Pests" for details.

Pruning

Start thinning and pruning **Red Raspberry** plantings as the snow begins to recede. Prune any plantings not managed in summer now until growth begins. See the general information in the "Training" section of this chapter's introduction and July's "Pruning."

- Start with **Summer** and **Everbearing Raspberry** crops. Remove all the older canes that bore fruit that summer. Cut these back to ground level. Thin the plantings to three to four canes per foot or six to eight canes per hill. Cut back long canes and side shots. Remove no more than onefourth of the total height. The more you prune, the smaller the harvest.

- Now prune your **Fall-bearing Red Raspberries**. See November "Pruning" for details.

Helpful Hints

Spend a few minutes now to review the training method for tree fruits. It is easier to read and study the information in a warm house than try to remember when you are standing in front of the tree, cold wind blowing, and saw in hand.

Consider training your tree fruits in the Central Leader System. It is easy for you and good for the tree. Follow this step-by-step process:

- ***At planting:*** Prune whips (thin, unbranched stems) back to 30 or 45 inches at planting. Do minimal pruning on branched trees. Remove only the damaged or broken branches at this time.
- ***1st spring after planting:*** Prune in late winter or early spring before growth begins. Evaluate the tree and branching structure. Look for evenly spaced branches with wide crotch angles (angle between branch and trunk). Leave four to five of the strongest and most evenly spaced branches with the lowest being 24 to 36 inches above the ground. These branches (scaffolds) should be evenly spaced around the trunk and located within 18 inches of the lowest branch. Prune the other branches back to the branch bark collar. See the "Trees" chapter for more information on pruning.
- ***2nd and 3rd years:*** Remove broken and damaged branches each spring before growth begins. Remove suckers (shoots that arise at the base of the tree) just below ground level. Prune off watersprouts (branches that grow straight up from scaffold branches) that interfere with growth and fruit development. Remove any drooping, crossing, and parallel branches. Remove branches back to the point where they join another branch. Prune flush with the branch bark collar (the swollen area at the base of the branch).

24" to 36"

Central Leader Tree—Apple

- ***3rd or 4th year:*** Select another set of scaffold branches 24 inches above the first. This will allow light to reach the first set of scaffold branches. Keep the upper tier of scaffolds shorter than the bottom set, allowing light to reach all parts of the tree. Spurs (the short fruiting stems) will begin to form along the branches.
- ***5th year and beyond:*** Maintain the leader as the tallest branch. Prune back any side branches that are starting to reach the height of the leader. Cut the tip of the branch back to a side branch. Slow down tree growth once it reaches the desired height. Most gardeners like to keep dwarf trees 8 to 10 feet tall and semi-dwarf trees 12 to 16 feet tall. Prune the tip of the leader back to a weak side branch to slow upward growth. Repeat yearly as needed.
- ***Yearly:*** Remove watersprouts, suckers, broken, and damaged branches. Watch for and prune out crossing and parallel branches that will eventually rub. Remove all inward- and downward-facing spurs and branches. Do the heaviest pruning just before the bearing season on alternate bearing **Apples.**

Planning

Call or visit your local county office of the University of Minnesota Extension Service. Ask to see a list of their fruit publications. They have many excellent publications that can provide more detail and pictures than I can in this chapter. Or check their website at www.extension.umn.edu/. You can view many of the publications and print out many useful tips on selection, planting, care, and harvest.

Planting

Let the weather and plant availability be your guide. Some years, gardeners in the southern part of Minnesota can begin planting dormant tree fruits and **Raspberries**. Other years, and for those in the north, we may still be waiting for the snow to melt. Prepare a storage area for any early arrivals that cannot be planted right away. Find a cool (not freezing) location. An unheated garage, enclosed porch, or root cellar would work. See the "Planting" section in the chapter introduction for specifics.

Care

Take a walk around the landscape. *Clean up* any debris that may have collected over winter. Check the base of trees for signs of vole and rabbit damage. This may influence your plant order. You may need a few extra replacement plants after a bad winter.

Watering

Water overwintered container plants whenever the soil is thawed and the top 4 to 6 inches are dry. Water thoroughly so that the excess runs out the bottom.

Keep the roots moist of those bare-root plants you have in storage. Pack roots in moist sawdust or peat moss to help retain moisture.

Fertilizing

Start fertilizing the end of this month or early April after the ground thaws and before growth begins. This is usually the best time to fertilize most fruit trees and berries. See the "Fertilization" sections in the chapter introduction for specific recommendations.

Pests

Continue looking for egg masses of tent caterpillar and gypsy moth. Look for mudlike globs (tent caterpillars) on stems and branches. Prune out the egg mass and discard the stem or smash the eggs with your hand. Check the trunks and major branches for the yellow, hairy egg masses of gypsy moth. Remove and destroy these as well.

Prune out cankered (sunken, discolored areas) or oozing (bacterial gummosis) stems. Make your cut 9 to 12 inches below the damage. Disinfect tools between cuts with rubbing alcohol or a solution of one part bleach to nine parts water.

Check **Plums**, **Cherries**, and other stone fruits for black knot. This fungal disease causes stems to swell and develop black lumpy growths. Prune out the old black knots and the new (swollen stems), less visible, knots. Complete removal of knots by April 1st to prevent the release of spores and reduce future infections.

Pruning

Continue pruning. This will be one of the busiest times of the year for you and your pruning tools.

MARCH

Helpful Hints

Late March is the time to start training and pruning **Grapes.** Train your plants over an arbor, across a fence, or on a trellis constructed for this purpose.

***Select a training system for your* Grapes.** The Four-cane Kniffen System is one of the most popular, though some of the newer systems allow more sunlight to reach the plants.

- ***At planting:*** Start training your **Grapes** now. Cut the stem back leaving only two buds above the soil. These two buds will produce new stems and leaves the first summer. Secure the trunk to the trellis.
- ***2nd year:*** Get out the pruning equipment in late March. Select one or two straight canes to be your permanent trunk. Remove other stems back to the main trunk.
- ***3rd year:*** Select the four strongest and best placed side branches in late March. Attach these to the trellis. Cut these side branches back to 8 to 12 buds each. These will be the fruiting canes that produce this season's harvest. Select secondary side shoots close to each of the first ones selected. Prune these back to two buds. These are the renewal spurs that will be next year's fruiting canes. Prune off all other growth.
- ***4th year and beyond:*** Remove last year's fruiting canes. Replace them with the renewal spurs. Cut the new fruiting canes back to 8 to 12 buds. Select new renewal spurs close to the fruiting canes. Prune these back to two buds. Remove all other growth. See figure.

Fruiting Cane with 8 to 12 buds

Renewal spurs

Renewal spurs 2 buds each

Fruiting Cane with 8 to 12 buds

Finish pruning and thinning **Red Raspberries** if this has not been done. See February "Pruning" for specifics.

Continue pruning and training young fruit trees. Remove broken, crossed, and damaged branches on older trees. Remove suckers and watersprouts on both young and old

trees. See February "Helpful Hints" for year-by-year pruning guidelines.

Do not forget about your **Currants, Gooseberries, Elderberries,** and **Blueberries**. These benefit from yearly pruning. Remove the weakest and damaged branches. See the "Pruning" section of the chapter introduction for specific guidelines.

Sharpen your tools and contact the grapevine wreath makers in your family. It is time to prune the **Grapes**. Be aggressive and you will be rewarded with a large harvest. See "Helpful Hints" for pruning tips.

Planning

As the snow melts and the buds begin to break, check for winter damage and plant survival. Harsh winters bring the opportunity to add new plants to the landscape.

Planting

Prepare the soil for planting. Follow soil test results and add the needed organic matter and fertilizer.

- Add 2 to 4 inches of organic matter to the top 12 inches of soil when planting **Raspberries** and **Strawberries**. **Blueberries** require major steps to grow in most landscapes. See May "Planting" for details.

- Either amend the whole planting bed or none of it when planting fruit trees and shrubs. Do not add lots of organic matter to the planting hole. This results in girdling roots that fail to explore the soil beyond the planting hole. It is important to plant these fruits in a well-drained area.

Plant bare-root trees, shrubs, **Raspberries**, and **Strawberries** that arrived in a dormant state. Prepare the soil and plant as directed in the "Soil Preparation" and "Planting" sections of the chapter introduction.

Purchase and plant potted trees and fruits as they become available. Those grown outdoors locally can be planted as soon as the soil can be worked. Imported or greenhouse grown plants need to be hardened off and protected from freezing temperatures.

Wait until the end of this month or early May to plant **Blueberries**. This will prevent damage to the tender buds. Keep blankets or row covers handy to protect them from freezing temperatures. See May "Planting" for details.

Care

Remove winter mulches on **Strawberries** as the temperatures begin to hover near freezing or when the covered plants begin top growth. Rake the straw into the aisles between plantings. Leave it there to serve as a summer mulch, reducing weeds and conserving moisture. Or add the straw to the compost pile and let it decompose for future use in soil preparation.

Watering

Water new plantings thoroughly so that the roots and surrounding soil are moist. Check new plantings once or twice a week. Keep the soil surrounding bare-root plantings moist. Give tree fruits 3 to 5 gallons of water each week. Water small fruits when the top 4 to 6 inches of soil begin to dry.

Check established plantings throughout the season. Make sure plants receive 1 inch of water each week. Nature usually provides this in the form of melting snow and spring showers. Provide the needed water in one weekly application for plants growing in clay soils and two applications (of $1/2$ to $3/4$ inch each) in sandy soils.

Fertilizing

Fertilize fruits before growth begins. Err on the conservative side if soil test recommendations are not available. Follow recommendations in the "Fertilization" section in the chapter introduction.

Avoid complete fertilizers such as 10-10-10 or 12-12-12 unless recommended by your soil test. Most soils contain high to excessive levels of phosphorus and potassium (the last two numbers). Adding more can interfere with the uptake of other nutrients and reduce water quality.

Pests

Continue monitoring for and protecting plants from animal damage. Tender spring growth makes good meals for rabbits and deer. Secure fencing materials and apply repellents as needed.

Spray stone fruits that have continually suffered from brown rot disease. Spray trees with a fungicide (labeled for disease control on stone fruit) at the early bloom stage and three to twenty-one days prior to harvest if the weather is wet.

Begin scab control on **Apples** and **Pears** with a history of this disease. Infected plants have spotted leaves and fruits that often drop prematurely. Start spraying susceptible plants you want to treat as buds begin to swell. Repeat every seven to fourteen days until dry weather returns.

Pull or *cultivate* weeds as soon as they appear. Maintain a circle of mulch around fruit trees and shrubs to help reduce weeds. Keep a constant watch on **Strawberry** and **Raspberry** plantings. Once the weeds take over, it is time-consuming to try to reclaim the planting.

Pruning

Finish dormant season pruning before growth begins. Prune new

Helpful Hints

Overgrown Apple trees need to be pruned to improve their productivity and make maintenance easier for you. They tend to be too tall or too densely branched. Take several years to get these trees back in shape. Heavy pruning stimulates lots of leaf and stem growth and discourages fruiting.

1   Start by reducing the height of tall trees. Take a close look at the tree's structure. Remove one or two of the tallest branches back to the trunk. Then remove any damaged or diseased branches. Wait a year to do additional pruning.

2   Open up the dense canopy. This can be done the first year on short trees or the second and third year on trees for which you have reduced the height.

3   Remove deadwood, suckers, watersprouts (stems that grow straight up from branches) and broken branches.

4   Next remove crossing, rubbing, or parallel branches that will eventually grow together.

5   Always make cuts back to the trunk or where a branch joins another branch. Make the final cut flush to the branch bark collar. This is the swollen area that occurs at the base of a stem.

6   Use the three-step system when pruning larger (3 inches in diameter or greater) branches. See the Trees February "Helpful Hints" on page 295 for a detailed description and illustration.

7   Do not use pruning paints. Allow plants to naturally seal the wound and fight off pests on their own.

plantings according to the transplant's size and the crop being grown. Prune established plantings to maximize light penetration and fruit production.

See February "Pruning" and "Helpful Hints," and March "Helpful Hints" for additional pruning information.

Planning

Spring has arrived and you are busy doing instead of planning. Take a little time to record the work you are doing in your landscape. These records will help you continually improve your planting and maintenance practices. All this will result in a larger harvest.

Make a planting list. Record the name and variety of every fruit plant you add to the landscape. Record the planting date and place of purchase.

Note fertilizer practices. Later, you can compare the input of fertilizer to the output of healthy plants and produce. The recommended rates may need to be adjusted to better fit your growing conditions.

Record pest control methods used. Be specific and record the type and amount of materials used, time of application, and weather conditions. These should all be considered when evaluating the need for and effectiveness of your pest management system.

Planting

Continue planting. Container and balled-and-burlapped trees are more readily available. Keep the plants in a cool, shaded location until they can be planted. Cover the rootball with mulch and make sure the soil stays moist.

As the temperatures warm, it is a good time to plant **Blueberries.** Select the hardiest half-high varieties you can find. Prepare the soil as described here to increase your chance of success.

- Add several inches of organic matter, such as peat moss or compost, to the top 12 inches of soil. This will improve drainage in heavy soils and improve the water-holding ability of sandy soils.

- Some gardeners remove the existing soil and totally replace it with a more suitable planting medium. Remove the soil from an area 15 inches deep and 24 inches wide for each plant. Replace the existing soil with two bushels of peat moss or compost, one bushel of loam soil, and one-half cup of sulfur. Mix well and use this to fill the planting hole.

- Plant **Blueberries** deep enough to cover the top roots with 3 to 4 inches of soil. Firm the soil and water to remove any air pockets. Water often enough to keep the top 4 to 6 inches of soil constantly moist.

- Mulch with shredded leaves, woodchips, or other organic mulch. This will help keep roots evenly moist throughout the summer.

Care

Replenish woodchip and bark mulch around fruit trees, shrubs, and **Grape** vines. Add shredded leaves or similar material to **Raspberry** and **Strawberry** plantings.

Continue to pull or cultivate weeds as soon as they appear. Keeping the plantings weed-free will reduce pest problems and competition for water and nutrients. Mulch weeded gardens to reduce future weed growth.

Watering

Check new plantings once or twice each week. Water these plants whenever the top 4 inches of soil begins to dry. Give newly planted fruit trees 3 to 5 gallons of water each week. Be sure to moisten the rootball and beyond.

Most established fruit prefer one inch of water each week. Supply this in one watering in clay soils and two waterings in sandy soils. Adjust watering based on rainfall.

Fertilizing

Make a second application of fertilizer to bearing **Raspberries** in late May or early June. Apply 1 cup of ammonium nitrate (33-0-0) per 100 feet of row or $1/4$ cup per hill.

Apply post-planting fertilization for the following crops:

- Apply 2 tablespoons of ammonium nitrate fertilizer to **Grapes** planted two to three weeks ago.

- Give **Currants** and other fruiting bushes 2 tablespoons of ammonium nitrate three to four weeks after planting

- Fertilize new **Blueberries** two to four weeks after planting with 2 tablespoons of ammonium sulfate.

Pests

Continue spraying for apple scab. Use a fungicide labeled for scab control on fruit trees. Do not use home orchard sprays during bloom time. These contain insecticides that kill pollinating bees and prevent fruit formation.

Remove fireblight-infested branches. Look for hooked branches with brown or blackened leaves. Find the canker (sunken, discolored area) before removing the branch. Prune at least 9 inches below the canker. Disinfect tools with a solution of one part bleach to nine parts water between cuts.

Remove the webby nests of tent caterpillars. Prune out the tent or use a stick to knock it out of the tree. Destroy the insects. Or spray the nest and surrounding 2 feet with *Bacillius thuringiensis*. This bacteria kills true caterpillars, but does not harm other insects and wildlife.

Do not spray insecticides on flowering plants. This includes home orchard sprays that contain both fungicides and insecticides. These products kill nature's pollinators (bees) and can prevent fruit set.

Helpful Hints

After you fill your landscape with new pest-resistant trees, you may have a few old timers that are creating a mess in the yard and garden. You hate to cut them down because they are a family heirloom, sentimental member of the family, or a good source for shade. Keep the tree and flowers but eliminate the fruit. Timing and proper application are the key to success. You may want to hire a professional with the training and experience to do the job safely and effectively. ***To eliminate the fruit on old fruit trees:***

- Call local garden centers or check your favorite gardening catalog for Florel® fruit eliminator. This product can be used to eliminate unwanted fruit on **Apples, Pears,** and several other ornamental trees.
- Apply this growth regulator when trees are in full bloom. Make sure all flowers and buds are thoroughly covered. Early or late applications are not effective. Insufficient coverage and improper timing can result in fewer but larger fruits.

Pruning

Remove flowers that form on new plantings of **June-bearing Strawberries**. Remove all flowers that form on **Day-neutral** and **Everbearing Strawberries** the first six to eight weeks after planting. This allows the plant to expend energy on establishing a strong root system and hardy plant for winter survival and long-term production.

Pick any fruits that start to develop on young (first two years after planting) fruit trees. This directs the growth into root and branch development for longevity.

Planning

Continue writing in your journal. Your working records will help you plan what stays and what goes in the future. You may decide it is more fun to visit the farmer's market and buy a bushel of **Apples**; while harvesting your own **Currants** can't be beat.

Planting

Continue planting. See April and May "Planting" for details.

Care

Harvest **Strawberries** *every other day to ensure quality and reduce the number of overripe berries on the plants.* Overripe berries attract insects and increase the risk of disease.

• Harvest all large and small **Strawberries** when they are fully colored. Hold the berry in your hand, pinch the stem with your finger, and twist as you pull.

• Use quarts or pints to carry and store berries. These shallow containers prevent overstacking that can damage the tender fruit.

• Store berries in the refrigerator as soon as possible. Put cooled berries—containers and all—in vented plastic bags and store for up to four days.

Rake and *compost* all immature **Apples** that fall from the tree. This is a common phenomena called June drop. It occurs when **Apples** produce more fruit than the plant can support. The fruit drop is nature's way of thinning the crop to a more manageable size. Eliminate June drop by thinning young fruit.

Thin **Apples** by removing all but one or two of the developing fruit in each cluster. Or thin to one fruit every 6 to 8 inches along the stem. Remove and compost unwanted fruit by mid-June to increase fruit size and improve flower set next season.

Mulch new plantings and replenish mulch on existing plantings. Straw and shredded leaves are suitable for **Strawberries**. Shredded leaves and woodchips can be used around **Raspberries**, **Blueberries**, and other fruiting shrubs. Use woodchips or shredded bark for fruit trees and fruiting shrubs. Use a 1- to 2-inch layer of fine mulch materials, such as leaves, and a 3- to 4-inch layer of coarser materials, such as woodchips.

Watering

Continue watering as recommended in July "Watering."

Fertilizing

Make the second application of fertilizer for established **Raspberry** plantings if it was not done in late May. Apply 1 cup of (33-0-0) per 100 feet of row or 1/4 cup per hill.

Give new plantings of **June-bearing Strawberries** 1 cup of ammonium nitrate (33-0-0) fertilizer per 100 feet of row, or 1 teaspoon per plant, when the runners begin to form. Fertilize established plantings with 1 cup of (33-0-0) after harvest.

Apply 2 cups of ammonium nitrate per 100 feet of row to **Everbearing Strawberries** after their first crop.

Apply the second part (1/3 cup of 33-0-0 per plant) of the two-part fertilization for **Grapes** suffering from frost damage.

Pests

Pest management is a very personal decision. Some gardeners grow their own fruit to avoid pesticides. Planting disease-resistant varieties and sanitation will help reduce pest problems. It is impossible to grow perfect **Apples** without pesticides. If perfection is not your goal, do minimal or no pesticide spraying.

Insects:

Place sticky traps in fruit trees to monitor insect populations. Some gardeners use trapping for limited pest control, while other strictly use the traps to monitor insects for spraying.

Evaluate past damage, monitor traps, and decide whether you want to control these fruit damaging insects: apple maggots, codling moths, and plum curculio.

• Lumpy **Apples** with brown streaks through the flesh are the results of apple maggots. The adults lay their eggs in the developing **Apples**. The larvae feed through the fruit, causing the damage. Some people use these for sauces, cider, and baking, while other insist on their control.

• Codling moths are the "worms" in the **Apples**. Reduce problems by raking and destroying fallen fruit. Preventative sprays will help eliminate this pest.

• The plum curculio prefers **Plums**, but will damage **Apples** and **Pears** as well. Female curculio lay their eggs on the fruit surface. This scar results in lumpy and misshapen fruit. The surviving offspring feed inside the fruit, causing it to fall prematurely.

Harvest **Strawberries** as often as possible to keep overripe berries off the plants. The overripe fruits attract picnic (also called sap) beetles that feed on all the berries.

Minimize your pesticide use and still provide substantial control for these pests by following this program: Apply an insecticide labeled for insect control on fruit trees at petal fall, two weeks later, mid-July, and early August.

Diseases:

• Continue to prune out fire-blight and black knot cankers. See March "Pests" for more specific information.

• Check **Raspberries** for signs of cane blight and anthracnose. Infected canes are discolored, have yellow leaves, and produce crumbly fruit. Remove and destroy infected canes as soon as they are discovered.

• Renew **Strawberry** plantings infected with leaf spot fungal disease. Regular renewal (see Fruit "Helpful Hints" on page 356), sanitation, and proper spacing will usually keep this disease under control.

Animals:

Cover **Strawberries** and **Raspberries** with netting to protect your harvest from the birds. Anchor the netting securely to prevent the birds from going in under the netting to reach the fruit. Apply the netting early to encourage them to go elsewhere for their snacks.

Pruning

Continue to prune broken and damaged branches. Remove disease infested branches and canes as soon as they are found. Always disinfect tools between cuts with a solution of one part bleach to nine parts water.

Planning

Record harvest dates and time spent harvesting. This will help you plan for next year. You may want to recruit friends and neighbors to help in the harvest and share the produce. Consider sharing surplus fruits and vegetables with a local food pantry. The Second Harvest Food Bank can help you locate a food pantry in your community. This is a great way to share your love of gardening with people, especially children and seniors in need.

Planting

Finish renovating **Strawberries** (see "Helpful Hints" on page 356). Continue planting potted tree and shrub fruits. Make sure they are properly watered throughout the hot, dry part of summer.

Care

Harvest the summer crop of **Raspberries** *when the fruits are fully colored and pull easily off the core.* This often coincides with mosquito hatch. Try some of the mosquito netting clothes to make picking more enjoyable and the mosquitoes more tolerable.

- Try using a gallon milk jug to gather the **Raspberries**. Cut away the top front of the container. Leave the bottom and handle intact. Tie the jug around your waist so you can keep both hands free for picking. Pile the Raspberries in thin layers to prevent crushing the bottom layers of berries.

- Chill the berries within 2 hours of picking. Wash just before use.

Harvest **Cherries** *when they have colored up, and are flavorful and juicy.*

- Hold the **Cherry** between several fingers. Pull and twist to remove the fruit, but not the spurs and branches from the tree. Leave stems attached to **Sweet Cherries** for storing. Move to cool storage (32 to 40 degrees Fahrenheit) if you want to store for several weeks.

Check and harvest **Currants** *and* **Gooseberries** *when they are sweet and juicy.* Store these in shallow containers and refrigerate as soon as possible to increase storage life.

Watering

Adjust watering rates to compensate for weekly rainfall.

Apply needed water in one application to fruits growing in clay soils. Make two applications (of half the needed amount) in sandy soils. Refer to the chapter introduction for additional watering information.

Fertilizing

Apply 1 teaspoon of ammonium nitrate per plant, or 1 cup of ammonium nitrate per 100 feet of row, to **Day-neutral** and **Everbearing Strawberries** that are flowering and fruiting. Sprinkle fertilizer on the soil, brushing off any that lands on the foliage.

Pests

Diseases:

- Check **Raspberry** canes for insects and disease. Cane blight and anthracnose cause purple and brown spots on stems. Leaves yellow and brown, and the fruits are dry and crumby. Prune out and destroy infected canes as soon as they are found.

- Fireblight is a problem on **Raspberries**, as well as **Apples** and **Pears**. Wilted tips that quickly turn black indicate this disease is present. Check the stems or branches for sunken, discolored areas called cankers. Prune out infected Raspberry canes to ground level. Prune 9 to 12 inches below the canker on infected Apple and Pear branches. Disinfect tools between cuts to reduce the risk of spreading this disease. Use a solution of one part bleach and nine parts water.

- Continue treating for apple and pear scab during wet periods. This fungal disease causes black spots on leaves and fruits. Use a fungicide labeled for controlling this disease on fruit trees, every ten to fourteen days.

- Prune out black knot (black knobby growths) on **Plums**, **Cherries**, and **Peaches**. This reduces future infection.

- Spray stone fruits with a history of brown rot if the weather is wet. Use a fungicide labeled for controlling this disease on stone fruits. Apply when the fruits begin to turn from green to ripe color.

Insects:

- Prune out and destroy cane borer- and cane maggot-infested stems. Both feed inside the stem, causing it to wilt. Prune canes to ground level.

- Harvest **Raspberries** as often as possible to keep over-ripe berries off the plants. The overripe fruits attract picnic (also called sap) beetles that feed on all the berries.

- Treat tree fruits suffering from repeated insect infestations with an insecticide the middle of this month. This schedule will give you substantial insect control with a reduced amount of pesticide applications. Check label for wait times between spraying and harvesting. See June "Pests" for details on insects.

Protect the harvest from birds, squirrels, and other uninvited guests. See "Helpful Hints" for August.

Pruning

Prune **Summer-bearing** and **Ever-bearing Raspberry** plants right after harvest. Remove all the older canes that bore fruit that summer. Cut these back to ground level.

Thin **Summer-bearing Red Raspberries** at this time. Summer thinning increases airflow and reduces disease problems. Remove all but three to four canes per foot, or six to eight canes per hill. Secure the remaining canes to the stake or within the trellis.

Remove only disease- and insect-infected canes on **Fall-bearing Red Raspberries** that were cut to the ground over the winter. All these first-year canes will produce fruit this fall.

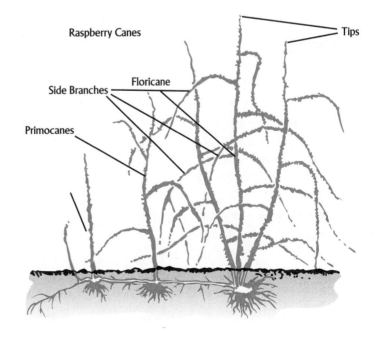

Raspberry Canes   Tips

Side Branches   Floricane

Primocanes

Planning

The big harvest season is quickly approaching. Soon your basement will be filled with **Apples** and **Pears**. Start making plans now for handling all this produce. Many gardeners turn their harvest into sauces, pie fillings, and preserves that can be canned and stored for winter. Others find a cool corner of their basement, or a second refrigerator to store fruits. Stock up on perforated plastic bags to help extend the life of your produce. Make a plan now so that you will not be overwhelmed when you are busy picking all those fruits.

Visit www.northerngardener.org for recent articles from *Northern Gardener*.

Planting

Garden centers and nurseries often have potted fruit plants for sale. Get these in the ground as soon as possible. This will allow the plants to get established before winter sets in. Make sure new plantings are watered throughout the remainder of the season. Check them more frequently during this hot, dry month.

Care

Follow these guidelines for harvesting:

- Harvest **Blueberries** when they are fully colored, sweet, and juicy. Like other berries, store them in shallow containers to prevent crushing the fruit.

- Harvest **Elderberries** throughout the month. Taste the fruit to check for ripeness. Pick when the berries are fully colored and juicy.

- Start harvesting **Apples** just before they are fully mature. Early season varieties will start ripening this month. Look for a color change in the indentation where the stem attaches to the fruit. The background color turns from a leafy green to a lighter green and eventually yellow in most Apples. Pick the fruit when this is just starting to turn yellow.

- Mature **Apples** will also pull off the tree easily. Hold the fruit in the palm of your hand, twist, lift, and pull. The fruit should come off with minimal resistance. Do not pull down on the tree, as this can damage the fruiting spurs and branches.

- Start harvesting **Pears** before they turn yellow and fall to the ground. Pick them when the skin turns from a dark green to

a lighter green or yellowish green. The dots on the skin—lenticels—will turn from white to brown. Ripe fruit will easily separate from the stem when gently twisted. Use the same technique used to harvest **Apples**.

- Monitor **Peaches** and **Plums** for ripeness. Peaches are in full production, if you are lucky enough to get a crop, and Plums are just starting to ripen. Harvest when the fruits are fully colored, sweet, and juicy. Harvesting at peak maturity maximizes flavor, but minimizes storage time. Store fruit immediately after harvest. These will keep several weeks in refrigeration. So be prepared to eat, preserve, and use the bountiful harvest.

Watering

Continue watering throughout the growing season. Late season water is important for next year's harvest. Properly watered plants are more winter hardy, better able to resist pests, and produce a larger crop the following year.

Fertilizing

Fertilize **June-bearing Strawberries** in early August. Apply 1 cup of 33-0-0 (ammonium nitrate) to 100 feet of row. This will aid in flower bud development for next June's crop.

Apply 1 cup of ammonium nitrate fertilizer per 100 feet of row, or 1 teaspoon of fertilizer per plant, to **Everbearing** and **Day-neutral Strawberries** that are flowering and fruiting.

Pests

Make the last of the insecticide applications for tree fruits suffering from repeat infestations. Apply insecticide early in the month. Check the label to make sure there is sufficient time between the last application and harvest. If not, skip this application. See June "Pests" for details on insect problems.

Make cleanup an ongoing part of your gardening routine. Remove fallen leaves and fruit to reduce the source of future pest problems.

Prune disease- and insect-infested **Raspberry** canes to ground level. Look for wilting, swellings, spots, or discoloration of the stems and leaves. Remove and destroy when found. Disinfect tools between cuts.

Helpful Hints

The sweet, juicy **Cherries**, **Raspberries**, and **Strawberries** are too much for anyone, including the wildlife, to resist. *Try these tips to protect your harvest from the birds and other unwanted guests.*

- Cover trees and bushes with bird netting. Secure the netting around tree trunks, the base of bushes, or the edges of your **Strawberry** bed. This will keep them from going under the netting to reach the fruit.
- Try scare tactics, such as whirligigs, clanging pans, rubber snakes, and blow-up owls. Vary scare tactics to keep the animals fearful. Make sure your scare tactics do not annoy the neighbors.
- Check the label before purchasing and using repellents on fruit trees. Most repellents cannot be used on food crops. Hot Pepper Wax™ and Hinder® are two that are safe to use on food crops.
- Try making your own repellents. Some gardeners report good success with hanging strongly scented deodorant soaps from fruiting trees and bushes. Others have used human hair in old nylon stockings to keep animals at bay. Vary repellents to increase the chance of success.

Continue spraying for apple scab. Treat susceptible plants every ten to fourteen days during wet weather. Do not spray if the disease has not been a problem or the weather is dry. Check the label for the waiting period between the last spray and harvest. Stop spraying so that the fruit can be harvested and enjoyed.

If the weather is wet, *treat* stone fruits that have suffered from brown rot in the past. Spray as the fruit begins to color. Stop spraying in time to allow for the waiting period between the last spray and harvest.

Pruning

Remove watersprouts (the branches that grow straight up from trunk and other branches) in early August. Prune early in the month and only if the weather is dry. Avoid pruning during wet weather, which can spread fireblight disease.

Finish pruning and destroy bearing canes of **Raspberries** and **Blackberries**. Summer pruning helps open up the plants and reduces pest problems.

Planning

Keep recording information in your journal as you harvest, store, and manage your fruit gardens. Be sure to record harvest and storage information. This will help you better prepare for next season's bumper crop.

Take a minute to evaluate new plantings. How are they doing so far this season? Make needed adjustments in care and be sure you build in time to give them proper care throughout the rest of the season.

Planting

Fall is not the best time to plant fruit trees, but you may find that you cannot resist the temptation. Follow planting directions given in the chapter introduction. Mulch to insulate roots, conserve moisture, and reduce weed problems. Keep the soil around the plant roots moist, but not wet. Water thoroughly enough to wet the root zone (6 to 12 inches deep). Water again when the top 4 inches begin to dry. Do not fertilize fall planted fruit trees.

Care

Follow these guidelines for harvesting:

• Continue harvesting **Apples**, **Pears**, and **Plums**.

• Pick **Apples** when the stem end indentation turns from green to yellow. The fruit should easily twist off the branch without breaking the spur or branch.

• Harvest **Pears** before they start falling from the trees. Remove fruit when they turn from a dark green to a yellowish green. The lenticels (small pores on fruit) should turn from white to brown.

• Pick **Plums** when they are fully colored, sweet, and juicy. You will get the best flavor by harvesting ripe Plums.

• Harvest **Grapes** as they reach maturity. Use your taste buds as your guide. Pick a Grape at the tip of a bunch that looks ripe. Harvest the bunch if the Grape is sweet and tasty.

• Harvest early ripening **Fall Raspberries**. Fruit should be fully colored and sweet. See July "Care" for harvesting tips.

Move the fruit into cold storage (the basement, root cellar, or spare refrigerator) as soon as possible after harvest. The cooler the temperature (near 35 degrees Fahrenheit), the longer the fruit will last in storage. Place fruit in perforated plastic bags to help retain moisture and reduce shrinkage. Do not store **Apples** with **Carrots** and other vegetables. **Apples** give off ethylene gas which encourages ripening and shortens storage life of other fruits and vegetables.

Mulch the soil around fruit trees, fruiting shrubs, **Raspberries**, and **Blueberries** with woodchips or shredded bark. Use shredded leaves or straw for **Strawberry** beds.

Move tropical fruit plants, such as **Grapefruit** and **Lemon** trees, indoors for the winter. Isolate the plantings for several weeks to avoid bringing unwanted insects into your houseplant collection. Grow in a sunny location, and water when the top few inches of soil begin to dry.

Watering

Continue watering whenever the top 4 to 6 inches of soil begin to dry. Give tree fruits 3 to 5 gallons of water and other fruit plantings 1 inch of water each week. Adjust the amount according to the rainfall received.

Fertilizing

Do not fertilize. Late-season fertilization can lead to late-season growth that is subject to winterkill.

Pests

Continue monitoring and controlling pests as needed. Sanitation, cleanup, and disposal of fallen leaves and fruit will greatly reduce future problems.

Avoid pesticide applications during harvest. Always check the label to make sure you allow the necessary time between spray and harvest.

Prune out the fireblight-infected branches. Fireblight bacterial disease attacks **Apples**, **Pears**, and **Raspberries**. Remove infected **Raspberry** canes to ground level. Prune 9 to 12 inches below the canker (sunken discolored area) on fireblight-infected Apple and Pear branches. Disinfect tools between cuts.

Remove and destroy black knot (black knobby growths) from **Plums**, **Cherries**, and other stone fruits. Prune 9 to 12 inches below the growth. Disinfect tools between cuts.

Helpful Hints

Can I start a tree from this Peach pit? Or how about that Grapefruit seed? Starting plants from kitchen scraps is fun if you have room to experiment. If your planting space is limited, stick to buying the most pest-resistant and productive variety available. But then again, part of the gardening appeal is trying to beat the odds, break the rules, and grow something from nothing. Try these:

- Keep in mind that the seed you plant may not look exactly like the fruit it came from or the plant it grew on. Offspring of hybrids do not always come true (look and taste like their parents) from seed.
- Take your clue from nature. If you are trying to start a tropical plant, it probably does not need a cold treatment. These plants do not naturally go through a cold period in their native lands. Fruits from more temperate areas that mature in fall probably need a cold treatment (stratification) to break dormancy and sprout. Place nuts in moist sand or peat moss in plastic bags during stratification.
- Plants with hard seed coats like the **Avocado** need a little help sprouting. Nick (scarify) or soak the seeds to absorb water and sprout.
- Give seeds their needed treatments. Plant treated seeds in a moist, warm soil. Once the seeds sprout, move them to a bright, sunny window.
- Grow as you would a houseplant until it is warm enough to move outside.

Pruning

Wait until the dormant season to do major pruning. Limit early fall pruning to repair and disease control. Remove broken, damaged, or diseased branches as soon as they are found. Prune back to a point where a branch joins a branch or next to the trunk.

Always cut flush with the branch bark collar, not the trunk of the tree. The branch bark collar is the swollen area that can be found at the base of branches. Do not treat with pruning paints. These compounds trap moisture and pests in, rather than keeping them away from the tree.

Planning

Winter is quickly approaching. Review last year's journal to see what winter preparation needs to be done. Check winter and spring comments to make sure you protect susceptible plants from winter cold and animal feeding.

Planting

Give the squirrels a hand and plant a few nut trees for the future. It may be easier to start them indoors than to fight the squirrels for them later.

- Collect nuts and remove the outer hull (fleshy covering). Wear gloves when cleaning **Black Walnuts**, otherwise your hands will match your walnut stained furniture. Pack the nuts in moist sand, peat moss, vermiculite, or sawdust. Store them in a plastic bag and place in a refrigerator for three to four months.

- Plant stratified seeds in the spring. Place them directly outside in their permanent location. Be sure to protect them from curious squirrels and rodents. Or plant the seeds in a deep container filled with well-drained potting mix. This allows you to get the plants started before adding them to the landscape.

- Or plant the seeds directly outside in fall. Cover the planted seeds with wire mesh to protect them from the squirrels and other rodents. Plant the seeds 2 inches deep in their permanent location or in deep pots for transplanting at a later date. Sink the pots in the ground for added insulation over the winter.

- Do not plant **Black Walnuts** in small yards and gardens. These plants contain juglone that is toxic to many other plants. Keep these large, long-lasting trees at least 50 feet, but preferably 200 feet, away from the garden.

Care

Follow these harvesting guidelines, and refer to September "Care" for more information.

- Check **Fall Raspberries** for ripeness. Harvest berries that are fully colored and pull easily off the core. Ripe fruit will be sweet and juicy. Pick often to prevent overripe fruit from collecting on the bushes. This reduces the risk of picnic beetles moving in to share the bounty.

- Harvest **Grapes** when the fruit is sweet and juicy. Pick one Grape from the tip of a bunch that looks ripe. Harvest the bunch if the sample Grape is sweet and tasty.

- Gather **Hickory** and **Black Walnuts** as soon as they drop from the tree.

  - Remove the hulls (fleshy covering) as soon as possible. Wear gloves to prevent staining your hands in the process.

  - Spread the nuts in a thin layer in a dry, airy location. Allow them to cure for four to six weeks.

  - Now comes the fun part—cracking the hard shells to get to the nutmeat. I have heard of gardeners spreading them on driveways, covering them with boards, and driving over them with their cars. Perhaps a bit drastic and very messy!

  - You may prefer my father's method. He used to keep a supply of **Black Walnuts** in his workshop. He could be found at the end of a hard day at work, his hammer in hand and the nuts secured in his vise. We would end the winter with a good supply of Black Walnuts for baking.

  - Separate the shells from the nutmeat. Dry the nutmeat thoroughly and refrigerate in an airtight jar.

OCTOBER

Check stored fruit. Remove any rotten or shriveling fruit. One bad **Apple** really does spoil the bunch, so get rid of the bad fruit before it ruins the rest of the fruit in storage.

Watering

Keep watering fruits during dry spells in the fall. Fruits need about 1 inch of water each week. Provide whatever nature does not. Water fruits growing in clay soils once a week. Apply the needed water in two applications, four to five days apart, in sandy soils.

Water aboveground planters anytime the soil thaws and the top 4 inches begin to dry. Water thoroughly so that the excess runs out the bottom.

Fertilizing

Do not fertilize. Take a soil test now if you have not already done so. Use this as a guide to help you plan next year's fertilization program.

Protect fruit trees and berries from hungry rabbits and deer.

- Start by placing cylinders of hardware cloth around the trees. Sink this heavy wire mesh several inches below the soil surface. Make sure it extends at least 4 feet above the ground. This creates a physical barrier between the animals (voles and rabbits) and your trees. Monitor plantings for damage throughout the winter. Keep in mind that the rabbits' reach extends as the snow accumulates.
- Try applying homemade or purchased repellents. Some gardeners swear by them while others swear at them. Try a variety of products, such as Ropel®, Hot Wax Pepper®, or Tree Guard® to increase your chance of success. Use only those products labeled for food crops during the growing season.
- Hang highly scented deodorant soap or handfuls of human hair in old nylon stockings from the trees and bushes. Research shows that these can help deter animals. I find they are not as effective in urban areas where animals are used to these smells.
- Try clanging pans, whirly gigs, or other scare tactics to discourage the animals. Vary techniques to keep them leery of the area.
- Fence small areas with 5-foot-tall snow or mesh fence to reduce the risk of deer damage. Even though they can jump the short fence, they seem to avoid going into these small areas.

Pests

Clean up and remove all fallen fruit and leaves. Discard or destroy pest-infested material. This reduces the risk of future infection.

Get out the repellents and fencing. Put animal protection in place for the winter. Protect new and young fruit trees and plantings from rabbits, deer, and voles. These are some of their favorite winter snacks. See the "Helpful Hints" for details.

Pruning

Remove any diseased, broken, or damaged branches. Save major pruning for late winter. This way you can see what the animals have destroyed (or left behind), eliminate winter damage, and take care of routine pruning all at one time.

Planning

Still some work left to do. Continue evaluating the health and productivity of your new and established plantings. Note any plants that will need moving or replacing next season. Though it is always sad to lose a plant, it is an opportunity to add something new to the landscape.

Note any crops that failed to produce. Did they receive the proper care? Or maybe you gave them a little too much kindness, in the form of water and fertilizer? Make a note to correct this next season.

Make sure you have the needed pollinators in place. Many fruits, such as **Apples**, some **Plums**, and **Pears**, need two plants for pollination and fruit production.

Planting

Wait until spring to plant fruit trees, shrubs, and berries. Protect any late purchases that did not get planted.

- Find a vacant garden location in a protected site. Sink the planting containers in the soil before the ground freezes.

- Protect the area with hardware cloth to keep out the voles and rabbits. Make sure the material is buried several inches in the soil and is at least 4 feet high.

- Mulch the soil with woodchips or shredded bark once the ground freezes.

Care

Mulch **Strawberries** with a 4- to 6-inch layer of straw or marsh hay for the winter. Apply the mulch after the top $1/2$ inch of soil is frozen. This is usually after the temperatures begin hovering around 20 degrees Fahrenheit in mid- to late November. Do not use tree leaves. They mat down when wet, trapping moisture and providing poor insulation.

Move aboveground containers into winter storage. An unheated garage makes a suitable location. Or move the planter to a protected outdoor location. Place bales of straw or hay around the planters. This will reduce the risk of root damage from cold winter temperatures. Use repellents, fencing, or other animal protection to protect these plants as well.

Keep checking and using stored fruit. Discard any damaged and rotting fruit. These can cause the other fruit to decline.

Use some of the surplus fruit for drying, canning, or creating edible holiday gifts. Nothing tastes better than a gift from the garden.

Watering

Keep watering until the ground freezes. Make sure new plants receive 1 inch of water a week either from rainfall or from your garden hose. Water established plants thoroughly before the ground freezes. Proper watering will improve winter survival and next year's harvest.

Water aboveground planters anytime the soil thaws and the top 4 inches are dry. Water thoroughly so that the excess runs out the drainage holes.

Check tropical plants moved indoors for the winter. Water thoroughly so that the excess runs out the bottom. Pour off the excess water. Or better yet, place pebbles in the drainage saucer. Allow the pot to sit on the pebbles and not in the excess water. As the water evaporates, it increases the humidity around the plants.

Drain and *store* your garden hose, sprinkler, and other watering tools for winter. Make sure faucets are shut off or properly insulated for winter as needed.

Fertilizing

Do not fertilize. Store fertilizer products in a cool, dark area away from children and pets. Keep liquids away from the sunlight and in an area where they will not freeze. Keep granular fertilizers in a dry area.

Pests

Finish fall cleanup. Remove brush piles that make a good habitat for rabbits and codling moths. Remove and destroy any cankered (sunken, discolored area) stems. Disinfect tools between cuts with a solution of one part bleach to nine parts water. Complete winter protection. Place cylinders of hardware cloth around trees and shrubs. Sink the wire mesh several inches into the soil to keep out voles. Make sure it is at least 4 feet high to discourage rabbits.

Start applying repellents before the animals begin feeding. Reapply after severe weather or as directed by the product label.

Store pesticides (fungicides and insecticides) in a locked area away from heat, freezing temperatures, and sunlight. Make a quick inventory of these products. Write it in your journal or other location. This will prevent you from purchasing more product than you need next year.

Helpful Hints

Grapefruit, Lemon trees, and **Avocados** are all fun plants for the family. In the summer, it is no problem finding growing space and keeping the plants healthy. Winter is a different story. Limited space, poor light, and low humidity add to the challenge of keeping these plants alive. ***Give your tropical fruit trees the best possible winter care.***

- Grow them in the sunniest location available. Supplement the natural light with artificial lights. Use spots or other fixtures to shine the light into large plants from the side. This will help ensure that light reaches all the leaves.
- Avoid drafts of hot or cold air. The plants can tolerate cooler temperatures, but not drafty locations.
- Group with other plants or use gravel trays to increase the humidity. Place pebbles in the drainage saucer. Place the pot on the pebbles. Allow the excess water to collect in the saucer. As the water evaporates, it increases the humidity around the plants.
- Water the soil anytime the top 2 to 3 inches begin to dry. Water thoroughly so that the excess drains out the bottom and collects in the gravel tray. Wait until the top few inches are slightly dry before watering again.

Pruning

Cut **Fall-bearing Raspberries** to the ground. This method of pruning eliminates the summer crop, but will give you a larger and earlier fall crop next year. Use sharp pruning tools or a mower with a heavy duty, sharp blade. Sharp tools make your work easier and reduce the risk of injury to the plants.

Check **Summer** and **Everbearing Raspberries** for pest-infested or old bearing canes. Look for spots, discoloration, and wilting. Cut these back to ground level. Destroy or discard canes to prevent the spread of insects and disease. Disinfect your tools between cuts with a solution of one part bleach to nine parts water.

DECEMBER

Planning

Start your planting list now. Write down the plants you want to add and the spaces you have available for planting. Review your journal to see what plants need to be moved in order to open up additional space for new plants. Use this as you review catalogs and put together your plant order for next season. Consider using the layering technique to start new **Grape, Kiwi,** or other vine crops next year. See May "Vines and Groundcovers" (page 331) for more details.

Planting

Just a few more months until planting time returns.

Care

Just a few things left in storage. Keep monitoring stored fruits and remove any that have rotted. Use the harvest for holiday dinners. What a nice way to share your garden with others!

Check on aboveground planters stored outdoors or in the garage. Make sure the roots are well insulated and plants are protected from animals.

Watering

Water aboveground planters whenever the soil thaws and the ground is dry. Water thoroughly so that the excess runs out the drainage holes. Water again when the top 4 to 6 inches begin to dry. Check these planters throughout the winter.

Water indoor tropical fruit plants throughout the winter. Water whenever the top 2 to 3 inches of soil begin to dry. Water thoroughly so that the excess runs out the bottom and collects in the gravel tray.

Fertilizing

No need to fertilize. The ground is frozen outdoors and the tropical plants are just trying to adjust to their new location. Fertilizing these plants could damage the tender roots.

Pests

Take a walk through the landscape and start looking for signs of pests. Check the twigs of **Apples**, **Plums**, and other fruit trees for eastern tent caterpillar eggs. These egg masses look like a shiny glob of mud on the stem. Smash or prune out the pest. This is the most environmentally friendly way to control this pest.

Check the trunks and major branches of trees and shrubs for gypsy moth eggs. The hairy yellow masses contain hundreds of eggs. Remove and destroy these as soon as soon as they are found. Check nearby trees and shrubs whenever you discover these pests.

Pruning

Finish pruning **Fall-bearing Red Raspberries** *if this has not yet been done.* Prune all the canes to ground level. Use sharp pruners or a mower with a heavy duty, sharp blade to avoid damaging the plants. Use this method of pruning when you only want a fall crop. Removing all the stems eliminates the summer bearing canes, but results in a larger and earlier fall harvest.

Remove any storm-damaged or pest-infested stems and branches. I like to wait until late winter to do major pruning. That way you can remove winter damage, assess animal damage, and take care of routine pruning all at one time.

Herbs and Vegetables

Spice up your cooking and your garden with vegetables and herbs. Try your hand at growing the ingredients for some of your favorite recipes. It is wonderful to be able to walk out your backdoor and harvest **Tomatoes**, **Eggplants**, **Basil**, or whatever herbs and vegetables you need to make dinner. And nothing improves your recipe better than the flavor of fresh vegetables from the garden. I am not a real cook, but growing herbs and vegetables takes the chore out of cooking in the summer.

You can also use herbs and vegetables to brighten up the landscape. Select plants with colorful fruits, fragrance, and other decorative features. I use herbs more for their fragrance and foliage texture than for cooking. If you visit my garden, you may find a small patch of **Purple Ruffle Basil** mixed with classic **Zinnia**, an edge of **Parsley** mixed with **Alyssum** around my vegetable garden, or a planter of **Chard** and **Pansies** in the spring.

Planning

Start with a plan before you dig up your backyard. Everyone is eager to plant, but you may find yourself all alone weeding in July—though that can be a nice escape from life's pressures and frustrations!

Take some time to meet with the family and friends who will help plant, maintain, and use the produce. Consider their eating habits, likes, and lifestyles as you plan your herb and vegetable additions. See January "Helpful Hints" and February "Planning" for more specific information.

Make sure the vegetables are suitable for our climate and your garden location. The vegetables need to tolerate our summer weather and start producing in our short season. Check the weather maps in the Appendix to help you calculate the average number of frost-free dates in your location.

Selecting a Growing Location

Find an area that receives full sun and has moist, well-drained soil. You may need to be creative if you have a small or shady yard or one with poor soil. Carve out small areas or use containers for your garden. I like to mix my herbs and vegetables with my flowers. It is attractive and saves space.

- Grow fruiting vegetables, such as **Tomatoes**, **Broccoli**, and **Squash**, as well as most herbs in full sun. These produce best when they receive 8 to 12 hours of full sun. Plant root crops, such as **Radishes** and **Beets**, in full sun to part shade. They need at least 6 hours of sunlight to flourish. Save leafy crops, such as **Spinach** and **Lettuce**, for the shadier areas. They can get by with as little as 4 hours of sun.

- Use a traditional garden style if space is not an issue. Plant vegetables in rows running east and west. Place the tallest vegetables in the back (north side) to reduce the shade cast on other, shorter plants.

- Try some of the space-saving techniques described in March "Helpful Hints" to get the most produce from your garden. Grow **Peas** and **Beans** on trellises, **Lettuce** in blocks, or three different crops in one row. All of these techniques can be used in either large or small gardens.

- Or try container gardening if you have limited or no space for gardening. It's simple. Just select a container with drainage holes. It can be decorative or as

Herbs and Vegetables

simple as a 5-gallon bucket with holes punched in the bottom. Fill it with a commercial or homemade potting mix. Try using equal parts blended topsoil, peat, or compost and vermiculite or perlite. I like to incorporate a slow-release fertilizer in my mix, so that every time I water it releases nutrients. Plant seeds and transplants just as you would in the garden. Leave enough room for the plants to reach mature size. Water thoroughly until the excess runs out the bottom of the container. Check daily.

• Map out your garden on graph paper. Use the squares to determine plant placement and spacing. This will help you determine the number of plants needed.

To prepare the soil for planting:

1 Remove or kill the grass and any weeds from new and existing gardens. Dig out sod and reuse it to fill in bare areas in the lawn. Kill the grass using chemical or nonchemical methods. Edge the garden with a spade or edger. Use a total vegetation killer, such as Roundup® or Finale®, to kill existing grass or weeds. Read and follow all label directions before using this or any chemical. Or cover the garden with black plastic for one year to kill grass and weeds without the aid of chemicals.

2 Take a soil test to determine how much and what type of fertilizer you should use on your garden. Take representative samples, 4 to 6 inches deep, from several areas of the garden. Send it to a state certified lab or contact your local County University of Minnesota Extension Service for details. The results will tell you how much and what type of fertilizer to add. If soil test information is not available, incorporate 1 pound of a low-nitrogen quick-release fertilizer or 3 pounds of a slow-release fertilizer per 100 square feet in spring.

3 Add several inches of organic matter, such as peat moss or compost, to the top 12 inches of soil. Organic matter helps improve the drainage of heavy clay soils and the water-holding capacity of sandy soils. Incorporate organic matter in fall or spring.

Use shredded fall leaves to improve the soil. Shred fallen leaves with your mower. Dig them into the top 12 inches of soil each fall. These will decompose over the winter. Incorporate fertilizer and finish soil preparation in spring.

Consider creating raised beds in poorly drained soils. Use existing soil or bring in new soil to create the raised bed. Raised beds can be fancy or strictly utilitarian. Raising the soil improves drainage and helps warm soils faster in the spring.

Raised-Bed Garden

Typical Dimensions: 3ft. × 8ft. Rows can be situated in any direction

Herbs and Vegetables

- Measure out the garden. Make raised beds within the garden 3 to 5 feet wide with 2- to 3-foot-wide aisles in between. Rake soil from the aisles into beds to create the raised area.

- Or add 6 to 8 inches of soil over the garden area. Create raised rows or a raised garden. Mulch the elevated soil to prevent washout along the edges of the beds. Or use long-lasting timbers or stones to create sides for the raised beds.

Starting Plants Indoors

Extend your gardening season by starting plants from seed. This may be the only way to get transplants of new and unusual plants and cultivars. You might want to use some of your saved seeds. See the "Helpful Hint" on page 362 for details. It can be challenging and a lot of fun.

1 Locate an area where you can place flats of plants and artificial lights. It can be next to a window on a table or on shelves in the basement. See January "Planting" in the "Annuals" chapter for details on setting up a light system.

2 Start with sterile containers, flats, and starter mix. Disinfect used containers with a solution of one part bleach to nine parts water.

3 Keep the soil warm and moist until the seeds sprout. Move containers to a well-lit location as soon as the green breaks the surface. A southern window will work for some plants, but artificial lights will give you better results. Keep artificial lights 4 to 6 inches above the tops of the seedlings.

4 Keep the soil moist, but not waterlogged. Excess water can lead to damping off (fungal disease) and root rot. Check plants daily to make sure they do not dry out. Seedlings do not develop well and often die if exposed to overly dry conditions.

5 Check the seed packets and the "Planting Chart" at the end of the introduction for planting times. Most packets will give you information on when to start seeds indoors or when to plant them outdoors in your part of the country.

Planting

Memorial Day is traditionally the biggest planting date. The worst of the cold weather has passed (we hope!) and the soil has started to warm. Adjust your planting times to better match the weather and crops you are planting.

- Cool weather crops, such as **Broccoli** and **Cabbage**, can be planted outdoors earlier. These plants tolerate cooler air and soil temperatures. They also taste better if they can be harvested before the heat of summer.

- Wait until both the air and soil warm to plant **Eggplants**, **Peppers**, and other warm weather crops. See the "Plant Chart" for outdoor planting dates for your part of Minnesota.

Get a jump on the season by using some of the homemade or commercial season-extending devices. Gardeners have long used glass bottles, plastic, cold frames, and other devices to trap heat and protect plants from frost.

- *Start* a month or more earlier than normal by warming the soil. Prepare the garden and cover it with clear plastic for two weeks. This warms the soil and helps germinate annual weed seeds. Lightly cultivate to remove weeds without bringing new seeds to the surface. See the illustration on the following page.

Herbs and Vegetables

Soil Solarization

- *Plant* seeds and transplants in the warm soil. *Cover* with a row cover fabric, such as ReeMay®, Grass-Fast®, or Harvest-Guard. These products let air, light, and water in while trapping heat near the plants.

Extending the Season

- *Leave* the row cover in place until both the day and night temperatures are warm. Covering plants through the early weeks of June can keep them warm on those cool nights, speed up growth, and reduce the time until harvest.

Watering

Proper watering is essential in growing healthy productive plants. Excess water can lead to root rot and other fungal diseases. Drought stress causes stunted growth and low productivity.

- *Check* seedlings and new plants several times a week. Water often enough to keep the top 3 to 4 inches moist. Reduce watering after the first few weeks as the root systems expand.

- *Water* established plants when the top 4 inches begin to dry. Water enough to moisten the top 6 to 8 inches where the roots are growing. This is usually done with 1 inch of water each week. Water gardens growing in clay soil once a week. Apply half the needed water twice a week in sandy soils. Always adjust watering to fit the soil, weather, and plant needs.

- *Water* early in the morning, if possible. This reduces water lost to evaporation in the heat of the day and disease problems caused by wet foliage at night.

- *Mulch* the soil with pine needles, grass clippings (herbicide-free), straw, or other organic material. A 2- to 3-inch layer will help conserve moisture and reduce weeds. Till the mulch into the soil each fall to improve drainage in clay soils and water-holding capacity in sandy soils.

Fertilizing

Start with a soil test. Take representative samples, 4 to 6 inches deep, from several areas of the garden. Send it to a state certified lab or contact your local county University of Minnesota Extension Service for details. The results will tell you how much and what type of fertilizer to add.

Or add a yearly total of 3 pounds of low-nitrogen fertilizer per 100 square feet. This can be applied in one or several applications. Use a slow-release formulation if applying all 3 pounds in the spring. Or add 1 pound at planting and follow-up applications in June and July.

Use a fertilizer spreader to apply needed nutrients to large gardens. Try a smaller hand spreader or perforated coffee can for small areas. Or sprinkle fertilizer by hand onto small areas.

Add several inches of organic matter to the top 6 to 12 inches of soil. This can be done in the fall or spring. Spring applications of organic matter and fertilizer can be tilled into the soil at the same time.

Herbs and Vegetables

Pests

A healthy plant starts with proper care. Prepare the soil, and grow herbs and vegetables in the best possible location.

- *Select* the most pest-resistant varieties available. New introductions of more pest-resistant varieties are made each year. Check the catalogs and The University of Minnesota planting guidelines for the most up-to-date information.

- *Rotate* crops to reduce the buildup and risk of disease and insects. Move **Tomatoes** and their relatives, such as **Peppers** and **Eggplants**, to an area where you grew **Cabbage** last year. Move the Cabbage and its relatives to the area where you had **Beans** last year. Since I have very little space, I move my Tomatoes to opposite ends of the garden each year. Do the best you can.

- *Adjust* planting times to avoid pests. Planting **Beans** too early results in poor germination and more risk of seed corn maggot damage. Their feeding causes poor germination and deformed seedlings that fail to develop. Wait for the soil to warm to avoid this problem.

- *Mix things up* to reduce pest problems. Plant unrelated crops near each other. They tend to have different pest problems, reducing the buildup of insects and disease. At the least, it makes the insects work a little harder for their favorite foods.

- *Go vertical.* Trellises and teepees help increase the light and air reaching **Pole Beans**, **Squash**, and other vine crops. This improves the growing conditions and reduces the risk of mildew, anthracnose, and other diseases.

- *Mulch* the soil to keep soil-borne fungi away from the plants. It also suppresses weed growth. Weeds not only compete with plants for water and nutrients, but they also harbor insects and diseases that can infect your herbs and vegetables.

- Keep water off the leaves. *Water* early in the morning so that leaves dry quickly. Or apply water directly to the soil, minimizing wet foliage. Use a watering wand to extend your reach and get the water to the soil. Or try a soaker hose or drip irrigation to make the job easier.

- Continual cleanup reduces insect and disease problems. Remove weeds and debris that can harbor pests. Clean the garden each fall to prevent disease spores and insects from over-wintering in the garden.

Once pests occur, you will need to decide on a course of action. First have the pest properly identified. Contact your local garden center or extension office for help. They can tell you whether control is needed. *Here are some ways to manage common pests:*

- Remove small infestations of insects or infected leaves. This is often enough to limit damage and still have a productive harvest.

- Use yellow pans filled with soapy water or sticky traps to trap aphids, white flies, and other common insect pests.

- Cover plantings with netting or row covers to keep out unwanted insects.

- Consider using some of the more environmentally friendly products on the market. Soaps, neem oil, *Bacillus thuringiensis*, and others control specific pests, while reducing the risk to beneficial insects, wildlife, and people.

- Use a pesticide as your last resort. Read and follow label directions carefully before applying any chemical—remember, you plan to eat part of the plant you are treating. Leave sufficient time between the last application and harvest.

Minnesota Vegetables

Vegetable	Planting Time Indoors/Outdoors*	Spacing Between Plants/Between Rows	Days to Harvest
Asparagus	+/April 15	18/36	1–2 years
Beans, Lima	+/May 25	3/24	70–80
Beans, Pole	+/May 10	3/30	60–65
Beans, Snap	+/May 10	3/18	50–60
Beets	+/April 15	3/15	50–60
Broccoli	March 15/May 1 (plants)	18/24	60–70
Brussels Sprouts	+/May 15 (seeds)	12/24	90–100
Cabbage, Chinese	+/June 20 (seeds)	10/24	90–100
Cabbage, Early	March 15/May 1 (plants)	12/18	60–70
Cabbage, Late	+/May 15 (seeds)	18/24	90–100
Carrot	+/April 15	2/15	60–70
Cauliflower	March 15/May 1 (plants)	12/24	50–60
Celery	March 15/May 20 (plants)	6/30	100–110
Chard	+/April 15	4/15	40–50
Collards	+/June 20 (seeds)	12/24	60–85
Corn, Sweet	+/May 10	8/30	65–90
Cucumber	+/May 20 (seeds)	6/36	50–60
Eggplant	March 15/June 1 (plants)	18/30	70–80
Kale	+/June 25	8/24	50–70
Kohlrabi	+/April 15	4/15	50–60
Lettuce, Head	March 15/May 1 (plants)	8/15	60–70
Lettuce, Leaf	+/April 15	3/15	40–50
Muskmelon	May1/May 20 (plants or seeds)	24/36	80–90
Okra	+/May10	12/36	60
Onion	February 15/May 1 (plants)	4/15	110–120
Onion, Sets	+/April 15	1/15	40–50
Parsnip	+/April 15	3/24	100–120
Pea	+/April 15	2/15	60–70
Pepper	April 1/June 1 (plants)	18/30	60–70
Potato, Early	+/April 15	12/30	80–100
Potato, Late	+/April15	12/36	130–140
Pumpkin, Pie	May 1/May 10 (seeds) 20 (plants)	24/48	90–110
Radish	+/April 15	2/15	25–30
Rhubarb	+/April 15	36/48	1 year
Spinach	+/April 15	2/15	40–50
Squash, Summer	+/May 20	24/48	50–60
Squash, Winter	May 1/May 20 (plants)	24/72	90–120
Tomato	April 15/May 20 (plants)	24/36	65–80
Turnip	+/April 15	3/18	60–70
Watermelon	+/May 20	96/96	65–90

*Plant one week later in southern and central Minnesota and areas along Lake Superior. Plant about two weeks later in northern Minnesota.
+Plant directly outdoors.
Adapted from the University of Wisconsin Extension Publication A1653, *Vegetable Cultivars and Planting Guide for Wisconsin Gardens*.

Minnesota Herbs

Common Name	Hardiness	Exposure	Height	Space	Comments
Basil	Annual	Full sun	20–24 inches	12 inches	Mulch to keep roots moist.
Chives	Zones 3–4	Full sun	12 inches	12 inches	All parts are edible.
Dill	Annual	Full sun to part shade	3 feet	12 inches	Reseeds readily.
Fennel	Annual	Full sun	2–3 feet	12 inches	Bronze variety makes nice addition to flower garden.
Lavender	Zone 4	Full sun	24 inches	18 inches	Needs good drainage for winter survival.
Marjoram, Sweet	Annual	Full sun	18 inches	12 inches	Preferred marjoram for cooking. Substitute for oregano.
Mints	Zones 3–4	Full sun	2 feet	2+ feet	Aggressive plant that must be contained.
Parsley	Annual	Full sun	6 inches	6–8 inches	Makes a nice edging in flower and vegetable gardens.
Sage	Zone 4	Full sun	18 inches	12 inches	Attractive foliage makes it a nice addition to containers and flower gardens.
Tarragon, French	Zone 3–4	Full sun	24 inches	12 inches	Reseeds readily.
Thyme	Zone 4	Full sun	4–8 inches	6–12 inches	Needs good drainage for winter survival. Wait until leaves sprout to prune back.

Planning

It's time to plan this year's vegetable garden. Gather the family and review last year's harvest. Make a list of all the vegetables you want to grow again. Adjust the number of rows and plants to include. Reduce the number of those vegetables that were more productive than you needed or not very popular with family and friends. See February "Planning" for help on designing the garden.

Take a look through all those catalogs that accumulated during the holidays. Find a few new and fun things to try in this year's garden. Get the whole family involved. (Those who help plan the garden are more likely to help weed it!) See "Helpful Hints" for ideas on designing kid-friendly gardens.

Planting

Gather and organize seed starting equipment and supplies. Find an area where you can place flats near a window or under artificial lights.

Consider using a shelving system to maximize growing space. Mount fluorescent lights on the underside of each shelf. Place planted flats on the shelves beneath the lights. Raise and lower the lights so they are 4 to 6 inches above the tops of the seedlings.

See January "Planting" in the "Annuals" chapter for more details on lighting systems. Select the method that best fits your space and gardening style. Or try combining these and other ideas to create a system of your own.

Care

Harvest herbs from your windowsill herb garden as needed for cooking. You may need to add some extra light during these short, dark days of January. Add artificial light to improve growth and productivity.

Harvest **Carrots** and **Parsnips** that have been stored in the garden for winter. Dig carefully to avoid damaging these root crops. Enjoy their sweet flavor.

Check on stored vegetables. Continue using them to bring back memories of last summer. Discard any that are shriveled or rotten.

Watering

Keep the soil slightly moist in windowsill gardens. Water thoroughly, allowing the excess to drain out the bottom of the pot. Check twice a week and water whenever the top 2 inches of soil start to dry.

Fertilizing

Watch indoor herbs for signs of nutrient deficiencies. Pale leaves and poor growth may be a result of poor light as well as a lack of nutrients. Try improving the light before fertilizing the plants. Go light on the fertilizer for better flavor.

Pests

Monitor herbs and other indoor plants for aphids and mites. These insects suck out plant juices, causing them to yellow and brown. You may see a clear, sticky substance on the leaves. Spray infested plants with insecticidal soap. You may need to apply severaly applications one week apart for adequate control. This is safe for the herbs and all who eat them.

Watch for fungus gnats and whiteflies. These insects can be seen flitting around the plants. Try catching them with yellow sticky traps. Buy them at a garden center or make your own by coating pieces of yellow paper with Tanglefoot® or another sticky substance. Place them near the plants.

Preparing Whitefly Trap

Make sure cats and other pets are not enjoying more of the harvest than you are. Keep tempting plants out of reach of these animals. *Consider planting a pot of* **Ryegrass** *to give cats their own herbal fix.*

1 Fill a 6-inch pot with a well-drained potting mix. Sprinkle **Ryegrass** seeds on the soil surface. Lightly rake the surface to ensure good seed-to-soil contact.

2 Water thoroughly until the excess runs out the bottom of the pot. Cover with plastic, or water often enough to keep the soil surface moist.

3 Move to a warm, sunny window. The grass should sprout in one to two weeks. Water less frequently once the grass begins

Helpful Hints

Plan some kid-friendly features in this season's garden. It is a great way to get your children, grandchildren, or neighborhood kids to share your passion. Make gardening fun for everyone involved.

*   Start with a fun planning activity. Get out some paper, scissors, old catalogs, and glue. Have each family member cut out pictures of the vegetables they want to grow and eat.
*   Create a teepee made of stakes and **Pole Beans**. Use them to shade **Lettuce** planted in the center. Or better yet, make it a hiding place in the garden.
*   Include a **Sunflower** maze to add mystery in the garden. Plant **Sunflowers** in narrow rows and patterns to create a mazelike walkway through the garden. Use the maze to direct children from planting to planting or from one side of the garden to the other.

Plant Staking in Teepee-Shape

*   Try designing and planting theme gardens. The pizza garden is a favorite. Include all the fresh ingredients you will need to make your own pizza—except for the cheese and pepperoni, of course! You may want to plant the garden in the shape of a pizza for additional fun.
*   Or give your children a little gardening space of their own. Let them plan, plant, and harvest their own garden. We did this for our daughter when she was about seven years old. She chose the seeds and plants for her own garden plot. Then she asked for a 10-foot-high fence—to keep her parents, not the rabbits, out!

to grow. Water until the excess runs out the drainage hole. Water again when the top few inches begin to dry.

Be sure to check with your vet first!

Pruning

Cut back leggy herbs to a set of healthy leaves. This will encourage branching and more growth for harvest. Dry or use these pieces for cooking.

Planning

Start finalizing your garden plan.

- **List** the vegetables your family likes to eat. Be sure to include the ingredients for your favorite recipes. Star the ones that taste best grown in the garden or that are more expensive to buy. Also consider the work involved compared to the price. I love to grow **Beans**, but when life is busy I would rather pay the growers at the farmer's market to do all the picking. They are inexpensive and just as tasty, and it only takes a few minutes to fill my bag. But I always find time for growing **Tomatoes**.

- **Consider** the space each plant needs. One **Tomato** plant produces lots of fruit, but one **Corn** plant produces one, maybe two ears. Plus, you will need at least a 4-by-4 block for pollination and fruit production. But nothing beats the taste of freshly harvested Corn prepared immediately.

- **Evaluate** how much of the various vegetables your family will eat. I like the look and flavor of **Okra**, but my family does not. This means one plant takes care of all our needs. See the "Planting Chart" for help in what vegetables to plant and how much space each plant needs.

- Make a list of herbs you use for cooking, crafts, and gifts. Flavored vinegars and oils are easy to make and great to give as gifts. Consider using bunches of dried herbs for decorations, deodorizers, or potpourri.

- **Decide** how many vegetables and herbs you need for fresh use and preserving. Most vegetables can be canned or frozen for later use. Consider purchasing a food dryer to dry vegetables and herbs. Or let nature, the oven, and microwave dry herbs for later cooking and crafts. See Herbs and Vegetables "Helpful Hints" on page 359.

- Always **add** a few fun vegetables for the children in your family and neighborhood. Try growing **Popcorn**, **Pumpkins**, and **Watermelons** to get the kids interested in gardening. Do not forget to grow **Radishes**, **Bibb Lettuce**, and other short-season vegetables that will give quick results. See January "Helpful Hints" for more ideas.

- Try something new and different. Check out the garden catalogs to find a new **Tomato**, more heat-tolerant **Lettuce**, or hot **Pepper**. Look for new colors, shapes, and sizes to add interest and fun to the garden.

- Make sure the vegetables are suited to our climate and your garden location. The vegetables need to thrive in our weather and be able to reach maturity and produce within our short season. **Check** the weather maps in the Appendix to help you calculate the average number of frost-free dates in your location.

- **Visit** your local garden center to see if they have the seeds you need for starting indoors. Order any unusual or hard-to-find seeds from a reliable company. Select one with a good reputation with family, friends, and fellow gardeners.

- **Write** your plan on paper. Use it to record cultivars grown, successes, and failures. Consider it the start of next year's plan.

Planting

Break out the garden journal, or warm up the computer, and start recording planting information. List when and what you plant this spring. Keep it handy so you can continue to add to it throughout the season. Include successes and failures to help with future projects.

Start **Onions** indoors from seeds. Plant them the middle of the month in the western part of the state. Wait a week if you live along Lake Superior; wait two weeks if you are in the northern part of Minnesota.

Care

Continue harvesting indoor herbs. Try freezing excess harvest in ice cubes for later use.

Finish using stored vegetables. Harvest **Carrots** and **Parsnips** stored in the garden for winter. Try digging them during a winter thaw. Share the wonderful sweet flavor with family and friends.

Clean and inventory tools. Use a wire brush to remove excess soil. Follow this with steel wool to remove any rust that formed on metal surfaces. Sharpen the soil cutting edge of trowels and shovels with a triangular file. Rub in a couple of drops of oil to prevent further rusting.

Watering

Check seeded flats every day. Keep the soil surface moist by covering the flat with plastic or misting the soil daily.

Water windowsill herb gardens thoroughly so that the excess water

runs out the bottom of the container. Wait until the top few inches start to dry before watering again.

Fertilizing

Monitor indoor herbs for nutrient deficiencies. Fertilize plants that are pale, stunted, or showing other signs of nutrient deficiencies. Make sure it is a lack of nutrients, not light, causing these symptoms. Use a dilute solution of any houseplant fertilizer. Avoid excess fertilization that can ruin the flavor.

Let **Onions** start growing before fertilizing the soil. Fertilizer can harm the sprouting seedlings.

Pests

Control insects that are damaging herbs and other indoor plants.

- Continue monitoring for aphids, mites, and whiteflies. These insects suck out plant juices, causing them to yellow and brown. See January "Pests" for control information.

- Use yellow sticky traps for fungus gnats. These are annoying insects that look like miniature fruit flies and flit around the

house. They feed on organic matter but do not harm the plants.

Avoid damping-off disease of seedlings by using sterile planting mix and clean containers. Keep the soil moist, but not too wet. Remove infected plants as soon as they are found. Diseased plants suddenly topple and collapse. Use a fungicide labeled to control damping off on seedlings.

Pruning

Prune back overgrown and leggy herbs. Use clippings for seasoning or dry and freeze them for later use.

Helpful Hints

Share the joy of gardening with those less fortunate. Plant an extra **Tomato**, row of **Beans**, and more for the hungry in your neighborhood. Your surplus produce can provide hungry seniors and children in your community with nutritious food. Plus, it is a great excuse to expand the garden and buy a few more vegetables.

Planning

Finish your garden plan. Check February "Planning" and January "Helpful Hints" for suggestions.

Take a look at your plan and the garden. Plan and locate needed expansions. Decide what type of soil preparation is needed. *Locate sources for topsoil, compost, and other amendments you might need. Calculate the amount needed before you go shopping.*

1 A cubic yard of soil covers over 300 square feet at a 1-inch depth.

2 Multiply the length of the garden by the width. This gives you the square footage of your garden. Write this on your plan; it will be useful now and in the future.

3 Next, multiply the depth of the material (in feet) you want to incorporate. Convert inches into feet by dividing the number of inches you want to add by 12. Label this number as cubic feet needed.

4 Convert cubic feet to cubic yards by dividing the volume in cubic feet by 27 (that is the number of cubic feet in a cubic yard). This is the amount of material you will need to order.

For example: Let's say your garden is 10 by 15 feet. You want to add a 2-inch layer of organic matter to the garden. Your equations would be:

10 feet × 15 feet =
   150 square feet
2 inches ÷ 12 = 0.17 feet
150 × 0.17 = 25.5 cubic feet
25.5 cubic feet ÷ 27 cubic feet per cubic yard = 0.9, or about 1 cubic yard

5 Lost in the math? See the "Ordering Chart for Soils and Mulch" in the Appendix.

Repair, locate, or replace cold frames, row covers, and other season-extending materials if you plan an early start to the season.

Planting

Get busy adding to your indoor garden. Fill clean flats or small containers with sterile starting mix. Plant seedlings in rows in flats or place one or two seeds in each container. Check the seed package for planting recommendations. Most seeds like to be planted twice as deep as they are thick.

Plant the following in March.

March 1: **Parsley** and **Celeriac**
March 15: **Broccoli, Early Cabbage, Cauliflower, Celery, Eggplant,** and **Lettuce**

Adjust these planting times to fit your part of Minnesota. Wait a week if you are by the lake; wait two weeks if you are in the northern part of the state.

Care

Keep the soil warm and moist when germinating seeds. Keep the seedlings in a bright window or better yet, under artificial lights. Adjust lights as the seedlings grow so they are always 4 to 6 inches above the top of the plants.

Start cleaning up and preparing your garden for planting. Take advantage of any snow-free days to remove debris, take a soil test, and get started. The soil can be worked any time it is not frozen and is only slightly moist. Check soil moisture by taking a handful of soil and gently squeezing it into a ball. Tap the ball with your finger. If it breaks apart, it is ready to work. Otherwise, wait a few days for the soil to dry. Working wet soil results in clods that last all season. See "Soil Preparation" in the chapter introduction for more details.

Watering

Cover seed trays with plastic or mist the soil to keep it moist during the germination process. Remove the plastic once the seeds sprout. Water flats and containers thoroughly. Pour off any excess that collects beneath the container. Check seedlings every day.

Fertilizing

Use a dilute solution of any complete (10-10-10 or 12-12-12) fertilizer on established seedlings. See the chapter introduction for additional information.

Pests

Get a jump on the growing season and this year's weeds. Prepare the garden for planting as soon as the soil thaws and can be worked. Cover the garden with clear plastic. Wait two to three weeks for the soil to warm and the weed seeds to sprout. Remove the plastic and lightly cultivate. Avoid deep hoeing that can bring new weed seeds to the surface. You will have both removed many weeds and warmed the soil for early planting.

Helpful Hints

Do not panic if your garden plans are bigger than the available planting space. *Try these space-saving techniques:*

- Grow plants in blocks or wide rows instead of single rows. Blocks can be several feet wide. Make sure you can easily reach all the plants for maintenance and harvest. Space plants just far enough apart to allow for the mature plant size. Make the aisles wide enough for you to work the surrounding rows.
- Make the most of all available space. Try growing **Pole Beans**, **Cucumbers**, and other vine crops on fences, trellises, and other vertical structures. Growing vertical not only saves space, it can help reduce disease and make harvesting easier.

Vertically Staking Plants with Wires

- Consider planting short-season crops, such as **Radishes** and **Beets**, between long-season crops of **Tomatoes**, **Peppers**, and **Broccoli**. The short-season plants will be ready for harvest just about the time the long-season plants need the extra space. Interplant **Lettuce** for added shade from heat and sun that can give the lettuce a bitter flavor.
- Grow several crops throughout the season in the same row. Start with cool weather-tolerant crops, such as **Radishes** or **Leaf Lettuce**. Harvest the first plant and replace it with a second planting. Try growing an unrelated crop (to reduce the risk of disease), such as **Beans** or **Cucumbers**. Plant a third crop if time allows.

Pruning

Trim **Onions** that are getting long and leggy. Continue to harvest and trim back your windowsill herbs.

Planning

Gather and order all the needed materials. Create a tentative schedule for site preparation and planting. Allow time to kill or remove existing weeds and grass, work in needed amendments and fertilizer, and get started with early plantings.

Be flexible. The best-laid plans can be set back by our unpredictable spring weather.

Locate an area to harden off transplants. A vented cold frame, shaded area near shelter, or under the tree will work. Make sure it is convenient and in plain view so that it will not be forgotten.

Planting

Make room under the lights for more seedlings. Follow these dates if you live in southern Minnesota away from the lake. Wait a week if you are near Lake Superior; wait two weeks if you garden in northern Minnesota.

April 1: Plant **Pepper** seeds indoors. Sprout in a warm location to speed up germination.

April 15: Seed **Tomatoes** indoors. Starting earlier results in long, leggy plants that suffer more transplant shock.

Transplant seedlings from flats to single-plant containers. Move the seedlings after they have two sets of leaves. Fill small, clean containers with sterile, well-drained potting mix. Punch a hole, large enough to accommodate the seedling's roots, in the soil. Place the seedling in the hole and gently tamp the soil to ensure good root-to-soil contact. Water thoroughly until the excess runs out the drainage holes.

April 15th is the start of outdoor planting for some gardeners. Once the soil is prepared, you can start planting some cool-season vegetables and dormant perennial herbs and vegetable plants outdoors. *Beginning in mid-April, start planting the following:*

- Plant **Asparagus** roots 12 inches apart in trenches 36 inches apart. Dig the trenches 6 to 8 inches deep and 9 to 12 inches wide. Set the Asparagus in the trench, spreading the roots away from the crown of the plant. Cover with 2 inches of soil. Gradually add soil throughout the season until the trench is filled. Wait several years to harvest.

- Dig and divide existing **Rhubarb** plants, or plant roots with the crown buds 2 inches below the soil surface. Space the plants 3 feet apart. Grow in full sun to light shade in well-drained soils. Wait one year to make your first (light) harvest.

- Plant seeds of cool-season crops from mid- to late April for central and southern Minnesota and mid-May in northern Minnesota. These include **Beets, Carrots, Chard, Kohlrabi, Leaf Lettuce, Mustard Greens, Onion Sets, Parsnips, Peas, Potatoes, Radishes, Rocquette, Salsify, Spinach,** and **Turnips.** Remember that weather controls the seasons, not the calendar. Planting dates can vary as much as two to three weeks from year to year. Contact your local Extension Office for more information. Dig a shallow trench using a hoe handle. Sprinkle seeds in the bottom of the trench. Cover with soil and water thoroughly. Water lightly until the top 2 to 3 inches of soil is moist. See the "Planting Chart" in the introduction for spacing.

Get an early start on the rest of your crops by using some of the new and old season-extending techniques. Gardeners have long used cloches, hotcaps, and cold frames to lengthen the growing season. New fabrics are making it even easier and less time consuming. See "Planting" in the chapter introduction for more ideas.

APRIL

Care

Prepare the garden for planting. Work the soil as soon as the ground thaws and the soil is ready to work. Add needed fertilizer and amendments. See "Selecting a Growing Location" in the chapter introduction for details.

Begin hardening off transplants two weeks before planting them outdoors.

Begin harvesting three-year and older **Asparagus** when spears are 6 to 8 inches long. Snap or cut the spears off below the soil surface. Harvest three-year-old plantings for just one month. Four-year and older planting can be harvested for six to eight weeks through May or June.

Harvest established **Rhubarb** for six to eight weeks. See May "Care" for details.

Watering

Keep the soil moist for seedlings growing indoors and out. Water thoroughly enough to moisten all the soil in the container or the top 2 to 3 inches outdoors.

Check new plantings of **Asparagus** and **Rhubarb** several times a week. Wet the top 4 to 6 inches (the root zone) of soil. Water whenever this area begins to dry.

Fertilizing

Apply fertilizer during the soil preparation just prior to planting. Make one application of a slow-release, low-nitrogen fertilizer in spring for season-long benefits. Additional applications can be made as needed for individual crops.

Use a dilute solution of water-soluble fertilizer at transplanting. Follow label directions for dilution rates for starter solutions

Spread well-rotted manure around **Rhubarb** in the spring before growth begins. Or wait until after harvest (June) to apply fertilizer.

Fertilize young **Asparagus** plantings (one to three years old) with the rest of the garden. Add 1 pound of a low-nitrogen fertilizer per 100 square feet of garden. Wait until after the final harvest to fertilize four-year and older plantings.

Pests

Protect new plantings from birds and animals. Spread bird netting or season-extending fabric over the garden. Anchor the sides securely. This will keep birds out and may discourage other animals.

Install a fence around the garden to keep rabbits out. Use chicken wire or hardware cloth (finer mesh and heavier wire) to make a fence. Sink the bottom several inches into the soil. Make the fence at least 4 feet high to keep out rabbits. Bury at least 12, preferably 18, inches of the fence beneath the ground to discourage woodchucks.

Try repellent, such as Hinder and Hot Pepper Wax™, that are labeled for use in food gardens. Or try placing handfuls of hair in old nylon stockings or slivers of deodorant soap throughout the garden. The smell may help discourage animals.

Helpful Hints

Prepare transplants (harden off) for the drastic change in growing conditions they will undergo when moving outdoors into the garden. The intense sunlight, cooler nights, and drier conditions can stunt and even kill tender indoor-grown and greenhouse plants.

Pruning

Examine **Lavender**, **Sage**, and **Thyme** for winter damage. Look for healthy buds (firm and plump) and pliable branches. Wait for new growth to begin. Remove dead tips and trim as needed. Always leave some healthy buds for new growth.

Planning

So you've made a plan, included intensive planting techniques, and still have extra plants or plans and no space. Consider planting containers filled with herbs and vegetables. It is a great way to maximize planting space and extend the growing season. See "Selecting a Growing Location" in the chapter introduction for details on planting and caring for container gardens.

Planting

Adjust indoor and outdoor planting dates based on your location. Add a week if you live near the lake; two weeks if you live in the northern part of the state.

Beginning May 1:

- Transplant seedlings from flats into small containers filled with a sterile potting mix. Follow planting guidelines in the April "Planting" section.

- Check seedlings planted directly in small containers. Remove all but one seedling per container. Cut off, at ground level, the smaller and weaker seedlings.

- Continue moving transplants outdoors. Harden off transplants prior to moving them

outdoors. Start the process two weeks prior to moving transplants into the outdoor garden.

Beginning in early May:

- Plant **Parsley**, **Head Lettuce**, **Cauliflower**, **Early Cabbage**, **Broccoli**, **Brussels Sprouts**, **Collard**, **Kale**, and **Onion** plants in the garden. Use a trowel to dig a small hole large enough for the roots. Loosen roots of potbound transplants. Place the roots in the hole and backfill with soil. Gently tamp to remove the air pockets and to ensure good soil-to-root contact. Water thoroughly until the top 4 to 6 inches are moist.

Beginning in mid-May:

- Plant seeds of **Brussels Sprouts**, **Snap Beans**, **Late Cabbage**, and **Sweet Corn**.

- Plant **Muskmelons**, **Pumpkins**, and **Winter Squash** indoors. Use peat pots to reduce transplant shock. Fill the peat pots with sterile planting mix. Plant two seeds per pot at a depth twice the diameter of the seed. Cover with soil and water. Moisten the soil until the pot is wet.

Beginning in late May to early June:

- Place transplants of **Muskmelons**, **Pumpkins**, **Winter Squash**, **Celeriac**, **Celery**,

Tomatoes, and herbs in the garden. Remove the upper lip and bottom of peat pots before planting. You may want to slice through the side to encourage quick rooting.

- Sow seeds of **Lima Beans**, **Cucumber**, **Melons**, and **Summer Squash**. Select short-season varieties of **Squash** and **Melons** that will reach maturity and be ready for harvest before the first fall frost.

- Gardeners in northern Minnesota (Zones 2-3) should wait to transplant any warm season plants (**Melons**, **Tomatoes**, etc.) outdoors until June 5th when all danger of frost has passed.

Care

Harden off transplants before moving them from indoors or a greenhouse to the outdoors. Allow two weeks to complete this process. See Bulbs May "Helpful Hints" on page 60 for a detailed step-by-step description of this process.

Harvest **Asparagus** when the spears are 6 to 8 inches long. Break or cut them just below the soil surface. Do not harvest new plantings. Harvest three-year-old plantings for only four weeks. Harvest four-year and older plantings for six to eight weeks.

Do not harvest new plantings of **Rhubarb**. Harvest two-year-old plants for one or two weeks. Keep harvesting older, established plantings for eight to ten weeks. Pull or cut the leafstalks from the plants when they are 12 to 15 inches high. Remove the leaf (it is toxic), and just use the stem.

Remove all flower stalks as soon as they appear on **Rhubarb** plants. Cut them back to the base of the plant. These typically appear in unseasonably hot weather, in overcrowded plantings, on old plants, or in infertile soil. Correct the cause to reduce the problem in the future.

Watering

Continue checking seedlings every day. Keep the soil surface moist while germinating seeds both indoors and out. Once the seedlings sprout, water thoroughly to encourage deep rooting. Keep the soil around the roots of recent transplants slightly moist. Water enough to moisten the top 4 inches of soil. This encourages deep rooting. Water again as the top 1 to 2 inches begin to dry. Reduce watering frequency as the root system develops in several weeks.

Check containers daily. Water anytime the top 2 to 3 inches begin to dry. Apply enough water so that the excess runs out the bottom.

Fertilizing

See April "Fertilizing."

Pests

Some common insect pests and possible solutions include:

- Avoid seed corn maggot damage on **Corn** and **Beans** by waiting until the soil warms for planting. Quick-germinating seeds are less susceptible to this damage. Seed corn maggots feed on germinating seeds, preventing germination or causing deformed seedlings that never develop.

- Cover **Broccoli**, **Cabbage**, **Turnips**, and **Radishes** with one of the season-extending fabrics. They create a barrier, preventing harmful insects including cabbage worms from reaching the plants.

- Rotate **Onions** with other unrelated crops to prevent problems with onion maggots. The immature stage of this insect feeds inside the Onion bulb.

- A thorough spring cleanup will reduce problems with the asparagus beetle. These orange and black beetles feed on emerging spears. Handpick and destroy or use an insecticide labeled for use on beetles in **Asparagus**.

- Handpicking is also the best control for the Colorado potato beetle. Many of the insecticides do not provide adequate control. Watch for yellow and black striped beetles or the red humped larvae feeding on the leaves.

- Place white sticky traps in the garden if flea beetles have been a problem in the past. Otherwise handpick and allow healthy transplants to outgrow the damage.

- The yellow and green striped or spotted cucumber beetles can be found on vine crops in spring or late summer. Remove and destroy these insects as soon as they appear. The cucumber beetles not only feed on leaves and fruit, but also transmit a deadly bacterial disease to the plant.

See April "Pests" for ideas on preventing bird and animal damage.

Pruning

Prune off damaged, dried, or discolored leaves at planting.

JUNE

Planning

Locate an area for your compost pile. It can be in either sun (dries out quickly) or shade (decomposes slower), but should be in a well-drained location. Place the pile in the middle of a large garden, along-side the garage, or tucked away in the corner of your landscape.

Planting

Finish planting your garden. I often wait until early June when the soil warms to plant **Tomatoes**, **Peppers**, **Eggplants**, **Melons**, and **Squash**. They suffer less transplant shock and grow much faster when planted in the warmer soil.

Plant annual and perennial herbs. Most prefer full sun and well-drained soils. Follow the same steps used for vegetables.

Sow seeds of **Chinese Cabbage**, **Endive**, **Kale**, **Rutabaga**, and **Collards** at the end of the month. These seeds will sprout quickly, and the plants will be ready for a fall harvest. Their flavor is usually much better when they mature and can be harvested in the cooler temperatures of fall.

Care

Thin rows of seeded vegetables. Reduce seedlings to recommended spacing. I know it is tough to do, but it will pay off with larger, more productive plants. Recycle the seedlings in the compost pile. Or try adding some of the edible ones, such as **Radishes** and **Beets**, to salads and sandwiches.

You can begin to harvest some plants, using the following guidelines:

- Harvest **Green Onions** when the greens are 6 inches tall. Use them fresh or for cooking when the flavor gets too strong. Leave some Onions to grow and develop for dry bulbs.

- Pick and use the outer leaves of **Leaf Lettuce** as soon as they reach 4 to 6 inches. Continue to harvest to encourage new tender and flavorful growth.

- Harvest **Spinach** plants as the outer leaves reach 6 to 8 inches in length. Remove larger plants until all the Spinach is harvested.

- Stop picking **Rhubarb** after eight to ten weeks of harvesting. Allow the leaves to grow and produce energy to build a strong plant for next season's harvest. Eating summer **Rhubarb** is not harmful to you (it is not poisonous), but it can weaken the plant and reduce future harvests.

Remove any flower stalks as soon as they appear.

- Allow the leaves (green fluffy growth) to develop on the **Asparagus** plants when you are finished harvesting. They help replenish energy supplies and keep the plant productive for seasons to come.

Mulch herb and vegetable gardens in mid- to late June when the soil has warmed. Use shredded leaves, cocoa bean shells, pine needles, straw, or herbicide-free grass clippings. A 2-inch layer will help conserve moisture, reduce weeds, and moderate soil temperature. Mulching cold soil can stunt the growth of **Tomatoes**, **Melons**, and other warm-season crops.

Stake or *cage* **Tomatoes** at or just after planting. See July's "Helpful Hints."

Watering

Water less frequently as your plants become established. Apply enough water to moisten the top 6 inches of soil. Allow the top 2 to 3 inches to begin to dry before watering again.

Check container gardens daily. Water thoroughly until the excess water runs out the bottom of the pot.

Fertilizing

Give transplants a starter solution of fertilizer at transplanting. This gives the plants a boost. Read and follow all label directions for mixing rates and application recommendations.

Fertilize **Rhubarb** and **Asparagus** plantings after the last harvest. Follow soil test recommendations. If these are not available, apply 2 to 3 pounds of a low-nitrogen fertilizer per 100 square feet.

Pests

Pull weeds as soon as they appear. Pull them the morning after a gentle rain or other time when the soil is moist. The weeds will be much easier to remove. Or use a hoe or cultivator between rows. Be careful not to damage the roots or weed out any vegetable plants. Apply a mulch to reduce future weed sprouting.

Common insect pests and solutions include:

- Continue monitoring and protecting plants from corn seed, cabbage, and onion maggots. Delay plantings, cover seedlings, and rotate crops to prevent problems. See May "Pests" for more specifics.

- Continue picking and destroying asparagus beetle, flea beetle, cucumber beetle, and Colorado potato beetle (both the adult and larvae). Remove them as soon as they are found to reduce damage.

- Cover **Broccoli**, **Cauliflower**, **Cabbage**, and **Brussels Sprouts** to prevent cabbage worms from reaching and feeding on the plants. These insects eat holes in the leaves and add a little unwanted protein (wormlike larvae) to the dinner table. Use cheesecloth or a lightweight row cover to form the barrier.

- Or treat susceptible plants with *Bacillus thuringiensis*, sold as Dipel® or Thuricide®, to control cabbage worms. This bacteria kills only the larvae of true caterpillars and is safe for people, other insects, and wildlife.

- Set out shallow, covered containers of beer or boards between rows to capture slugs. The slugs will crawl into the beer and drown. Or they will hide under the board in the morning so you can remove and destroy the unwanted pests. I know a gardener who feeds them to her water-garden fish.

- Watch for squash vine borer. This orange and black day-flying moth lays its eggs at the base of vine crops. Remove and smash any that are found. Check for sawdust and holes at the base of the plant. This means the borers have entered the stem and are causing damage. Slice the stem lengthwise and kill any borers you find. Bury this portion of the stem, keep the soil moist, and hope it develops new roots. Reduce damage with three weekly applications of an insecticide to the base of the plant when the adults can be seen and are laying eggs.

- See August "Pests" tips on controlling leafhoppers, aphids, and other pests.

Pruning

Remove suckers (side shoots) that form between the leaf and stem on staked **Tomatoes**. This gives you an earlier, but smaller harvest. Snap the small shoots off by hand when they are 1 to 2 inches long.

Planning

Take some time to update your journal and evaluate the garden. Include the names of all the herb and vegetable varieties you are growing so that you will be sure to repeat this year's success and avoid repeating failures.

Planting

The garden season is well under way, but there is still plenty of time to plant. Add seeds and transplants to the garden. Use vacant spots and harvested rows for these late additions by growing in containers. See Appendix (page 358) for planting dates.

Care

Mulch the garden with straw, evergreen needles, shredded leaves, or herbicide-free grass clippings. Spread a 2- to 3-inch layer over the soil surface. Mulching helps keep roots cool and moist, while reducing weeds and improving the soil.

Blanch Celery and Cauliflower to keep the stems and flowers white and flavor less bitter. Cover stems of Celery with soil or cardboard to block out the sunlight and keep the

stems white. Many Cauliflower cultivars are self-blanching. The leaves naturally fold over the flower bud, blocking the light. You need to lend a hand for the other types. Start blanching when the flower bud (the part you will eat) is about 2 inches in diameter. Tie the outer leaves over the center of the plant. Check often; it will be ready in seven to twelve days when the head is 6 to 8 inches in diameter.

Follow these harvesting guidelines:

- Harvest **Spinach** when the outer leaves are 6 to 8 inches long. Remove the whole plant as days get longer and hotter and the plants get larger. Plan a late planting for fall harvest.

- Continuing picking **Leaf Lettuce** as the outer leaves reach 4 to 6 inches. Replant for a fall harvest.

- Pick **Summer Squash**, such as **Zucchini**, when the fruits are 6 to 8 inches long, or 3 to 6 inches in diameter for the round scalloped types. Keep picking to keep the plants producing.

- Dig or pull **Beets** and **Radishes** when the root is full size. Proper thinning and well-drained soil are important for proper root development. No roots? Use the greens to spice up your salads.

- Check **Broccoli** every few days once the flower buds (the part

we eat) form. They quickly go from quarter size to harvest size. Harvest when the head is full size, but before the yellow flowers appear. It is still edible, just not as tasty. Cut the stem 6 to 7 inches below the flower. Leave side shoots that will develop into smaller heads for later harvest.

- Pick herbs as needed. Cut short pieces off the ends of the stem. Make the cut just above a set of leaves. It looks neater, and the plant recovers faster. Wait until the plants start blooming for the most intense flavor. Preserve this flavorful harvest for later use. See Herbs and Vegetables "Helpful Hints" on page 359.

Watering

Provide 1 inch of water each week. Adjust the amount of water based upon rainfall and temperatures. You will need to water more often in extremely hot weather and less frequently in cooler temperatures.

Fertilizing

Fertilize leafy vegetables, **Sweet Corn**, and root crops when they are half their mature size. Apply fertilizer to **Tomatoes**, **Peppers**, **Cucumbers**, **Beans**, and vine crops when they have started producing fruit.

Sidedressing
Fertilizing

Sprinkle small amounts of fertilizer in a band on the soil about 6 inches from the plant. Use about 2 cups of a low-nitrogen fertilizer or $1/4$ to $1/3$ cup of ammonium nitrate or ammonium sulfate for every 100 feet of row.

Pests

Continue pulling weeds as soon as they appear. Remove by hand or lightly cultivate the area between the plants. Be careful not to injure the shallow roots or accidentally "weed out" your vegetable plants.

Insects and disease continue to be a problem. Monitor the garden for the following pests: cabbage worms, root maggots, Colorado potato beetles, squash vine borers,

picnic beetles, slugs, aphids, leafhoppers, and plantbugs. See June and August "Pests" for more specific information.

Check the lower leaves on **Tomato** plants and vine crops for discoloration, yellowing, and spotting. See August "Pests" for specifics on disease control.

Do not be discouraged if the bottoms of your first few **Tomatoes** are black. Blossom end rot commonly affects the first few fruit. See August "Pests" for details.

Pruning

Cut back leggy annual herbs. Use hand pruners or sharp garden scissors to cut the stems back to just above a set of leaves. Use the cuttings for cooking, wreaths, or the compost pile.

Annual
Pinching Back

Planning

Plan a harvest party and share your fresh produce with friends and relatives. Have everyone bring their favorite recipe for **Zucchini** or other vegetables that tend to overproduce.

Visit the farmer's market. This is a great source of fresh vegetables and a good place to try some new vegetables you may want to grow in your own garden next season.

Planting

Keep planting seeds of short-season crops that can be harvested before the first killing frost. Calculate the number of days left before the first killing frost and compare it to the needed growing dates for the crop. See the "Late Planting Chart" on page 358 in the Appendix.

Care

Check late plantings for overcrowding. Remove excess plants (thin) so the remaining seedlings have enough space to reach mature size. Use the thinned **Turnip**, **Beet**, and **Radish** seedlings to spice up your salads.

Protect ripening **Melons** and the fruit of other vine crops from rot. Slide a downturned plastic lid under the fruit or mulch the soil under the fruit. This keeps the fruit dry and reduces the risk of rot.

Follow these harvesting guidelines:

- Harvest **Potatoes** as the tops die and tubers reach full size. Dig carefully to avoid damage. Gently remove excess soil and store surplus Potatoes in a cool, dark location.

- Dig **Onions** when the tops fall over and begin to dry. Use those started from sets first; they do not store as well as those started from seeds or plants. Cure the bulbs you plan to store. Braid the tops and hang them to air dry. Or spread them on a screen in a dry location. Give them one to two weeks to dry before storing in a cool, dry location.

- Pick **Peppers** when the fruits are firm and fully colored. Separate the hot and mild Peppers during harvest and storage to avoid surprises.

- Harvest **Tomatoes** when they are fully colored. Leave ripe Tomatoes on the vine for an extra five to eight days to enhance their flavor.

- Remove **Summer Squash** when the fruits are 6 to 10 inches long or 3 to 6 inches in diameter. Use the tender Summer Squash fresh, steamed, or fried. Wait to harvest **Winter Squash**. Pick them when the rind is firm, glossy, and the portion touching the soil has changed from cream to orange.

- Harvest **Cucumbers** based on their use. Pick for sweet pickles when they are $1^1/2$ to $2^1/2$ inches long. Allow those for dill pickles to reach 3 to 4 inches in length, and pick slicing Cucumbers when they are firm, bright green, and 6 to 9 inches long. Harvest **Burpless Cucumbers** when they are 10 to 12 inches long.

- Harvest herbs for fresh use and drying. See Herbs and Vegetables "Helpful Hints" on page 359 for drying herbs.

Watering

Make sure plants receive sufficient moisture throughout the growing and harvest season. See "Watering" in the chapter introduction for details.

Fertilizing

Fertilize container gardens that did not have a slow-release fertilizer incorporated into the soil at planting. Use a dilute solution of any flowering fertilizer (higher in phosphorus). Follow label directions for application rates and timing.

Pests

Continue pulling weeds before they flower and set seed. Remove weeds now to reduce weeding chores next season.

Insects:

- Continue removing and destroying cucumber beetles, Colorado potato beetles, and cabbage worms as soon as they are found. See June "Pests" for more control options.

- Monitor and control squash vine borer. Remove and destroy infested vines this fall. Cleanup will help reduce next season's population. See June "Pests" for tips on managing animals, slugs, and this pest.

- Keep picnic beetles out of the garden with timely harvest. These ¼-inch, black-with-four-yellow-dots beetles do not harm the fruits, but they are attracted to overripe or damaged fruits. Attract them out of the garden with a mixture made of 1 cup water, 1 cup dark corn syrup, one cake of yeast, and a spoonful of vinegar. Place the mixture in a container outside the garden. Use it to attract the beetles away from the garden, trap, and drown them.

- Watch for signs of aphids, leafhoppers, and tarnished plantbugs. These insects suck out plant juices, causing the leaves to yellow and bronze. Severe damage can stunt plant growth. Use several applications (five to seven days apart) of insecticidal soap to treat these pests.

Diseases:

- Check the lower leaves of **Tomatoes** for yellowing and brown spots. Septoria leaf spot and early blight are common causes of these symptoms. Remove and destroy infected leaves as soon as they are found. Fall cleanup, proper spacing, staking, and full sun will reduce the risk of these diseases, as will sterilizing tomato cages from year to year. Regular applications of a fungicide, labeled for use on vegetables, can be used to prevent the spread of this disease. Read and follow label directions carefully.

- Be patient when dealing with blossom end rot. The blackened ends of fruit are caused by a calcium deficiency. Do not add calcium; our soils have plenty. Instead, avoid root damage caused by late staking and cultivating. Mulch the soil to keep it consistently moist, and wait. Once the soil moisture is consistent, the plants will adjust and the remaining fruits will be fine. Cut off the black portion and use the remaining red **Tomato** for sandwiches and salads.

- Watch for mildew (white or gray film on the leaves) and leaf spots on vine crops. Try growing them on trellises or fences to increase light and air flow and to reduce disease problems. Remove infected leaves as soon as they appear. You can use a fungicide labeled for use on vine crops to prevent further spread of these diseases. Read and follow label directions carefully and allow the required waiting time between the last spray and harvest.

Pruning

Continue removing unwanted suckers on staked **Tomato** plants. Check the plants every five to seven days and remove the side shoots (suckers) that form between the stem and leaf. This reduces the amount of fruit and increases the risk of cracking, but it speeds ripening and increases fruit size.

SEPTEMBER

Planning

Plan to extend the season using cold frames, hotcaps, and season-extending fabrics. A little frost protection on those first frosty nights can extend the harvest through the warm weeks that always follow.

Or let nature end the season with the first killing frost. Use this as an excuse to end a troublesome growing season full of insects, disease, and weeds. Then you can start planning for next year's garden.

Planting

Add short-season and frost-tolerant plants to the garden. You can still plant **Lettuce**, **Greens**, **Spinach**, and **Onion Sets**. Try growing them in containers that can be moved in and out according to the weather. Or have some frost protection handy for covering plants on frosty nights to extend the harvest season.

Dig and *pot* **Parsley** and **Chives** to bring indoors and grow for winter. Or start new plants from seed for even better success.

Take cuttings of **Marjoram**, **Mints**, **Oregano**, **Rosemary**, **Sage**, and **Winter Savory** for your indoor winter herb garden. Take 3- to 4-inch cuttings from healthy plants. Stick the cut end in moist vermiculite or perlite. Keep the vermiculite moist and the plant in a bright, not sunny, location. Plant the rooted cutting in a small container of moist, sterile potting mix. Grow them in a sunny window and enjoy the fresh herbs.

Plant **Garlic** in the first half of this month. Fall planting is risky but can—not always—reward you with a larger and tastier harvest next season. Plant the cloves in an upright position, 3 to 5 inches apart and 1 inch deep. Protect the young plants with winter mulch. With some luck, they will survive winter and start growing again in early spring. Replace failed plantings in early spring.

Care

Store leftover seed in an airtight jar in the refrigerator. The controlled environment will help keep the seeds viable for next season.

Follow these harvesting guidelines:

- Harvest **Eggplants** when the fruits are 6 to 8 inches long and glossy. Use a knife or pruning shears to cut the fruits off the plant. This will prevent damage to the plant.

- Pick **Muskmelons** when the fruit stem starts to separate from the fruit. Wait for the crack to appear all around the stem for a fully ripe, great tasting melon.

- Harvest **Watermelons** when the fruits are full sized, dull colored, and the portion touching the ground changes from white to cream. Check the tendrils nearest the fruit for confirmation. These will curl and dry when the fruit is ripe.

- Pick **Pumpkins** when they are full size, the rind is firm and glossy, and the area touching the soil changes from cream to orange.

- Continue harvesting **Tomatoes**, **Pepper**, and **Squash**. See August "Care" for tips.

- Make one fall harvest of **Rhubarb** before the first killing frost. The stalks are safe to eat and the plant has had ample time to replenish its energy supply. Cut the rest of the stalks back after a hard freeze.

- Keep cutting, using, and preserving herbs. Harvest most leafy herbs just prior to blooming when they have the greatest oil content and strongest flavor. **Sage**, **Rosemary**, **Thyme**, and other strongly scented herbs can be harvested almost anytime. For maximum flavor and fragrance, pick herbs in the morning after the dew has dried.

Prepare for the first fall frost. Move tender potted plants indoors. (See October.) Cover plants with sheets or season-extending fabrics whenever frost is predicted. Cover plants in late afternoon or early evening. Remove sheets in the morning when the temperatures warm. Season-extending fabrics can stay on plants throughout the fall. They let air, light, and water through, while trapping heat near the plants.

Watering

Continue watering the garden as needed. See the chapter introduction for more information.

Check container gardens every day and water whenever the top 2 to 3 inches of soil are dry. Water thoroughly so that the excess runs out the drainage hole.

Fertilizing

No need to fertilize the garden. Enjoy the benefits of your soil preparation efforts in the spring.

Helpful Hints

Do your **Cucumbers, Zucchini,** and other vine crops have lots of flowers, but no fruit? Be patient. The first set of flowers is all male. The next flush is a mix of male and female flowers so pollination, fertilization, and fruit formation can occur.

Male Squash Blossom

Female Squash Blossom

Keep fertilizing container gardens that did not have a slow-release fertilizer incorporated at planting or showing signs of nutrient deficiency. Use a complete (equal parts of nitrogen, phosphorus, and potassium) or flowering plant fertilizer to encourage both fruiting and leaf growth.

Pests

Keep pulling weeds and removing insects and diseased leaves as soon as they are discovered. See June, July, and August "Pests" for ideas on managing insects and disease.

Remove and destroy all pest-infested plant debris in fall. A thorough cleanup is your best defense against insects and disease. Do not compost pest-infested material unless you have an active compost pile that reaches 160 degrees. That leaves most of us out. Contact your local municipalities for disposal options.

Pruning

Prune out the stem tips on **Tomato, Squash,** and **Melon** plants early this month. This will allow the plant to expend its energy on ripening the existing fruits instead of producing more fruits that will not have time to mature.

Cut back **Rhubarb** foliage once it is killed by frost.

Leave ferny **Asparagus** leaves and stems standing for the winter. The standing stems help capture snow that will insulate the roots for winter.

Planning

Sit down now, before you forget what a wonderful and challenging garden season you have had. Record all your successes and failures—I actually learn the most from the failures—in both the herb and vegetable gardens. Record and note the varieties you want to plant again next year as well as those to avoid in the future.

Planting

Finish planting **Garlic** cloves. See September 'Planting' for details.

Start a windowsill garden for fresh seasonings all winter long. Try **Thyme**, **Parsley**, and **Sage** in small individual pots or planted together in a larger container.

Finish planting perennial herbs early in the month so that the plants have a chance to root before winter arrives. Try growing **Mint** as a container sunk in the soil. Leave the top inch or two of the pot exposed. The sunken pot will help slow the spread of this aggressive plant.

Plant annual **Rye**, **Oats**, or **Buckwheat** as a green manure crop. These plants will provide a green ground cover for the winter garden. Dig or till these plants into the top 6 inches of soil next spring. They add nutrients and help improve the soil. Check your favorite garden catalog, local farm supply store, or garden center for seed.

Care

Move **Rosemary**, **Sweet Bay**, and other tender herbs indoors. Place them in a bright, sunny window or under artificial lights for the winter. Keep the soil moist, but not too wet.

Cover tender plants in late afternoon whenever there is a danger of frost. See September "Care" for details.

Follow these harvesting guidelines: Pick mature **Green Tomatoes** when the blossom end is greenish white, or showing color before the plants are killed by frost. Ripen these Tomatoes indoors for an added enjoyment. Store unripe Tomatoes in a 60- to 65-degree Fahrenheit location. Spread them out on heavy paper so that the fruits do not touch. Or wrap each one in newspaper if they have to touch in storage. They will ripen over the next few weeks. Speed up the process by moving a few Tomatoes to a bright, warm location a few days prior to use. My dad always had the Ping-Pong table covered with unripe Tomatoes through- out the fall. You can also use **Green Tomatoes** to make relish or fried green tomatoes.

Check your favorite cookbook, community garden coordinator, or University of Minnesota Extension Service for ideas.

Dig **Radishes**, **Beets**, and **Turnips** when they reach full size. Leave some **Carrots**, **Turnips**, and **Parsnips** in the garden for winter storage. Mulch the plantings after the soil is a little crunchy with frost. Harvest them throughout the winter for a little fun and fresh-from-the-garden flavor.

Harvest **Pumpkins** when the fruits are full size, the rind is firm, and the spot touching the ground turns from cream to orange. Clean Pumpkins to help extend their longevity. Dip harvested Pumpkins in a solution of 4 teaspoons of bleach per 1 gallon of water. Allow the Pumpkin to dry and cure at room temperature for one week. Move it to a cool location. With some luck, it should last at least two months.

Leave **Asparagus** stems and leaves intact. These help catch the snow, which provides an excellent winter mulch for the roots.

Make one last harvest if your **Rhubarb** plant is still around. One fall harvest just prior to a killing frost will not harm the health and vigor of the plant. The stems are safe to eat and tasty this time of the season. Plus your family and friends are not tired of yet another Rhubarb dish. Cut the plants back and remove debris after a hard frost. See August and September "Care" for harvesting tips.

Check stored vegetables throughout the fall and early winter. Discard any damaged or rotting fruit. One bad **Apple**, **Onion**, or **Squash** really does spoil the bunch. See this month's "Helpful Hints" for storage tips.

Watering

Make sure perennial herbs and vegetables are well watered before the ground freezes. Keep the roots of young seedlings for indoor gardens moist. Check daily and water whenever the top 1 inch of soil starts to dry. Reduce watering frequency once the seedlings root. Water windowsill gardens thoroughly until the water runs out the bottom. Pour off excess water. Wait for the top 1 or 2 inches of soil to dry before watering again. Check small pots and young plants every few days. Larger containers may go a week or more between waterings.

Fertilizing

Take a soil test to find out what your garden needs. See the chapter introduction for details.

Helpful Hints

The days of root cellars in every home are long gone. Most of us have warm basements that make storing produce difficult. Find a cool corner or invest in an extra refrigerator to extend your eating enjoyment. *Try these storage tips:*

- Increase nonrefrigerated storage space by insulating a basement room with two outside walls. I have met gardeners who created a "storage cooler" in the basement using this technique.
- Or store **Carrots** and other root crops in the garden for winter harvest. Harvest any root crops you want to use. Mulch the remaining plants after the ground is crunchy with frost. Cover with straw or evergreen branches. Harvest root crops throughout the winter. You may need to adjust use based on weather and your ability to dig through the snow to get to the garden.
- Store **Beans, Cucumbers, Eggplants, Okra, Sweet Peppers,** and firm, ripe **Tomatoes** at about 45 degrees Fahrenheit in a humid environment. Keep **Winter Squash, Sweet Potatoes,** and mature **Green Tomatoes** in a 55-degree Fahrenheit, humid location.

Pests

Monitor seedlings for damping off. This fungal disease causes seedlings to collapse and die. See February 'Pests' for details.

Harvest time is fun for the wildlife as well as your family. Monitor plantings, secure fencing, and use scare tactics to keep animals from taking more than their fair share of the harvest. Whirly gigs, plastic owls, and noisemakers may provide some relief. Vary tactics to keep the animals guessing. Commercial and homemade repellents may also provide relief. Make sure that whatever you use is safe for people. Hinder® and Hot Pepper Wax™ are labeled for use in food gardens. Avoid rotten eggs and other homemade remedies that could cause a health risk to your family.

Pruning

Cut back and remove vines and stalks from the garden to reduce the risk of reinfesting next year's garden.

Planning

The growing season is not over. You still have a few things to harvest and much more to do to prepare for winter. Make a list of all the end-of-the-season chores. Prioritize those that must be done before the snow flies and others that can wait if you run out of time. *What follows is a list of some end-of-season chores to get you started:*

- *Collect*, *clean*, and *store* tools. Check the yard, porch, and other areas your tools tend to collect. Clean them if you have time, and store them a dry place for winter. Try to clean and sharpen tools prior to storage; otherwise, add this to your late winter list of chores.

- *Store* pesticides in a cool, dark, dry location. Liquids must not freeze or be exposed to sunlight. Keep granules dry. Secure all products from children and pets.

- *Empty* pots and flats you plan to reuse next spring. Wash with a solution of one part bleach to nine parts water before reusing them. Share excess pots with school groups, master gardeners, and community gardeners who can put them to good use growing their own plants.

- *Start* a compost pile. You do not need anything fancy. Remember, the compost bin is just a structure meant to contain and hide your pile from view. It should allow easy access and be large enough to hold your materials. Buy or build your own compost bin. All you need are discarded pallets, chicken wire, lattice, or just some space to pile green garbage and let it rot. See "Composting" in the book introduction for more details on building and using a compost bin.

- *Look* for plans for a cold frame. This is a great winter project that can help you get an earlier start and a later finish to the growing season. Most cold frames are 3 feet by 6 feet or made to fit the window sash or other material used as a cover. The back of the cold frame should be 18 to 30 inches high and taller than the front at 12 to 24 inches. The slanted side should face south or toward the sunniest exposure available.

Planting

Consider planting an indoor herb and vegetable garden. Leafy crops like **Lettuce** and **Spinach**, root crops like **Radishes**, as well as herbs mentioned in September "Planting" will survive most indoor growing conditionsl.

Care

Continue frost protection for cool-season crops that you are trying to save. I know quite a few gardeners who serve a fresh-from-the-garden salad of **Leaf Lettuce** and **Radishes** at Thanksgiving. They use cold frames; homemade, plastic, greenhouse-type structures; and season-extending fabrics to make this happen.

Harvest **Lettuce** when the outer leaves are 4 to 6 inches long. Dig **Radishes**, **Carrots**, and **Turnips** when the roots are full size. Make one last, crispy, fresh salad for family and friends to enjoy.

Mulch **Carrots**, **Parsnips**, and other root crops left in the garden for winter storage. Cover the lightly frozen (crunchy) soil with straw or evergreen branches. This insulates the soil, protecting the vegetables and making it easier to harvest in winter.

Mulch fall planted **Garlic** for winter protection. Cover young plants with straw or evergreen branches after the ground lightly freezes.

Finish cleanup and start preparing the garden for next spring. Shred fallen leaves with your mower or leaf shredder. Dig a 3- to 4-inch layer of shredded leaves into the top 6 to 12 inches of soil. These will decompose over the winter, improving the drainage of heavy clay soils and the water-holding capacity of sandy soils.

Watering

Water perennial herbs, **Rhubarb**, and **Asparagus** thoroughly before the ground freezes. Apply enough water to moisten the top 6 to 8 inches of soil.

Water plants in cold frames, under plastic, or under other season-extending devices whenever the top 4 to 6 inches of soil are dry.

Drain and store the water hose for the winter. Pick a warm day to make the job easier and less damaging to the hose.

Check young seedlings daily and indoor gardens several times each week.

Fertilizing

Do not fertilize the garden now. Concentrate on improving the soil with the addition of shredded leaves, well-rotted manure, and other organic matter. Spade several inches of these materials into the top 6 to 12 inches of soil. Add the fertilizer in spring prior to planting.

Helpful Hints

Did your **Tomatoes** wilt, **Beans** die, and garden perform badly? *Check surrounding yards and your own for Black Walnut trees.* The roots, leaves, and nuts of these trees contain juglone. This substance is toxic to many plants, including vegetables. The roots can travel hundreds of feet beyond the tree, killing any susceptible plants in their way.

- Avoid planting Black Walnut trees in small landscapes where you are trying to grow other trees, flowers, and vegetable gardens.
- Plant vegetable gardens at least 50 feet, preferably further, from these trees.
- Grow vegetables in containers or create a raised-bed garden. Cover the ground and inside of the raised-bed walls with weed barrier fabric. Fill with 8 to 12 inches of soil. This will help keep the tree roots out of the raised bed garden.
- Do not use Black Walnut leaves to amend soil. Compost them until they are unidentifiable. Once decomposed, they will not be harmful to susceptible plants.
- Consider removing the Black Walnut tree for long-term, not short-term, benefits. It takes five to ten years for the roots and debris to decompose and become nontoxic to susceptible plants.

Use a complete fertilizer, low in nitrogen (10-10-10 or 12-12-12), for seedlings and windowsill gardens. Follow label directions for rates and times of applications.

Pruning

Trim herbs as needed for cooking. Allow young plants to establish themselves before harvesting large amounts.

Pests

Clean up the garden if you have not already. Remove debris that harbors insects and diseases for next season.

DECEMBER

Planning

Grab a cup of tea, coffee, or eggnog. Then find your garden journal, pen, and garden plan. Now sit down and take a few minutes to review the season. Make sure your garden records are up to date. Record the varieties grown, the source, and success rates. Revise your garden plan to reflect what you really did, not just what you planned.

Planting

There is still time to start a windowsill garden. It is a great distraction for the whole family. Use leftover seeds or scour the garden centers for their leftover inventory. See page 362 for seed longevity. Leafy crops, such as **Lettuce**, do well in the low light indoors. Mix in **Radishes** and miniature **Carrots** for some zing. **Onions**, **Parsley**, **Basil**, **Chives**, and other herbs are always good suggestions for indoor gardens.

1 *Locate* small pots for individual plants or large containers for mixed plantings. Use clean containers with drainage holes. Fill with sterile soil.

2 *Plant* seeds or rooted cuttings. Water thoroughly so that the excess water drains out the bottom. Pour off any excess water.

3 *Place* the garden in a sunny, south-facing window. Or place it under artificial lights for the best results. Keep lights 4 to 6 inches above the tops of the plant.

Consider making several gardens with various plant combinations. They make great holiday gifts for both cooks and gardeners.

Care

Thin out seedlings in your newly planted windowsill garden and continue harvesting herbs as needed for seasoning.

Watering

Check indoor plantings several times a week. Keep the soil moist for seedlings. Allow the top 1 or 2 inches of soil to dry before watering small pots. Wait for the top 3 inches of soil to dry before watering larger containers.

Water thoroughly until the excess runs out the bottom of the pot. Water often enough to meet the plants' needs.

Fertilizing

Herbs and indoor vegetables need very little fertilizer. Use a diluted solution of any complete fertilizer (10-10-10) for over-wintering herbs and windowsill gardens. Read and follow the label directions.

Pests

Watch for fungus gnats, whiteflies, aphids, and mites. These insects are commonly found on indoor plants, including herbs and windowsill gardens. See January "Pests" for descriptions of the insects, their damage, and control options.

Pruning

Remove any damaged or diseased leaves as soon as they are found.

Houseplants

Indoor gardens are the perfect way to make gardening a year-round avocation. When the rest of your garden is buried under snow, you can catch a little green relief from your houseplants.

Do not worry if you have been unsuccessful in the past. Most good gardeners have killed their share of houseplants along the way to developing green thumbs. The key to success is finding the right plant for your growing conditions and gardening style.

Planning

Start by *evaluating* the growing conditions in your home. Look at the available light, temperature, and humidity. Select plants that can tolerate the existing conditions. You will need to adapt your watering schedule to the plant's needs. This will vary somewhat with each plant and each growing location.

Helping plants adapt to the growing conditions relates to your gardening style. If you like to water, groom, and generally fuss over your plants you can select **Orchids**, **Ferns**, and other houseplants that need a little extra care. If you prefer the benign neglect plan, you need to select plants such as **Cacti**, **Cast-iron Plant**, and **Snake Plant** that thrive with limited care.

The plant must also fit in the space available. Some houseplants become trees, while others crawl their way across the room. Select plants that fit your indoor dècor and available space.

Now *buy a healthy plant.* Investing a little extra money up front can save you a lot of frustration as well as money spent on replacement plants. Purchase plants that are acclimatized and are free of pests and signs of neglect.

Most houseplants are raised outdoors in southern, more tropical areas. They need to be acclimated to the lower light of indoor growing conditions. Quality plant growers have done this for you. Check with the florist or garden center where you purchase your plants.

Avoid plants that show signs of insects or disease. Plants should have lots of leaves with good color and should be free from spots, blotches, and insects. You do not need to pay for added challenges. Gardening indoors offers challenges enough on its own. *Avoid plants with:*

- Sticky leaves from honeydew secreted by mites, aphids, whitefly, or scale.

- Fine webs in the leaf joints from spider mites.

- Small, hard-shelled bumps (scale insects) on stems and leaves.

- Soft spots on leaves and stems from rot.

- Yellow leaves and brown tips from pest damage or poor care.

The Growing Environment

Light is usually the key factor in raising healthy plants. Unfortunately light is not always plentiful indoors. Select plants that will thrive in the available light, or consider growing some plants under artificial lights. Here are some general categories for light requirements. You will have to monitor and experiment with the plants and lighting in your home to make a good match.

- *High-light plants* must be in or next to a south-, east-, or west-facing window. Make sure there are no trees, buildings, awnings, or other structures diffusing the light.

- *Medium-light plants* need bright (less direct) light all day. Place them within 3 feet of an unobstructed south-, east-, or west-facing window. Move plants closer to the window if the light is somewhat obstructed.

- *Low-light plants* need to be within 6 feet of a well-lit (south-, east-, or west-facing) window or next to a north-facing window. Seldom do houseplants suffer from too much light.

Temperature can also be difficult to control. Matching the needs of plants and people can be challenging. Most houseplants survive in normal household temperatures—they just do not like the low humidity that goes with them. Cooler temperatures increase humidity and help slow down plant growth to match the lower light conditions. Keep houseplants in cool, bright locations during the winter. Avoid drafts of hot or cold air.

Humidity, like light, is a difficult environmental factor to change. *You can help increase the humidity near your plants with one of these techniques.*

- Group plants together. As one plant loses moisture from the leaves and soil, the nearby plants will benefit.

- Place pans of water on radiators. The added moisture is also good for the people in the house.

- Place plants on saucers filled with pebbles and water. The pot sits on the pebbles above the water. As the water evaporates, it increases the humidity around the plant.

- Create a terrarium for your plants. Buy one—yes they are back in style—or create your own. Use an old aquarium or other large glass container. Cover for high humidity lovers, but leave open for most plants.

Soil

Soil provides support and a reservoir of nutrients and water for your plants. Select a sterile, well-drained potting mix. Soil-less mixes are the most common potting mix on the market. They contain a mixture of peat moss, vermiculite, and perlite. These mixes are lightweight and well drained. They are perfect for gardeners who tend to overwater. Once these mixes dry, however, they are difficult to rewet. Your plant will be sitting in a block of hard, dry peat. Place it in a tray of water and let it gradually absorb the moisture.

Many gardeners concoct their own potting mix. Start with $1/3$ sterile soil, $1/3$ peat moss, and $1/3$ vermiculite or perlite. Adjust the proportions to your gardening style. Once you find a blend you like, mix extra. Store the soil in sealed 5-gallon buckets for later use.

Houseplants

Watering

Always water plants thoroughly and allow the excess to drain out the bottom. Keep pebbles in the plant saucers so that the plants sit above, not in, the excess water. Growing conditions, the container, and the plant will influence how often you need to water.

Plants growing in bright light, high temperatures, and low humidity will need to be watered more frequently than those in low light and cool temperatures. Plants in glazed ceramic or plastic containers dry out more slowly than those in porous clay pots. The bigger the container, the slower it will dry out.

The potting mix will also influence watering. Soil-less mixes need to stay slightly moist. Their built-in drainage makes it difficult to over-water. Potting mixes containing soil are less forgiving. Waterlogged soils can mean death to your plants.

Water plants when:

- The top few inches of the soil-less mix are slightly moist. Wait to water until the top few inches of the soil-based mix are slightly dry. Use your finger to monitor soil moisture; it is the best moisture meter on the market.

- The container is lightweight due to the decrease in moisture.

- The leaves turn a bluish-green.

Fertilizing

Consider growing conditions, plant needs, and your growing goals when fertilizing plants. Houseplants in difficult conditions grow slowly and need little fertilizer. Increasing the fertilizer without improving the growing conditions can harm the plant. Most fertilization should be done in spring and summer when the growing conditions are better and the plants are actively growing.

Do not fertilize new plants for at least four months. Give them time to adjust to the new, usually less than ideal, growing conditions.

Plants growing in soil-less mixes need to be fertilized regularly. These mixes do not hold the nutrients like mineral soils. Some mixes come with slow-release fertilizers added, or you can add them yourself at planting time. Slow-release fertilizers provide needed nutrients for several months or the whole fertilizing season. Check label directions.

Some gardeners prefer to have a little more control. Use a dilute solution of houseplant fertilizer once or twice a month. The more often you fertilize, the bigger and faster your plants will grow. Reduce fertilizing frequency to control plant growth.

Repotting

Do not be anxious to repot your houseplants. Most plants can spend months and even years in the same container. Plants like **African Violets**, **Hoyas**, **Spider Plants**, and **Clivia** actually flower better when they are slightly potbound. Let the plant tell you when it needs to be moved.

Repot houseplants when:

- The roots fill the container. Carefully slide the plant out of the pot. If you see nothing but roots, it is time to transplant.

- Water runs right through the soil and out the drainage holes. This can also occur when soil-less mixes dry out.

Houseplants

- The new growth is stunted. Undersized growth and pale leaves can be caused by a lack of nutrients or lack of soil to hold those nutrients.

Move plants to a slightly larger (1 to 2 inches larger in diameter) container with drainage holes. Avoid over-potting. Many gardeners like to transplant once and be done. Unfortunately this is not best for the plant. Over-potting can cause a decline in growth and waterlogged soils that lead to root rot and death of the plant.

Transplant in early spring when the light is increasing, days are lengthening, and plants are beginning to grow.

1 *Select* a clean container with drainage holes. Use a pot that is no more than 1 to 2 inches larger in diameter than the original container.

2 *Use* a sterile potting mix. Select or mix one that best suits your gardening style. Do not put gravel or clay pot chips in the bottom. These actually decrease drainage and lead to waterlogged soils. Cover the drainage hole with a coffee filter if you are concerned about soil spilling out the bottom.

3 *Massage* the sides of the pot to loosen the roots. Tip the pot over and slide the plant out of the container. Do not pull on the stem as this can damage the roots.

Removing Plant from Pot

4 *Free up* potbound roots. You can lightly massage the rootball of slightly potbound plants; otherwise, use a knife to make shallow cuts on opposite sides and the bottom of the rootball. This frees up the roots, allowing them to grow into the new soil.

5 *Cover* the bottom of the pot with fresh soil. Place the plant in the new container. *Adjust* the height by adding or removing soil from the bottom layer. The ultimate soil surface should be 1 inch below the lip of the container.

Replanting

6 *Fill in* around the sides with fresh soil. Gently firm the soil in place with your fingers or by tapping the pot on the tabletop.

7 *Water* thoroughly to settle the soil and remove air pockets. Do not fertilize for at least one month.

8 *Adjust* the watering schedule to accommodate the change in potting mix, larger size container, and additional soil.

Care

Clean and groom your houseplants regularly. It improves the plants' health and appearance.

- Wipe dust off smooth leaves with a damp sponge or cloth. Use a soft cosmetic brush to dust **African Violets** and other hairy-leafed plants.

- Check under the leaves and along the stem for any unwelcome insects. It is much easier to control a few aphids than the large colony that can quickly develop.

Houseplants

- Remove any dying, damaged, or diseased leaves. These will be pale green, yellow, brown, or full of holes. The plant will look better, and you will reduce the risk of further problems.

- Move the plants for even exposure to the sun. Turn the pot so that all sides eventually face the window.

- Exchange plants in poor light conditions with those growing in more suitable conditions. A monthly switch can keep both plants growing despite the less than desirable conditions.

Pruning

Houseplants, like any other plants, benefit from pruning. Save the majority of pruning for late winter or early spring before new growth begins. Remove broken, dead, or damaged stems as soon as they are found. Fall pruning should be reserved for plants that outgrew their home during summer vacation outdoors.

To prune houseplants:

- *Remove* damaged, diseased, or dead branches.

- *Remove* crossing and rubbing branches. This prevents injury and opens up the center of the plant for better light penetration.

- *Pinch out* growing tips or cut back the stems of leggy plants to encourage branching and fuller growth.

- *Cut back* stems just above a healthy bud or leaf, where one branch joins another or where the branch joins the main stem.

- Play it safe and *remove* no more than $1/3$ of the total growth.

- Severely overgrown plants can be air-layered. This technique is used to start new plants and rejuvenate old overgrown specimens. See Houseplants "Helpful Hints" on page 360 for details.

Pests

A healthy plant is your best defense against pests. Select the plant that is most suited to your home and provide it with proper care. Check frequently for insect and diseases. Small infestations can often be picked off by hand or pruned off and destroyed. See the monthly Pests sections for common houseplant pests and their control.

Propagation by Air-Layering

Gardening Tips

- Visit www.northerngardener.org
- Purchase a gardening book or two!
- Read recent articles from *Northern Gardener.*

Minnesota Houseplants

Common Name (Botanical Name)	Light	Moisture	Comments
African Violet (*Saintpaulia*)	High to medium	Moist	Needs bright light or artificial light to flower. Warm temperature. Keep cold water and soil salts off leaves.
Aloe/Burn Plant (*Aloe vera*)	High	Dry	Tolerates neglect as long as it receives good light. Plant juices soothe burns.
Asparagus Fern (*Asparagus densiflorus* 'Sprengeri')	High to medium	Slightly moist	Good bright light and cool temperatures. Often loses leaves in winter, but will recover if moved outdoors for summer.
Begonia (*Begonia* species)	Medium	Moist	Likes warm temperatures, high humidity, and moist organic soils.
Boston Fern (*Nephrolepsis exaltata* 'Bostoniensis')	High to medium	Moist	Bright light and high humidity. Summer outdoors if plant declines over winter.
Bromeliad (*Bromelia, Tillandsia,* and more)	High to medium	Moist to slightly dry	See August "Helpful Hints."
Cactus (*Cereus, Mammillaria, Opuntia,* and more)	High	Dry	Summer outdoors or in a sunny south-facing window inside. Cool, bright location for winter to encourage bloom.
Cast-iron Plant (*Aspidistra elatior*)	Medium to low	Well drained to dry	Tough plant that tolerates a lot of abuse. May be hard to find.
Chinese Evergreen (*Aglaonema* species)	Medium to low	Well drained	Tough plant. Avoid wet soils and drafts.
Christmas Cactus (*Schlumbergera*)	High to medium	Well drained	See October "Helpful Hints" for reblooming information.
Clivia (*Clivia miniata*)	High	Moist, well drained	Blooms best when potbound.
Dumb Cane (*Dieffenbachia*)	High to medium	Moist, well drained	Needs bright light to maintain even bottom leaves. Air-layer to renew. Keep out of children's reach. It's poisonous.
Dracaena (*Dracaena* species)	Medium to low	Moist, well drained	Lots of varieties. Water and light needs vary with species. Brown leaf tips due to fluoride and chlorine in water. Keep soil slightly moist.
English Ivy (*Hedera helix*)	High to medium	Moist	Watch for mites. Keep soil slightly moist and wash leaves occasionally.
Grape Ivy (*Cissus rhomifolia*)	Medium to low	Moist, well drained	Tough plant. Be careful not to overwater in low-light situations
Hibiscus (*Hibiscus rosa-sinensis*)	High to medium Prefers high to flower	Moist, well drained	See September "Helpful Hints."

Minnesota Houseplants

Common Name (Botanical Name)	Light	Moisture	Comments
Jade (*Crassula ovata*)	High	Well drained to dry	Summer outdoors or in a southern window. Bright light, cool temperatures, and dry soil for winter for blossoms.
Norfolk Island Pine (*Araucaria heterophylla*)	High to medium	Moist	Needs bright light and high humidity to keep lower branches and prevent drying.
Orchids (*Cattleya*, *Dendrobium*, *Phalaenopsis*)	High	Moist	Blooms over long period with little care.
Palm (*Areca*, *Chamaeodorea*, *Howea*, and more)	High to medium	Moist	Tough plant. Watch for mites and brown leaf tips if soil goes too dry.
Peace Lily (*Spathiphyllum*)	Medium to low	Moist	Check often; this plant dries out fast. It will forgive you the first few times and then leaves start yellowing and browning.
Philodendron (*Philodendron*)	High to low	Well drained	Tough plant. Prefers benign neglect; usually killed with kindness.
Pothos (*Epipremnum aureum*)	High to low	Well drained	Tough plant. Avoid overwatering.
Rubber Tree (*Ficus elastica*)	High to medium	Well drained	Loses leaves when adjusting to new location. Pinch out growing tip to encourage branching.
Schefflera (*Schefflera actinophylla*)	High	Moist, well drained	Avoid wet soggy soils and drafts. Watch for mites.
Snake Plant (*Sansevieria*)	Medium to low	Well drained to dry	Tough plant that is difficult to kill. Will bloom when grown potbound in bright light.
Spider Plant (*Chlorophytum comosum*)	High to medium	Moist	Avoid brown tips (caused by chemicals in the water) by keeping soil slightly moist.
Wax Plant (*Hoya carnosa*)	High	Well drained	Summer outdoors to encourage blooming. Leave long, leafless stems intact for flowering. Watch for mealybugs.
Weeping Fig (*Ficus benjamina*)	High to medium	Moist	Drops leaves with any change in the environment. Can lose 95 percent of its leaves and still recover. Watch for scale insects.

Planning

The short, dark days of January are hard on gardeners and houseplants alike. Consider moving your houseplants south for the winter—to a south-facing window, that is, where the plants will receive the most sunlight. Move low-light plants closer to the window and those near east- or west-facing windows to a south-facing window. Or move them under artificial lights. A combination of natural sunlight supplemented with artificial lights will help your houseplants survive the dark days of winter.

Avoid drafts of hot and cold air. Cold drafts from patio doors and windows can chill the foliage and lead to root rot. Drafts of hot air from heating ducts create lower humidity. The drier air is hard on the plants, but is a great environment for mites and aphids.

Planting

Pot up purchased or stored **Amaryllis** bulbs. See January "Planting" in the chapter on bulbs for details. Wait until the light increases, days lengthen, and temperatures warm to propagate and transplant other houseplants.

Care

The holidays may be over but your **Poinsettia** and other holiday plants are still blooming. Keep these in a cool, bright location to prolong flowering. Once the bloom cycle is complete, remove faded flowers, decrease the watering, and move to a sunny window.

You may need to sacrifice some sunlight during extremely cold weather. Move plants away from the window or keep the curtains and blinds between the cold window and the plants. *Never trap plants between the curtain and the window where they can suffer cold damage.*

Increase the humidity around your plants. Group plants together, place them on gravel trays, or place pans of water on your radiator. See "The Growing Environment" in the introduction to this chapter for more details.

Some gardeners like to move their plants to a cool room for winter. The cooler temperatures slow the plants' metabolism and allow them to better tolerate the low light.

Clean your plants. Removing dust and debris increases the light reaching the leaves and helps remove any insects that may be present. Use a damp cloth or sponge to clean smooth leaves. Brush dust off hairy-leafed plants using a soft cosmetic brush.

Plants growing under fluorescent lights need 12 to 16 hours of light each day. Give plants at least 6 hours of dark each night. Use a timer to automatically turn lights on and off. It makes your job easier and eliminates the problem of forgetfulness.

Watering

Adjust your watering schedule to meet the needs of the plants. Always water thoroughly until water runs out of the pot. Pour off the excess. Wait until soil-less mixes are slightly moist and soil-based mixes are slightly dry to water again.

Plants growing in a warm house with low humidity will need to be watered more frequently than those growing in a cool house. Light intensity also influences watering. The more light plants receive, the more often you will need to water.

Fertilizing

Do not fertilize. Most houseplants are in a resting stage for winter. Plants growing in soil-less mixes under artificial lights may benefit from a dilute solution of fertilizer.

Use the same dilute solution to fertilize holiday plants that have finished blooming.

Pruning

Remove the faded flowers on holiday plants. Prune off insect-infected, broken, or wayward branches. Save major pruning for late February.

Pests

Insects: Indoor growing conditions are tough on plants, but they are great for all the insects that like to feed on them, such as fungus gnats, aphids, mites, mealybugs, and scale.

Check under the leaves and along the stems for signs of problems. Look for speckling, yellowing, spots, or a clear, sticky substance on the leaves. Handpick or prune off small populations of insects. See January and February "Helpful Hints" for more details.

Diseases: Powdery mildew, leaf spot, and root rot can affect houseplants. See February "Pests" for more information on the diseases and their control.

Animals: Curb your cat's love for your indoor garden by planting him a garden of his own. A 6-inch pot of **Ryegrass** will be fine. If this does not work, contact your vet or try one of the commercially available cat and dog repellents.

Insects: Part I

Fungus gnats are often misidentified as fruit flies. These insects feed on the organic matter in moist soil. They do not harm the plants, but they can be annoying. ***Tips for controlling fungus gnats include:***

- Try living with them. The populations will rise and fall and eventually disappear.
- Allow the soil to dry slightly between watering. Fungus gnats thrive in moist, organic soils; keeping it dry helps reduce their population.
- Try an environmentally friendly product sold as Gnatrol®. The active ingredient is ***Bacillus thuringiensis israelensis***. This particular bacteria only kills the larvae of fungus gnats and mosquitoes. Check your local garden center or catalogs for this product.
- As a last resort, you can use an insecticide labeled for indoor use. I find the smell of some of these more offensive than the gnats. And as always be sure to read and follow all label directions before purchasing and using any pesticide. Spray in an area with good air circulation.

Speckling or bronzing of leaves means you have aphids or mites. Aphids are small ($\frac{1}{8}$-inch), teardrop-shaped insects that suck out the plant juices. Their feeding can cause yellowing and distorted growth. Mites are much smaller but cause similar damage. Use the white paper test to discover if mites are present. Shake a leaf over a sheet of white paper. If you see small specks moving, your plants have mites. Even though these are different types of pests, ***both aphids and mites require the same control.***

- Regular cleaning will help remove small populations.
- Spray plants with a strong blast of water to dislodge these pests. Place the pot in a bag and secure it around the stem. Place it in the sink or shower and spray with water. This allows you to wash off the plants without washing the soil down the drain.
- Treat with insecticidal soap. You may need several applications to get these pests under control.

Planning

Sit down, grab your journal, and start writing. Make notes on the winter survival strategies that you tried this year. Record pest problems, controls used, and the results. This will help reduce guessing and improve results next winter.

Now is also a good time to prepare for all the grooming and transplanting activities that will start next month. Locate, clean, and sharpen your hand pruner or garden scissors. Clean and sterilize the pots you plan to use. Use a solution of one part bleach to nine parts water. Rinse and store pots for later use. Purchase or mix your own potting mix.

Planting

Force some Paper-whites *for indoor bloom.*

1 *Fill* a shallow container with pea gravel. Add enough water to reach the top of the gravel. Place the bulbs on the gravel and cover with just enough gravel to hold them in place. Or *plant* them in a container of any well-drained potting mix. Leave the tops of the bulbs exposed. Keep the planting mix moist, but not wet.

2 *Move* the potted bulbs to a cool location for rooting.

3 *Place* them in a cool, bright location as soon as the leaves start to grow. It takes just a few weeks to get flowers. This is a great project for kids—or any anxious gardener!

Care

Continue cleaning plants once a month. Wipe off smooth leaves with a damp sponge or cloth. Use a cosmetic brush to dust **African Violets**, **Gloxinias**, and other hairy-leafed plants.

The dry winter air is hard on tropical plants. Increase the humidity around your plants by grouping plants together, placing them on gravel trays, or placing pans of water on your radiator. See "The Growing Environment" in the introduction to this chapter for more details.

Watering

Water plants as needed. Always water thoroughly until water runs out of the pot. Pour off the excess water. Wait until soil-less mixes are slightly moist and soil-based mixes are slightly dry to water again.

Plants growing in a warm house with low humidity will need to be watered more frequently than those growing in a cool house. Light intensity also influences watering. The more light plants receive, the more often you need to water.

Fertilizing

Do not fertilize plants. Those growing under lights in a soil-less mix can be fertilized with a dilute solution of houseplant fertilizer.

Check plants for salt buildup. This appears as a crusty, white substance on the soil surface or as white ring stains on clay pots. Scrape off the crusty salt buildup on the soil, then leach the soil by watering thoroughly. Wait 20 minutes and water thoroughly again. This helps dilute and wash the salts out of the soil.

Pruning

Remove faded flowers, brown leaves, and pests. The end of the month is a good time to prune **Hibiscus**. Cut stems above a healthy bud or leaf, where one branch joins another, or back to the main stem. Remove crossed, inward growing, and damaged branches first. Next, thin out the branches and shape. Remove only one-third of the plant.

Pests

Insects: Continue to monitor plants for pest problems. Consult January and February "Helpful Hints" for details on insects and their controls.

Diseases: Powdery mildew (looks like someone sprinkled baking powder on your leaves) problems should be decreasing with the increase in light. Continue to remove infected leaves and provide plenty of space for air circulation.

A variety of leaf spot diseases attack houseplants, especially those that have been overwatered. Reduce watering frequency and remove infected leaves. This is usually enough to correct the problem.

Root rot can also infect overwatered houseplants. Correct your watering habits. As a last resort, you can use a fungicide labeled for use as a soil drench on houseplants. If rot continues, you will need to remove the infected plant from group plantings or discard rotted plants. If you decide to use a pesticide, be sure to read and follow all label directions carefully. Spray in an area with good ventilation.

Animals: Cats love indoor gardens—for eating, digging, and other inappropriate purposes. Here are some tips for discouraging your feline friends:

Insects: Part II

Mealybugs look like little pieces of cotton and are found in the leaf joints and on the stems of a variety of houseplants. **African Violets, Hoyas, Jades**, and **Cacti** are favorites of this pest. Treat with alcohol. Dip a cotton swap in rubbing alcohol and apply it to each mealybug. The alcohol dissolves the fuzzy covering and kills the insect below. Insecticidal soap can be used to treat the immature mealybugs that have not formed the cottony covering. Repeated applications are needed.

Scales are hard-shelled insects. They suck out the plant juices causing stunting and poor growth. The immature stage is translucent and hard to see. The hard shell develops as the insect matures. This shell protects it from insecticides. Gently scrape off the scale using an old toothbrush or your thumbnail. Spray the plant with insecticidal soap to kill the immature scale. Persistence is the key to success. It takes several treatments and lots of scraping to get this pest under control.

Whitefly is a descriptive name for this insect. The tiny whiteflies suck out the plant juices and cause stunting. Use yellow sticky traps to reduce the population to a tolerable level. Buy traps at your local garden center or make your own. Spread Tanglefoot on a small piece of yellow poster board. Place several traps in your houseplant collection. You may choose to treat high populations of whiteflies if they are causing significant damage. Use an insecticide containing Resmethrin or Permethrin that is labeled to control whiteflies on houseplants. Make three applications, five days apart. If you miss an application, start over.

- Train cats to stay away from houseplants. Use a squirt gun to discourage plant-damaging activities.

- Try one of the commercially available cat and dog repellents.

- Use large chunks of mulch or wire screening to keep cats from digging in the soil.

- Plant a pot or tray of **Ryegrass** for your cat. Let him eat these greens so he will not need to eat your plants. Consult your vet.

Planning

Houseplants are beginning to show signs of life. Start preparing them for their growing season. It is time to take action on all the observations that you have made throughout the winter.

Planting

Start repotting houseplants that have outgrown their containers. Potbound plants have stunted growth or roots growing out of the bottom of the pot. See the "Repotting" section in the introduction to this chapter.

Use kitchen tongs or a strip of newspaper to transplant a **Cactus**. Gently grasp the **Cactus** with tongs or wrap the paper around it. Tilt the pot and slide the plant out of the container. Be careful not to crush the stem or spines.

Pot up any annuals such as **Geraniums** that were kept in dormant storage for winter. Cut the stems back to 4 inches above the soil surface. Water thoroughly and repeat when the soil starts to dry. After growth begins, fertilize with a dilute solution of any flowering houseplant fertilizer.

This period of new growth makes it a great time to propagate houseplants.

1   *Fill* a container with moist vermiculite, starter mix, or soil-less potting mix.

2   *Use* a sharp knife, pruners, or garden scissors to take a 4- to 6-inch cutting. Cut just above a leaf.

3   *Remove* one or two lower leaves. This is where the roots will form.

4   *Dip* hard-to-root cuttings in a rooting hormone. This product contains hormones that promote root development and fungicides to prevent rot. Be careful not to get rooting hormone in your eyes.

5   *Stick* cuttings into the rooting mix so at least one node (leaf joint) is buried. Water until the excess drains out of the bottom of the pot.

6   *Place* the pot in a loose plastic bag—do not seal it—and move it to an area away from direct light.

7   Once the roots develop, *transplant* rooted cuttings to a small container of potting mix.

Care

Monitor changes in the growing conditions. The light is improving and the days are getting longer. By late March, you may be able to move plants back to their original locations.

Continue cleaning plants once a month. Wipe off smooth leaves with a damp sponge or cloth. Use a cosmetic brush to dust **African Violets**, **Gloxinias**, and other hairy-leafed plants.

Watering

Adjust your watering schedule for recently repotted plants. The increased amount of soil usually means you need to water less frequently. The type of soil used can also either increase or decrease frequency.

You will also need to adjust your watering schedule to match the changes in light, temperature, and humidity.

Fertilizing

You can start fertilizing plants. Fertilize if the plants show signs of nutrient deficiencies, or if you want to promote growth. Use a diluted solution of any houseplant fertilizer.

Do not fertilize newly repotted plants. Give them a month or so to adjust to their new container.

Pruning

Use a hand pruner or garden scissors to shape plants and reduce their size. Cut stems above a healthy bud or leaf, where one branch joins another, or back to the main stem. Remove crossed, inward growing, and damaged branches first. Next, thin out the branches and shape. Remove no more than one-third of the plant.

Overgrown and leggy vines and hanging baskets can be pruned back severely. Cut above a healthy set of leaves. Cut trimmings into shorter pieces (4 to 6 inches long) and use to start new plants.

Sterilize pruners after each use to avoid spreading diseases.

Pests

Continue to monitor and control insects and diseases as needed. A spring cleaning under the shower will help wash away the dust

Helpful Hints

African Violets do not always age gracefully. As the oldest leaves yellow and drop, a bare-stem "neck" develops. This leafless stem is topped with healthy leaves and beautiful flowers. You can save the plant and improve the appearance.

Short-necked African Violets can be planted deeper by following these steps:

1 **Remove** the plant from its container. **Cut away** the bottom half of the rootball.

2 **Position** the plant in the container so that the lower leaves will be just above the soil. Add soil below and above the rootball as needed. Water thoroughly so that the excess runs out the drainage holes in the bottom of the pot.

African Violets with longer necks (3 inches or more of bare stems) can be propagated.

1 **Cut off** the rosette of leaves with 1 to 2 inches of stem attached. Stick the stem in an African Violet or well-drained potting mix.

2 **Water** and place the pot in a loose plastic bag. The bag will help trap moisture without causing rot that often occurs in sealed bags.

3 **Grow** in indirect light until the plant is well rooted. Then remove the bag and provide normal care.

4 **Save** the original plant. **Cut** the stem back to 1 inch above the soil surface. Keep the soil moist and wait. In several weeks, you will see new leaves sprouting from the stem.

and some of the insects. See January and February "Helpful Hints" and "Pests."

Animals: Curb your cat's love for your indoor garden by planting him a garden of his own. A 6-inch pot of **Ryegrass** will be fine. If this does not work, contact your vet or try one of the commercially available cat and dog repellents.

Planning

Summer is on its way. Start evaluating where your plants will spend the summer. Moving houseplants outdoors often revives winter-weary and declining plants. It also increases the risk of insects infesting your indoor garden. These unwelcome guests often hitch a ride with the houseplants when they move back indoors. See September "Pests" for tips.

Planting

Finish repotting plants that have outgrown their containers. Large plants with nowhere to go (they have reached the maximum pot size) can be topdressed or root-pruned.

Topdressing—a short-term solution—is done by carefully removing the top 1 to 2 inches of soil. Replace it with fresh soil and water.

Root pruning will give longer-lasting results. It is a bit riskier but can be done successfully. Post-transplanting care is critical to success. Move plants to the best possible growing location to encourage new root growth.

1 Take cuttings from valuable specimens, just in case this process does not work.

2 *Massage* sides of the container and slide the plant out of the pot.

3 *Prune off* a thin layer of roots around the sides and bottom of the rootball.

4 *Repot* in the same or similar container. Make sure the container is clean and free of pests. Water until the excess runs out the drainage holes in the bottom of the pot.

Divide and plant divisions of large plants that spread by increasing in diameter or by rhizomes. Ferns, Snake Plants, and Peace Lilies are just a few plants that can be divided.

1 Loosen and *remove* the plant from its container.

2 *Use* a sharp knife to cut the rootball in halves or quarters.

3 *Repot* divisions in smaller containers that are slightly larger than their rootballs.

4 *Water* and *move* plants to a location with the best available growing conditions.

Finishing planting any **Annuals** that were kept in dormant storage

for winter. See March "Planting" for details.

Continue propagating houseplants. *Stem cuttings described in March "Planting" are the most common and successful ways to start new plants.*

Leaf cuttings of **African Violets**, **Begonias**, *and* **Snake Plants** *require a little more effort and some patience.*

- Cut 3-inch sections of **Snake Plants**. Notch the bottom of the stem. Bury the bottom inch in vermiculite or a well-drained potting mix. Keep it slightly moist and out of direct sun. Wait for a new plant to develop.

- Remove a healthy leaf from an **African Violet** plant. Bury the leaf stem in vermiculite or a well-drained potting mix. Keep it moist and out of direct sun. New plants will develop in one to two months.

- Remove a **Begonia** leaf. Slice through several large veins. Lay the leaf (top side up) on the soil surface. Use hairpins or small stones to anchor the leaf in place. Keep the soil moist. Cover with a loosely tied plastic bag to increase humidity and chance of success. Be patient; this process takes one to two months.

Plant rooted cuttings started last month. Plant in a small container filled with a well-drained, sterile potting mix.

Care

Continue cleaning plants once a month. Wipe or brush off dust.

Watering

Adjust your watering schedule to match the change in growing conditions. Use your finger to measure soil moisture. Soil-less mixes should be watered when they are barely moist. Soil-based mixes should be allowed to go slightly dry before watering. Keep in mind the differences in individual plant requirements.

Reduce brown tips on **Spider Plants**, **Dracaenas**, and **Prayer Plants** by keeping the soil slightly moist. This dilutes the fluoride and chlorine in the water, preventing tip burn. Or use rainwater, dehumidifier water, or distilled water for these plants.

Fertilizing

Do not fertilize recently repotted, divided, or propagated houseplants. Give them time to establish new roots. Established houseplants can be fertilized as needed.

Pruning

Prune back **Poinsettias** to 4 to 6 inches above the soil surface. This will encourage branching and help control the growth for the coming season. The trimmings can be rooted and used to start new plants.

Clip off brown tips of **Spider Plants**, **Dracaenas**, and **Prayer Plants**. Change watering practices to reduce this problem.

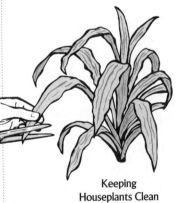

Keeping
Houseplants Clean

Shape and reduce the size of overgrown and leggy houseplants. See March "Pruning" for directions.

Pests

Continue to monitor plants for pest problems. Check under the leaves and along the stems for hidden pests. Remove insects and infected leaves as soon as they are discovered. See January and February "Pests" for more details.

Insects: Mites and aphids cause speckling on the leaves. Aphids can be seen with the naked eye. You need a hand lens or the paper test to detect mites. Shake an infested leaf over white paper. If you see specks moving, the plant has mites. Several applications of insecticidal soap will control these pests.

Aphid

If you find holes in the leaves of outdoor plants but no insects are present, the culprit is probably slugs, caterpillars, or earwigs. Check for these pests at night. A few insects can cause significant damage. Remove and destroy any offenders you discover. High populations may need additional treatment. Use beer bait for slugs and insecticides for earwigs and other beetles. Select a product labeled for use on tropical plants. As always, read and follow all label directions carefully.

Planning

Start making plans for moving. Survey your indoor garden and decide which houseplants will stay inside and which ones will move outside for the summer. Wait until the daytime and nighttime temperatures are warm before moving these tropical plants outdoors. This is usually the end of May in the southern part of the state and early June in the northern part of the state. Do not let a few warm days in early May coax you into a premature move.

Plan for new additions to the outdoor patio garden. Tropicals are quite popular and readily available at many garden centers. **Bougainvillea**, **Oleander**, **Hibiscus**, and other tropicals can add beauty to the landscape. Just make sure you have indoor space, a friend with a greenhouse, or another alternative if you plan on keeping these large plants over winter.

Planting

Continue repotting and dividing plants. See "Repotting" in the introduction to this chapter and April "Planting" for detailed directions.

Plant recently rooted cuttings in a small container filled with a well-drained potting mix.

Use a few tropical plants as accents in your flowerbeds. A **Banana Plant** or an **Ornamental Taro** growing in a bed of annuals can really attract attention. Wait until the weather warms—late May or early June—to plant these outdoors. Leave the plants in the container and sink the pot into the garden. This makes it easier on you and the plant when it is time to move the plant indoors for winter.

Smaller tropical plants, such as **Rex Begonias** and **Ferns**, make great companions for more traditional **Annuals** and **Perennials**. Treat these like bedding plants. Space them so that the plants have room to mature, and plant them directly in properly prepared soil. No need to leave them in the pot if you do not plan on digging them up and moving them indoors for winter.

Care

Harden off (acclimatize) houseplants you plan on moving outdoors. Hardening off allows the plants to gradually adapt to the outdoor environment—just like Northerners must do when they travel to Florida for the winter. I keep my houseplants in a shady spot all summer. The slight increase in light and humidity still revive the plants, but the change is less drastic.

This is less stressful for plants moving outside and then back inside in fall.

Indoor plants may also need some relocating.

- Move plants away from air conditioner vents. Blasts of cold air can be drying and can cause damage to houseplants.

- Adjust location according to heat and light. A south- or west-facing window may be too warm or sunny for some low-light plants. Move them away from the windows or into an east-facing window. Sheer curtains can also be used to reduce the intense heat and sun.

Watering

Check the soil moisture before watering. The changing environment will change your watering schedule. Air conditioning, higher humidity, and more sunlight all influence how quickly the soil will dry out.

Soil-less mixes should be watered when they are barely moist. Soil-based mixes should be allowed to go slightly dry before watering. Keep in mind the differences in individual plant requirements.

Check houseplants moved outdoors daily. These plants dry out quickly and may need to be watered every day. Water plants when the top few inches of soil are just starting to dry.

Fertilizing

Continue to fertilize indoor plants as needed. Do not fertilize recently repotted, divided, or propagated houseplants. Give them time to establish new roots. Houseplants summering outdoors benefit from regular fertilization. Use a dilute solution of houseplant fertilizer once or twice a month, according to label directions.

Pruning

Do minimal pruning on flowering houseplants. Most of them will be blooming soon. Pruning now can delay or eliminate the bloom period. Prune off only broken, dead, or wayward branches.

Pinch out the growing tips or prune back the stems of leggy foliage plants. This will promote branching and give you a fuller plant.

Pests

Continue monitoring pests on houseplants located inside and outside. Outdoor houseplants are exposed to many more problems and should be monitored more closely. Cover the bottoms of buried pots with a piece of old nylon stocking to prevent slugs, centipedes, and sow bugs from moving in through the drainage holes.

Helpful Hints

Summering plants outdoors can help rejuvenate declining plants. It also adds some challenges to your gardening efforts. You will need to monitor and control insects that catch a ride on the plants when they move back indoors. Small populations of mites, aphids, and whiteflies can quickly grow and damage your indoor plants. The plants will also need to be gradually *acclimated* to the change in environment when moving outdoors for summer and indoors for fall.

- Move plants outdoors to a shaded location once the temperatures stay above 50 to 55 degrees Fahrenheit.
- Bring plants inside the house or garage on cold nights.
- Gradually increase the amount of sunlight these plants receive each day.
- By the end of two weeks, the plants should be ready to stay in their permanent location.

Some of my favorite spots to summer my plants include:

- Under the filtered shade of a honeylocust or other tree that casts light shade. The high humidity and diffuse light is perfect for reviving houseplants.
- On a screened-in porch. Even in the shade, the light is better than indoors and the plants are protected from harsh weather and are somewhat protected from insects.
- Displayed with other container gardens. The tropical foliage can add lots of interest and variety to the garden.
- In existing gardens or container plantings for added interest. Burying the pot makes the plant look like it is part of the garden and reduces watering frequency.

Planning

As the outdoor gardening season becomes our primary focus, it is easy to neglect our houseplants. Take advantage of rainy days to catch up on your indoor garden care.

Keep writing in your journal. Make notes on how things are growing indoors and out. Note planting locations and the use of tropical plants in your landscape. Record how the plants looked and how well they thrived in their outdoor location. This will help you repeat or improve plant placement next season.

There is still time to make changes and additions to your indoor and outdoor gardens. Be sure to consider the winter growing space needed for your existing plants and the new additions.

Planting

It is usually safe to move tropical plants into the outdoor landscape in early June. They will need to be protected or moved indoors if cold or frost is predicted.

Use large tropical plants as accents in your flowerbeds. Leave the plants in the container and sink the pot into the garden. This makes it easier on you and the plant when it is time to move them indoors for winter. Cover the pot with an old nylon stocking to help keep slugs, sow bugs, and other soil-residing insects from entering through the drainage hole.

Smaller tropical plants, such as **Boston Ferns**, **Pink Polka-dot Plants**, and **Asparagus Ferns** make great companions for more traditional annuals and perennials. Mix **Rex Begonias** with **Japanese Painted Ferns** and **New Guinea Impatiens** for a nice shade garden combination. Treat the smaller tropicals like bedding plants. Space them so that the plants have room to mature, and plant them directly in properly prepared soil. No need to leave them in the pot if you do not plan on digging them up and moving them indoors for winter.

Care

You can move houseplants outdoors when the temperatures are at least 50 to 55 degrees Fahrenheit and the danger of frost has passed.

Move indoor plants away from air conditioner vents. Blasts of cold dry air can be drying and damaging to houseplants.

Monitor the growing conditions. The increased light and temperatures outdoors will affect plant growth indoors. South- and west-facing windows can get pretty warm on sunny days. Low-light plants may need to be moved away from the window or into an east-facing location. Sheer curtains and awnings also reduce the available light. Match plants to their growing requirements.

Clean smooth-leafed houseplants with a damp sponge or cloth. Brush dust off hairy-leafed plants with a soft cosmetic brush.

Watering

Water indoors as needed. Improved growing conditions usually mean you need to water more often. Plants in an air-conditioned or low-light environment will need less frequent watering.

Check outdoor plants daily. The soil dries quickly, and the plants use more water in these good growing conditions. Shade plants will need to be watered less often than those in full sun. Water as the top few inches of soil begin to dry. Check twice a day in extremely hot, dry weather.

Fertilizing

Continue to fertilize indoor houseplants as needed. Those growing outdoors for the summer will benefit from regular fertilization. Apply a diluted solution of any houseplant fertilizer once or twice a month. Use a flowering plant fertilizer, one higher in phosphorus, for flowering houseplants. Consult label directions for specific information. Those planted in the ground can be fertilized with the other annuals and perennials in the garden.

Pruning

Remove faded flowers on blooming plants.

Pinch out the growing tips or prune back the stems of leggy foliage plants. This will promote branching and give you a fuller plant in the future.

Prune off any broken, dead, or wayward branches.

Helpful Hints

Houseplants summering outdoors need more frequent watering than those inside. Reduce the watering needs by:

- Placing plants under the filtered shade of trees or porches.
- Sinking the pots in the ground. The soil insulates the pot and reduces the need for water. Cover pots with an old nylon stocking to keep sow bugs, millipedes, and other insects from crawling in through the drainage hole.
- Mulch the soil surface. A thin layer of cocoa bean shells or twice-shredded bark will help conserve moisture and reduce the need for water.
- Double pot for added insulation. Select a container at least 2 inches larger in diameter. Use one with a drainage hole to avoid overwatering. Line the bottom with gravel, Styrofoam packing peanuts, or other drainage material to elevate the pot to the correct height. Place the potted houseplant inside the larger container. Cover the pot and line the sides with sphagnum peat. You will need to pour off the excess water that collects in containers without drainage holes.

Pests

Monitor both indoor and outdoor houseplants. Insects can move indoors through screens, on gardening tools, and with new plants. Isolate insect-infested plants as soon as they are discovered. This reduces the risk of them spreading to other plants. Control insects and monitor for several weeks before returning the plant to its permanent location.

Holes in the leaves of outdoor plants can be caused by slugs, earwigs, caterpillars, or beetles. Check for these pests at night. Remove any offenders. Use beer to trap slugs or insecticides to treat high populations of earwigs, caterpillars, and beetles. Read and follow all label directions.

Animals often damage houseplants summering outdoors. Birds often try to nest in and chipmunks often dig in hanging baskets. Cover the planter with bird netting to discourage this behavior. Remove the netting once the animals find another gardener to bother.

Weed seeds may blow in and sprout in houseplants summering outdoors. Pull weeds as soon as they appear.

Planning

Keep monitoring and evaluating houseplants growing indoors and out. Record the plants' response to their summer environment. This information will help you decide where to place plants next summer.

Planting

Continue propagating plants. Overgrown **Dumb Canes** (*Dieffenbachias*) can be air-layered and propagated by cane cuttings. See Houseplants "Helpful Hints" on page 360 for details on air-layering. *To make cane cuttings:*

1 *Fill* a flat with a mixture of ¹/₂ peat and ¹/₂ vermiculite or perlite.

2 *Cut* long, leafless stems of **Dumb Canes** into 3-inch sections (must contain bud).

3 *Lay* the cane sections, lengthwise, on the soil surface so that a bud is facing up. Press the bottom half of the stem into the potting mix.

4 *Store* the flat of cuttings in a bright location out of direct sun. Keep the potting mix moist, but not wet.

5 *Watch* for new shoots to develop. It takes four to eight weeks for canes to root and new plants to develop.

6 *Move* the new plants to a small container filled with any well-drained potting mix. Give small plants the same care as the parents—bright light and slightly moist soil.

Take cuttings of **Poinsettias** now so you will have more to give and enjoy this Christmas. See March "Planting" for details on starting plants from stem cuttings.

Care

Keep grooming and cleaning both indoor and outdoor plants. Indoor plants collect dust, pet dander, and other airborne particles on their leaves. Cleaning removes it, allowing more light to reach the leaves. Outdoor plants may need an occasional cleaning from dust, splashing soil, and such. Use a damp sponge or cloth to wipe off glossy leaves. A soft cosmetic brush works well for removing debris from hairy-leafed plants.

The heat of midsummer often means houseplants, indoors and out, need a break from the heat. Make sure plants are well watered.

Outdoor containers may need to be watered twice a day, or move them into a partially shaded area until the extreme heat has subsided. Indoor plants may need to be moved away from hot locations as well. Adjust watering to adapt to the changes in the environment.

Hibiscus plants should be in full bloom. Late pruning, excess nitrogen, or lack of light can prevent flowering. Plants pruned after the middle of March will eventually bloom, just be patient. Fertilize **Hibiscus** and other blooming tropical plants with any flowering houseplant fertilizer. These fertilizers are higher in phosphorus (the middle number on the container) and promote flowering.

Watering

Water plants as needed. Check plants growing outdoors every day. Indoor plants will not need to be watered as often. Check these plants once or twice a week. Remember the bigger the container, the less often they will need watering.

Double pot houseplants when using decorative containers or baskets that lack a drainage hole. Fill the bottom of the decorative container with pebbles. Place your houseplant (in a plastic pot) on top of the pebbles inside the decorative container. Mask the plastic pot with sphagnum moss. The pebbles will collect the excess water while keeping the plant from sitting in the water and rotting. Occasionally pour off the excess water that collects in the pebbles.

Fertilizing

Continue fertilizing as needed. Plants with stunted growth may benefit from fertilization. Fertilizer also promotes faster growth. This may not be what you really want for some of the bigger plants that barely fit in your home.

Outdoor houseplants benefit from regular fertilization. Frequent watering and the good growing conditions outdoors increase the need for nutrients.

Pests

Monitor all your houseplants, indoors and out, for pests. Check under the leaves, along the stems, and throughout the plants for signs of pests.

Helpful Hints

It is difficult, sometimes impossible, to find a dependable sitter for your plants when going on vacation. I am lucky enough to have a green thumb neighbor to water and tend my garden. If this is not the case for you, try these suggestions:

- Fill the sink or tub with an inch or so of water. Elevate houseplants on empty containers so that they sit above, not in, the water. Water the plants thoroughly. Cover the sink or tub with plastic sheeting. This creates a moist, humid environment reducing the plants' need for water.
- Double pot houseplants. Plant your houseplants in a clay pot. Set the clay pot in a larger plastic container. Fill the empty spaces with damp peat moss. Water the peat moss. Moisture will move from the moist peat moss, through the clay pot, and into the soil.
- Make your own self-watering container. You will need an old margarine container; a strip of felt, string, nylon stocking, or other wicking fabric; and a houseplant (see Figure 1). The margarine tub serves as the water reservoir, and the wick moves the water from the container to the potting mix for the plant to use.

End of wick pushed with tweezers through hole. Must be in contact with potting soil

Hole cut in lid. Pour water through here

Water

Plastic margarine tub

Wick cut from pair of nylon tights

Figure 1

- Frequent travelers might want to invest in self-watering pots or switch to growing only **Cacti** and **Succulents**.

Diseases: Yellow, brown, or spotted leaves are common symptoms of fungal disease. Remove infected leaves as soon as they appear. Adjust watering so that the plants are watered thoroughly, but not so often that the soil stays wet. Pour off the excess water that collects in the plant saucer.

Pruning

Remove faded flowers on blooming tropical plants. Prune off damaged, diseased, or wayward branches.

Pinch and prune **Poinsettias** and **Azaleas** to the desired size and shape.

Planning

Fall is quickly approaching. Soon it will be time to move all your houseplants and tropicals indoors. Take inventory and make a list of what you plan to bring indoors and possible indoor growing locations. If you are like most gardeners, you probably have more plants coming indoors than you moved out in the fall.

Find an area to quarantine plants as they move indoors. It should be an area with good, bright light but separate from your indoor houseplants. Keep plants in this area for several weeks. Check along the stems and under the leaves for insects. Control any pests found and continue to monitor. Once the plants are free from insects, it is safe to move them in with the rest of your houseplant collection.

Planting

Take cuttings of **Coleus**, **Geraniums**, **Vinca**, and other annuals you want to overwinter indoors. This method reduces the space needed and the risk of bringing insects indoors with the plants. *Here's how to start new plants from cuttings:*

1 *Fill* a container with moist vermiculite, starter mix, or soil-less potting mix.

2 *Use* a sharp knife, pruners, or garden scissors to take a 4- to 6-inch cutting. Cut just above a leaf.

3 *Remove* one or two lower leaves. This is where the roots will form.

4 *Dip* hard-to-root cuttings in a rooting hormone. This product contains hormones that promote root development and fungicides to prevent rot.

5 *Stick* cuttings in rooting mix so that at least one node (leaf joint) is buried. Water thoroughly, allowing excess water to drain out of the bottom of the pot.

6 *Place* the pot in a loose plastic bag—do not seal—and move to an area away from direct light.

7 Once roots develop, *transplant* rooted cuttings into a small container of potting mix.

Care

The hot days of early August can cause heat stress and may result in scorch. Move plants to a partially shaded area and keep the soil moist during times of extreme heat.

Going on vacation means you will need to find a plant sitter or set up your plants to be self-sufficient. Make the plant sitter's job easier by writing down directions for care. You may want to spend some time showing and telling your friend how to water. It will reduce your concern and his or her anxiety over this responsibility. See July "Helpful Hints" for more details.

Reduce brown tips on **Spider Plants**, **Dracaenas**, and **Prayer Plants** by keeping the soil slightly moist. This dilutes the fluoride and chlorine in the water, preventing tip burn. Or use rainwater, dehumidifier water, or distilled water for these plants.

Watering

Check outdoor plants daily. Indoor plants do not dry out as quickly. Water as often as needed to keep the soil slightly moist.

You will need to water more often in hot, dry weather. Plants in small containers dry out faster than those in large containers. Water plants growing in a soil-less mix often enough to keep the soil slightly moist. Those growing in a soil-based mix should be allowed to dry slightly between waterings.

160

Fertilizing

Continue fertilizing plants as needed. Over-fertilization can damage plants or cause unwanted growth on already large plants. Those growing outdoors or in soil-less mixes need more frequent fertilization. Soil-less mixes do not retain the nutrients like soil-based mixes do, so they need to be replenished more frequently. Nutrients are leached out of the soil by frequent watering on outdoor plants.

Pruning

Remove faded flowers to improve appearance and flowering. Use a hand pruner or garden scissors to remove damaged or pest-infested stems. Clip off brown tips common on **Spider Plants**, **Dracaenas**, and **Prayer Plants**.

Keeping
Houseplants Clean

Helpful Hints

Bromeliads are fun and beautiful plants that can brighten up any indoor garden. Add these members of the pineapple family to your collection. Purchase a healthy, flowering **Bromeliad** from a garden center or florist. The flowers are so large and colorful you will think they are artificial.

- Grow **Bromeliads** in a bright location indoors. Keep the soil evenly moist for all but those **Bromeliads** that have thick, fleshy leaves. Water the soil until the excess runs out the drainage hole. Water again as the top 2 inches begin to dry.
- Fertilize spring through fall with any dilute solution of a flowering houseplant fertilizer. Only fertilize in winter if the plants are growing but showing signs of nutrient deficiency. Apply fertilizer if the leaves are yellow and stunted.
- Enjoy the **Bromeliad** flower–it can last a month or more! Remove the faded flower, but leave the foliage intact.
- Soon the mother plant may begin to fade as small plants form around its base. Remove and plant the small offshoots individually in smaller containers.
- Force the offspring to flower once they reach full size and their roots fill the pot. Place a piece of **Apple** in the plant and cover with a plastic bag. Keep the bag sealed and the plant out of direct light for three days. Remove the bag and Apple. Now wait (it takes weeks) for your flowering reward.

Pests

Monitor both indoor and outdoor houseplants. Insects can move indoors through screens, on gardening tools, and with new plants. Isolate insect-infested plants as soon as they are discovered. This reduces the risk of them spreading to other plants. Control insects and monitor plants for several weeks before returning them to their permanent locations.

Weed seeds may blow in and sprout in houseplants summering outdoors. Pull weeds as soon as they appear.

Planning

Identify an area in which to isolate plants as they move indoors. This will reduce the risk of contaminating your indoor houseplant collection. Select a well-lit location that can accommodate all the plants moving indoors.

Review your garden journal to see where your houseplants thrived last year. Avoid or alter problem areas. You may need to invest in artificial lights if your houseplant collection has outgrown the available windows.

Record the highlights, both successes and failures, from the summer season. Note pest problems, plant locations, and maintenance strategies. This will help you plan and care for your houseplants next summer.

Planting

You can still take cuttings of annuals that you want to overwinter indoors. Impatiens, Coleus, Vinca, and others can be started from cuttings and grown as houseplants for winter. See August "Planting" for more details.

Pot up rooted cuttings of annuals. Plant them in small containers filled with a well-drained potting mix. Grow them under artificial lights or in a sunny window. Even shade plants such as **Impatiens** prefer a sunny window indoors in winter. Keep the soil slightly moist.

Plant cane cuttings that have developed roots and shoots. These also prefer a well-drained potting mix. Plant single cuttings in small containers or several cuttings in a larger (6 to 8 inch), pot. Extras make nice gifts for friends or trading material to use with other gardeners. Move these to a bright location and keep the soil slightly moist.

Care

Isolate and acclimatize your plants as you move them indoors. Plants summered outdoors have developed sun leaves. They are not efficient at capturing the available sunlight. These leaves cannot support the plant in the low-light conditions found indoors.

- *Isolate* plants from your indoor houseplant collection. Monitor and control insects.

- *Place* plants in the sunniest south- or west-facing window available, or grow them under artificial lights. Leave plants here for several weeks.

- Next, *move* them into an east-facing or well-lit north-facing window. Leave them here for several weeks.

- Gradually *decrease* the light until the plants reach their final locations. This helps the plants develop new, shade-tolerant leaves that are more efficient at capturing what little light is available.

- Failure to acclimatize plants results in yellow leaves and massive leaf drop. This is stressful on the plants—and most gardeners as well!

Move **Amaryllis** indoors before the first fall frost. Store the bulb in a cool, dark location or continue to grow it indoors. See the January "Helpful Hints" in the "Bulbs" chapter for information on reblooming your **Amaryllis**.

Watering

Adjust your watering schedule to accommodate the changes in climate and location. Plants moved indoors will need less frequent watering. Check the soil moisture on all your plants before watering.

Soil-less mixes should be watered when they are barely moist. Soil-based mixes should be allowed to go slightly dry before watering. Keep in mind the differences in individual plant requirements.

Fertilizing

Cut back or stop fertilizing houseplants. This is a time of adjustment. Plants are adapting to their new indoor location and the change in the climate. Fall means shorter days and less intense sunlight. Houseplants will grow less and need less frequent fertilization.

Plants growing in soil-less mixes may benefit from an occasional dilute solution of fertilizer. These mixes do not retain nutrients like the soil-based potting mixes. Fertilize plants that show signs of nutrient deficiencies.

Pruning

Limit pruning to broken, damaged, or pest-infested branches. You may need to prune large plants to fit their indoor location. Cut stems above a healthy bud or leaf, where one branch joins another, or back to the main stem.

Pests

Quarantine houseplants moving indoors.

- Maintain the plants in a well-lit location away from your indoor plants. They may need to stay here for several weeks or months.

- Check under the leaves, along the stems, and throughout the plant for signs of insects.

- Remove and destroy any insects that are found. Insecticidal soap will control aphids, mites, immature scale, and other soft-bodied insects. See January and February "Helpful Hints" for specifics of controlling houseplant insects.

- Evaluate the success of your treatment and continue to monitor for additional pest outbreaks.

- Move plants to their permanent location once they have been acclimatized and pests are under control.

Helpful Hints

Overwintering Hibiscus can be challenging and often frustrating. Evaluate the available growing space. Hibiscus plants prefer a sunny window, moist soil, and the same care as your houseplants. They will, however, tolerate less than ideal conditions and survive, though not thrive, over the winter. For the best results, follow these tips:

- *Acclimatize* (see the "Care" section) the plants to their winter location. This gradual reduction in light will help minimize leaf loss.
- **Hibiscus** growing in an unobstructed south-, west-, or east-facing window should be *watered* often enough to keep the soil slightly moist, not wet.
- **Hibiscus** moved to a cool, low-light location need much less water. The goal is survival, not growth. *Water* often enough to prevent the soil from drying.
- Prune as needed in February. *Move* the plants back outdoors in late May or early June. You will be amazed by their recovery and bloom.

I place my **Hibiscus** in an east-facing basement window in the laundry room. It is cool, and I am there often enough to remember to water. My plants lose some leaves but bloom profusely all winter. This makes laundry a little less of a chore!

Planning

This month marks the beginning of the most difficult growing period for indoor plants. The short days, low light, and decreasing humidity make it hard to create a plant-friendly environment. Add to this the addition of holiday decorations that may occupy some prime indoor growing space.

Now may be the time to consider installing artificial lights. A standard, two-bulb fluorescent fixture will provide additional indoor growing space. Look for existing tables, benches, or other areas where a light garden can be installed. Check garden catalogs for some of the new and different lighting options. New plant stands and clip-on light fixtures allow greater flexibility even where space is limited.

Planting

Plant rooted cuttings. Place one cutting in a small pot, or several cuttings in a larger container, filled with a well-drained potting mix. Move plants to a sunny window or under an artificial light. Water often enough to keep the soil moist, but not wet.

Care

Yellow falling leaves are a common sight on houseplants and tropicals that have been moved indoors for the winter. The plants are shedding their sun leaves and soon will start producing more shade-tolerant leaves. Reduce leaf drop by acclimatizing plants to their indoor location. See the September "Care" section for details.

Your **Weeping Fig Tree** may also be losing leaves. These plants are sensitive to any change in their environment, including the decrease in day length and light intensity. As the light intensity outdoors decreases, so does the light reaching indoor plants. This causes leaves to drop. Fortunately **Weeping Figs** can lose up to **95** percent of their leaves and still recover. Adjust watering for the change in light and wait for new, more shade-tolerant leaves to appear.

Wipe off glossy leaves with a damp sponge or cloth. Dust hairy-leafed plants with a soft cosmetic brush. This improves the appearance and health of your plants.

Now is the time to begin forcing **Poinsettias** and **Christmas Cacti** into bloom for the holidays. These plants need several months of specific growing conditions to initiate flowering. See "Helpful Hints" for details.

Move **Azaleas** to a cool (40 to 50 degrees Fahrenheit), sunny location for the fall. The cooler temperatures help promote bloom. Keep the soil slightly moist. They will need less frequent watering in this cooler environment. Move them to a warmer location after the first of the year. Or try finding a cool, sunny window to grow them year round. I have been rewarded with a scattering of flowers year round under these conditions.

Move **Cacti** and **Succulents** to a cool location for the winter. Grow them under artificial lights in a cool basement or in a sunny window in a cool, vacant room. The cooler conditions will help them adapt to the low light and encourage flowering.

Watering

Adjust your watering schedule to fit the plants' needs in their new growing conditions. Cooler temperatures, decreasing humidity, and lower light all impact watering.

Water soil-less mixes often enough to keep the soil slightly moist. Soil-based mixes should be allowed to dry slightly before watering. Keep the individual plant needs in mind.

Cacti and **Succulents** in cool locations need little water. Water these plants thoroughly, but only often enough to prevent shriveling.

Fertilizing

Stop fertilizing. Plants growing under artificial lights or in soil-less mixes may benefit from an occasional application of a dilute solution of houseplant fertilizer. Only fertilize actively growing plants that show signs of nutrient deficiency.

Pruning

Limit pruning to the removal of dead, damaged, or pest-infested branches. Wait until February or March for major pruning work.

Pests

Watch all your houseplants for uninvited guests that may have hitched a ride on plants that were moved back inside. Isolate pest-infested plants as soon as they are discovered. This reduces the risk of infesting nearby plants.

Remove insects. A strong blast of water followed by insecticidal soap will help control aphids, mites, and immature mealybugs and scale. Repeated applications may be necessary. See January and February "Helpful Hints" for details on insects and their control. Always read and follow all label directions carefully. Never apply pesticides indoors without adequate ventilation.

Remove spotted and yellow leaves as they appear. These fungal diseases often occur when plants are overwatered, overcrowded, or growing in low light. Improving the growing conditions is often enough to eliminate the problem.

Helpful Hints

Reblooming **Poinsettias** and the **Christmas Cactus** can be a fun family activity. The challenge and sense of accomplishment is something the cost of a new **Poinsettia** cannot replace.

Rebloom Poinsettias by modifying the growing conditions.

1 *Provide* plants with 10 hours of light and 14 hours of total darkness each night.

2 *Move* plants to an unused closet or room each night. Even a reading light or streetlight can interfere with the dark treatment and delay flowering. Or *cover* the plant with a cardboard box to keep out any artificial light.

3 Cool night temperatures and slightly dry soil help stimulate bloom.

4 *Continue* dark treatments until the bracts (upper leaves) are fully colored. Then move to an area for everyone to enjoy.

5 Each missed or interrupted dark period delays the blooms by one day. Do not give up if this happens to you. Keep up the event and enjoy your flowering **Poinsettia** for Valentine's Day.

Christmas Cacti *are usually treated like* **Poinsettias** *to initiate flowering.* There has been some recent debate as to whether or not they really need the dark treatment. I find that keeping the plants cool and dry in fall helps promote bloom. You may want to do both to ensure success.

Planning

Cut flowers and flowering plants are traditional hostess and holiday gifts. *Use the following suggestions to add a new look to plant gifts:*

- Dress up a houseplant with cut flowers. Place cut flowers in water picks and stick these into the soil. When the flowers are gone, the houseplant will continue to add beauty.

- Fill a large basket with a collection of potted houseplants and flowering plants. The flowering plants can be replaced as the seasons change or the plants decline.

- Create a changeable planter. Plant several compatible houseplants in a large container. Sink a small, empty pot in one area. Set a small, potted, flowering plant inside this empty container. Replace it occasionally with fresh flowering plants.

- Consider giving a terrarium or dish garden. These are both back in style.

- Consult your local professional florist for other new and creative gift-giving suggestions.

Planting

Purchase and plant **Amaryllis**, **Paper-whites**, and **Hyacinths** for holiday bloom.

See the January and February "Planting" sections in the "Bulbs" chapter for details on forcing **Amaryllis** and **Paper-whites**. **Hyacinths** will need a cold period in order for them to bloom. Follow the planting directions included with the bulbs.

Care

The light and humidity are decreasing, and it is time to move plants to the best possible growing conditions. Move low-light plants closer to the window and those near east- or west-facing windows in front of a south-facing window. Or move them under artificial lights. A combination of natural sunlight supplemented with artificial lights will help your houseplants survive the dark days of winter.

Avoid drafts of hot and cold air. Cold drafts from patio doors and windows can chill the foliage and lead to root rot. Drafts of hot air from heating ducts create lower humidity. The drier air is hard on the plants, but great for mites and aphids.

Continue giving your **Poinsettia** and **Christmas Cactus** 14 hours of total darkness each night. Uncover or move plants into the sunlight each day.

Increase the humidity around your plants. Group houseplants together so that as one plant loses moisture the others will benefit. Or use gravel trays, terrariums, and other techniques described in "The Growing Environment" section in the introduction to this chapter.

Watering

Water houseplants as needed. Always water plants thoroughly. Overwatering is caused by watering too often or allowing houseplants to sit in excess water. *Here is a simple way to deal with the excess water that collects in the plant saucer:.*

1 *Place* a few pebbles in your plant saucers.

2 *Water* plants thoroughly so that the excess collects in the pebble-filled saucer. The pot will sit on the pebbles, not in the water.

3 As the water evaporates, it will increase the humidity around the plant. This will create a better environment for your plants and make less work for you.

Under-watering plants is common during the hectic holiday season. Soil-less mixes turn into a solid block of peat when they are allowed to dry out completely. To re-hydrate, place the pot in a container of water. It will take several hours for the soil to rehydrate. Check plants more often, and water when the soil is slightly moist.

Helpful Hints

Always protect houseplants, flowering plants, and cut flowers being moved from one location to another during cold winter weather.

- Wrap plants in paper or plastic. Remove plastic sleeves as soon as the plants move indoors.
- Move plants in a warm car and never leave them in the car while you run errands.
- Move chilled plants into warmer locations. The cold temperature injury usually appears later as a graying or blackening of the foliage. Remove dead leaves and wait to see if the plants recover.

Fertilizing

Do not fertilize plants. Those growing under lights in a soil-less mix can be fertilized with a dilute solution of houseplant fertilizer.

Check plants for salt buildup. This appears as a crusty, white substance on the soil surface or as white stains on clay pots. Scrape off the crusty salt buildup on the soil, then leach the soil by watering thoroughly. Wait 20 minutes and water thor-oughly again. This helps dilute and wash the salts out of the soil.

Pruning

You can trim off brown tips on **Spider Plants**, **Dracaenas**, and **Palms**. It is not necessary, but it improves the appearance and makes many gardeners feel better.

Pests

Continue to monitor and control pests as needed. A shower will help wash away the dust and some of the insects. Place the pot in a plastic bag before hosing plants down in the sink or shower. This will keep the soil in the pot and out of the drain. See January and February "Helpful Hints" for common insects and their controls.

Diseases: Powdery mildew problems may start appearing with the decrease in light and poor air circu-lations. Move plants to a sunnier window or under artificial lights. Increase the space between plants to increase air circulation. Remove infected leaves to reduce the spread of this disease.

A variety of leaf-spot diseases attack houseplants, especially those that have been overwatered. Reduce watering frequency and remove infected leaves. This is usually enough to correct the problem.

Root rot can also infect overwatered houseplants. Correct your watering habits. As a last resort, you can use a fungicide labeled for use as a soil drench on houseplants. If the rot continues, you will need to remove the infected plant from group plant-ings or discard rotted plants.

Animals: Curb your cat's love for your indoor garden by planting him a garden of his own. A 6-inch pot of **Ryegrass** will be fine. If this does not work, contact your vet or try one of the commercially available cat and dog repellents.

DECEMBER

Planning

Do not worry if you are tired of red **Poinsettias**. You are in luck. You can find curly and variegated Poinsettias, speckled and marbled, as well as pastels and even yellow-flowered varieties.

Planting

You still have time to purchase, plant, and force **Amaryllis** and **Paper-whites** into bloom for the holidays. Flowering plants or "bloom-it-yourself" kits make great gifts for others. See the January and February "Planting" sections in the "Bulbs" chapter for details.

Care

Continue dark treatments for your **Poinsettia** and **Christmas Cactus** until they are in full bloom. Then move them to a cool, bright location where you can enjoy the colorful display.

Wipe dust and insects off glossy leaves with a damp sponge or cloth. Use a soft cosmetic brush to dust off hairy leaves.

Helpful Hints

December often means a houseful of flowering holiday plants. ***Get the most out of your holiday plants by following these simple guidelines:***

1   ***Remove*** plants from protective sleeves as soon as they arrive. ***Bend*** foil edges down so that light can reach all of the leaves, or remove the foil altogether.

2   ***Punch*** holes in the foil to allow excess water to drain out the bottom. Be sure to place the plant on a saucer to avoid water damage.

3   ***Pour off*** excess water or place pebbles in baskets and saucers to prevent plants from sitting in excess water. Keep soil moist and plants in a cool, bright location.

Watering

Water as needed. Keep the soil moist for holiday plants. **Poinsettias** and **Christmas Cacti** like to be slightly dry during the dark treatment. Once flowering, you can keep the soil slightly moist.

Water **Cacti** and **Succulents** growing in cool locations only as often as needed to prevent shriveling.

Fertilizing

Do not fertilize. The low light and poor growing conditions mean plants need very few nutrients.

Pruning

Only remove dead, damaged, or pest-infested branches. Pinch out growing tips of houseplants and **Annuals** that are growing tall and leggy.

Pests

Keep watching plants for signs of insects. Fungus gnats often move in with holiday plants and new additions to the indoor garden. They are annoying but not harmful to the plants. See January "Helpful Hints" for details on controlling these and other insects.

Lawns

Whether you view your lawn as a matter of pride or as something to keep your feet from getting muddy when it rains, a healthy lawn will give you the results you want. Lawns have long been viewed as a status symbol. In ancient times the amount of lawn (cut grass) you owned reflected your wealth. The more money you had, the more sheep you owned; and therefore, the more "mowed" grass you had on your property. Lawns made their way from the castle grounds to urban and suburban landscapes. Now, instead of sheep we have mowers, weed whips, and bagged fertilizer. We spend our weekends mowing, watering, and fertilizing.

Some gardeners feel like slaves to their lawns while others find great satisfaction in managing the turf. Minimize your efforts and maximize your results by matching mowing, fertilizing, and watering to the grass's needs, your quality goals, and time available. Keep the grass healthy and you will reduce the time needed to rid it of insects, diseases, and weeds.

The amount of effort needed to manage your lawn depends somewhat on the level of quality desired and the amount of use your lawn receives. A golf course quality lawn will require more care than a lawn maintained at a lower quality level. A well-used lawn, with space for kid's play and sports, will also require more care than one merely viewed from the porch or only occasionally walked upon. Look at how you use your lawn and what quality level you desire to determine your yearly care schedule.

High-quality lawns with dense weed-free grass will receive the maximum number of fertilizations, four or five times per year, and the most pesticide use. Those interested in a nice looking, less-than-perfect lawn can get by with fewer fertilizer applications and less pesticide use. No matter what quality level you desire, proper care and properly timed management are the keys to building a healthy and attractive lawn.

Selecting the Right Grass

Putting the right plant in the right location applies to lawns as well as to other garden plants. Cool-season grasses are the best choice for Minnesota landscapes. These grasses provide some of the first and last glimpses of green in our cold northern climate.

- **Kentucky Bluegrass** is the most popular lawn grass in Minnesota. It has a fine texture (thin leaf) and a good green color. It is best suited for sunny locations.

- **Fine Fescues** are more shade- and drought-tolerant than **Kentucky Bluegrass**. They look similar to and are generally mixed with Bluegrass.

- Turf-type **Perennial Ryegrass** is quick to germinate and short-lived in Minnesota. It is blended with other grass seeds to provide quick cover until the other grasses germinate. It gradually dies out and is replaced by the desirable grasses over the next several years.

- **Tall Fescue** is a tall, coarse-textured (wide leaf) grass used for high-use areas in full sun to part shade and in dry soils.

Starting a Lawn

A healthy lawn starts from the ground up. Investing time and effort now will save you a lot of frustration in the future. Both seeding and sodding require proper soil preparation for good results. Seeding a lawn takes more time, but it saves you money and increases your selection of grass-seed mixtures. Sodded lawns give you instant beauty at a price. See April "Planting" for directions on installing sod.

To seed a lawn:

1 *Take a soil test* to determine what nutrients and soil amendments should be added to the soil prior to planting. See "General Horticultural Practices" in the book introduction or contact your local county office of the University of Minnesota extension service for soil testing information.

2 *Kill* the existing grass and weeds with a total vegetation killer such as Roundup® or Finale®. Old fields, neglected, or extremely weedy areas may benefit from two applications made two weeks apart. *Read and follow label directions exactly. Increasing the concentration will burn off the tops and not kill the roots. Lower rates will not kill the weeds and make additional applications (more product in the long run) necessary.* You must wait four to fourteen days after treatment before tilling the soil.

3 *Cultivate* the top 6 inches to loosen compacted soil and turn under dead weeds and grass. This is your rough grade. But remember, only *work* the soil when it is moist. Grab a handful of soil and gently squeeze. Tap it with your finger. If it breaks into smaller pieces it is dry enough to till. Working wet soil results in compaction and clods, while working dry soil breaks down the soil structure.

4 *Rake* the area smooth, removing any rocks and debris. Allow the soil to settle. Time, rainfall, or a light sprinkling with water will help the soil to settle.

5 *Fill* in any low spots. *Slope* the soil away from the house and make the final grade 1 inch lower than adjacent sidewalks and drives.

6 *Till* the recommended amount of fertilizer, organic matter, and any other needed amendments into the top 6 inches of the soil. In general, new lawns need 1 pound of actual nitrogen per 1000 square feet and several inches of organic matter such as peat moss or compost. See chart on page 350.

7 *Rake* the soil smooth and make any final adjustments to the final grade.

8 *Spread* grass seed at a rate of 3 to 4 pounds per 1000 square feet for sunny mixes and 4 to 5 pounds per 1000 square feet for shade mixes. (See August "Helpful Hints" for seed selection tips.) Using a drop-type or rotary spreader. *Sow* half the seed in one direction and the remainder at right angles to the first.

Fertilizer Spreaders

Rotary (centrifugal or cyclone) spreader   Drop-type (gravity) spreader

Lawns

9 Lightly *rake* seeds into the top $^1/_4$ inch of soil. *Roll* the seeded area with an empty lawn roller to ensure good seed-to-soil contact. Borrow an empty lawn roller from a friend or rent one from a local tool rental center.

10 *Mulch* the area to conserve moisture and reduce erosion. Use weed-free straw, hay, or floating row covers sold as GrassFast® or ReeMay® for mulch. Cover the area with the row cover and anchor the edges with stones, boards, or wire anchors. Or spread the straw and hay over the soil surface. Apply a thin layer so some of the soil is still visible through the mulch. Thin layers of these materials can be left on the lawn to decompose naturally.

11 *Water* after seeding and frequently enough to keep the soil surface moist, but not soggy. You may need to water once or twice a day for several weeks. Once the grass begins to grow, you can reduce the watering frequency. Established seedlings should still be watered thoroughly, but less frequently.

12 *Mow* the grass when it is one-third higher than your normal mowing height of $2^1/_2$ to $3^1/_2$ inches tall. Cut 4-inch-tall seedlings back to 3 or $3^1/_2$ inches and continue mowing as needed.

Caring for Your Lawn

Proper care is the best defense against weeds, disease, and insects. The three major practices include watering, fertilizing, and mowing. Manage these properly and you will be rewarded with a beautiful, healthy lawn.

- Established lawns need about 1 inch of water per week from rain or irrigation. On clay soils, apply the needed water once a week. Sandy soils should receive $^1/_2$ inch of water twice a week. See July "Helpful Hints" for watering tips.

- Your soil test results will tell you what type of fertilizer to use and the amount to apply for every 1000 square feet. High-quality and high-use lawns require more fertilizer than most residential lawns.

Spreading Seed

Lawns

- Keep the grass 3 to $3^1/_2$ inches high. Taller lawns will be healthier and better able to fight off weeds and disease. Mow frequently enough so that you remove no more than one-third (about 1 inch) of the total height. Leave these short clippings on the lawn. Rake and compost longer clippings, run the mower over long clippings or use a mulching mower to cut them down in size.

Fertilizer Guidelines

Most Minnesota lawns are a blend of **Kentucky Bluegrass**, **Fine Fescues**, and **Perennial Ryegrass**. These lawn areas need 1 to 3 pounds of nitrogen (N) per season. Most soils have high to excessive levels of phosphorus (P) and potassium (K) and need little or none of these nutrients. Select the fertilizer recommended by your soil test or use one high in nitrogen with little or no phosphorus and potassium. Avoid midsummer fertilization on nonirrigated lawns as it can damage turf and encourage weed growth.

To calculate your fertilizer needs:

- Calculate your lawn area by measuring the length and width of each section. Multiply the length times width to find the square footage of that portion of lawn. Approximate the area of irregularly shaped parcels.

- Highly managed and frequently-used lawn areas should receive several applications of fertilizer. Nice looking lawns with less activity can get by with just one or two applications of fertilizers. See the "Fertilization Schedule" on the facing page for more details.

- Calculate the fertilizer needed. Most fertilizer spreaders' settings are based on applying 1 pound of actual nitrogen per 1000 square feet. You can calculate the amount of fertilizer needed with this formula:

Divide 100 by the percentage of nitrogen in the fertilizer that you are using. Multiply that number by the amount of actual nitrogen recommended by the results of your soil test or Fertilization Schedule. This will give you the amount of fertilizer needed per 1000 square feet. Or use the "Common Fertilizers" chart.

- Use low-nitrogen or slow-release fertilizers to avoid burning the lawn.

- Apply half the needed fertilizer in one direction and the remaining half in the other direction. This will reduce the risk of striping and fertilizer burn. Be careful not to overlap or leave the spreader open when making your turns.

Pests

A healthy lawn is your best defense against weeds, insects, and diseases. Mow high, fertilize properly, and water during droughts to keep weeds and other pests under control. If a problem is discovered, find out why it has developed. Correcting the cause, not just killing the pest, will give you better long-term results.

Minnesota Lawns

Fertilization Schedule

Dates and Rates (Actual Nitrogen Per 1000 Square Feet) of Application

Number of Applications	May/June	July	September	Late October
1				1 to 1¹/₂
2	¹/₂			1 to 1¹/₂
3	¹/₂	1		1 to 1¹/₂
4	¹/₂	¹/₂	1	1 to 1¹/₂

Common Fertilizers

Fertilizer Analysis (N-P-K)	Pounds of Fertilizer Needed to Supply		
	¹/₂ lb. N*/1000 sq. ft	1 lb. N*/1000 sq. ft.	1¹/₂ lb. N*/1000 sq. ft.
45-0-0	1.1 (100/45 × 0.5)	2.2 (100/45 × 1)	3.3 (100/45 × 1.5)
24-8-6	2.1 (100/24 × 0.5)	4.2 (100/24 × 1)	6.3 (100/24 × 1.5)
16-4-8	3.1 (100/16 × 0.5)	6.25 (100/16 × 1)	9.4 (100/16 × 1.5)
6-2-0	8.3 (100/6 × 0.5)	16.7 (100/6 × 1)	25 (100/6 × 1.5)

*Actual Nitrogren

Planning

January is the time for resolutions, and maybe one of yours is to hire someone to care for your lawn.

Selecting the right lawn care professional is not just about price. Here are some additional factors to consider:

- Know what services you want performed and contact several companies for cost estimates.

- Ask friends and relatives for recommendations.

- Get a written service agreement. Ask about automatic renewals and penalties for discontinuing the service.

- Pesticides, including herbicides, insecticides, and fungicides, should only be applied as needed. Ask what chemicals they plan to use and why.

- Make sure the company will provide advance notice of chemical applications. This will allow you to get the dog, toys, and lawn furniture away from the areas to be treated.

- Seek a company that belongs to a professional organization, such as the Turfgrass Association, Minnesota State Horticultural Society, Professional Grounds Management Association, or Minnesota Nursery and Landscape Association.

- Ask about the staff's training and qualifications. Do they have any Certified Landscape Technicians (individuals who have demonstrated a standard of competency through a certification program)?

- Ask the company for references from local customers and check with the Better Business Bureau.

- The University of Minnesota Sustainable Urban Landscape Information website has great lawn maintenance advice. Visit www.sustland.umn.edu.

Planting

Still in our dreams for now—so sit back and relax!

Care

Shovel walks and driveways before using deicing salts. This will help reduce damage to lawns and other valuable plants.

Watering

No need to water; the grass is dormant and the ground is usually frozen or covered with snow.

Fertilizing

Do not fertilize. Applying fertilizer to frozen soil can pollute the water. Melting snow and winter rains wash the fertilizer off the frozen soil surface and into nearby storm sewers, rivers, and lakes.

Mowing

Nothing to cut, so enjoy the break!

Pests

Make a note of areas where snow and ice tend to linger. These are prime candidates for snow mold. Damaged turf will be matted and covered with a gray or pink fungus in spring.

Watch for mole activity. These rodents scurry beneath the snow eating weeds, chewing on bark, and wearing trails in the lawn. Be prepared to do a little raking and overseeding in the spring.

Planning

Draw a sketch of the lawn.
Mark areas where water and ice collect, snow is slow to recede, and deicing salts may cause damage. Plan on filling low spots in spring to reduce future drainage problems. Areas where ice and snow collect will benefit from a light raking soon after the spring thaw. Raking also helps reduce snow mold disease. Grass along the driveway and sidewalks will benefit from a thorough watering in the spring to leach (wash) the salts through the soil. Consider using magnesium chloride, calcium acetate or other more plant-friendly deicing compounds.

Helpful Hints

Nothing beats a nice stand of shade trees when it comes to beating the summer heat—unless you are trying to grow grass under those trees, that is! The lack of sunlight and competition for water make it difficult, if not impossible, to grow grass under some shade trees. But you do not have need to sacrifice the shade or give up on the lawn. ***Here are some tips for getting both the shade and the lawn you want:***

· ***Plant shade-tolerant grass seed mixes in these areas.*** They contain a high percentage of **Fine Fescue** grass. This shade- and drought-tolerant grass is the best choice for shady locations.
· ***Plant shade-tolerant groundcovers in heavily shaded areas.*** **Hostas, Pachysandra, Deadnettle (*Lamium*),** or **Variegated Archangel (*Lamiastrum*)** are just a few of the shade-tolerant groundcovers you can try. Start with just a few plants to make sure there is enough sunlight and moisture for the groundcovers.
· ***Mulch densely shaded areas.*** Spread 3 to 6 inches of woodchips under the tree. Keep the woodchips away from the tree trunk. The woodchips improve the growing conditions, while keeping the lawn mower and weedwhip away from the trunk of the tree.

Planting

Do you plan on expanding any planting beds this season? The sod removed (with a sod cutter) to create these beds can be used to repair problem areas in other parts of the lawn. Look at the season ahead. Tentatively plan a block of time when you can do both tasks.

Watering

Watering now is not practical and usually not needed.

Mowing

Mowing is not needed in February—not even when El Niño was around!

Fertilizing

Do not fertilize. Applying fertilizer to frozen soil can pollute the water. Melting snow and winter rains wash the fertilizer off the frozen soil surface and into nearby storm sewers, rivers, and lakes.

Care

This is a great time to take your lawn mower to the repair shop and beat the spring rush.

Pests

Minnesota landscapes, especially those in the southern half of the state, often experience a winter thaw. Use this break to survey the lawn for signs of winter damage.

175

Planning

In March, spring still seems far away. Those up north may still be staring at an endless expanse of snow, while the rest of the state is being teased with a mixture of spring days and snowstorms. *Now is a good time to get your lawn mower ready for the season ahead. Take it to a repair shop, or get out the owner's manual and do it yourself. These are a few of the things that will need your attention:*

- For safety's sake, if you are new at this job, consider asking an experienced friend or relative for help. Always disconnect the spark plug wire when working on your mower.

- Clean or replace the spark plug and air filter.

- Drain the oil from the crankcase of a mower with a four-cycle engine (not needed for two-cycle engines). Refill with the type and amount of oil recommended by the manufacturer.

- Replace bent, cracked, or damaged blades. Sharpen or have a professional sharpen the mower's blades.

- Check the tires for wear and replace them as needed.

- Check for loose nuts, bolts, and screws, both now and throughout the season.

Planting

Try to contain your enthusiasm. It is still a little early to plant grass seed, and sod is usually not available until April.

Care

Get out the rake and start work as soon as the snow and ice melt. Use a leaf rake to fluff and dry the grass to reduce the risk of snow mold. *Remove* any leaves and debris that may have collected prior to the snowfall. Never work on frozen or waterlogged soils. This can lead to damage and death of the grass.

Watering

Watering is usually not needed. In dry springs, *water* areas exposed to deicing salts. This will help wash the salts through the soil and reduce damage caused by the salt. Water grass along sidewalks, drives, and steps. Salt damaged grass won't green up in spring. Water areas of the lawn that were seeded or sodded at the end of last season. This will reduce the stress on the young, developing root systems. Water only if the top 4 to 6 inches of the soil are starting to dry. Make sure any recently seeded repair jobs are kept moist.

Fertilizing

This is a good time to take a soil test. See "General Horticultural Practices" for tips on taking a soil test. Contact your local Extension office for details on taking and submitting soil for testing.

Pests

Lightly *raking* the lawn helps dry out the grass and reduce problems with snow mold. Tamp down runways formed by vole activity over winter. A light tamp is often enough to get the roots back into the soil, allowing the grass to recover. Severely damaged areas may need to be reseeded. Fill in any holes dug by animals or created by winter activities.

Mowing

Mowing is usually not needed. Wait until the grass greens and starts to grow.

Helpful Hints

Should you *core aerate* or *dethatch* your lawn this season? All the neighbors are doing it, so how about you? These practices have become a common part of the lawn care scene. Make sure you have a problem that these practices will solve before renting the equipment or hiring a professional. *Dethatching and core aeration are both used to control thatch.*

- Thatch is a layer of partially decomposed grass plants. It is not caused by short grass clippings left on the lawn to decompose.
- A thin layer, $1/2$ inch or less, of thatch is good for the lawn. It conserves moisture and reduces wear.
- Thick layers, greater than $1/2$ inch, should be removed.

Dethatching machines, called vertical mowers, are used to physically remove the layer of thatch. These machines cut through the thatch and pull it to the surface. This is stressful on the lawn and should only be done in early September or May when the lawn is actively growing. Rake and compost the thatch removed during this process. This is also a good time to overseed thin lawns. Spread the seed over the recently dethatched lawn. The disturbed lawn provides a good surface for the seed to contact the soil and germinate. See September "Helpful Hints" for tips on renovating the lawn.

Core aerators remove plugs of soil from the lawn. They open up the soil surface, allowing the thatch to decompose. Breaking up the cores and spreading the soil over the lawn surface helps speed up the process.

Aeration also reduces soil compaction. Compacted soils are poorly drained, limit root growth, and result in thin, unhealthy lawns. Lawns growing in clay soils or in high traffic areas are subject to compaction. Make sure the aerator cores through the thatch layer and several inches into the soil. This process opens up the soil, allowing air, water, and nutrients to reach the plant roots. Aeration is less stressful on the lawn than dethatching, but it is most effective when done in early September or May.

To prevent thatch from becoming a problem:

- Do not overwater or overfertilize the lawn.
- Avoid excessive use of insecticides that may reduce earthworm populations. Earthworms are nature's aerating machines.
- Leave short clippings on the lawn to decompose. Mulch, or remove and compost long clippings (only those free of herbicides).

Vertical Mower

Planning

Depending on the weather, mowing can begin anytime this month. Make sure your lawn mower is ready to go. See March "Planning" for details on preparing your mower for the season.

You should have a schedule and strategy for accomplishing your lawn maintenance tasks throughout the growing season. Use your gardening journal to record successes, failures, discoveries, pests, and significant weather events encountered this year. This information will help you or your lawn care professional revise and improve your lawn maintenance program in the future.

Do not succumb to ads for fantastic, no-maintenance grasses and groundcovers. If it sounds too good to be true, it probably is. Every living thing, plants included, requires some care and attention. Those that can manage on their own are often aggressive or invasive and can take over your landscape and nearby native areas. See Vines and Groundcovers "Helpful Hints" on page 356.

Planting

This is a good time to repair damaged areas in the lawn. As the grass greens, it will be easier to spot these problems. You can purchase lawn repair kits. These contain the seed and mulch needed to repair problem areas. Remove the dead turf, loosen and amend soil as needed, and then apply the patch. You can make your own lawn patch by mixing a handful of a quality grass-seed mix into a bucket of topsoil. Prepare the soil and spread the seed and soil mixture. Mulch to conserve moisture.

Start laying sod as soon as the snow disappears and the sod is available for sale. Site preparation is the same whether seeding or sodding a lawn.

1 Prepare the planting site and soil as directed in "Starting a Lawn" in the introduction to this chapter. Soil preparation is just as critical for sodding as it is for seeding.

2 Calculate the square footage of the area to be sodded. A roll of sod is usually $1^1/_2$ feet wide by 6 feet long. It will cover 9 square feet.

3 Order sod to be delivered or plan on picking it up just prior to installation,

4 Select freshly cut sod with a good green color. Be sure it is free of weeds and pests. Use sod that has a blend of several grass varieties and is grown on a soil similar to yours.

5 Keep sod in a cool, shady place to prevent it from overheating and drying out. Lay it as soon as possible.

6 Use a driveway, sidewalk, or curb as your starting point. Lay the first row of sod next to the longest of these straight edges. Butt sod ends together and make sure the roots contact the soil. Stagger the seams, as if you were laying bricks. Use a knife to trim the sod to fit.

7 Lay the sod perpendicular to the slope on steep hills. Use wooden stakes to hold it in place.

8 Run an empty lawn roller over the sod. Push it perpendicular to the direction that the sod was laid. Rolling removes air pockets and ensures good root-to-soil contact.

9 Water immediately. Moisten the sod and the top 3 to 4 inches of soil. Keep the sod and soil surface moist until the sod has rooted into the soil below. Continue watering thoroughly, but less frequently once this happens. Mow the sod once it is firmly rooted in place.

Care

Rake out any dead grass and be patient. Wait for grass roots to resprout and surrounding grass to fill in these areas.

Watering

Water newly sodded or seeded areas of the lawn. Keep the soil surface moist in these areas. In dry springs, water areas exposed to deicing salts. This includes the grass along walks, drives, and roadways. Spring irrigation helps wash the salts through the soil and reduces the damage caused by the salt.

Fertilizing

Wait until late May. Fertilizing now means more grass to cut. Lush, succulent spring growth increases the risk of disease and creates more work for you.

Mowing

Start mowing as soon as the grass greens up and starts to grow. Keep the grass at least 2½ inches tall, but preferably 3 to 3½ inches

---

Helpful Hints

Proper mowing is one of the keys to a healthy lawn. Set your mowing height at 3 or 3½ inches tall. Taller grass forms a deeper root system. The stronger plants are better able to fight off insects, disease, and weeds. Mow often enough so that you are removing no more than ⅓ of the total height. This reduces the stress on the plants and results in shorter clippings that can be left on the lawn. These short clippings add nitrogen, moisture, and organic matter to the soil. Vary the direction and pattern of mowing. It reduces the wear and tear on the lawn.

Sod Placement

---

tall. Mow often enough so that you remove no more than ⅓ of the total height. You may be cutting the grass several times a week in the spring.

Pests

Prevent crabgrass problems with proper care. Keep the grass tall, and water during droughts. If this has not worked, you may choose to use a crabgrass pre-emergent. Apply it to problem areas, about the time that the **Forsythia** start to bloom. This is usually mid- to late April. Do not use these products if you plan to seed or overseed the lawn

this spring. Pre-emergents will kill the desirable grass seeds as well as the weed seeds.

Minnesota lawns seldom suffer severe insect damage. Always make sure insects are causing damage before using an insecticide. Unnecessary use of pesticides kills the beneficial insects that help create a good growing environment for the lawn.

This is the time to watch for adult billbugs. These small insects can be seen on the sidewalks. Treat them only if your lawn has suffered from browning or dieback damage that you know was caused by this insect.

Planning

The pace is picking up with time spent mowing, trimming, and planting. Monitor the health and vigor of your grass as you work your way through the landscape. Watch for changes in color, density, and overall vigor. Problems caught early are easier to control. Contact a lawn care professional or your local county University of Minnesota Extension Service for help diagnosing problems.

Planting

This is the second-best time to seed or overseed lawns in Minnesota. (Mid-August through mid-September is the best time.) Proper soil preparation is the key to creating a healthy lawn that can withstand pests and the rigors of Minnesota weather. See "Starting a Lawn" in the introduction for details on preparing the soil and seeding.

Use a grass mix suitable for your light conditions. Use a grass mix containing about 60 percent **Bluegrass**, 30 percent **Fine Fescue**, and 10 percent turf-type **Perennial Ryegrass** for sunny areas. Use a mix with 60 percent **Fine Fescue**, 30 percent **Bluegrass**, and 10 percent turf-type **Perennial Ryegrass** for shady areas. Select a quality grass seed that contains several varieties of each type of grass.

This is still a good time to install sod. See April "Planting" for details.

Care

May is also the second-best time to control thatch and soil compaction. (The best time is in the fall.) Thatch is a brown, spongy layer of partially decomposed grass. Thick layers prevent water and nutrients from reaching the grass roots. Dethatching physically removes this layer of organic matter. Core aeration removes plugs of soil, allowing the thatch to break down. The openings also help repair soil compactions. See March "Helpful Hints" for more details on thatch, core aeration, and dethatching.

Watering

Newly planted lawns need extra attention. Keep the soil surface moist until the sod is well rooted or the grass seed has sprouted. Established lawns need an average of 1 inch of water each week. Spring rains usually provide the needed moisture. You can step in with the sprinkler as needed.

Fertilizing

Late May or early June is the first time to fertilize your lawn. Apply 1/2 pound of actual nitrogen per 1000 square feet. This is equal to 5 pounds of a fertilizer containing 10 percent nitrogen or 3 pounds of a fertilizer with 16 percent nitrogen. See the "Common Fertilizers" chart in the introduction to this chapter for details. Consider using a low-nitrogen slow-release fertilizer to reduce the risk of burn on nonirrigated lawns.

Mowing

Keep the grass at least 2 1/2 inches tall, preferably 3 to 3 1/2 inches tall. Mow frequently so that you remove no more than 1/3 of the total height at each mowing.

Pests

A healthy lawn is the best defense against weeds. Broadleaf weedkillers can be used to get problem areas under control. Creeping Charlie, also known as Ground Ivy, is one of the more common and perhaps most irritating of these weeds. It has round scalloped leaves that smell somewhat minty when crushed. The purple flowers appear in mid-to late May. There is good news for those who are losing the battle. Broadleaf weedkillers containing 2-4D and MCPP (yes, I know you've tried them) will work. Timing is the key. Treat Creeping Charlie when it is in full bloom. Spot treat problem areas only. This will reduce the amount of pesticide used. It may take several years to eliminate the offspring of these weeds.

Insects are not usually a major threat to Minnesota lawns. Sod-webworm feeding can cause thin patches, brown trails, or patchy lawns. Treat these insects only if you find more than 1 per square yard. See June "Helpful Hints" for more information on monitoring turf insects.

Wisconsin's cool, wet springs often increase the risk of lawn disease. Helminthosporium leaf spot and necrotic ring spot (formerly known as fusarium blight) are probably the most common diseases of home lawns. Proper care and over-seeding with resistant grass varieties can minimize the damage. See this month's "Helpful Hints" for more information on these and other turf diseases.

Helpful Hints

Common Diseases:

- Helminthosporium leaf-spot and melting-out diseases cause irregular patches of brown and dying grass. A close look at nearby blades reveals brown to black spots on leaves. As the disease progresses, the patch gets larger and the grass begins to disintegrate and disappear (melt away). Overseed areas with resistant grass varieties. Heavy infestations can be treated with a fungicide labeled for use on turf and melting-out disease.

- Snow mold is most evident in the spring as the snow and ice melt. Infected lawns have small to large patches of white or gray matted turf. The grass thins and is slow to recover in spring. Rake the lawn in early spring, and avoid overuse of nitrogen in the spring.

- Powdery mildew looks as though someone has sprinkled baby powder on the leaves. It is most common on shady lawns in the fall, but it can appear anytime during the growing season. Over-seed shady areas with **Fine Fescue**, or increase the sunlight by thinning the crowns of trees.

- Rust-infected lawns have brown, orange, or yellow spots on the leaves. A walk through a rust-infected lawn will result in red shoes. This is a common problem on newly seeded lawns due to the high percentage of rust-susceptible **Ryegrass**. As the **Bluegrass** and **Fescue** increase, the rust usually becomes less of a problem in the future. Proper care increases turf health and allows it to tolerate the damage. Treatment is usually not needed.

- Necrotic ring spot (formerly known as fusarium blight) appears as circles or irregular patches of dead grass with tufts of green grass in the center. All **Bluegrass** and **Fescue** varieties appear to be susceptible. Overseeding with **Perennial Ryegrass** may help mask symptoms. Proper care and time for the disease to run its course is usually the most successful treatment.

- Fairy ring is not life threatening, but it can cause aesthetic concerns. Infected lawns have rings of dark green, yellow, or dying turf. The rings appear for a short time, disappear, and then return—slightly larger in diameter—later or the next season. During wet periods, mushrooms will appear within the ring. No control is needed (or effective). Water fairy rings during drought to minimize the symptoms.

Planning

As the temperatures rise, grass growth slows. Keep monitoring the lawn for weeds, insects, and disease. Draw a sketch of the lawn area, and record any problems that may require further evaluation or treatment.

Planting

You can still lay sod. Lawns installed now will need a little extra water as the weather turns hot and dry.

Care

A spongy lawn surface may mean you have a thatch problem. Confirm your suspicions with this simple test. Remove several 3- by 3-inch plugs of grass. Take these samples from several areas throughout the lawn. Measure the thatch layer. If it is greater than $1/2$ inch you should consider taking action in the fall. See March "Helpful Hints" for more details on thatch prevention and control.

Watering

Be sure to provide new lawns with adequate moisture. *Established lawns generally need 1 inch of water each week. June rainfall often provides enough moisture.* Water established lawns only as needed. If your footprints remain in the lawn, the color turns a dull bluish-gray, or the leaves start to roll, it is time to water the lawn. Water thoroughly, but less frequently to encourage deep roots for drought tolerance.

Fertilizing

Apply $1/2$ pound of actual nitrogen per 1000 square feet, if it was not done in late May. This is equal to 5 pounds of a fertilizer containing 10 percent nitrogen or 3 pounds of a fertilizer with 16 percent nitrogen. See the "Common Fertilizers" chart in the introduction to this chapter for details. Consider using a low-nitrogen slow-release fertilizer to reduce the risk of burn, especially on nonirrigated lawns.

Mowing

Mow often enough so that you remove only $1/3$ of the total grass height at each cutting.

Removing less leaf surface minimizes the stress on the plant. Keep the grass $2^{1/2}$ to $3^{1/2}$ inches tall. The taller grass shades the soil, keeping grass roots cool and preventing weed seeds from sprouting.

Pests

Check for symptoms and monitor the occurrence and spread of disease. A cool, wet spring means you will be seeing more problems. Proper care and drier weather often are sufficient to stop or slow down the spread of disease. Keep cutting the grass high, water during droughts, and overseed damaged areas in late August or early September. See May "Helpful Hints" for more details.

Insects are not usually a severe problem in Minnesota lawns.

- Greenbugs, a type of aphid, occasionally feed on the grass under trees in southern Minnesota. If you find 30 or more aphids on each grass blade, it is time to treat. Spray the infested areas and the surrounding 6 feet with insecticidal soap.

- Sodwebworm feeding can cause thin patches, brown trails, or patchy lawns. Treat these insects only if you find more than one insect per square yard.

- Turf-damaging grubs are the immature larvae of several different beetles. They feed on grass roots, causing the turf to be uniformly thin, droughty, or dead. Treat only if three or four grubs are found per every 1 square foot of turf sampled.

- Anthills may sporadically appear throughout the lawn. They generally do not harm anything, but just annoy some home- owners. If their activity is damaging the turf roots, or if your family cannot abide their presence, you may chose to use an insecticide. Spot treat to minimize the use of pesticides. Remember, insecticides also kill or reduce the population of the good insects living in the soil. Select an insecticide labeled for use on lawns to control the problem pest. And as always, be sure to read and follow all label directions carefully.

Helpful Hints

Insects do not generally pose a threat to Minnesota lawns. Before reaching for the can of insecticide, make sure insects are really the problem. *Here are some easy tests you can conduct to determine if insects are damaging your lawn:*

- *Flotation Test:* This test is used for chinch bugs. Remove both ends of a coffee can or similar container. Sink the can in the grass at the edge of the dead area. Fill the can with water and agitate the grass. Chinch bugs will float to the surface. Test several areas. Treatment is needed if you find two or three of these insects per test.
- *Irritation Test:* This test will detect sodwebworm larvae. Mix 1 tablespoon of dishwashing detergent in 1 gallon of water. Sprinkle the soapy water over 1 square yard of lawn. Conduct the test in several areas, both damaged spots and areas adjacent to the damaged grass. Check the treated areas several times over the next 10 minutes. Treat if one or more sodwebworm larvae are present.
- *Turf Removal:* This is done to confirm the presence of grubs. Cut out and remove 1 square foot of turf. Check the top 4 to 6 inches of soil for white grub larvae. Replace the sample and keep the soil moist until it re-roots. Treat if three or four grubs are found per 1 square foot of turf.

The warm weather is perfect for most weeds. As grass growth slows, the weeds seem to appear and grow overnight. Do not use herbicides (weedkillers) in the summer. They can damage your lawn when applied in hot, dry weather. New weeds will fill the voids left by the dead weeds faster than the grass. Dig small numbers of weeds or those in bloom. Removing their flowers will help reduce future weed problems. You may be able to convince the neighborhood kids it is fun to pull or "decapitate" weeds. No? Then how about a penny or two for each weed removed?

Dogs often cause brown spots of dead grass in the lawn. Their nitrogen-rich urine acts just like fertilizer burn. The treatment is the same. Thoroughly water the area to dilute the urine and wash it through the soil. It may not be practical, but it is effective. Some gardeners have trained their dogs to go in a specific area. They may have several mulched areas for this purpose. The surrounding grass will eventually fill in these brown areas. Nature and time do heal many landscape problems. I have had mixed reports on some of the new urine-neutralizing products. Several people have reported great success while others find the watering works just as well. Contact your vet for more information.

Planning

Keep evaluating your lawn. Make notes on the areas that need work. Late summer through early fall is the best time to repair, over-seed, and start a new lawn. Use the summer months to find ways to reduce your workload or to make it more enjoyable. Consider creating beds around groups of trees and shrubs to reduce mowing and hand trimming. Eliminate tight areas that are hard to reach with the mower. Write down these ideas in your journal. You can implement them as time allows.

Make plans for lawn care while on vacation. If you plan on being gone more than a week, you will need someone to cut the grass. Vacationing during the hot, dry months of July and August may mean you need someone to water the lawn—or you could just let it go dormant for this portion of the growing season.

Planting

You can still lay sod. Use fresh sod and install it as soon as possible. Stored sod can overheat and damage or kill the grass plants. Once installed, the new lawn will need extra care during this often hot, dry month. Make sure the soil surface stays moist until the sod roots into the soil below. Once rooted, it will still need thorough, though less frequent watering.

Care

Right now, you just want to sustain your lawn. As the heat increases and the weather turns dry, you will need to decide how you will manage your lawn through droughts. Some gardeners prefer to let their lawns go dormant. They stop watering and let the lawns shut down and turn brown during this stressful period. As the weather cools and the rains return, the lawn will green up and begin to grow again. Others choose to keep watering to prolong the growth and green in their lawn. The choice is yours.

Watering

Growing lawns need 1 inch of water per week. You may need to step in and give nature a hand during July and August. In clay soils give lawns a good soaking once a week. Lawns in sandy soils should be watered $1/2$ to $3/4$ an inch twice a week. During an extended drought of three or more weeks, water dormant lawns $1/4$ inch. This is enough water to prevent the plants from drying, while still keeping them dormant. Once the rain returns, the lawn will turn green. Do not water and bring the lawn out of dormancy unless you can maintain a regular watering schedule throughout the drought. Allowing the lawn to go in and out of dormancy several times during the season stresses and can even kill the grass.

Fertilizing

Only irrigated and highly managed lawns can be fertilized this month. Use $1/2$ pound of actual nitrogen per 1000 square feet. This can be accomplished by using 5 pounds of a fertilizer containing 10 percent nitrogen. See the "Common Fertilizers" chart in the introduction for more details. Do not fertilize dormant or non-irrigated lawns. This can damage and even kill the grass.

Mowing

Keep the grass 3 to $3^1/2$ inches tall. Taller grass is more drought-tolerant and better able to compete with pests. Remove no more than $1/3$ of the total height with each cutting. The warmer, drier weather means you will probably be mowing less frequently.

Pests

Proper care is the best defense against pests. Always properly identify the pest, determine if control is needed, and evaluate your options before treating. Nature is the best pest manager for your lawn.

Insects:

- Grub damage becomes obvious during the dry months of July and August. Their feeding causes the turf to be uniformly thin, appear droughty, or die. Only treat if you find three or four grubs per 1 square foot of turf.

- Small patches (2 to 4 inches) of dead grass may indicate billbug damage. Check the soil for the larvae before treating.

- Watch for pale or yellowing turf under trees. Greenbugs, a type of aphid, can cause this type of damage. Treatment is only needed when you find 30 or more greenbugs per grass

blade. Always read and follow label directions before purchasing or using any pesticide.

Diseases are usually less of a concern on home lawns at this time of the year. See May "Helpful Hints" for more information.

Helpful Hints

Improperly watered lawns suffer more problems than those that depend on rainfall as the sole source of water. *Make the most of your efforts by watering properly.*

- Lawns need to be watered when your footprints persist, the grass turns bluish-gray, or the leaves start to roll.
- Lawns will typically need 1 inch of water each week. Water lawns on clay soils once a week. Water lawns on sandy soils with about 1/2 inch of water twice a week.
- Set several straight-sided cans under the sprinkler to measure the water applied. Once filled with the required amount of water, turn off the sprinkler and move it to the next location. Note the pressure used and the time it took to apply the needed water. Now you have an idea of how long you need to water.
- Water early in the day for best results. Watering early reduces disease problems and water lost to evaporation.

To help control weeds, continue to mow high. Taller grass is better able to out-compete the weeds. Continue to dig offensive weeds as time allows. Crabgrass is just starting to appear. Mark locations of problem areas on your lawn map. This will make it easier to target pesticide applications next spring, reducing the amount of chemical you will have to use.

White Grub

Crabgrass

Planning

Early August is often the peak of hot, dry weather. Keep monitoring the health of your lawn. By mid- to late-August, the weather usually begins to cool. This is a good time to review your journal entries, evaluate needed repairs, and make plans for the remainder of the season. *Mid-August through mid-September is the best time to repair, replace, or start a new lawn.* Lawns with 50 percent or more weeds should be replaced. Those with compacted soils, some weeds, or bare spots would benefit from some renovation and repair. See September "Helpful Hints" for details on renovating lawns.

Planting

Begin seeding lawns in mid- to late-August as the weather starts to cool. This is the best time to seed lawns. The soil is warm, so the seeds germinate quickly. The temperatures are cooling and perfect for growing grass. See "Starting a Lawn" in the chapter introduction for details on seeding.

This is also a good time to lay sod. The cooler temperatures promote rooting and mean you will need to water less frequently than lawns sodded in July. See April "Planting" for details on installing sod.

Bare areas can also be repaired. Remove dead grass, amend soil as needed, and roughen the soil surface. Purchase a lawn patch kit or make one yourself. Mix one handful of a quality lawn-seed mix into a bucket of topsoil. Sprinkle this over the soil surface, rake smooth, and mulch. Water often enough to keep the soil surface moist.

Overseed thin lawns. Creating a denser stand of turf will help reduce weeds, fight pests, and improve the overall appearance. See September "Helpful Hints" for details.

Care

The early part of the month is focused on sustaining the lawn. Proper care, whether the grass is dormant or growing, will help the lawn survive the heat and drought often experienced in early August. As temperatures cool, you will notice the improvement in the health and appearance of your lawn.

Watering

Established lawns should receive 1 inch of water when it shows signs of wilting. Use a rain gauge or coffee cans to measure the amount of water applied (see July "Helpful Hints").

Grub-infested, disease-damaged, or stressed lawns should be watered. Watering helps reduce stress and mask pest damage.

Dormant lawns should be left dormant until the drought conditions pass. Give them $1/4$ inch of water during extended (three to four weeks) drought periods. This is enough moisture to keep the grass alive while still allowing it to remain dormant.

New lawns should be watered often enough to keep the soil surface moist. Reduce watering frequency once the sod has rooted into the soil and the grass seed begins to grow.

Fertilizing

Wait until September to fertilize established lawns. Incorporate fertilizer into the soil prior to seeding or sodding new lawns.

Mowing

Keep the grass 3 to $3^1/2$ inches tall. Taller grass is more drought-tolerant and better able to compete with pests. Remove no more than $1/3$ of the total height with each cutting. Start cutting newly sodded lawns as soon as they are well rooted.

Pests

Insects may be more of a problem if the summer has been hot and dry. Continue monitoring for grubs, billbugs, sodwebworms, and greenbugs. Make sure the insects are present and the damage is severe enough to warrant treatment.

Skunks, raccoons, and moles can damage lawns with their digging and tunneling. These critters are searching for big, fat, tasty grubs. Continual damage means they have found a food source and plan to stay. Get rid of the food—the grubs—and you will solve the problem. Squirrels can also be found digging in the lawn. They are storing nuts and seeds for future meals. The damage is irritating, but not a threat to the health of the lawn. Gently tamp down disturbed areas.

Newly seeded lawns are often infected with rust. This fungal disease causes the grass to turn yellow, orange, or brown. The symptoms will soon disappear and the grass will begin to recover on its own. Treatment is usually not needed.

Powdery mildew often appears in August. Like rust, it is more of an aesthetic problem than a threat to the lawn's health. See May "Helpful Hints" for more information on turf diseases.

Helpful Hints

A quality lawn starts with good soil preparation and a quality lawn seed.

- Use a mixture of approximately 60 percent **Bluegrass**, 30 percent **Fine Fescue,** and 10 percent turf-type **Perennial Ryegrass.**
- Seed shady areas with a mixture of approximately 60 percent **Fine Fescue**, 30 percent **Bluegrass**, and 10 percent turf-type **Perennial Ryegrass.**
- All grass seed mixes should contain several varieties of each type (**Bluegrass, Fescue,** and **Ryegrass**) of grass. This increases disease resistance and reduces the risk of losing your whole lawn to a pest infestation.
- Purchase a high quality seed. Select seeds with a high rate of germination. The higher the germination rate, the more viable (living seeds) the mix contains. The purity rate tells you what percentage of the mix is desirable grass seed. The remainder includes other grass seeds, weed seeds, dirt, and chaff. A high percent of purity means you are paying for seeds and not unwanted "other ingredients."
- Seed sunny grass seed mixes at a rate of 3 to 4 pounds per 1000 square feet. Apply shady mixes at a rate of 4 to 5 pounds per 1000 square feet.

Grass	Minimum Seed Germination	Minimum Purity
Kentucky Bluegrass	75–80%	90–95%
Fine Fescue	80–85%	95–97%
Perennial Ryegrass	90–95%	95–98%
Tall Fescue	85–90%	95–98%

Measuring 1-inch of Water

Planning

Labor Day marks the beginning of increased lawn care activity. Cooler temperatures and regular rainfall make this a good time to start a new lawn or repair an existing one.

Planting

Whether you are renovating an existing lawn, starting a new one, or just patching bare spots, early to mid-September is the best time to plant grass seed. The warm soil speeds up germination while the cooler air temperatures aid in growth and development. Do not seed after September 20th. Late plantings do not have time to establish and may be winterkilled.

You still have time to sod. The good growing conditions speed up the root development of newly laid sod.

Care

Now is the time to correct compacted soils and thatch problems. Both problems interfere with root growth and result in thin lawns. Removing the thatch or removing plugs of soil allows water and fertilizer to reach the roots. The actively growing grass will quickly recover from the stress of these operations. (See March "Helpful Hints" for more information on dethatching and core aeration.)

Watering

Water new plantings often enough to keep the soil surface moist. Reduce watering frequency once the grass seeds have sprouted or the sod has rooted into the soil below.

Fertilizing

Apply 1 pound of actual nitrogen per 1000 square feet. This is equivalent to 10 pounds of a 10 percent nitrogen fertilizer. The September fertilization helps lawns recover from the stresses of summer.

Incorporate fertilizer in the soil prior to seeding or sodding a new lawn.

Mowing

Things should start slowing down. See August "Mowing" for more information.

Pests

A healthy lawn is your best defense against pests. Review your maintenance practices to be sure you are mowing, fertilizing, and watering correctly. If not, make needed adjustments. This should always be your first step in pest control.

Weeds:

- Fall is the best time to control perennial weeds, such as dandelions and plantain. The chemicals are usually more effective, and the actively growing grass will quickly fill in the empty spaces.

- Replace lawns that contain more than 50 percent weeds. Starting over gives you quicker and more effective results. Reclaiming a weed-infested lawn often requires more pesticides and gives poor results over a long period of time. Kill the existing lawn and reseed or sod.

- Add a wetting agent or dishwashing detergent to liquid herbicide mixtures. The wetting agent breaks down the surface tension of the water, providing better coverage. Even pesticide coverage helps in the control of waxy leafed, hard-to-eliminate weeds, such as clover and violets.

- Control violets in the lawn with a broadleaf weedkiller containing triclopyr, such as Weed-B-Gon® for difficult weeds. Make the first application in mid-September. Repeat in late October if weeds are still present.

- Wait to treat Creeping Charlie. Late fall applications, after a hard frost, of broadleaf weedkillers will kill this weed. Do not be alarmed if the weed begins to grow next spring. Fall-treated Creeping Charlie often starts to grow but quickly dies. Keep in mind there are hundreds of seeds just waiting to sprout. It may take several years to get this pest under control.

Insects:

Grubs are starting to move deeper into the soil for winter. Complete all grub treatments by September 15th. Only treat lawns that have been diagnosed with a problem that needs control.

Diseases:

The cool, wet weather of fall increases the risk of disease. Watch for leaf spot, mildew, and rust. Fall fertilizations and proper care are usually enough to control these diseases. See May "Helpful Hints" for more on turf diseases.

Helpful Hints

September is a great time to renovate poor quality lawns. Renovation is the last step before replacement. Use this method on lawns that are thin, have lots of bare spots, or are full of weeds. Consider hiring a professional for large jobs. They have the equipment, training, and staff to get the job done efficiently. ***To renovate your lawn:***

1 *Cut* the grass as short as possible. It will act as a living mulch. Rake off and compost clippings.

2 *Remove* the thatch layer if it is greater than $1/2$ inch thick. Use a vertical mower to lift the thatch. Set the revolving blades to slice into the top $1/2$ inch of soil. This will remove the thatch while creating grooves or slits in the soil surface. These slits make a good seedbed. Rake up and compost the debris.

3 *Core aerate* compacted soil to improve drainage. Core aerate in several directions. See March "Helpful Hints."

4 *Spread* grass seed over the renovated area using a broadcast or drop-type spreader. Use 3 to 4 pounds per 1000 square feet of sunny grass-seed mixes or 4 to 5 pounds per 1000 square feet of shady mixes. Apply half the total amount in one direction and the remainder at right angles to the first. Rake for good seed-to-soil contact.

5 *Fertilize* renovated lawns next month.

6 *Raise* the mower back to the recommended 3 or $3^1/2$ inch mowing height. *Cut* the grass once it reaches 4 inches.

Animals:

Skunks, raccoons, and moles damage lawns in their search for food. Continual damage means they have found some tasty grubs and plan to stay. Get rid of the food—the grubs—and you will solve the problem. Squirrels can also be found digging in the lawn. They are storing nuts and seeds for future meals. The damage is irritating, but is not a threat to the health of the lawn. Gently tamp down disturbed areas.

Planning

Many plants are shutting down for the season, but your lawn is still growing full force. Fall is the time when lawns use their energy to spread and develop deeper root systems instead of top growth. This is good for the grass and even better for the mowing crew!

Planting

You can still lay sod to establish new lawns or to repair existing ones. Weed removal and soil preparation are important whether you are repairing a small area or installing a 1-acre lawn. See "Starting a Lawn" in the introduction to this chapter and April "Planting" for detailed tips on preparing the soil and laying sod.

Once in place, *water* the sod often enough to keep the soil surface moist. Reduce watering and begin mowing the sod once it has rooted into the soil below.

Care

Fall has arrived, and you may be tired of raking all those leaves. And, of course, there is that **Norway Maple** that just will not let go of its leaves. Put away the rake and break out the mower. *Shredded leaves make a great amendment for gardens and lawns.*

- *Shred* leaves with the mower the next time you cut the grass. You may need to make several passes with the mower during peak leaf drop. As long as you can see the grass blades, the lawn will be fine. In fact, the leaves add nutrients and organic matter to the soil.

- *Mow* and *collect* the clippings (herbicide-free) and leaves. This makes a great addition to the compost pile or vacant garden. Spade this mix into the top 6 inches of an annual or vegetable garden this fall.

- Or *use* them to mulch the soil around your perennials. Don't use them as a winter mulch over the plants. They mat down, hold moisture, and lead to disease. Save this for straw and evergreen branches, which work better than leaves as a winter mulch over the plants.

- *Store* dry leaves in bags over winter for use next spring. Do not store wet leaves. The weight can be difficult to manage and the smell that develops in the bag will turn most gardeners' noses. You can tuck the leaf-filled bags behind the bushes next to your home's foundation. This is an out-of-the-way storage area that provides added insulation for winter.

Gardeners in the southern part of the state can still *core aerate* the lawn. You get the best results when the lawn has at least four weeks of good growing weather to recover. Do not dethatch the lawn using a vertical mower at this time of the year. The lawn will not have enough time to recover before winter.

Watering

Make sure new plantings are watered. Keep the soil surface moist under newly laid sod. Continue to water thoroughly, but less frequently, once the sod is rooted into the soil below.

Established lawns should be watered when they show signs of wilting.

Fertilizing

Late October is the most important fertilizer application for your lawn.

Apply 1 to 1½ pounds of actual nitrogen per 1000 square feet. This can be obtained by applying 2 to 3 pounds per 1000 square feet of sulfur-coated urea (45-0-0) or $5^{1}/_{2}$ to 8 pounds per 1000 square feet of an 18 percent nitrogen fertilizer.

Use a slow-release nitrogen fertilizer for best results. The actively growing plants will use some of the nutrients now. The unused nitrogen will remain in the frozen soil over winter. As soon as the ground thaws, the grass will begin growing. This fertilizer will be available for the grass early in the season. Avoid winterizing fertilizers that are high in phosphorus and potassium.

Mowing

Keep cutting the grass as long as it keeps growing. Remove no more than $^{1}/_{3}$ of the total height at each cutting.

Pests

Apply a broadleaf herbicide (weed-killer) to Creeping Charlie and other difficult to control weeds in mid- to late October after a hard frost. Make a second application to violets if needed. The triclopyr-containing herbicide will also work on Creeping Charlie and other broadleaf weeds. Spot treat problem areas to reduce the amount of chemicals needed.

Squirrels are still stashing their nuts and bulbs in the lawn for safekeeping. Enjoy all the surprises that appear in the lawn next spring.

Planning

It is almost time to pack away your lawn care equipment. Our work is about done, even though the grass keeps growing until the ground freezes. Though we do not see much happening, there is a lot growing underground. Take one last look at the lawn. Make notes on any needed changes, improvements, or repairs.

Purchase a good snow shovel or snow blower and plant-friendly deicing salt. Removing the snow before salting saves you money and reduces salt damage to the lawn.

Planting

Dormant seeding is risky. You might want to risk a little seed and some time on small areas, but think twice before seeding large areas or new lawns.

- Sprinkle seed over bare or thin areas of the lawn.

- The fluctuating winter temperatures will help work the seed into the soil.

- Don't worry about the snow, it makes the best winter mulch. Hope for consistently cold weather until spring.

Unseasonably warm weather can extend the landscaping season. Sod can be laid as long as the ground is not frozen and the sod is available. Keep the soil surface moist until the sod roots into the soil below. Make sure it is well watered before the ground freezes. Poorly rooted sod is subject to winter drying. Snowfall is the best protection for late-season plantings.

Care

Keep raking leaves. **Norway Maples** and **Callery Pears** are reluctant to give in to winter. *Rake and remove leaves from the lawn. If left on the lawn, large leaves block the sunlight and trap moisture, increasing the risk for disease and death of turf.*

1 *Shred* leaves with the mower the next time you cut the grass. You may need to make several passes with the mower to chop up thick layers of large leaves like **Norway Maple** and **Oak.** As long as you can see the grass blades, the lawn will be fine. In fact, the leaves add nutrients and organic matter to the soil. This is a great way to improve the soil while reducing time spent on lawn care.

2 *Mow* and *collect* the clippings (herbicide-free) and leaves in

your mower's bag. This makes a great addition to the compost pile or vacant garden. Spade this mix into the top 6 inches of an annual or vegetable garden this fall. See October "Care" for additional ideas for using fallen leaves in the landscape.

Watering

Newly planted lawns benefit from regular watering throughout the fall.

Established lawns should only be watered in dry falls when they show signs of wilting.

Drain and pack away the garden hose after the final watering.

Fertilizing

Didn't get the fertilizer applied in October? *There is still time to apply fertilizer in early November before the ground freezes and snow begins to cover the ground.* Apply 1 to $1^1/2$ pounds of actual nitrogen per 1000 square feet. This is equal to 2 to 3 pounds per 1000 square feet of sulfur-coated urea (45-0-0) or $5^1/2$ to 8 pounds per 1000 square feet of an 18 percent nitrogen fertilizer.

Avoid winterizing fertilizer that are high in phosphorus and potassium, the last two of the three numbers on the fertilizer bag. Our soils tend to be high to excessive in these nutrients. Adding more can pollute the ground water and interfere with the uptake of other needed nutrients.

Consider using a slow-release nitrogen fertilizer for best results. The actively growing plants will use some of the nutrients now. The unused nitrogen will remain in the frozen soil over the winter. As soon as the ground thaws, the grass will begin growing. This fertilizer will be available for the grass early in the season before we can get out and fertilize. Have your soil tested if you're not sure. Contact your local University Extension office and see "General Horticultural Practices" at the beginning of the book for more information.

Mowing

Keep cutting the grass as long as it keeps growing or until the snow starts flying. Your final cut does not need to be shorter. *Once the mowing season is over, you can clean up and pack away the mower until next spring.*

Helpful Hints

Now that the mower is safely stored, *it is time to locate, organize, and safely store fertilizers and pesticides.*

- Always leave pesticides in their original containers. It is illegal– and unwise–to transfer them to a different container.
- Pesticides should be stored in a locked area, away from pets and children.
- Store granular formulations in cool, dry locations.
- Liquids should be kept out of direct sunlight and freezing temperatures. Freezing and UV light can diminish their effectiveness.

- Empty the gas tank, or fill it with a gas preservative. The tank can be emptied by running the engine until it stalls. Or add a gas preservative and run the engine for a few minutes to distribute it throughout the gas.

- Disengage the spark plug wire for safety.

- Drain and replace the oil. This should be done at least once a year. Check the owner's manual for specific information.

- Clean off any dirt and matted grass.

- Sharpen the blades or make a note in your journal to do that before the next mowing season begins.

- Buy replacement belts, spark plugs, and an air filter as needed and store them for spring.

Pests

Work on your journal. Record all pest problems encountered this season. Evaluate the possible cause and the solutions tried. Do a little research over the winter to try to reduce future problems.

Watch for voles. These small rodents are active all winter. They scurry across the turf and under the snow in search of seeds, bark, and roots to eat. Protect trees and shrubs from these critters. Lawn damage can be repaired in the spring.

Planning

This is a good time to make a Christmas list. Maybe you need a new fertilizer spreader, an environmentally friendly push mower to work off the winter bulge, or just the promise of a helping hand.

Helpful Hints

Winter, snow, and deicing salts have a major impact on our landscape. Identify any lawn areas that are killed each year by deicing salt. Then evaluate your snow removal technique. Consider alternatives such as adding a border of annuals, expanding the walk, or incorporating some other landscape feature instead of grass in these areas.

Planting

Dormant seeding is risky. You might want to risk a little seed and some time on small areas, but think twice before seeding large areas or new lawns.

- Sprinkle seed over bare or thin areas of the lawn.

- The fluctuating winter temperatures will help work the seed into the soil.

- Do not worry about the snow; it makes the best winter mulch. Hope for consistently cold weather until spring.

Care

All of your hard work can be damaged with a quick toss of deicing salt. A little care now will eliminate the frustration and time needed next spring to repair winter-damaged turf.

- Shovel before applying deicing salt. This reduces the amount of salt needed to control ice on walks and drives. It also eliminates salt-laden snow from ending up on the lawn.

- Use plant-friendly deicing compounds. Calcium chloride is more expensive, but it is easier on your plants. Calcium magnesium acetate is also safe for both concrete and plants. Watch for new, more plant-friendly products entering the market.

- Apply deicing compounds down the middle of walks and drives, avoiding the grass.

- Consider using sand or kitty litter to provide traction and reduce the use of salt.

- Note the areas most impacted by deicing salts. Water these areas in spring to dilute the salts and wash them through the soil.

Watering

No need to water. Drain and store the hose for winter.

Fertilizing

Do not fertilize frozen lawns. Winter rains and melting snow can wash the fertilizer off the frozen soil surfaces and into our waterways.

Mowing

The mowing season is over. (There are some good things about winter!) Clean and store your mower if you have not done so already.

Pests

Take a break!

Perennials and Ornamental Grasses

Perennials have started moving in and taking over many Minnesota landscapes. People have converted their annual gardens and lawn areas to large perennial gardens. English cottage gardens, filled with a collection of colorful blossoms; the New American Gardens, composed of masses of **Ornamental Grasses** and perennials; and mixed borders have started filling Minnesota landscapes.

No matter the garden style, everyone seems to want season-long blooms with no maintenance. While many perennials require less maintenance than other landscape plants, they do require some yearly care. You will need to prune back in the fall or spring and divide occasionally. Some perennials need fertilizing, deadheading, and winter protection. (See Perennials "Helpful Hints" on page 361 for some low-maintenance recommendations.)

Very few perennials bloom from spring through fall. But a well-planned garden can provide year-round interest from the foliage, flowers, and seedpods. Some gardeners, including myself, like to mix a few annuals in with their perennials. Annuals can fill in voids left by winter damage, empty spots between new plantings, and planning mistakes. Use tall cultivars of **Ageratums**, linear-leafed **Zinnias**, and other perennial-looking plants. Or use individual plants, rather than mass plantings, to help them blend into your design.

Planning

The joy of flower gardening is personal expression. I like the subtleties of a mixed border, while others prefer dynamic masses of bloom. Both are fine. Select the style that fits your landscape, interest, and desires. *Try a few of these design ideas to make maintenance easier:*

- Select and plant the right perennial for your growing conditions. A healthy plant will look more attractive, flower longer, and need less care.

- Start small and expand your garden as time allows. Evaluate the time needed for care and maintenance. It is better to end the season wanting more than to be overwhelmed with weeds and work in July.

- Consider using fewer species, but more of them. A garden with ten different types of perennials is easier to maintain than one with 30 different species. Remember, you will have to distinguish each species from the weeds in spring, decide the type of care each species needs, and do the work.

- Plan for year-round interest. You have several options. Use a mixture of spring-, summer-, and fall-blooming perennials in each garden. Or design individual gardens for display at a specific time of the season. Perhaps place the spring garden outside the kitchen window, the summer garden next to the deck, and the fall garden outside the family room. Select the design strategy that best fits your family's likes and habits.

- Include some perennials that provide winter interest and food for wildlife. Add **Ornamental Grasses**, **Rudbeckias**, **Coneflowers**, and other plants that have attractive seedpods.

- Consider the foliage, as well as the flowers, when planning your garden. Some plants, such as **Coralbells,** have attractive foliage all season long. Others, such as **Poppies** and **Bleeding Heart**, fade away in midsummer. And do not forget about fall color. Many perennials, such as **Willow Amsonia**, **Evening Primrose**, and some

Sedums, have colorful fall foliage.

Soil Preparation

Take time to properly prepare the soil before planting. Investing the time and effort up front will minimize future maintenance and pest problems. Begin preparing soil in the spring or fall prior to planting.

1 **Remove** the grass from the area to be developed. Cut it out with a sod cutter, kill it off with a total vegetation killer, or cover the area with black plastic for a season. Select the technique that best fits your time frame and gardening style.

2 **Take** a soil test if you plan on gardening in the existing soil. Wait to take the test if you are creating a garden with purchased topsoil. Contact your local county University of Minnesota Extension Service for soil test information.

3 **Add** 2 to 4 inches of compost, peat moss, or other organic matter to the top 12 inches of soil. The organic matter improves drainage in heavy clay soils, increases water-holding capacity in sandy soils, and adds nutrients.

4 **Only add fertilizer** if it is recommended by your soil test report. Recent research has found that organic matter usually provides sufficient nutrients for perennials. Excess fertilizer can cause poor flowering, leggy growth, and stunted root systems. Use no more than 1 pound of a 10 percent, or 2 pounds of a 5 percent, nitrogen fertilizer per 100 square feet if your plants need a boost.

5 **Level** and rake the soil smooth. Lightly sprinkle with water or wait several days for the soil to settle.

Planting

Purchase perennials as bare-root plants from catalogs or garden centers in 4-inch, 1-gallon, or 2-gallon containers. The smaller plants may look a little sparse at first, but leave sufficient room for these to reach full size.

- **Plant** bare-root perennials as soon as they arrive in spring. If the weather is bad, store them in a cool location—such as a root cellar or refrigerator—until they can be planted outdoors. Keep the packing material around the roots moist.

- **Pot up** any bare-root perennials that have begun to grow. Keep them in a cool, bright location free from frost. Gradually introduce them to the outdoors.

- **Plant** container-grown perennials spring through fall. Do the majority of planting in the spring and early summer. This allows plants to become established before the heat of summer and the cold of winter. Perennials are tough and can be planted just about anytime that proper post-planting care can be provided.

- **Loosen** potbound roots on container plants prior to planting. Use a sharp knife or hand pruners to slice through the rootball in several places. This encourages the roots to grow into the surrounding soil.

- **Place** the plant in a hole the same depth but at least twice as wide as the root system. Avoid shallow planting that causes plants to dry out and deep planting that leads to crown rot and plant death. Fill with soil and gently tamp.

- **Water** thoroughly, wetting the top 6 to 8 inches of soil. Water the planting hole and the surrounding soil. This will encourage rooting beyond the planting hole.

Water

Give special attention to new plantings. Check them every other day for the first few weeks. Water thoroughly when the top 4 to 6 inches

Perennials

of soil start to dry. Gradually increase the length of time between waterings. Provide young plantings with 1 inch of water per week.

- Established perennial gardens can get by with less water. Water thoroughly so that the top 8 inches of soil are moist. This encourages deep, more drought-tolerant roots. Water thoroughly as needed.

- Water early in the day to reduce the risk of disease and the amount of water lost to evaporation. Consider using a watering wand or drip irrigation system to keep the water off the plants and on the soil where it is needed.

- Mulch the soil surface to conserve moisture and reduce the watering frequency. Use a thin layer of cocoa bean shells, shredded leaves, or twice-shredded bark.

Ongoing Care

Overgrown perennials fail to bloom, open in the center, and tend to flop. Dig and divide overgrown perennials in early spring as new growth is emerging or in early September. Most perennials are tough and can be divided at other times during the season as long as proper post-transplant care is provided. *To divide perennials:*

1 *Cut back* mature plants by one-half to two-thirds. This reduces transplant stress and makes the job easier for you.

2 Use a shovel or garden fork to dig up the perennial. *Dig out* the clump and place it next to the hole. Use a knife or two shovels to divide the clump into several pieces.

Methods of Dividing Perennials

3 *Prepare* the new planting location. Amend the existing area by working compost, peat moss, or other organic matter into the soil. Plant one of the divisions in the original location. Use the remaining pieces in other gardens or for trading with friends.

4 *Water* thoroughly. Check every few days, and water whenever the top 4 inches of soil begin to dry.

Pruning

Control plant height, reduce floppiness, and delay flowering with proper pruning. Cut back **Sedum**, **Coneflower**, **Asters**, and **Mums** early in the season. This encourages shorter, stiffer branches. Stop pruning by July to avoid delaying bloom until frost.

Pinch out the growing tips on small plants or prune back taller plants halfway down the stem. Prune above a set of healthy leaves. See May and June "Pruning" for details on pruning specific perennials.

Pinching Back

Perennials

Deadhead—remove faded flowers—to lengthen bloom time and improve the appearance of some perennials. Deadheading allows the plant to put energy into forming new flowers instead of setting seed. Stop deadheading at the end of bloom time to encourage seed formation when you want bird food or winter interest.

- Use a garden scissors or hand pruners to make the cuts. Remove the flower stem just above the first set of leaves or side shoots.

Deadheading

Pinching Back

- Prune back further on the stem after the second flush of flowers. This encourages branching and new, more attractive foliage.

- If you're tired of deadheading, turn to the Perennials "Helpful Hints" on page 361 for a list of perennials that do not require deadheading.

Pests

Perennials are fairly pest free. Minimize problems by doing the following:

- Select the most pest-resistant species and varieties available. Plant them in a location with the right type of soil and light conditions as specified on the label.

- Provide proper care to keep the plants healthy and better able to resist plant damage.

- See May through August "Pests" for more information on pests and their control.

To keep weeds under control, try the following suggestions:

- Start with a weed-free garden. Take time to control weeds before they take control of your garden. Eliminate quackgrass, ground ivy, and other perennial weeds prior to planting. Spray the actively growing weeds with a total vegetation killer. Wait four to fourteen days (check label) before tilling and preparing the soil.

- Spot treat invasive weeds as they appear. See July "Helpful Hints" for tips on controlling perennial weeds in an established garden.

- Mulch the soil with shredded leaves, cocoa bean shells, or twice-shredded bark to suppress weed seeds.

- Be careful using pre-emergent weedkillers to control weed seeds. They can prevent some perennial reseeding and may injure some plants.

- Pull or lightly cultivate young weed seedlings as soon as they appear. Remove all weeds before they go to seed. This means several hundred fewer weeds to pull next season.

- Visit the Yard and Garden website each month. You'll be kept up-to-date by reading their electronic newsletter as well as specialized pages on insects and diseases. Go to www.extension.umn.edu, then click on Yard and Garden Line.

Minnesota Perennials

Common Name (Botanical Name)	Hardiness	Light	Bloom Time	Comment
Artemisia (*Artemisia*)	2 to 4	Full sun	Summer	Grown for foliage, not flowers. Needs well-drained soil.
Aster (*Aster* species)	2 to 4	Full sun	Late summer to fall	2 to 5 feet tall. Prune back to 6 inches through June to control height. Good fall interest.
Astilbe (*Astilbe* species)	3 to 4	Part to full shade	Summer	1 to 4 feet tall. Good color for shade garden; attractive foliage all season. Needs moisture.
Balloon Flower (*Platycodon grandiflorus*)	3 to 4	Full sun	Midsummer to early fall	2 to 3 feet tall. Balloonlike flower buds. Pinch back in early June to encourage branching. Plant is late to emerge in spring.
Black-Eyed Susan (*Rudbeckia*)	3 to 4	Full sun	Summer and fall	2 to 3 feet tall. Attractive flowers and seedpods for winter. Quickly fills in available space.
Bleeding Heart (*Dicentra spectabilis*)	3 to 4	Full to part shade	Spring	2 to 3 feet tall. Foliage dies back in midsummer. *D. eximia* is smaller with good foliage all season; it repeats bloom throughout the season.
Bugbane (*Cimicifuga racemosa*)	3 to 4	Part shade	July	4 to 6 feet tall with white bottlebrush blooms. Nice summer bloomer for shade. *C. simplex* is a fall-blooming species.
Butterfly Weed (*Asclepias tuberosa*)	4	Full sun	Summer into fall	18 to 30 inches tall. Plant in well-drained soil. Slow to establish from transplants. Allow seedlings to develop where they decide to thrive.
Columbine (*Aquilegia* species)	3 to 4	Full to part sun	Late spring to early summer	1 to 3 feet tall. Attracts butterflies and hummingbirds. Prune back miner-infested foliage for a fresh look.
Coralbells (*Heuchera* species)	3 to 4	Full to part sun	Spring to summer	12 to 15 inches tall and wide. Nice foliage and small, bell-shaped flowers. Purple foliage types scorch in full sun.
Coreopsis (*Coreopsis verticillata*)	3 to 4	Full sun	Mid-June to frost	2 to 3 feet tall. Attractive foliage and yellow blooms. Low maintenance; no deadheading needed on young plants.
Corydalis (*Corydalis lutea*)	4	Part shade	Late May to frost	Nonstop yellow bloom. Either thrives and spreads or fails to survive. Invasive.
Daylily (*Hemerocallis* species)	3 to 4	Full to part sun	Summer to fall	1 to 4 feet tall. Tolerates a wide range of soils. Select repeat bloomers or a variety of cultivars for season-long blooms.

Minnesota Perennials

Common Name (Botanical Name)	Hardiness	Light	Bloom Time	Comment
Gayfeather (*Liatris* species)	3 to 4	Full sun	Midsummer to fall	2 to 3 feet tall. Prefers moist, well-drained soils to dry soils. Attracts birds and butterflies.
Geranium (*Geranium sanguineum*)	3 to 4	Full to part sun	Summer	6 to 15 inches tall. Deadhead or clip back by 4 inches after main bloom.
Hosta (*Hosta* species)	3 to 4	Full to part shade	Summer or fall	Grown for foliage. Watch out for slugs, earwigs, rabbits, and deer.
Oriental Poppy (*Papaver orientale*)	3 to 4	Full to part sun	Late spring to early summer	2 to 4 feet tall. Feathery foliage and paperlike flowers. Foliage dies early in the season; cut back for regrowth or mask with nearby plantings.
Peony (*Paeonia* hybrids)	3 to 4	Full sun	Early to late spring	3 feet tall. Good foliage all season with red to purple fall color. Flowers for fragrance and cutting.
Phlox (*Phlox* species)	3 to 4	Full sun	Spring or summer	Creeping, running, or upright types. Well-drained soils. Deadhead for repeat blooms.
Purple Coneflower (*Echinacea purpurea*)	3 to 4	Full sun	Summer to fall	2 to 4 feet tall. Good for well-drained to dry soils. Good winter interest and food for birds.
Russian Sage (*Perovskia atriplicifolia*)	4	Full sun	Midsummer to fall	3 to 5 feet tall. Silvery gray foliage and blue flowers; fragrant. Cut back to 4 to 5 inches in late March.
Salvia (*Salvia* species)	3 to 4	Full to part sun	Summer	2 to 3 feet tall. Deadhead for continuous bloom. Prune back to prevent floppiness. Leave standing for winter hardiness.
Sedum (*Sedum* species)	2 to 4	Full to part sun	Summer to fall	3 inches to 2 feet tall. Various foliage colors and textures. Some have fall color and winter interest.
Shasta Daisy (*Chrysanthemum × superbum*)	4	Full to part sun	Summer to frost	1 to 3 feet tall. Divide every other year for improved hardiness and vigor.
Veronica (*Veronica* species)	2 to 4	Full to part sun	Late spring to summer	4 to 36 inches. Deadhead for repeat blooms. Divide floppy and over-grown plants every two to three years.
Yarrow (*Achillea filipendulina*)	3 to 4	Full sun	Early summer to early fall	6 to 36 inches. Clump forms. Long-lasting blooms. Excellent for drying.
Yucca (*Yucca filamentosa*)	4	Full sun	Mid- to late summer	2- to 3-foot-tall foliage and up to 12-foot-tall blooms. Evergreen foliage; often a biennial bloomer.

Minnesota Ornamental Grasses

Common Name (Botanical Name)	Hardiness	Light	Bloom Time	Comment
Blue Fescue (*Festuca cinerea*)	4	Full sun	Midsummer	12-inch clump grass with blue-green foliage; evergreen. Needs well-drained soil. Salt tolerant.
Blue Oat Grass (*Helictotrichon sempervirens*)	4	Full sun	Summer	2 to 3 feet tall; wide clump grass. Blue-green foliage; evergreen. Tolerates clay soil.
Feather Reed Grass (*Calamagrostis × acutiflora*, 'Stricta')	4	Full to part sun	Midsummer	4 to 5 feet; upright clump. Prefers well-drained soils, but tolerates moist soils. Salt tolerant. Has winter interest.
Hakonechloa (*Hakonechloa macra*, 'Aureola')	4	Part shade	Late summer	2 feet tall and wide. Small mound of variegated foliage that combines well with **Hostas**.
Little Bluestem (*Schizachyrium scoparium*)	3 to 4	Full sun	Fall	$1/2$- to 3-foot-tall native grass. Needs well-drained soils. A fine-textured grass that is good for naturalized and perennial gardens.
Miscanthus (*Miscanthus sinensis* species)	4	Full sun	Fall	3 to 7+ feet tall. Good vertical and winter interest in any landscape.
Moor Grass (*Molinia caerulea*)	4	Full to part sun	Midsummer	1- to 2-foot-tall foliage and 5- to 8-foot-tall blooms. Light, airy, see-through blooms.
Spike Grass (*Spodiopogon sibiricus*)	3 to 4	Full sun	Summer	4 to 5 feet tall. Fall color. Falls apart in winter.
Switchgrass (*Panicum virgatum*)	3 to 4	Full to part sun	Mid- to late summer	5- to 6-foot-tall native grass. Tolerant of a wide range of soil conditions. Spreads quickly by roots and seeds. Consider using one of the tamer cultivars for small areas.

Planning

Pack away the holiday decorations and break out the photos, video, and journal of last year's gardens and landscape. Review these materials before you start planning this year's additions. Look for areas to convert to perennial gardens as well as locations for adding a few new plants. See February "Planning" for more ideas on designing perennial gardens.

Planting

Perennials can be started indoors much like annuals. Some seeds need to be *stratified* (a cold treatment) for weeks, *soaked* in tepid water overnight, or *scarified* (the seed coat scratched) prior to planting. Check the label directions for seed treatment, timing, and planting directions. See the January and February "Planting" sections in the "Annuals" chapter for details on starting plants from seed.

Care

Winter mulch helps protect plants from fluctuating temperatures. Nature provides the best mulch—snow—for much of central and northern Minnesota. Lend

nature a hand if this is not the case in your area.

- Apply winter mulch after the ground freezes. Some years the ground freezes by Thanksgiving, while other years it does not freeze until January. The goal is to prevent temperature extremes caused by winter thaws and fluctuating spring temperatures—*not* to keep the soil warm.

- Recycle your holiday trees and trimmings by converting them into windbreaks and mulch. Cut branches off the trees and lay them over your perennial gardens.

- Relax and enjoy the scenery if nature mulched the garden with snow. Keep a few branches handy in case there is a winter thaw and nature's mulch disappears. I often place a few holiday trees in a snow bank for storage. They provide shelter for the birds and easy storage, just in case I need to convert them into mulch.

Watering

The ground is frozen, so there is no need to break out the sprinkling can.

Fertilizing

Perennials and other outdoor plants should not be fertilized while the ground is frozen.

Pests

Check for tracks, chewed bark, and other signs of vole (meadow mouse) damage. High vole populations may start nibbling on the roots of **Siberian Iris** and **Hostas**. Chipmunks and squirrels can also damage perennials by digging up the plants and leaving the roots exposed to cold winter temperatures. There is not much you can do when the plants are buried in the snow. Next year, plan ahead and try to prevent the damage. See November "Pests" for information on managing voles.

Pruning

No need to prune. Enjoy the seedpods, form, and winter interest provided by the perennials. Note areas that need a little lift. Perhaps you need a few more perennials or the addition of dwarf conifers, small trees, or ornamental shrubs.

Helpful Hints

Consider adding a few of the Perennial Plants of the Year. These plants were selected by members of the Perennial Plant Association for their low maintenance, ease of propagation, multi-season interest, and suitability to a wide range of climates. See www.perennialplant.org for more information. Past winners of the Perennial Plant of the Year include:

- 1990 **Native Creeping Phlox** (*Phlox stolonifera*): This winner is hardy in zones 4 through 8. It grows 6 to 12 inches tall and 12 inches wide with blue flowers in spring. Grow in part shade to full sun for best results.

- 1991 **Palace Purple Alumroot** (*Huechera micrantha*, 'Palace Purple'): The 1991 winner is hardy in zones 4 through 9. It grows 15 to 18 inches tall and wide. It is grown for its attractive greenish-purple foliage that looks best when grown in part shade.

- 1992 **Moonbeam Coreopsis** (*Coreopsis verticillata*, 'Moonbeam'): This threadleaf coreopsis is rated hardy in zones 4 through 8, though it does not always prove this hardy, especially in heavy soils. The plants produce creamy yellow flowers summer through fall on 18- to 24-inch-tall plants.

- 1993 **Sunny Border Blue Speedwell** (*Veronica*, 'Sunny Border Blue'): The dark green, wrinkled leaves make a nice contrast to the blue spike flowers on this Speedwell. The plant produces flowers throughout the summer in zones 3 through 8. Divide every three or four years to keep it vigorous and long blooming.

- 1994 **Sprite Astilbe** (*Astilbe*, 'Sprite'): This Astilbe has lacy leaves and a late bloom of pale pink flowers that make it a nice addition to the shade garden. Hardy in zones 4 through 8, it grows 20 inches tall and up to 36 inches wide.

- 1995 **Russian Sage** (*Perovskia atriplicifolia*): The fragrant silvery foliage combined with the airy blue summer flowers makes this plant a good addition to many perennial gardens. The plant is hardy in zones 4 through 9 and reaches heights of 4 to 5 feet. Grow in full sun with well-drained soil.

- 1996 **Husker Red Beardstongue** (*Penstemon digitalis*, 'Husker Red'): The maroon foliage of this winner is topped by white flowers, tinged pink in midsummer. It is hardy throughout the state and should be grown in full sun and well-drained soils.

- 1997 **May Night Salvia** (*Salvia*, 'May Night'): This Salvia was selected for the deep indigo flowers produced in summer on 18-inch-tall plants. It is hardy in zones 3 through 8 and grows best in full sun.

- 1998 **Magnus Purple Coneflower** (*Echinacea purpurea*, 'Magnus'): This winner has large, rosy purple flowers with non-drooping petals. It grows to 4 feet tall and is hardy throughout the state. Grow in full sun for best results.

- 1999 **Goldsturm Black-Eyed Susan** (*Rudbeckia fulgida* var. *sullivantii*, 'Goldsturm'): This variety is a nice compact (24 inches tall), powdery mildew resistant Rudbeckia with bright yellow flowers. Blooms through fall and is hardy throughout the state.

- 2000 **Butterfly Blue Pincushion Flower** (*Scabiosa columbaria*, 'Butterfly Blue'): This season-long bloomer tends to bloom itself to death. Not reliably hardy in Minnesota, it does put on a good show in its first and possibly only season. Grow this 12-inch-tall plant in full sun and well-drained soils.

- 2001 **Karl Foerster Feather Reed Grass** (*Calamagrostis* × *acutiflora*, 'Karl Foerster'): This winning grass is a nice grass for small and large landscapes. It grows 4 to 5 feet tall and 2 feet wide and flowers in early summer. This tough grass grows best in full sun and is hardy in zones 4 through 8.

Planning

Continue to review photos and videos of last year's landscape. Start sketching areas you would like to add perennial gardens. Locate the garden in areas that have good soil drainage and that receive sufficient sunlight for the plants you want to grow. *Some additional tips for developing the plan for your perennial garden include:*

- Create perennial borders by designing planting beds in front of hedges, walls, or buildings. Island beds are surrounded by turf or pavement. I find these a little more formal in appearance.

- Make sure all parts of the garden can be reached for maintenance chores. Add steppers or walkways in large gardens for easier access.

- Check out catalogs for newer and harder to find perennials. Catalogs are also a great source of information. If you do not currently receive catalogs, surf the Internet or order the book *Gardening by Mail*. Once you order a few catalogs, a hundred others will follow.

- Plan for year-round interest. Try using a variety of perennials that bloom at different times in one garden or create several different gardens that each peak at different times of the season.

- Create dramatic impact by placing plants in large masses and drifts. These large sweeps of color will be visible from great distances.

- Use a mixture of bulbs, perennials, shrubs, and small trees to take advantage of all planting and vertical space.

Once you have a plan, you can start ordering plants and seeds. Talk to friends to see if they want to share an order. This is a great way to get the benefits of quantity discounts without having to order more perennials than you can fit into your landscape.

Planting

Start perennials from seed indoors the same way you grow annuals. The soil needs to be warm and moist. Check seed packets and garden catalogs for specific information on starting times and seed treatment requirements. Grow seedlings under lights for stronger and stouter plants. See January and February "Planting" in the "Annuals" chapter for details on building your own light stand and growing plants from seeds.

Care

Transplant seedlings from flats into individual containers as soon as the first set of true leaves appear. Adjust your watering schedule to fit plant needs. Continue to keep the soil moist, but not wet.

Check winter mulch if the snow has disappeared. It can always be added after snow melts. Remember, the goal is to keep the soil temperature consistent and avoid those January and February thaws.

Monitor plantings for frost heaving caused by the freezing and thawing of unmulched gardens. The fluctuating temperatures cause the soil to shift and often push shallow-rooted perennials right out of the soil. Gently tap these back into the soil as soon as they are discovered. Make a note to mulch these areas next fall after the ground lightly freezes.

Watering

Check perennial seedlings growing indoors every day. Keep the soil moist, but not wet. Insufficient water can stunt and kill seedlings while excess moisture can cause rot.

Fertilizing

Fertilize young seedlings with a dilute solution of a complete fertilizer every other week.

Pests

Avoid damping off (a fungal disease) of seedlings by using sterile containers and seed starter mix. Infected plants suddenly collapse and rot at the soil line. Remove any diseased seedlings as soon as they appear. Apply a fungicide as a soil drench to infected plantings. Make sure the product is labeled to control damping off disease on perennial seedlings.

Continue monitoring for rodent and animal damage. See January "Pests" for more information.

Pruning

Be patient. Wait for the worst of winter to pass before cleaning out the garden. Many borderline hardy perennials, such as **Salvias**, seem to survive better when the stems are left standing. The standing plant stems and the snow help provide extra winter insulation.

Helpful Hints

My planting list always seems small until it is time to plant. At that point, I seem to have more plants than available space! Luckily, I can always find a willing gardener to take the extras off my hands.

Avoid overbuying and the temptation to overplant by buying the right number of plants for the available space. Consider planting groups of odd-numbered plants (one, three, five) for a more informal appearance. Use larger groupings for a bolder display of color. *To calculate the number of plants you will need:*

1 *Measure* the length and width of the garden. Multiply these numbers for the total square footage of the perennial garden. This will give you an idea of the total space available for planting.

2 Now *review* your garden design. *Calculate* (length times width) the planting area of each drift, mass, or cluster of plants. Then evaluate the area you have for each plant.

3 *Check* the space requirements of the individual plants. Use the spacing chart below to calculate the number of plants you will need.

4 *Multiply* the square footage of the planting area times the number of plants needed per square foot to get the number of plants needed for your garden. For example, if your garden is 100 square feet, and you decide to cover 9 square feet with **Spike Speedwell** at 18 inches apart, then your calculation would be:

9 square feet × 0.45 = 4 plants of Spike Speedwell

Plant Spacing	Number of Plants Per Square Foot
12 inches	1.0
15 inches	0.64
18 inches	0.45
24 inches	0.25
36 inches	0.11

Planning

Get out your garden journal and start watching for the first signs of spring. Take one last look at the winter garden and make notes on any changes that should be made. Now check this against your planting plans for this year. Make any needed adjustments.

Remember to keep your plans simple if you are a beginner gardener or one with limited time. Gardens with fewer species, but more of each species, are easier to maintain. Those with botanical zoos (that's me!) need to spend a little more time giving the wide range of plants the care they need.

Finalize your plant list. Include the number of each plant species that you need. See February "Helpful Hints" for details on calculating this number. A plant list is like a grocery list: they both keep you from buying the wrong items or more than you need. You may still succumb to the temptation of new plants, but the list will help you keep overbuying to a minimum.

Planting

Starting plants from seeds may be the only way you can get some of the newer and harder-to-find perennial varieties. Check the catalogs and seed packets for starting times. *Continue planting seeds and transplanting seedlings.*

- Take a soil test of new garden areas. Follow the test results to ensure that you are adding the right amounts and types of fertilizer and organic matter to your garden. Soil test information is available from your local county office of the University of Minnesota Extension Service.

- Wait until the soil thaws and dries before getting out the shovel. Working wet soil causes damage that takes years to repair. Be patient and keep looking at those garden catalogs and planting plans.

- Most catalogs send bare-root plants just prior to the planting time for our area. Dormant plants can be planted directly outdoors if the soil is workable.

- Sometimes the plants arrive early or winter stays late. Store dormant bare-root plants in a cool, dark location. A root cellar or refrigerator works fine. Keep the roots moist.

- Pot up bare-root plants that started to grow during shipping or storage. Grow these plants indoors in a sunny window or under artificial lights. Move outside after the danger of frost.

Care

Continue to check unmulched gardens for signs of frost heaving. Replant any perennials that were pushed out of the soil.

Wait until temperatures consistently hover near freezing before removing the mulch. This is usually late March in the southern part of the state and early April in the north.

Remove the mulch if plants are starting to grow. Keep some handy to protect the tender tips of early sprouting **Hostas**, **Primroses**, and other early bloomers that may be damaged by a sudden drop in temperature.

Watering

Check seedlings every day. Keep the soil moist, but not wet. As the plants grow and develop larger root systems they will need less frequent watering.

Water potted bare-root perennials often enough to keep the soil moist, but not wet. Continue to water thoroughly but less frequently as the plants begin to grow.

Keep the packing material around the roots of stored bare-root plants moist.

Fertilizing

Take a soil test of new garden areas as soon as the ground thaws. Retest the soil in established gardens every three to five years or when problems develop.

Pests

Continue to monitor for damping off in seedlings. Watch for collapsing seedlings and stem rot at the soil line. See February "Pests" for management strategies.

Pruning

It is time to get busy cleaning up the garden!

• Remove any stems and seedpods left for winter interest.

• Cut back **Ornamental Grasses** before the new growth begins. Use a weedwhip, hedge shears, or hand pruners to clip the plants back to several inches above the soil. Smaller grasses, such as **Blue Fescue** and **Blue Oat Grass**, can be clipped back or left intact. The new growth will quickly cover the old leaves in the spring.

Helpful Hints

Cleanup of large perennial gardens can be a fair amount of work. I find it comes in late March when most of us are anxious to get busy outdoors and are not yet bored with maintenance tasks. Spring cleanup is also a great uncovering and discovery of the first signs of life in the garden.

Use the proper tool to make the cleanup job easier on your back.

• Hand pruners will take care of most of the cleanup jobs. Use these to cut back perennials and sub-shrubs such as **Russian Sage** and **Butterfly Bush**. I do break out the loppers on some of the larger and harder-to-reach stems.

• Use an electric hedge shear or weedwhip with a rigid plastic blade for mass planting of perennials and grasses.

Compost pest-free materials. See "General Horticultural Practices" at the beginning of the book.

• Prune back **Russian Sage** and **Butterfly Bush** to several inches above the soil. Both plants (often classed as sub-shrubs) usually die back in winter. Use a lopper or hand pruners to cut stems above an outward facing bud.

• Cut back only the dead tips of **Candytuft**, **Lavender**, and **Thyme**. Cut them back even further in late spring if the plants become leggy.

• Remove dead foliage and stems of all perennials. Be careful not to damage the leaves of early emerging perennials during the cleanup process.

• Remove only the dead leaves on evergreen perennials, such as **Lungwort** (*Pulmonaria*), **Barrenwort** (*Epimedium*), and **Coralbells** (*Heuchera*). This makes a more attractive display as the new foliage fills in.

• Remove dead foliage on **Lamb's Ear**. The old leaves tend to mat down over winter and will lead to rot if not removed.

Planning

Take a walk through your landscape. Note what survived and what may need replacing. Adjust your landscape plans to accommodate these changes.

Start a bloom chart in your garden journal. Record the name and bloom time of various plants in the landscape. This will help you fill any flowering voids when planning next year's additions.

Planting

Start the planting process by properly preparing the soil.

1 *Remove* the existing grass with a sod cutter. Use this to patch problem areas in the lawn. Or treat the grass with a total vegetation killer. The grass and weeds must be actively growing for these chemicals to be effective. Wait four to fourteen days (check the label) before completing soil preparation.

2 *Work* the soil when it is moist, but not wet. Grab a handful of soil and gently squeeze. Tap on the clump you just formed. If it breaks into smaller pieces, it can be worked. If it stays in a clump, it is too wet; wait a few days before working the soil.

3 *Add* 2 to 4 inches of organic matter to the top 8 to 12 inches of soil. Use compost, peat moss, or aged manure to improve the drainage of clay soil and to increase the water-holding capacity of sandy soil.

4 *Follow* soil test recommendations for fertilizer. Recent research indicates that amended soils need little if any fertilizer. Use a starter solution at planting and wait to see if more is needed.

5 *Rake* the garden smooth and allow the soil to settle. Lightly sprinkle the prepared site with water to speed up settling.

Begin planting once the soil is prepared and the plants are available. This is usually the middle to the end of the month in southern areas and late April to early May in the northern areas. Purchase plants as bare root, field grown in pots, or greenhouse plants. See May "Planting" and this month's "Helpful Hints" for tips on transplanting.

Care

Continue removing winter mulch. Let the weather and plant growth be your guide. Remove mulch as temperatures consistently hover near or above freezing. Check under mulch for plant growth. Remove mulch as soon as plants begin growing. Keep some handy to protect tender plants from sudden and extreme drops in temperature. Use a cold frame for starting seeds outdoors and hardening off transplants. Check the cold frame daily. Vent by opening the lid when temperatures get too warm. Close the lid in late afternoon to keep plants warm during the cold nights. Water plants as needed. See March "Helpful Hints" in the "Annuals" chapter for more details on making and using a cold frame.

Watch for late-emerging perennials, such as **Butterfly Weed**. Use a plant label or consider adding spring-flowering bulbs next fall to mark their location. This will help you avoid damaging them in the spring.

Watering

Thoroughly water transplants and divisions at the time of planting. Water when the top few inches of soil begin to dry. Always water thoroughly enough to wet the top 4 to 6 inches of soil. Reduce watering frequency as the plants become established.

Fertilizing

Perennials grown in properly amended soil need very little fertilizer. Always follow soil test recommendations. A starter solution of fertilizer (follow label directions) can be used to give new transplants a bit of a boost.

Spread several inches of compost or aged manure over the surface of existing gardens. Lightly rake this into the soil surface. Apply organic matter every three to four years to keep perennials healthy and well fed.

Pests

Complete garden cleanup. Sanitation is the best defense against pest problems.

Inspect new growth for signs of pests. Remove insects and disease-infested leaves as soon as they are found. Make this a regular part of your gardening routine.

Use netting and repellents to protect emerging plants from animal damage. Start early to encourage animals to go elsewhere to feed. Reapply repellents after severe weather or as recommended on label directions.

Helpful Hints

Divide perennials that have poor flowering, open centers, or floppy growth. Some plants, such as **Shasta Daisy** and **Moonshine Yarrow**, benefit from transplanting every few years. Others, such as **Purple Coneflower** and **Perennial Geraniums**, can go many years without division. Let the plant, not the calendar, be your guide.

To divide perennials:

*   Begin digging and dividing existing plants as new growth appears. Try to move them when they are less than 3 to 4 inches tall. Cut back taller plants to reduce the stress of transplanting.
*   Early spring is a good time to transplant summer- and fall-blooming perennials. Transplanting spring-blooming perennials now may delay or eliminate this year's flowers.
*   Dig and divide spring-flowering plants in late August or early September. You can dig and divide most perennials anytime as long as you can give them proper post-planting care.
*   Use a shovel or garden fork to dig the clump to be divided. Lift the clump and set it on the soil surface. Use a sharp knife or two shovels or garden forks to divide the clumps. Cut into smaller pieces. Plant one division in the original hole. Use the others in new and existing gardens, or share them with your friends and neighbors.
*   Amend the soil when dividing and transplanting perennials. Add several inches of compost, peat moss, or other organic matter into the soil. Plant the division at the same depth as it was growing originally. Gently tamp the soil, and water to remove any air pockets.

Division of Perennials

Pruning

Finish cleanup early in the month. Cut dead stems back to ground level and remove dead leaves on evergreen plants. See March "Pruning" and "Helpful Hints" for more specifics.

Planning

Use your landscape and garden design as a working document. We all make changes to our plans. Sometimes the plants we wanted are not available—and then there are those few unplanned additions that we just could not resist at the garden center.

Continue to check your garden for losses and voids that need filling. Look at these losses as an opportunity to try something new.

Record bloom times in your journal. This will be useful in planning future gardens—and fighting the winter blues next January.

List all your new additions to the garden in your journal or on your landscape plan.

Planting

Complete soil preparation. Invest time now to ensure many years of success with your perennial garden. See April "Planting" for soil preparation information.

Plant dormant bare-root plants as soon as they arrive and the weather permits. Soak the roots several hours prior to planting. Trim off any broken roots. Dig a hole large enough to accommodate the roots. Place the plant in the hole and spread out the roots. Fill the hole with soil, keeping the crown of the plant (where stem joins the roots) just below the soil surface. Gently tamp and water.

Move field-grown container plants right into the garden. See "Planting" in the chapter introduction.

Harden off plants started indoors or in the greenhouse before planting outdoors. Use a cold frame or protected location for this process. Stop fertilizing and reduce watering as you harden off the plants. Move transplants outdoors on warm, frost-free days. Cover or bring them indoors when there is danger of frost. Start in a shaded location. Gradually increase the amount of light the plants receive each day. This process takes about two weeks.

Cut back any overgrown and leggy transplants. Prune the stems back by one-third to one-half at planting. This encourages new growth and results in a fuller, sturdier plant.

Label plants and record the planting information on your landscape plan and in your journal. Make a note of the cultivar (variety), planting date, and plant source.

Dig and *divide* overgrown perennials or those you want to propagate.

Spring is the best time to divide summer- and fall-blooming perennials. Wait until after flowering or late August to divide spring-flowering perennials. See April "Helpful Hints" for specifics.

Dig and *divide* your woodland wildflowers after blooming. Do this only to move existing plants or to start new plantings; otherwise, leave your wildflowers alone.

Care

Move or remove unwanted perennial seedlings. **Coneflowers**, **Black-Eyed Susans**, and other prolific seeders may provide more offspring than needed. Dig and share with friends or donate surplus plants to nearby schools, community beautification groups, and master gardeners.

Put stakes, **Peony** cages, and trellises in place. It is always easier to train young plants through the cages or onto the stakes than manipulate mature plants into submission.

Wait for the soil to warm before adding mulch. Apply a thin layer of cocoa bean shells, twice-shredded bark, or chopped leaves to the soil surface. Do not bury the crowns of the plant. This can lead to rot.

Watering

Check new plantings several times a week and water only as the top few inches of soil start to dry. Established plants need less frequent watering.

Fertilizing

Perennials need very little fertilizer. Incorporate organic matter at the time of planting. Topdress established plantings with several inches of compost every three to four years. Use a starter solution of fertilizer (per label directions) at planting to give transplants a boost.

Pests

Monitor the garden for pests. Remove infected leaves when discovered. Watch for four-lined plantbug, slugs, and aphids. See July "Pests" for more identification guides and control information.

*Check **Columbine** plants for the following specific pests:*

- Check for leafminer. The leafminer causes white, snake-like lines in the leaves. Prune back badly infested plants after flowering. The new growth will be fresh and pest free.

- Watch for **Columbine** sawfly. This wormlike insect eats holes in the leaves so quickly that it seems to devour the plants overnight. Remove and destroy any that are found. You can use insecticides labeled for controlling sawflies on perennials.

- Check wilted **Columbine** plants for stalk borer. Look for hole- and sawdust-like droppings at the base of the plant. Remove infested stems and destroy the borer.

Pull weeds as soon as they appear. dandelions, thistle, and quackgrass are among the first to appear. Removing weeds before they set seed saves pulling hundreds more next year.

Continue to minimize animal damage by fencing and using repellents on susceptible plants.

Pruning

As the garden comes to life, so does the opportunity to spend time in the garden. *Deadhead (remove faded flowers) of early blooming perennials.*

- Shear **Phlox**, **Pinks**, and **Candy-tuft** to encourage a new flush of foliage. Use hand pruners or pruning shears.

Helpful Hints

Save yourself the headaches and frustration caused by accidentally removing **Butterfly Weed, Balloon Flower,** and other late-emerging perennials by making a note to mark their spot with spring-flowering bulbs. Next fall, plant bulbs next to these plants. As the bulbs fade in spring, the perennials will begin to grow. You will get twice the beauty and less risk of digging up your perennials.

- Pinch back **Mums** and **Asters**. Keep them 4 to 6 inches tall throughout the months of May and June.

- Pinch back **Shasta Daisy, Beebalm, Garden Phlox,** and **Obedient Plants** to control height and stagger bloom times.

- Disbud (remove side flower buds) **Peonies** if you want fewer but larger flowers.

- Thin **Garden Phlox, Beebalm,** and other powdery mildew-susceptible plants when the stems are 8 inches tall. Remove one-fourth to one-third (leaving at least four to five) of the stems. Thinning increases light and air to the plant, decreasing the risk of powdery mildew.

- Trim any unsightly frost-damaged leaves.

Planning

Summer is a great time to plan next year's garden. Evaluate the success and beauty of your spring garden. Be sure to take photographs or videotape your ever-changing landscape.

- *Record visitors to your garden.* Note in your journal the birds, butterflies, and beneficial insects stopping by to nest or feed. You may want to add water, birdhouses, and butterfly houses to encourage your guests to stay.

- *Visit botanical and public gardens to see new and different plants.* Participate in the local garden tours. This is a great way to support community beautification efforts and charities while getting a peek into fellow gardeners' backyards. Record planting combinations that you want to use in future gardens.

- *Harvest flowers for arrangements and drying.* Experiment with different flower combinations. If they look good in the vase, they will probably look good as planting partners in the garden.

- *Start a wish list for new plants for future gardens.* Add to this throughout the season. Record the name, bloom time, size, hardiness, and other features of

the plant. This will help when planning new additions.

Planting

Keep planting. The soil is warm, and there are still lots of perennials available at local garden centers and perennial nurseries. Label new plantings, write their locations on your garden design, and record critical information. See the label for any specific planting and care information. Consider saving these for future reference. Write the plant name, variety, source, and planting date in your garden journal. This will help you track the plant and its success in your garden.

This is a good time to transplant **Bleeding Heart.**

Dig and divide overgrown perennials. Dig a hole slightly larger than the plant. Lift the plant out of the hole. Cut it into several smaller pieces. Replant one of the divisions in the original hole and use the other pieces to fill in voids, start new gardens, or share with friends. Amend the soil with organic matter prior to planting.

- *Cut back* taller plants to 3 to 4 inches, and provide shade for those showing signs of transplant stress.

Care

Put stakes and cages in place. Tuck plants in place or carefully tie them to the support as needed. Twine or other soft bindings work best. Loop the twine around the stem and then around the support.

Thin **Garden Phlox** and other overgrown perennials subject to mildew and leaf spot diseases. Remove one-third of the stems.

Remove dead or declining foliage on spring-blooming perennials.

Mulch perennials with cocoa bean shells, twice-shredded bark, or shredded leaves. Apply 1 to 2 inches of these materials to conserve moisture and reduce weeds—but be careful not to bury the plant with mulch.

Watering

As a general rule, perennials need 1 inch of water per week.

Check new plantings several times a week. Water thoroughly whenever the top few inches of soil start to dry. Established plants can tolerate drier soils.

Do not overwater new or established plantings. Perennials, like other plants, often wilt in the heat of day. This is their way of conserving moisture. As soon as the temperatures cool, the plants recover.

Fertilizing

Perennials usually get enough nutrients from the soil and need very little supplemental fertilization. Let the plants be your guide. Use a liquid fertilizer for plants needing a quick boost. Topdress established beds once every three to four years by working several inches of compost into the soil surface.

Pests

Cool, wet springs mean lots of diseases. Remove spotted, blotchy, or discolored leaves as soon as they are found. *Sanitation is the best control for disease problems.*

Watch for leafhoppers, aphids, mites, and spittlebugs. These insects all suck out plant juices, causing leaves to yellow, brown, and die. Control high populations with insecticidal soap. Repeat weekly as needed. See July "Pests" for more details on controlling these pests.

Get out the flashlight, and check your garden for nighttime feeders.

Slugs and earwigs eat holes in leaves and flowers at night. See Annuals "Helpful Hints" on page 45 for more information.

Check the garden for signs of wildlife. Deer and rabbits love **Hostas, Phlox**, and other perennials. Apply repellents or use scare tactics such as noisemakers and whirligigs, and fence gardens to discourage feeding.

Pull weeds as soon as they are found.

Pruning

Continue deadheading plants to prolong bloom, prevent unwanted seedlings, and improve the overall appearance.

- Deadhead **Columbine, Valerian,** and other heavy seeders to prevent unwanted seedlings.

- Do not deadhead **Siberian Iris**. Leave seedpods to provide added interest in the summer, fall, and winter garden.

- Consider removing the flowers of **Lamb's Ear** as soon as they form. This encourages better foliage while removing the flowers that lead to open, less attractive growth.

- Pinch back perennials to control height or delay bloom.

Keep **Mums** and **Asters** 6 inches tall throughout the month.

- Cut back **Amsonia** and **Wild Blue Indigo** (*Baptisia*) by one-third to prevent sprawling, open centers.

- Pinch or cut back an outer ring of stems or scattered plants of **Purple Coneflower, Heliopsis, Garden Phlox, Balloon Flower,** and **Veronica**. The pinched-back plants will be shorter and bloom later. They act as a living support for the rest of the plant and extend the bloom period.

- Pinch out the growing tips or cut back 8-inch stems to 4 inches on 'Autumn Joy' Sedum that may have tended to flop in your garden. Or try moving it to a sunnier location with less fertile but well-drained soil.

- Shear dead or miner-infested foliage on **Columbine**. The new growth will be fresh and pest free.

- Cut back unsightly foliage on **Bearded Iris** and **Perennial Geraniums** after bloom.

- Cut back **Bleeding Heart** as the flowers fade. This reduces reseeding and encourages new growth that may last all season. Mulch the soil and water to help preserve the leaves.

Planning

Continue evaluating the garden—yours and other gardeners'. Take pictures and videotape so that it will be easier to recreate the good ideas and avoid repeating mistakes.

Planting

Keep planting as long as you have space, time, and plants. Give July transplants extra attention during hot dry spells. Mulch new plantings to conserve moisture and keep soil temperature cool. Label, map, and record all new plantings. This will make spring cleanup and weeding much easier.

Dig and divide or take root cuttings of spring-blooming **Poppies**, **Bleeding Heart**, and **Bearded Iris**.

Care

Mulch bare soil. A thin layer of cocoa bean shells, twice-shredded bark, or leaves will help keep the soil cool and moist during hot, dry weather.

Finish staking. Carefully maneuver plants around trellises and into stakes.

Evaluate the light and growing conditions in your perennial gardens. Note the plants' response and any future changes you need to make.

Watering

Check new transplants several times per week. Water thoroughly anytime the top few inches start to dry. Established plants need less frequent watering.

Reduce the need to water by planting the right plant for your growing conditions. Apply a thin layer of organic mulch to help conserve soil moisture. Water thoroughly, but less frequently, to encourage deeper, more drought-tolerant roots.

Fertilizing

Avoid overfertilizing your plants. Most perennials can get all the nutrients they need from the soil. Give stunted, less vigorous plants a boost with a dilute solution (one-half the recommended rate) of liquid fertilizer.

Consider fertilizing heavy feeders and those cut back for rebloom. Use a low-nitrogen, slow-release fertilizer to avoid burn.

Pests

Continue removing spotted and diseased leaves as soon as they are found. Deadhead plants during wet weather to further reduce the risk of disease.

To control insects:

- Check the upper and lower leaf surfaces and stems for aphids and mites. These pests suck out plant juices, causing leaves to yellow and brown. Spray plants with a strong blast of water to dislodge these insects. Use insecticidal soap to treat damaging populations. This is a soap formulated to kill soft-bodied insects, but it is not harmful to the plant or the environment.

- Check for plantbugs whenever you see speckled and spotted leaves and stems. These insects suck out plant juices, causing leaves to discolor and brown. Insecticidal soap or other insecticides labeled for controlling plantbugs on flowers can be used.

- Monitor for spittlebug, earwigs, and slugs. See "Annuals" December "Helpful Hints"s on page 45 for additional information.

- Watch for lacy leaves caused by Japanese beetles and rose chafers. Handpick and destroy these pests. Insecticides labeled for controlling these pests on flowers can also be used to reduce their damage.

Pruning

Continue deadheading and pinching back straggly plants, such as **Lavender**. See the Perennials Helpful Hints on page 361 for a list of perennials that either don't require deadheading or have a long season of bloom even without deadheading.

Prune back **Silvermound Artemisia** before flowering. Prune back to fresh new growth to avoid open centers.

Cut back old stems of **Delphiniums** to the fresh growth at the base of the plant. This encourages new growth and a second flush of flowers.

Prune back yellow foliage of **Bleeding Heart** to ground level. This is normal and no cause for concern—your plants will be back next spring.

Stop pinching fall-blooming perennials at the beginning of the month.

Remove insect-infested, diseased, or declining foliage. This reduces the source of future infection.

Helpful Hints

Ground ivy, Quackgrass, and Bindweed are perennial weeds that can quickly take over your garden. Hand pulling does not usually work on these deeply rooted plants. Cultivation just breaks the plants into smaller pieces that can start lots of new plants. Use a total vegetation killer to control these pesky weeds. These products kill the tops and roots of the weeds and any growing plant they touch. Several applications may be needed to control Bindweed, as well as other tough and established weeds.

Paint, sponge, or wipe the total vegetation killer on the weed leaves. Be sure to wear protective gloves when mixing or applying these and other pesticides. The chemical moves through the leaves, down the stems, and into the roots. Be careful that none of the weedkiller touches your perennials-the herbicide will kill them as well. *Here is a quick tip for making the job easier:*

1 *Remove* the top and bottom of a plastic milk jug.

2 *Cover* the weed with the plastic milk jug.

3 *Spray* the total vegetation killer on the weed inside the milk jug. The jug will protect the surrounding plants from the harmful weedkiller. Remove the jug after the herbicide on the weed dries.

Weed Control

Planning

Continue evaluating your garden. Take pictures and videotape both the good and bad parts of your landscape. These records will help you correct problems and duplicate successes in next year's landscape.

Take advantage of the heat. Grab a cold drink, find a little shade, and write in your journal. Make sure you have recorded all your new plantings, pest problems, and other useful information.

Create or add to your planting wish list. Write down the plant name, variety, bloom time, and other features that caught your attention. Use this list when planning changes and additions to next year's garden.

Look for bare areas for new plants or planting beds. Late summer is a great time for adding new plants or preparing the soil for new perennial gardens.

Planting

Keep making additions. Be sure to label, map, and record the location of all new plantings.

Dig and **divide** overgrown **Iris**, **Poppies**, and other spring-blooming perennials.

Care

Mulch perennial gardens if you have not yet done so. Apply a thin layer of cocoa bean shells, twice-shredded bark, shredded leaves, or other organic matter. This will help keep perennial roots cool and moist.

Lightly **rake** mulch during wet periods to prevent slime mold. This fungus develops and feeds on the mulch. It looks disgusting—in fact, its common name is dog vomit fungus—but it does not harm the plants.

Watering

Check new plantings several times a week. Water when the top few inches start to dry. Apply enough water to wet the roots and surrounding soil. New plantings need about 1 inch of water per week. Apply needed water in one application in clay soils and in two applications in sandy soils.

Water established and mulched plantings thoroughly but less frequently. They can last several weeks with very little water. Pay special attention to moisture-loving plants. Use a watering wand to spot water these plants. Consider moving them to areas that tend to stay wet for longer periods.

Water your gardens early in the morning to reduce the risk of disease and water loss to evaporation. Use a soaker hose or watering wand to get the water to the soil and roots where it is needed.

Fertilizing

Do not fertilize. Late-season fertilization encourages problems with winter survival. Use this time to evaluate the health and vigor of your plantings. Make note of those areas that need topdressing or fertilization next spring.

Pests

Continue monitoring perennial gardens for disease and insect problems. Catching the problems early may mean the difference between removing a few sick leaves and spraying the whole garden.

- Check **Beebalm, Garden Phlox**, and other perennials for signs of powdery mildew. Look for a white, powdery substance on the leaves. This fungal disease causes leaves to eventually yellow and brown. Consider moving infected plants into an area with full sun and good air circulation.

- Substitute mildew-resistant cultivars of mildew-susceptible plants in next year's garden. Use **'Bright Eyes'**, **'David'**, or **'Starfire'** cultivars of **Garden Phlox** (*Phlox paniculata*). Or substitute the mildew-resistant **Wild Sweet William** (*Phlox maculatum*).

- Try **'Marshall's Delight'**, **'Gardenview Scarlett'**, **'Vintage Wine'**, and other mildew-resistant cultivars of **Beebalm** (*Monarda didyma*).

To control weeds, try these tips:

- Continue pulling weeds as soon as they appear. Remove weeds before they set seed to avoid adding hundreds of new problems to next year's garden.

- Remove or kill perennial weeds such as Quackgrass, Bindweed, and Creeping Charlie. Be sure to remove all roots and stems when pulling these weeds. Any little piece that remains can start a new plant. See July "Helpful Hints" for ideas.

Pruning

Continue *deadheading* for aesthetics, to prevent reseeding, and to prolong bloom. Leave the last set of flowers intact to allow the formation of seedpods that add interest to the winter landscape.

Cut back declining plants to improve the overall appearance of your perennial garden. Remove insect-damaged, declining, and dead foliage.

Do not prune sub-shrubs such as **Butterfly Bushes** (*Buddleja*), **Blue Mist Spirea** (*Caryopteris*), and **Russian Sage** (*Perovskia*). Enjoy the late-season blooms and allow plants to start hardening off for winter. I prune these only once a year, in late March, and enjoy a long flowering display and attractive seed set for winter.

Try cutting back short-lived perennials, such as **Blanket Flowers** (*Gaillardia*). Late-season pruning will stimulate new green growth and may help extend the plant's life.

Harvest flowers to use fresh and dried.

- Harvest flowers in the morning for fresh use. Take a bucket of water with you to the garden. Place cut flowers in the water while collecting the remaining flowers. Remove the lower leaves and recut the stems just prior to arranging them in the vase. Keep the vase full of fresh water to extend your enjoyment.

- Wait until midday to harvest flowers used for drying. Remove leaves and combine in small bundles. Use rubber bands to hold the stems together. As the stems shrink, the rubber bands will contract, holding the stems tight. Use a spring-type clothespin to attach drying flowers to a line, nail, or other support.

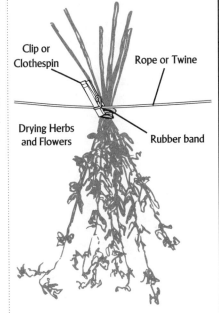

Clip or Clothespin

Rope or Twine

Drying Herbs and Flowers

Rubber band

Planning

Fall is for planting and planning. Evaluate your fall perennial garden. Do you need more **Mums**, **Asters**, or fall-blooming **Anemones**? Record bloom and fall color. **Hosta** leaves turn a beautiful yellow, while **Evening Primrose** and **Peonies** add a touch of purple and red to the fall perennial garden.

Continue evaluating the bloom and performance of the perennials in your landscape and gardens. Note the results of pinching back **Sedum 'Autumn Joy'**, **Coneflower**, and other fall bloomers. Make a list of changes you want to implement in next year's garden.

Add to your wish list of plants for next year's garden. Record bloom time, care, and other plant features that will help you plan.

Take pictures and videotape of the fall garden. These will make for nice memories and easier planning next winter.

Planting

Keep adding perennials to your garden and landscape. The warm soil and cooler air temperatures are great for planting and establishing new perennials.

Move self-sown biennials to their desired location. Transplant early in the month so the seedlings will have time to get re-established before winter.

Finish transplanting **Iris** early in the month. This gives them time to put down roots and prepare for winter.

Transplant **Peonies** now until after the tops are killed by frost. Dig and divide, leaving at least three to five eyes per division. Replant so that the eyes are no more than 1 to 2 inches below the soil surface.

Add **Mums** to the fall garden. Fall planted **Garden Mums** are not always hardy in our area. Many botanical gardens and estates use them as an annual for fall interest.

- *Consider planting your bulbs and **Mums** at the same time.* Dig a hole for the bulbs in late September (a week earlier in the northern part of the state). Place the bulbs in the bottom of the hole and lightly cover with soil. Set the Mum in the same hole above the bulbs. Make sure the Mum will be planted at the same depth as it was growing in the container. Backfill with soil and gently tamp. Water and enjoy the fall display.

- *Or consider using the sunken-pot technique.* Sink empty planting pots, with drainage, in

groundcover and other planting areas. Set potted **Mums** in the sunken pot. This method eliminates the need to dig and disturb surrounding plant roots. Replace the **Mums** with **Pansies**, summer annuals, or other seasonal displays.

Finish digging and dividing perennials as soon as possible. Northern Minnesota gardeners should try to finish this task early in the month. Those in southern Minnesota should try to finish by the end of the month. Wait until spring to divide **Siberian Iris**, **Astilbe**, **Delphinium**, or other slow-to-establish, less hardy perennials.

Consider preparing the soil for new garden areas. Kill or remove the grass, take a soil test, and amend the soil as needed. Shredded fallen leaves make a great soil amendment. Spade several inches of this free material into the top 12 inches of soil. They will disintegrate over the winter and will improve the drainage and water-holding capacity of your soil. Starting now gives you a jump on next season.

Care

Winter is quickly approaching, especially for those in the north. Make note of new and tender plantings that will need winter protection. Look for sources of straw, marsh hay, evergreen branches, or other winter mulch materials. Wait until the ground freezes to apply them to the soil.

Watering

Water as needed. As the temperatures cool, you will need to water less frequently. Check new plantings several times a week. Keep the top 4 to 6 inches slightly moist. New gardens need about 1 inch of water every seven to ten days. Established plantings should be watered when the top few inches of soil are dry.

Fertilizing

Do not apply fertilizer. This is a good time to take a soil test if your plants are showing signs of nutrient deficiencies. Poor flowering, discolored leaves, and generally poor growth may indicate a need to fertilize. Start with a soil test before adding fertilizer. Excess nutrients can cause floppiness, poor flowering, and other problems. Contact your local county office of the University of Minnesota Extension Service for more information.

Pests

Continue weeding all your gardens. Removing weeds now can reduce the amount of weeds you will have to pull next year.

Monitor plants for insects and disease. Fewer harmful insects are present during the cool temperatures of fall. See July "Pests" for more details on pests and their control.

Continue removing spotted and diseased leaves as soon as they are found. Water early in the day or use a watering wand or drip irrigation to reduce moisture on the leaves. This helps reduce disease problems. Make note of mildew-infested plants. Consider amending your care (thinning young plantings) to reduce mildew, moving susceptible plants to a sunnier location, or replacing them with mildew-resistant plants such as *Phlox maculatum* and 'Gardenview Scarlet' Bee Balm.

Remove plants with rotting roots and stem. Amend the soil to improve drainage, adjust watering, and replace with a plant more suited to the location.

Pruning

Stop deadheading plants you want to develop seedpods for winter interest, such as fall-blooming **Sedums**, **Astilbes**, **Coneflowers**, and **Rudbeckias**.

Continue deadheading to prevent seed set on perennials that are overtaking your garden. Or plan to invite gardening friends over for a digging party next spring.

Cut back faded summer-blooming plants as needed. This improves their appearance and opens up space for the fall flower display.

Planning

Make your final review of the garden during the growing season. Take a few minutes to record what worked and what needs improvement for next season. But do not put your notes away; you will want to evaluate them during the coming winter months.

Review your wish list. Add some outstanding fall bloomers and evaluate some of the early bloomers on your list. Remove any that have not lived up to their early season performance.

Evaluate future planting locations and look at next year's landscape plans. Consider preparing new perennial gardens now, when the list of garden chores is much shorter.

Planting

Finish planting early in the month. The later you plant, the less time your perennials will have to get established and the greater the risk of winterkill. Try to limit planting to hardier perennials that are suited to our cold winters.

Locate a place to overwinter less hardy transplants and those scheduled for spring planting. I always have more plants than time left in the fall. I locate vacant garden space

in a protected location for these and other transplants slated for spring planting. Sink the pots into the ground. Once the soil freezes, mulch with evergreen branches or straw for extra protection.

Collect and *sow* seeds of **Coneflowers**, **Rudbeckias**, and other late summer- and fall-blooming perennials. Spread the seeds outdoors on well-prepared soil.

Dig and *divide* **Peonies** after the tops have been killed by frost. Use a spading fork to dig the rhizomes. Dig a hole wider than the plant to avoid damaging the root system. Cut the clump into smaller pieces, leaving at least three to five eyes per division. Prepare the planting site by adding several inches of compost into the top 12 inches of soil. Replant the divisions, keeping the eyes no more than 1 to 2 inches below the soil surface.

Perennial
Division

Care

Clean up and remove any diseased or insect-infested leaves,

stems, and flowers. You need to decide what "look" you want for your winter garden. Some gardeners like the neat and tidy look and prefer not to have standing "dead stuff." I prefer to leave my perennials standing for winter interest and improved hardiness. Many plants such as **Salvia** and **Mums** seem to overwinter better when the dead stems are left standing for the winter. (A friend reading my first book thought I was just lazy. But he followed suit and discovered that the perennials not only provided visual relief for the winter garden, but they also attracted birds to his landscape. He still claims it is laziness, but with a purpose!)

Carefully *blow* or *rake* tree and shrub leaves off your perennial gardens. Large leaves get wet, mat down, and provide poor insulation for your plants. Shred fallen leaves and use them as a soil mulch or amendment for new plantings. Or rake and bag them for use in next year's garden.

Collect dried pods, grasses, and other materials for fall and winter arrangements.

Remove stakes and supports as plants decline. Clean and store for next year's garden.

Start preparing the soil for next year's gardens. Remove or kill the grass and weeds. Take a soil test.

Add organic matter such as compost, aged manure, and shredded leaves to the top 12 inches of soil. Wait until spring to add the fertilizer recommended by your soil test report.

Watering

Water established plants thoroughly before the ground freezes.

Keep watering until the ground freezes. New plantings and transplants need your attention throughout the fall. Make sure they receive 1 inch of water every seven to ten days. Adjust your watering schedule to fit the weather and soil. Give plants the needed water in one application in clay soils and in two applications in sandy soils.

Fertilizing

Take a soil test of new and existing gardens. Test older gardens every three to five years or whenever you suspect a nutrient problem. Alternate years for testing to help spread out the cost.

Wait until spring to fertilize. You can topdress the soil with compost or organic matter. Consider shredding fallen leaves and using them as

Helpful Hints

Winter interest is not just "dried stuff" peeking through the snow. It can also be a way of attracting birds that brings color, motion, and life to the winter landscape. ***Break out the journal and start recording the plants that feed and attract songbirds to your garden. Here is a start for your list:***

Black-Eyed Susan	*Rudbeckia*
Gayfeather	*Liatris*
Hosta	*Hosta* species
Little Bluestem	*Schizachyrium scoparium*
Purple Coneflower	*Echinaceae purpurea*
Switchgrass	*Panicum virgatum*

a soil amendment for new plantings. Work the shredded leaves into the top 12 inches of soil in empty gardens. These will break down over winter and improve the soil for future planting. Or spread the shredded leaves on the soil surface for mulch. Do not use leaves to cover the plants for winter protection.

Pests

Remove diseased or insect-infested foliage, flowers, and stems. Fall cleanup will reduce the risk of pest problems next season.

Check last winter's notes on wildlife damage. Consider control options if voles have been a problem in the past. Some gardeners choose to cut down their gardens in fall to eliminate the vole's habitat. Others depend on nature, hawks, owls, temperature extremes, and the neighbors' cats to control these rodents. See November "Pests" for more details.

Pruning

Leave stems, flower heads, and seedpods standing for winter interest. Remove only those infected by pests or those that tend to reseed more than you desire.

Cut back the foliage of **Peonies** and **Hostas** to reduce the risk of fungal leaf disease in next year's garden. I leave the flower stems of **Hostas** standing for winter interest. In fact, you may find birds feasting on the seeds over the winter.

Planning

You have spent the season evaluating the beauty of your garden. Continue doing this through the winter, but take some time now to evaluate the amount of work spent to keep the garden looking good.

Keep adding to and amending your wish list. Consider maintenance and year-round interest as you add to your list.

Planting

It really is too late to plant. Every gardener occasionally pushes the limit and plants later than they should, but you know you are taking a risk. *Increase success by overwintering transplants for spring planting.*

1 Find a vacant planting space in a protected location. Look for areas near your house, shed, or fence that are sheltered from winter wind and sun.

2 Sink pots into the soil in this protected location. The soil will insulate the roots from our cold winter temperatures.

3 Wait until the ground freezes to apply winter mulch. This usually occurs after a week of freezing temperatures.

4 Use evergreen branches, straw, or marsh hay as winter mulch for added insulation.

Collect and save seeds of Coneflowers, Black-Eyed Susans, and other perennials you want to plant next spring. Remove seeds from the seedpod and allow them to dry, then place the seeds in an envelope. Write the seed name and the date they were collected on the outside of the envelope. Place the envelope in an airtight jar in the refrigerator. This gives the seeds their needed cold treatment (stratification) while storing them at a consistent temperature. The seeds will be ready to plant next spring.

Care

Soil preparation can be done until the ground freezes. In some years, November is the end of the season, and in other years, we can still work in the gardens into December. *Following are some tips for preparing your soil and plants for the coming cold weather:*

• *Spread* a 2- to 3-inch layer (topdress) of organic matter on the soil of your perennial gardens now or in the spring. Do this every three to four years to keep your perennials healthy and beautiful.

• *Apply* winter mulch to your perennial gardens after the ground freezes. This occurs after a week of freezing temperatures. The goal of winter mulch is to prevent the freezing and thawing of the soil. Apply anytime after the ground freezes and before the winter thaw occurs. Waiting until after the soil freezes also gives the wildlife a chance to find another place to spend the winter—as opposed to under your mulch and near your plants.

• Do not worry if it snows before you put the mulch in place. Snow is the best mulch. Keep the other materials handy for late applications needed when the winter thaw melts the snow. *Apply* the mulch after the snow melts and before the soil thaws.

• Give your perennials growing aboveground extra care for the winter. *Place* planters in an unheated garage, porch, or other protected area where temperatures hover near freezing. Insulate the roots with packing peanuts or other material. Water whenever the soil is thawed and dry.

• Or *sink* the containers into a vacant garden area for the winter. This is perfect for double-potted containers. Slide the ugly inner pot out of the decorative planter. Bury the ugly pot in a protected area of the landscape. Next spring, lift the pot out of the soil, repot or divide as needed, and place in the decorative container. Or **add** potted perennials to the garden. Store decorative containers in the potting shed or garage. Now you have an excuse to buy new plants next season!

- Leave the stems or place markers by **Butterfly Weed, Balloon Flower**, and other late-emerging perennials. *Plant* bulbs next to these perennials to marks their locations and to prevent accidental damage in early spring.

Helpful Hints

You may have used **Garden Mums** for a burst of color in the fall garden; however, these late additions often fail to survive the winter. Most botanical gardens and professionals treat them as annuals. They add them to the fall garden and replace them each year. *Following are some suggestions for overwintering* Mums:

- Improve hardiness by planting **Garden Mums** in spring. Check with your favorite garden center. Many are now selling **Mums** for spring planting.
- Leave the **Mums** standing for winter. The dried stems help catch snow and hold winter mulch in place. Cover plants with evergreen branches after the soil freezes.
- Increase winter protection by mounding 6 to 8 inches of soil over the dormant plants. Remove in spring as the temperatures hover near freezing.
- Or try planting its hardy relative *Chrysanthemum* × *rubellum*. 'Clara Curtis', 'Duchess of Edinburgh', and 'Mary Stoker' are popular cultivars.

Watering

Water the perennial garden thoroughly just before the ground freezes. Monitor poor drainage and ice buildup.

Fertilizing

Do not fertilize. Fertilizing frozen soil can lead to groundwater pollution.

Pests

Monitor for animal and rodent damage. Fall cleanup may help reduce the damage. Try trapping voles (meadow mice) with snap traps baited with peanut butter and oats. Tuck the traps in a pipe or under cover to prevent birds and desirable wildlife from accidentally being injured. Keep in mind there may be more than 400 voles per acre. That's a lot of peanut butter and snap traps!

Cut back and remove disease- and insect-infested perennials.

Pruning

Finish cleanup and enjoy the winter interest.

Remove seedpods from heavy seeders that procreate more than you want. Consider saving some for birds.

Leave tender perennials—those subject to winterkill—standing for winter. The standing stems will catch the snow for better winter insulation. This, along with the intact plant, seems to increase winter hardiness.

DECEMBER

Planning

The holidays are quickly approaching, and all thoughts are turning to preparation for the holiday season. Help make gift giving easier for your family and friends by making a wish list—a new journal, plant labels, hand pruners, flower scissors, a harvest basket, a new shovel, a gift certificate to your favorite garden center or catalog, a load of manure (to be delivered at a later date!), and much more.

Planting

Pull out your garden pictures and dream of the planting season. Keep exercising and stretching to keep those planting muscles toned until spring returns.

Care

Finish garden cleanup. Do not worry if you have waited too long and the snow has buried all your good intentions. Wait until the first thaw or spring to finish garden cleanup.

Use evergreen branches, straw, or marsh hay for winter mulch. These will protect tender perennials and prevent frost heaving.

Watering

Make sure the garden hose is safely stored for winter. *Turn off* the water or insulate outside faucets to prevent freezing.

Fertilizing

Review soil tests and make a list of fertilizing and soil amendment needs. Make a note on next year's calendar so that you will not forget to implement your soil improvement plans.

Pests

Wildlife can be a wonderful addition to the landscape. Their movements and antics can be entertaining. Make a list of the visitors to your winter garden. Note what plants helped bring them into the landscape.

Unfortunately, some wildlife visitors do more damage than we want to tolerate. Watch for tracks, droppings, and other signs of wildlife. Monitor for damage done by squirrels digging and voles eating roots.

Helpful Hints

Don't throw away that holiday tree. Use it in your winter landscape. I collect all the discarded trees in my neighborhood to use as mulch in my garden. Prune off the branches and cover perennial and bulb gardens. The soil is usually frozen by the holidays and we have not yet had the damaging winter thaw.

Or leave the tree intact and use it as a windbreak for other plants in the landscape. In snowy winters, I prop our trees in a snowdrift for winter interest. The trees provide shelter for the birds that like to feed on the seeds of **Coneflower**, **Rudbeckia**, and **Liatris** in the perennial garden.

Repellents may discourage squirrels and deer. Treat before feeding and digging begins. Reapply repellents as needed. Check label for more specific directions.

Pruning

Sit back and relax. Enjoy the winter interest your perennial garden provides. Make notes about which plants add to and which ones detract from your winter landscape.

Roses

When you think of roses you probably picture 'Peace', 'Mr. Lincoln', or other **Hybrid Tea Roses**. Until recent times, these have dominated the rose-growing scene. Though beautiful, they require a fair amount of work to remain attractive and survive our cold winters. Recent attention, however, has focused on many of the outstanding **Shrub Roses**. Gardeners are finding gems from the past as well as new introductions to help them enjoy roses with a minimum amount of effort.

There are many ways to divide and categorize roses. Here, we will use the three broad categories of species and shrub roses, old garden roses, and modern roses. **Species Roses** are naturally occurring, propagated from roses found growing wild. **Shrub Roses** are close relatives of these. They are hybrids that have been bred from species roses. **Old Roses**, or **Old Garden Roses**, are varieties that have been around since 1867. **Modern Roses** are any roses, including **Hybrid Teas**, introduced after this date. This category also includes **Polyantha**, **Floribunda**, and **Grandiflora** roses. **Rose Trees**, **Climbers**, and **Miniature Roses** are garden forms of roses.

Planning

Roses are often relegated to a garden of their own. This is fine, but diversity in growth habit and size makes roses a good addition to the beauty as well as the function of the landscape as a whole. Use roses as specimens in the perennial garden. **Shrub Roses** can be used as informal flowering hedges or backdrops for flowerbeds. **Climbers** make nice vertical accents and privacy screens.

Location is important for the health of the plant. Decrease pest problems and frustrations while increasing satisfaction by growing your roses in the right conditions. Proper site selection and care will give you beautiful results.

- Plant roses in sunny locations that receive at least 6 hours of sunlight each day. Sunlight is important for both flowering and disease control. A south- or east-facing location is ideal. The morning sun dries the dew, reducing disease problems.

- Grow roses in well-drained, fertile soil. Add a 2- to 4-inch layer of organic matter to heavy clay soils to improve drainage, as well as to sandy soils to improve water and nutrient-holding capacity. Sulfur can be added to alkaline soils to reduce pH, and lime can be added to acid soils. Aim for a pH between 5.5 and 7.0. Use your soil test as a guide. Work these materials into the top 12 inches of soil.

- Maximize the beauty and minimize pest problems by giving roses enough room to grow and spread. Proper spacing will allow roses to develop a more natural appearance with minimal pruning on your part. The needed space will also increase air circulation and assure that light reaches the plants. This means fewer pests problems. Consult plant tags and rose catalogs for information on the mature size and spread of specific rose varieties.

Roses

Selection

Select the rose that gives you the desired flower color, fragrance, and plant size. Always select the hardiest and most pest-resistant variety available. Botanical gardens, the county extension service, garden centers, and nurseries can help in the selection process.

Many roses are grafted onto hardy rootstocks; these are called **Grafted Roses**. A small bud is attached to the roots of another rose. The roots are hardy, but the graft and above-ground growth can be damaged over the winter. Protect the graft by planting it 2 inches below the soil surface.

Bare-root Roses are available through garden centers and catalogs. Select Grade 1 roses. These have several long, stout canes and a larger root system. You will pay more for these plants, but you will be rewarded with the best possible bloom. They are sold and shipped with their roots packed in moist peat moss and the canes are dormant. Plant these in early spring for best results.

Potted **Hybrid Tea Roses** are usually bare-root plants that were potted by the nursery or garden center in early spring. They are often placed in the greenhouse to encourage leaf and root growth. These can be planted spring through early summer. Special care must be taken at planting to avoid

damaging the developing root system. See the following section on "Planting" for more information.

Planting

Properly *prepare the soil* prior to planting. Work needed organic matter and amendments into the top 12 inches of soil. Sprinkle the area with water or allow the soil to settle for several days before planting.

Plant dormant **Bare-root Roses** in spring after severe weather has passed.

1 Unwrap the roots and *soak* for several hours before planting.

2 *Dig* a hole 12 inches deep and at least 2 feet wide. Create a cone of soil in the middle of the hole. Tamp down the cone of soil to reduce settling.

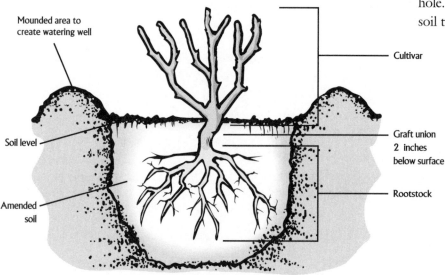

Mounded area to create watering well

Cultivar

Soil level

Graft union 2 inches below surface

Amended soil

Rootstock

Rose-Graft Union Reduced Mound

Roses

3 Remove damaged or broken roots. *Drape* the roots over the cone so that the graft union will end up 2 inches below the soil surface. Use your shovel or other long-handled tool to measure the planting depth. Lay the handle over the hole and make sure the graft is 2 inches below the soil surface.

4 *Fill* the planting hole with soil. Water to help settle the soil; add more soil if needed.

5 *Mulch* the soil with woodchips, shredded bark, or other organic matter.

Bare-root Roses that began to grow during shipping or while in storage should be potted and grown in a protected (frost-free) location. These plants can be planted outdoors after the danger of frost.

Potted Roses growing in greenhouses need to be hardened off before moving outdoors. Many garden centers will do this for you. Wait until after the danger of frost has passed to plant these roses.

1 *Dig* a hole several feet wide and deep enough to plant the graft union 2 inches below the soil surface. Many potted roses are growing with the graft union above the soil. Use special care when transplanting potted

roses. The root system is not always established.

2 Move the rose near the planting hole. Cut off the bottom of the container.

3 Set the rose, pot and all, in the planting hole. Adjust the planting depth so the graft union is 2 inches below the soil surface.

4 Slice the side of the pot and peel it away. This reduces the risk of damaging the developing root system.

5 *Backfill* the planting hole with the amended soil. Water to help settle the soil.

6 *Mulch* the soil with a 1- to 3-inch layer of cocoa bean shells, woodchips, or shredded bark. The coarser the material used, the thicker the layer of mulch should be.

See September "Planting" for specific information on planting **Shrub Roses**.

Watering

Roses need an average of 1 inch of water each week. This is about 5 to 6 gallons of water per plant, so you may need to supplement rainfall. Water established roses when the

top 2 to 4 inches of soil are dry. Apply needed water in one application each week to roses growing in clay soil and in two applications for roses growing in sandy soils.

To help reduce the spread of disease, use a watering wand or soaker hose to water roses. This allows you to put the water where it is needed—on the soil, not the leaves.

Water new plants often enough to keep the roots and surrounding soil moist. As the plants become established reduce the frequency of watering.

Fertilization

Start with a soil test to determine how much and what type of fertilizer your roses need. Our soils are generally high to excessive in phosphorus and potassium. Adding more of these elements can interfere with the uptake of other nutrients.

- *Apply* a low-nitrogen (5 to 6 percent), slow-release fertilizer at a rate of 2 pounds per 100 square feet or 1 heaping tablespoon per plant.

- Use a complete fertilizer (one that contains nitrogen, phosphorus, and potassium) such as 5-10-10 or 6-12-12 only if all three elements are needed.

Roses

- Fertilize **Species**, **Shrub**, **Old Roses**, and **Climbers** once in early spring as the buds begin to swell.

- Fertilize repeat-blooming **Old Roses** in early spring and again after their first bloom period.

- **Hybrid Tea Roses** should be fertilized after the new spring growth has developed. Reapply every 5 to 6 weeks. Stop fertilizing August 1st. Late season fertilization leads to late season growth that is more likely to be killed over the winter.

- *Apply* the recommended amount of fertilizer twice as often to **Container Roses**.

Pests

Pest management is important for the health and beauty of roses. A healthy rose is more likely to survive our harsh winters. It used to be that weekly sprays were needed to control blackspot, mildew, aphids, mites, and all the other pests that attack roses. The increased use of pest-resistant **Shrub Roses** and new introductions have brought about a reduction in pest problems and the need to spray. Select the most pest-resistant rose that fits your landscape needs. See May and July "Helpful Hints" for specifics on pests and their control.

Winter Care

Hybrid Teas, **Floribundas**, **Grandifloras**, **Tree Roses**, and most **Climbers** benefit from winter protection. There are many different ways to overwinter roses. Some years, one method seems to fit the weather and work better than others. Soil mound, leaves, rose cones, and shelters are a few of the methods used by rose enthusiasts. Select the method that fits your gardening style and growing conditions.

The Do-Nothing Method leaves survival to chance. Roses are managed properly throughout the growing season. When winter arrives, they are on their own. In mild years, this works great; in other years, you have plenty of new planting locations when spring arrives.

See September, October, and November "Helpful Hints" for more detailed descriptions of the various types of winter protection.

Climbing and **Tree Roses** need special care for winter, however, some **Climbers** and **Ramblers** are hardy and will survive the winter on their own. **Climbers** growing against the south side of a home may survive with minimal protection. Mound soil around the base. Leave the rose attached to the trellis. Wrap with fabric and fill with evergreen branches.

Container Roses need added protection for winter. Their roots are in small amounts of soil and are exposed to the harsh weather.

- *Bury* the **Container Rose** in an unused, but protected spot in the landscape. An eastern location or other area protected from the northwest wind works well. Provide winter protection for the plant. Potted **Tree Roses** would benefit from the Minnesota Tip Method described in September "Helpful Hints."

- Or, *move* **Container Roses** into an unheated garage. Place the pot in a box or larger container filled with Styrofoam peanuts or other insulating material for added insulation. Water anytime the soil is dry and not frozen.

- Or, *move* **Container Roses** indoors to a cool sunny location. This can be tricky since the house is usually not cool enough to keep the roses dormant, and the poor growing conditions will make it hard to keep the roses growing and healthy.

Minnesota Roses

Variety	Type	Color	Comments
All That Jazz™	Shrub	Coral to salmon	Old-fashioned look with a light fragrance. Needs winter protection.
Carefree series™	Shrub	Pink	Repeat blooming. Hardy with good pest resistance.
Dream series™	Shrub	Orange, pink, red, and yellow	A new introduction you may want to try in your garden.
Explorer series	Shrub	Red, pink, and white	Small to large roses used as shrubs and climbers. Bred in Canada for winter hardiness.
Flower Carpet series™	Shrub or groundcover	Pink, red, and white	Low grower under 3 feet tall. Good disease resistance. Benefits from winter protection in severe winters and in the northern part of the state.
Knock Out™	Shrub	Cerise to cherry red	2000 AARS winner developed in Wisconsin. Good repeat bloomer. Bred for pest resistance and winter hardiness. Winter mulch is advisable.
Meidiland series™	Shrub	Pink, red, and white	Showy and tough repeat bloomer for low maintenance situations. I have had mixed results with hardiness.
'Morden Blush'	Shrub	Light pink	One of the Parkland series developed for hardiness. Hardy to zone 3. Not disease resistant.
'Nearly Wild'	Floribunda	Medium pink	Tough, hardy, season-long bloomer.
'Peace'	Hybrid tea	Yellow blend	A popular, well-known hybrid tea due to its long-lasting flowers.
'The Fairy'	Polyantha	Light pink	Low, compact grower. May need winter protection in severe winters and the northern part of state.
'William Baffin'	Shrub	Pink	One of the more popular Explorer roses grown as a large shrub or climber. Hardy, repeat-blooming plant. The best hardy climber..

Planning

The catalogs are pouring in and, like all gardeners, you are planning all the new additions to your landscape. These plans may include some roses. Before placing the order, make sure the roses you select are suitable to our climate and will fit in the available space.

Notice that there are one-time, repeat, and continuous bloomers.

- *One-time bloomers flower on the tips and new side branches of the previous season's growth.* They usually start flowering the second year after planting. Most **Species** and **Old Garden Roses** are in this group. Some **Modern Roses** and **Shrub Roses** are one-time bloomers.

- *Repeat bloomers will bloom the summer they are planted.* They flower in spring on the tips of new growth or side shoots formed on the previous season's growth. Fall flowers develop on the tips of summer growth or side shoots. Some **Modern Roses** and **Shrub Roses** are repeat bloomers.

- *Continuous bloomers produce flowering canes and side shoots all season long.* **Hybrid Tea Roses** and some **Shrub Roses** such as 'Chuckles', 'Nearly Wild', 'Carefree Delight', 'Knock Out', and 'Ballerina' fit in this category.

You may consider adding a native rose to the landscape. Both the **Prairie** (*Rosa setigera*) and **Prairie Wild** (*Rosa arkansana*) are hardy native roses.

- Use **Prairie Rose** as a **Climber** on walls, fences, or trellises. It will brighten your landscape with single pink flowers in early to mid-July and small reddish fruit (Rose Hips) in fall. The fruits also help attract birds to the landscape.

- Try **Prairie Wild Rose** in your natural landscape. It is hardy to Zone 2 with a variable height of 6 to 12 inches. It works well in prairie restoration. The plants spread via suckers, sometimes traveling five feet under barriers before popping up to the surface. They are very drought tolerant.

Whatever rose you choose, select the most pest-resistant varieties available. Consult your local botanical garden or extension service for suggestions.

Planting

Consider areas that are suitable for roses. Evaluate growing conditions and your landscape plan. Select and place roses in areas where they will thrive, add beauty, and serve a function in the yard. Use **Climbers** for vertical accents, large **Shrub Roses** for screening, and fragrant **Species** for a little aromatherapy near a patio or screened porch.

Care

Check roses and make sure winter protection is secure. Locate and replace any rose shelters, rose cones, or mulch that may have blown away during a storm.

Vent rose cones on sunny days or during warm spells. Some cones come with precut or removable vents. If not, cut small holes on the side away from the wind and near the top of the cones.

Monitor the health and growing conditions of **Miniature** and **Tree Roses** that you are overwintering indoors. Keep plants in a cool room in front of a southern or other sunny window. Place plants on a pebble tray to increase humidity and to eliminate the need to pour excess water out of the saucer. As you water plants thoroughly, the excess will collect in the pebbles, allowing the pot to sit on the pebbles and not in the water. As the water evaporates, it will increase the humidity around the plants.

Watering

No need to water outdoor roses. Water those growing indoors as needed. Keep the soil slightly moist. Check on **Container Roses** stored in the garage. Water them whenever the soil is dry and not frozen.

Fertilizing

Do not fertilize. Roses should be tucked away for the winter. Wait until the indoor growing conditions improve before fertilizing indoor roses.

Pruning

Only prune off canes damaged by snow or ice.

Pests

Check outdoor roses for signs of animal damage. Rabbits, deer, and voles are major problems. Covered roses should be safe from rabbits and deer. Try repellents on uncovered roses that are suffering damage.

Voles are mouselike rodents that travel under the snow, feeding on seeds, roots, cambium, and bark. Poisonous baits or snap traps baited with peanut butter and oats can be used to manage these pests. Place traps and bait packets in pipes or otherwise out of reach of other wildlife, birds, and children. Read and follow all label directions on poisonous baits.

Check indoor roses for signs of mites and aphids. These insects suck out the plant juices, causing the leaves to be speckled, yellow, and stunted. Cover the pot with a plastic bag. Place plants in the shower and rinse with clear water. This helps dislodge many of the insects. Then spray the upper and lower leaf surfaces with insecticidal soap. This soap is effective at killing soft-bodied insects, such as aphids and mites, but it is safe for the plant. Insecticidal soap can be found at most garden centers and floral shops. Repeat once a week as needed. You will probably need at least two to four applications to keep these pests under control.

Helpful Hints

Make the most of this slow gardening period by preparing for the growing season ahead.

- Visit your local library and check out the many books on roses. This is a great place to get inspiration and ideas on how to use roses in the landscape.
- Attend meetings of the local Rose Society.
- Contact the American Rose Society, P.O. Box 30,000, Shreveport, LA 71130. They have several useful publications for home gardeners.
- Call the Yard and Garden Line for directions on sending soil samples to the University's Soil Testing Laboratory or to listen to dozens of Info U tapes about garden activities. Call 612-624-4771 (Metro) or toll-free 1-888-624-4771 (Greater Minnesota).

Planning

Begin finalizing your landscape plans. Double-check the list of roses against your landscape needs. Make sure they provide the seasonal interest you desire such as flowers all summer, rose hips for fall, and winter interest. Look for added features such as fragrance and flower color. Then evaluate the size and growth habits to make sure the rose will fit the space and the landscape design.

Attend a meeting of your local rose society. These local experts can give you great insight into growing roses in your part of the state.

Planting

Planting is still just a dream. Keep looking at the catalogs and reading books to find out more about the roses best suited to your landscape. In your search, you will notice the different classifications of roses. These include:

- **Species Roses**, which are varieties that are found growing in the wild. Many were used to develop modern roses. Some are still used in our modern landscapes.

- **Shrub Roses**, which are usually species roses that have been hybridized for gardening pur-

poses. They are usually hardy and require little maintenance. Some are one-time bloomers, while others will bloom several times in a season.

- **Old Garden Roses**, or **Old Roses**, which are varieties and species that were discovered and grown before 1867. This is when the hybrid tea roses were introduced. Old roses tend to be less showy and refined than the hybrid teas, but they are usually more fragrant, more disease resistant, and hardier.

- **Modern Roses**, which are those roses introduced after 1867. These include **Hybrid Teas**, **Polyanthas**, **Floribundas**, and **Grandifloras**.

  - **Hybrid Tea Roses** are grafted onto a hardy rootstock. They grow 3 to 5 feet tall and produce single or double flowers on long stems.

  - **Polyanthas** are hybrids that grow up to 2 feet tall and produce a proliferation of small flowers in clusters. They are hardier than hybrid teas but less popular than floribundas.

  - **Floribundas** are the result of crossing hybrid teas with polyanthas. These 3-foot-tall plants are usually grafted and produce many small flowers in clusters.

- **Grandifloras** are grafted and grow up to 6 feet tall. They produce flowers similar to the hybrid teas, though the blooms are smaller and are clustered in groups of five to seven.

- **Tree Roses** can be any type of rose, though **Hybrid Teas** and **Floribundas** are the most popular choices. A straight trunk is grafted onto a hardy rootstock. The desired rose is then grafted to the top of the trunk. During cold weather, both grafts need to be covered or the plants should be moved indoors for winter.

- **Climbing Roses** can grow to over 6 feet tall and can be trained over fences, on trellises, or up walls. These plants produce long canes that can be tied to the support structure.

- Large-flowered **Climbers** have thick stiff canes, bloom twice a season, and are climbing versions (mutations) of other roses. Some are grafted, and all benefit from winter protection.

- **Ramblers** are much hardier climbers. They flower once a year on long, thin, flexible canes.

- **Miniature Roses** are small versions of **Hybrid Teas** and **Floribundas**. They produce smaller leaves and flowers on 6- to 18-inch-tall plants.

Care

Continue monitoring roses under winter protection. Pick up and replace any rose cones, mulches, or protection that has blown off the plants.

Vent rose cones on warm sunny days to prevent heat buildup, which can damage rose canes. If necessary, you can cut small holes near the top of the cones and on the side facing away from the wind.

Watering

No need to water outdoor roses.

Water indoor roses as needed. Water thoroughly and frequently enough to keep the soil slightly moist. Set on a gravel tray to increase humidity around the plant.

Check on **Container Roses** stored in the garage. Water them whenever the soil is dry and not frozen.

Fertilizing

Do not fertilize outdoor roses.

Helpful Hints

Always select the hardiest and most pest-resistant rose available. Visit local botanical gardens to find out which roses perform the best for them. You may find that many of these are labeled AARS. This means they are one of the **All American Rose Selections.** These award-winning roses have been tested at over 25 locations in the United States. They were selected as winners based upon their flower form, pest resistance, fragrance, growth habit, or other feature. See http://www.rose.org/ for more information.

We are fortunate to have an AARS test garden at Lake Harriet Rose Gardens in Lyndale Park in Minneapolis. AARS varieties are on display at more than 138 gardens in 43 states.

Only fertilize indoor roses that are actively growing or showing signs of nutrient deficiency. Nutrient deficient roses have stunted, pale, or off-colored leaves. Fertilize with a diluted solution of any flowering houseplant fertilizer.

Pruning

Limit pruning to storm damaged stems.

Pests

Continue monitoring plants for animal damage. Watch for signs of rabbit and deer feeding. Use repellents to protect uncovered roses exhibiting damage. Use snap traps baited with peanut butter and oats or poisonous baits to control voles. Cover traps and baits to keep children, pets, and other wildlife away.

Continue checking indoor roses for signs of mites and aphids. These insects suck out the plant juices, causing the leaves to be speckled, yellow, and stunted. Cover the pot with a plastic bag. Place plants in the shower and rinse with water. Then spray the upper and lower leaf surfaces with insecticidal soap. Repeated applications will probably be needed.

Planning

Place your rose order if you have not already. Select a place to store roses that arrive prior to planting. **Bare-root Roses** should be kept in a cool, dark place until planting. Locate containers, potting mix, and other materials that will be needed for growing **Potted Roses**. Make a list of needed supplies.

Check stored pesticides and fertilizers. Take an inventory of the type and amount of each product you have in storage. This will save you time and money spent buying materials you don't really need. Make sure they are stored safely. See November "Care" for storage tips.

Planting

Most of the state is still covered with snow and the southern half is experiencing a mixture of spring and winter weather. In other words, it is too early to plant.

Repot indoor roses that have outgrown their pots and will remain in containers throughout the season. Carefully slide the plants out of the existing containers. Move them to slightly larger (about 1 to 2 inches bigger in diameter) containers and fill with a well-drained potting mix. Water, but do not fertilize for several weeks.

Store dormant **Bare-root Roses** in a cool, dark location until planting. Dormant roses can be stored in a spare refrigerator, root cellar, or other location where temperatures remain above freezing. Keep the roots moist and covered with peat moss or sawdust.

Or *heel in* **Bare-root Roses** outdoors if they cannot be planted within several days. Dig a trench with one sloping side. Place the roots and the graft in the trench with the plant leaning on the side. Cover with soil.

Check stored roses. Move to a cooler location if the buds begin to swell. Pot up any plants that begin to grow. Move them to a sunny location and keep indoors until the danger of frost has passed.

Roses that started to grow in transit or storage will need different care. Plant in pots and grow indoors. Keep them near a sunny window. Water thoroughly, and allow the top few inches of soil to dry before watering again. **Potted Roses** can be moved outdoors after the danger of frost.

Care

Continue to monitor winter protection.

- Keep mulch, shelters, and rose cones in place until weather begins to consistently hover near freezing.

- Continue to vent rose cones on warm or sunny days. The goal is to keep the roses cool and dormant. High temperatures can cause premature growth that can be killed by cold temperatures in spring. Close vents when temperatures drop.

- Remove cones and the outer layer of mulch after a week of temperatures above freezing, but keep the cones handy in case of an extreme drop in temperature.

- Gradually start removing the remaining layers of mulch. Many gardeners let the spring rains wash away the soil mounded over the crown.

Watering

Continue watering indoor roses as the soil dries.

Check on **Container Roses** stored in the garage. Water them whenever the soil is dry and not frozen.

You usually do not need to water outdoor roses. Check soil moisture once the ground thaws and roses are uncovered. Water only if the top 2 to 4 inches of soil are starting to dry.

Fertilizing

No need to fertilize yet. Wait until new spring growth is established.

Indoor roses can be fertilized with a diluted solution of any flowering houseplant fertilizer.

Pruning

Wait until the weather has warmed and the mulch is off to start pruning. Remove any damaged branches as they are found.

Check, clean, and sharpen hand pruners while waiting for the pruning season to begin.

- *Replace* the damaged or old blades that can no longer be sharpened. High quality pruners have replacement blades, while cheaper pruners must be replaced when damaged. Replacement blades are available through garden supply catalogs and many garden centers. Replace nicked and damaged blades.

- Use a three-cornered (tapered) metal file to *sharpen* the cutting edge of your hand pruner. Take the pruners apart for easier sharpening. Sharpen away from the blade for safety or toward the cutting edge for a sharpening edge—just be careful. Smooth off any burrs that form along the edge. Make a test cut to check for sharpness.

- *Clean* the blades with a lightweight oil. Spray to lubricate the working parts and prevent rust.

Helpful Hints

Deer and rabbits will feed on roses anytime they can reach the plants. A variety of techniques may be needed to control these pests.

- *Fence in small areas.* Use a black or green fine mesh material to fence in the garden. This material allows you to see the garden while providing a barrier to the animals. The fence should be 5 feet tall with the bottom few inches sunk into the ground. The deer will stay out of these small areas and the rabbits can't get in.

- *Homemade or commercial repellents may provide some relief.* Hot pepper sprinkled on the plants has provided some relief. One landscape professional swears by this method, while another says the deer prefer the "seasoned" plants. Or try bloodmeal, TreeGuard, Ropel, and other commercial repellents. Apply them early and repeat after heavy rains. Try a variety of products.

- *Scare tactics such as clanging pans, blasting radios, white balloons on a stick, and other devices may help keep animals away.* Vary these tactics for continued control. I find urban animals are not scared by people, noises, and smells. They are too used to dining undisturbed in our landscape.

- *Trapping is not always a humane method for controlling rabbits.* This practice can separate a mother from her young babies. Releasing animals in a strange environment can be stressful and even deadly. Besides, who needs more rabbits? Parks, farmers, and other gardeners probably have enough rabbits of their own.

Pests

Continue to monitor and control rabbits, deer, and voles as needed. Reapply animal repellents after heavy rains. Check on vole traps and baits.

Check indoor roses for aphids and mites. Treat with a strong blast of water and insecticidal soap as needed. Repeated applications are usually needed.

Planning

A trip to the local garden center and a look at the many **Bare-root Roses** will confirm that planting season is finally here. Select Grade 1 roses for the best quality. The bare-root roses should be dormant, have firm canes, and be free of pests.

Start plant records in your journal when you buy your plants. Record the plant's name, place of purchase, and planting date. As the year goes by, also record winter survival, care provided, pests encountered, and weather conditions in your journal. These notes will help you monitor and improve the health and winter survival of your roses.

Planting

Plant and transplant **Dormant Roses** after severe weather has passed and before new growth begins. *Prepare* the planting site by working the needed organic matter and amendments into the top 12 inches of soil. Sprinkle the area with water or allow the soil to settle for several days before planting.

See "Planting" in the introduction to this chapter for directions on planting **Bare-root Roses**.

Proper site preparation is also important when transplanting roses. Move plants in early spring before growth begins.

1 Make sure the soil around the rose is moist, not wet. *Water* dry soils the night before transplanting roses. The moist soil will hold together during transplanting.

2 *Dig* out as much of the root system (2 feet or more in diameter) as possible. Make the rootball only as large as you are able to handle. Digging and dropping a large rootball is worse than starting with a smaller one.

3 Use your shovel or spading fork to *lift* the rose out of the planting hole. You may need to cut attached roots with your pruning shears.

4 *Slide* a plastic or burlap tarp under the rootball. This makes transporting the plant easier and reduces the risk of damaging the rootball.

5 Slide the plant off the tarp and into the planting hole. *Plant* it at the same depth as it was growing before. The graft should be 2 inches below the soil surface.

6 *Fill* with amended soil and water.

Care

Start or continue removing winter protection as the temperatures consistently hover near freezing. Remove protection gradually. Continue to vent rose cones on warm sunny days until all protection is removed. If you have already removed the cones, continue to keep them handy in case of an extreme drop in temperature.

Tip **Climbers** and **Tree Roses** back into an upright position. Firm the soil around the roots and water. Attach climbing roses to trellises and tree roses to stakes as needed.

Move stored roses out of storage after severe weather has passed.

Indoor roses need to remain indoors. Their tender leaves are not ready for the unpredictable and often cold days of April.

Watering

Begin watering once the winter protection is removed and the ground begins to dry. Established roses need about 1 inch of water each week. Cool, wet springs often eliminate or reduce the need to water. Water plants thoroughly. Apply needed water in one application each week in clay soils and in two applications in sandy soils.

As roses are moved out of storage, they will need more frequent watering. Check plants daily and water as the soil dries. Keep the soil moist around newly planted roses. Once the plants are established, water deeply and less frequently.

Continue to water indoor roses as needed. With the increase in light they may need more frequent watering. Adjust your watering schedule so that the soil stays slightly moist.

Helpful Hints

Extremely harsh weather, improper winter protection, or shallow planting can cause the death of the bud graft (the swollen portion of the stem). This delicate union joins the hardy root system with the desired rose. Since the graft is planted below ground, the damage is not always discovered immediately. After the graft dies, the rootstock takes over. If the graft has died, replace the rose and plant the new rose with the graft 2 inches below the soil surface.

The following changes in growth may mean the graft has died:

- Canes are thicker, with more thorns and fewer leaves.
- The plant fails to bloom or produces flowers that are different than those produced in the past.

Fertilizing

Fertilize **Old Garden, Shrub, Species,** *and* **Climbing Roses** *as the buds begin to swell.* Apply the amount and type of fertilizer recommended by your soil test. If this information is not available, apply 2 pounds per 100 square feet or 2 heaping tablespoons per plant of a low-nitrogen, slow-release fertilizer. Wait to fertilize **Hybrid Teas.**

Apply a diluted solution of any flowering houseplant fertilizer to your **Indoor Roses.**

Pruning

Assess animal and winter damage. *Remove* only dead and damaged canes on **Old Roses,** including

Climbers. These roses bloom on the previous season's growth. Major pruning is done after flowering.

Prune **Hybrid Tea** and other **Modern Roses** just before growth begins.

1 Start by *removing* dead and winter damaged canes. Living canes are green with white pith in the center. Prune at least 1 inch below the darkened dead tissue.

2 *Cut* at a 45-degree angle above a healthy, outward-facing bud.

3 *Remove* all spindly weak growth, crossing stems, and canes growing toward the center of the plant.

4 *Prune* out any suckers that grow from beneath the graft.

Cut them off below the ground near the rootstock.

5 *Shape* the plant to 16 to 18 inches tall. After severe winters, there will be nothing left to shape after you remove all the winter damage.

Pests

Develop the habit of monitoring roses and other plants for pests.

Seal fresh pruning cuts to prevent cane borer. This is particularly important for roses with a history of this pest. Dab cut ends with pruning paint, yellow shellac, or white glue to prevent the borer from entering through this opening.

237

Planning

Evaluate the health and survival rate of existing plants. You may need to purchase some replacement plants for those that were killed over the winter. Watch for signs of new growth. The aboveground growth may be dead, but the graft and roots may still be alive. Watch for signs of new growth emerging above the graft union.

Continue evaluating your plan. Make sure you have room for the roses you have bought and those you plan on purchasing. I am always tempted by the plant tags, new introductions, and beautiful pictures and then end up buying more plants than I should.

Planting

Finish planting your **Bare-root Roses**. See "Planting" in the introduction to this chapter for details. Bare-root roses that began to grow during shipping or while in storage should be potted and grown in a protected (frost-free) location. These plants can be planted outdoors after the danger of frost.

Potted Roses are now available and can also be planted.

Dormant Roses should be planted as soon as possible. Those grown in greenhouses need to be hardened off before moving them outdoors. Many garden centers will do this for you. If not, you can *harden off* plants by gradually increasing their exposure to sunlight and cooler temperatures. Protect the new growth from freezing temperatures. After two weeks, the plants are ready to move outdoors.

1 *Prepare* the soil by working the needed organic matter and amendments into the top 12 inches of soil. Sprinkle the area with water or allow the soil to settle for several days before planting.

2 *Dig* a hole several feet wide and deep enough to plant the graft union 2 inches below the soil surface. Be aware that many **Potted Roses** are growing with the graft union above the soil.

Use special care when *transplanting* **Potted Roses**. The root system is not always established. See the introduction to this chapter for directions on how to plant potted roses.

See September "Planting" for details on planting **Shrub Roses**.

Care

Begin *hardening off* indoor roses and greenhouse roses in the middle of the month.

Stake or trellis **Climbing** and **Tree Roses** as needed. Use fabric, twine, or flexible ties to avoid damaging the trunk and stems.

Watering

Continue to water plants as needed.

Water **Potted Roses** as soon as the soil starts to dry. Check soil moisture daily and water as needed.

Keep the soil around newly planted roses moist. The new plants will begin to root into the surrounding soil in several weeks. At that time, water thoroughly but less frequently.

Fertilizing

Fertilize **Old Garden, Shrub Roses, Species,** and **Climbers** if you have not already. Follow soil test recommendations, or apply 2 heaping tablespoons per plant or 2 pounds per 100 square feet of a low-nitrogen, slow-release fertilizer.

Use the same rate to fertilize **Modern Roses** once their new spring growth is full size.

Fertilize **New Roses** three to four weeks after planting.

Fertilize **Container Roses** once or twice a month with any flowering houseplant fertilizer.

Pruning

Remove only dead and damaged canes on **Old Roses** and **Climbers**. Major pruning should be done after flowering.

Finish pruning **Hybrid Tea Roses**. See April "Pruning" for more detailed information.

Pests

Check for pests at least once a week. Small populations of aphids can easily be removed by hand.

Seal recent pruning cuts on roses that have suffered from cane borer in the past. Dab cut ends with pruning paint, yellow shellac, or white glue to prevent the borer from entering through this opening.

Helpful Hints

The best defense against pest problems is a healthy plant, but even healthy plants can be infested by disease. Sanitation is sometimes enough to keep diseases under control. If you chose to use a fungicide, be sure to read and follow all label directions carefully. Select a fungicide labeled to control several diseases. This will give you a great range of control with one product. Here are some of the more common rose diseases and the recommended controls:

- **Blackspot** is one of the most common and most serious fungal diseases on roses. It causes black spots and yellowing of the leaves. Once a planting is infected, it is likely to develop the disease in the future. Remove infected and fallen leaves throughout the season. Fall cleanup helps reduce the source of infection for the next season. Apply fungicides labeled to control blackspot on roses in mid-June or at the first sign of this disease. Repeat every seven days throughout the growing season. You can lengthen the time between applications during dry weather.

- **Powdery mildew** is a fungal disease that appears as a white powder on the leaf surface. It is a common problem during periods of fluctuating humidity. Properly spaced plants growing in full sun are less likely to develop this disease. Apply fungicides as soon as the disease appears and repeat every 7 to 14 days. Use a product labeled for controlling powdery mildew on roses. Several universities and botanical gardens have successfully used weekly applications of a mixture of 1 tablespoon baking soda, $\frac{1}{2}$ tablespoon lightweight horticultural oil or insecticidal soap, and 1 gallon of water to control both blackspot and powdery mildew.

- **Botrytis blight** is a fungal disease that causes flower buds to turn black and fail to open. It is most common on pink and white roses and occurs during wet weather. Prune off and destroy infected blossoms. Sanitation and drier weather are usually enough to keep this disease under control.

- **Cankers** are sunken and discolored areas that develop due to weather, mechanical injury, or disease. Prune out infected canes beneath the canker. Disinfect tools between cuts. Provide plants with proper care and winter protection to minimize this problem.

Clean up any dead leaves and debris near roses. This helps reduce the source of infection for this growing season.

JUNE

Planning

By early June there should be no doubt about winter survival. **Remove** dead and struggling plants. Select an appropriate replacement that may or may not be another rose. If roses keep dying in this location, it may be time to find another place for your roses.

Roses will start blooming this month. Take pictures of these blooming beauties; you have earned some bragging rights. **Record** bloom times and color. Make notes of any future changes you might want to make.

Visit area botanical and rose gardens. This is a pleasant way to spend a June afternoon while gathering ideas for your own garden.

Planting

June is a good time to plant **Potted Roses**. The weather is usually not too hot and dry, making it easier for plants to adjust to their new location. Plus, the plants have all summer to get established before the onset of severe winter weather. See "Planting" in the introduction to this chapter for specifics.

See September "Planting" for details on planting **Shrub Roses**.

Care

Tie canes of **Climbers** and **Ramblers** to a trellis, fence, or other support.

Watering

Water roses as needed. Use a watering wand or soaker hose to avoid wet foliage and splashing water that can lead to disease problems.

Check **Container Roses** daily and water as the soil begins to dry.

Water new plantings often enough to keep the planting area moist. Decrease watering frequency in several weeks once new rooting occurs.

Fertilizing

Follow soil test recommendations, or apply 2 pounds per 100 square feet or 2 heaping tablespoons per plant of a low-nitrogen, slow-release fertilizer. Select a fertilizer with at least one-third of the nitrogen in a slow-release form.

Fertilize repeat-blooming **Old Roses** after their first flush of flowers.

Fertilize **Hybrid Teas** four to six weeks after your first application.

Fertilize **Container Roses** once or twice a month with any flowering houseplant fertilizer, following label directions

Pruning

Leave the fading flowers on spring-blooming **Old Roses**. These one-time bloomers have finished their flower show, but not their beauty for the season. The faded flowers will soon be replaced by fruit known as rose hips. The hips will turn orange or red and will often persist through fall and winter. They are decorative in the landscape or floral arrangements, high in vitamin C, and help attract birds to the winter landscape.

Deadhead repeat bloomers and **Hybrid Tea Roses**. This improves the appearance and increases bloom time. Remove only individual flowers in the cluster as they fade. Once all the flowers in the cluster have bloomed, prune back the flower stem to the first 5-leaflet leaf. Deadhead single-flowered roses back to the first 5-leaflet leaf. This encourages stouter and stronger branch development.

Now is the time to prune **Old Garden**, **Species**, **Shrub**, and **Climbing Roses**.

Shrub and **Species Roses** are hardy and need very little pruning. They look best if allowed to grow to their normal size and shape. Do very little pruning on new plants. Once the plants have reached full size, they may need a little yearly pruning.

- Thin overgrown plantings by removing several of the older canes to ground level. This is often the only pruning that is needed.

- You can shorten overgrown stems by one-third. This helps contain plant growth and increase flowers for next season.

- Limit pruning on **Shrub Roses** that produce attractive rose hips. Excessive pruning will eliminate the fruit that provides added ornamental value and food for many birds.

Ramblers are tough, often hardy **Climbing Roses**. They bloom once and proceed to ramble at will. Pruning helps control their growth and improve the appearance.

1 *Deadhead* flowers as they fade. Prune the flowering stems back to the third or fourth set of leaves.

2 *Prune* out one-third of the older canes. This allows room for the new canes to grow and develop. New growth this year will be the flowering wood next spring. Some of the new

---

Helpful Hints

Enjoy your roses outdoors in the garden or inside in a vase.

- *Cut* rose flowers early in the morning just as the top of the bud is starting to open. Make the cut on a slight angle above an outward facing, 5-leaflet leaf. Cut flowers back to a 3-leaflet leaf on young flowers that may not tolerate this amount of pruning.
- *Remove* the lower leaves on the stem.
- *Recut* the bottom of the stem on an angle just before placing in a vase.

---

growth develops on older canes. So remove older canes that have very little new growth.

3 *Tie* new shoots to the trellis or wrap them around arches, fences, or pillars. Shoots bent sideways will produce flowers all along the stem.

4 *Remove* any long and wayward canes that have outgrown the available space.

Once-blooming **Climbers** also bloom on the previous season's growth but are not as vigorous growers as the ramblers. Be a little more selective in your pruning efforts with these plants.

1 *Deadhead* faded flowers. Prune the flowering stems back to the third or fourth sets of leaves.

2 Evaluate the health and vigor of the plant. The more new canes that are forming, then the more old canes you can remove.

Remove as many old canes as you have new canes to replace them.

3 *Prune* the less vigorous, thick, brown flowering stems to ground level.

4 *Tie* new canes to the trellis. Arrange them on the structure to fill in empty spaces left after pruning.

Pests

Sanitation and proper care are critical in pest management. Monitor plants for signs of blackspot and powdery mildew diseases.

Insect populations are also starting to build. See March, May, and July "Helpful Hints" for more pest information.

Planning

Continue to monitor the garden and record significant weather events, care strategies, and plant health. Evaluate the sun and shade patterns and make sure plants are receiving the amount of light they need. Record the information in your gardening journal.

Planting

You can still plant **Container Roses**. They may need a little extra attention if the weather turns hot and dry. See May "Planting" for details on planting **Grafted Roses** and September "Planting" for details on planting **Shrub Roses**.

Care

Mulch the soil with a thin layer of organic matter. A 1-inch layer of cocoa bean shells mixed with rice hulls makes an attractive mulch that helps suppress weed growth and conserve moisture. A thin layer of cocoa bean shells, if rice hulls aren't available, will also work. Or use a thicker, 2- to 3-inch layer of twice-shredded bark or woodchips.

Tie up new growth on **Climbing Roses**. Use string, cloth, or other flexible material to loosely tie stems to the trellis, fence, or other support structure.

Watering

Water new roses often enough to keep the roots and several feet of surrounding soil moist.

Water established plants as needed. Roses need about 1 inch of water (5 to 6 gallons per plant) per week. Supplement rainfall as needed. Apply all the needed water in one application to clay soils. For sandy soils, make two applications of half the needed water each week.

Check **Container Roses** daily. Water as the soil begins to dry.

Fertilizing

Make your next application of fertilizer to **Hybrid Tea Roses**, waiting at least four to six weeks after the last application.

Fertilize **Container Roses** once or twice a month with any flowering houseplant fertilizer. Follow label directions.

Pruning

Continue to *deadhead* roses. Remove only individual flowers in the cluster as they fade. Once all the flowers in the cluster have bloomed, prune back the flower stem to the first 5-leaflet leaf. Deadhead single-flowered roses back to the first 5-leaflet leaf. This encourages stouter and stronger branch development.

Cuting Roses

Pests

Weeds are starting to grow faster than your roses. Pull weeds growing in and around the plants. Or use a hoe to lightly cultivate these invaders. Be careful not to injure the rose roots. Mulching will help reduce weed problems.

Repellents, fences, and scare tactics may provide some relief from deer and rabbits. See March "Helpful Hints" for more information on reducing deer damage.

Helpful Hints

A variety of insects attack roses. Small populations can usually be removed by hand. You may choose to use an insecticide to control larger populations that are damaging the plant. Many rose fertilizers contain insecticides. Check your fertilizer and pesticide labels before applying these materials.

- Aphids and mites suck out the plant juices causing the leaves to appear speckled, yellow, and distorted. Many rose fertilizers contain insecticides labeled for controlling these pests. Lightweight horticulture (summer) oils and insecticidal soap are more environmentally friendly products that will control these pests.

- Leafhoppers often go undetected but can cause plants to be weak and stunted. These greenish-yellow insects feed on the underside of the leaves. They hop sideways when disturbed. Insecticidal soap and many other insecticides will control these insects.

- Budworms and other caterpillars feed on flower buds and leaves. Remove and destroy the caterpillars as they are found. *Bacillius thuringiensis*, sold as Bt, Dipel, or Thuricide will control these insects without harming other beneficial insects.

- Rose chafers are most common in areas with sandy soil. These beetles eat the leaf tissue, leaving the veins in tact. They feed on roses from late June through July. Small populations can be removed and destroyed by hand. Insecticides labeled to control chafers on roses may be used to control larger populations or insects on large plantings. Make sure the insects are still present prior to spraying. The damage is often noticed after the insects have left.

- Japanese beetles have been found in several areas of Minnesota. These small, metallic-green beetles seem to be moving in and adapting to our colder climates. Watch for this pest in June through August. Remove or treat with an insecticide when the adults are found feeding on the plants.

- Earwigs are reddish-brown beetles with pinchers on their back end. They eat holes in leaves and flower petals. To trap and kill damaging earwigs, set a crumpled paper under a flowerpot. The earwigs will hide in the folds of the paper during the day. Move fast to capture and crush the hiding earwigs. Insecticides can also be used to control these pests.

Continue monitoring plants for pests on a weekly basis. Early detection and sanitation can reduce pest populations with fewer pesticides. Always read and follow all label directions whenever using any chemical. Wear gloves, goggles, and long sleeves. Check label for any other safety precautions. Spray early in the morning when the air is still and there is less activity in the yard. This will help reduce spray hazards.

Watch for blackspot, powdery mildew, and canker diseases. Aphids, mites, leafhoppers, caterpillars, and beetle populations are starting to reach damaging levels. See May and July "Helpful Hints" for specific pest information.

Planning

Take a few minutes to survey your roses. Evaluate and record their growth rate, flowering, and pest problems. Many repeat-blooming roses are starting to put on their second show of the season. Take time to enjoy your roses as summer care begins winding down.

Planting

Finish planting potted **Hybrid Teas** early in the month. The later you plant, the greater the risk of winterkill. See May "Planting" for details on planting potted hybrid teas.

You can still plant hardy **Shrub Roses** throughout August and early fall. See September "Planting" for details.

Water and *mulch* the roses after planting. This helps plants adjust quickly to their new location. Use a transplant starter fertilizer at planting. The low nitrogen and higher phosphorus will help stimulate establishment without promoting late-season growth that can be winterkilled.

Care

It is not too late to mulch roses. A 1- to 3-inch layer of organic matter can help conserve moisture and suppress weeds. Weed the garden prior to mulching. Avoid piling the mulch around the crown of the plant.

Hybrid Tea Roses are often *disbudded* to increase flower size as well. Remove side buds that form along the stem. This allows the plant to send all its energy to one flower. The result is one large, long stem flower. Harvest or deadhead this back to the first 5-leaflet leaf.

Other roses, such as **Grandifloras** and **Floribundas**, produce several flowers in a cluster. *Remove* all but one bud for a single large bloom. Or allow the cluster to develop so you have several smaller blossoms. Deadhead the individual flowers as they fade. Cut the whole stem back once all the flowers in the cluster have faded.

Watering

Continue to water plants as needed. New plantings need special attention. Make sure the roots and surrounding soil stay moist. After two weeks reduce watering frequency, but continue to water deeply.

Continue to provide established plants with 1 inch of water each week. Early August is often hot and dry, meaning you may need to supplement the rainfall. Water the soil thoroughly until the top 8 inches are moist. Wait until the top 2 to 4 inches are dry before watering again.

Check **Container Roses** daily. Water often enough to keep the soil slightly moist. Use a watering wand or drip irrigation to avoid getting water on the leaves. Splashing water and wet foliage increase disease problems.

Fertilizing

Stop fertilizing. Late applications of fertilizer will encourage late season growth that is more susceptible to winter injury.

Pruning

Remove suckers that appear at the base of roses. Cut them off below ground to reduce the chance of re-sprouting. These canes are growing from the hardy rootstock and can diminish the vigor and beauty of the desired, grafted rose.

Prune off any cankered, dead, or damaged canes. Between cuts, disinfect tools with a solution of 1 part bleach to 9 parts water. This will help reduce the spread of diseases.

Continue to *harvest* or *deadhead* flowers. Regular deadheading keeps the plants producing more flowers. Remove individual flowers within clusters as they fade. Remove the whole flower cluster back to the first 5-leaflet leaf once all the flowers have faded. For long stem roses, cut the stem back to the first 5-leaflet leaf after this blossom has faded.

Pests

Deer and rabbits continue to feed on roses. Repellents, fences, and scare tactics may provide some relief. See March "Helpful Hints" for more information on reducing deer damage.

Continue controlling weeds. Remove these unwanted plants by hand or light cultivation. Be careful not to injure rose roots in the process. Add a layer of cocoa bean shells, twice-shredded bark, or other organic material. Mulching helps prevent weeds and conserve moisture. It also adds some nutrients and organic matter to the soil as it breaks down.

Helpful Hints

If your planting space is limited, or if you need a little color on your patio, consider growing **Container Roses. Tree Roses**, **Miniature Roses**, and **Hybrid Teas** can all be grown in containers.

1 Leave the rose in the nursery pot.

2 Select a decorative container with drainage holes that is one to two sizes larger than the original pot.

3 Place pebbles in the bottom of the decorative pot and set the rose on the pebbles inside the decorative pot.

4 Water when the soil dries.

5 Fertilize with any flowering houseplant fertilizer. The higher phosphorus will help promote flowering. Follow label for rate and frequency. Stop fertilizing in early August. See November "Helpful Hints" for details on overwintering **Container Roses**.

6 Next season move the rose into a larger pot filled with a well-drained potting mix. Incorporate a low-nitrogen, slow-release fertilizer into the soil at planting. This will eliminate the need to fertilize through most or all of the growing season.

Blackspot and powdery mildew may be causing significant damage by now. Most fungicides are preventatives and won't cure what is already infected. Make a note to start treatment earlier next season if this was a problem in your garden.

If the weather is hot and dry, the insect populations will be thriving. Watch for aphids, mites, and leafhoppers. Rose chafers have done their damage for the year, and

Japanese beetles are starting to disappear. See May and July "Helpful Hints" for more specifics on pests and their control.

Planning

The cooler days of September seem to bring out the best in our landscapes, and roses are no exception. Enjoy the beauty and fragrance roses provide. Make notes on the health and attributes of the roses in your garden. These notes will help when you need to decide what stays and what goes when planning next year's additions.

Planting

Wait until next spring to plant and transplant **Hybrid Teas**. Planting early gives them several months to establish a healthy root system before winter.

Hardy **Shrub** and **Landscape Roses** can still be planted. Make sure they get proper post-planting care. This will help reduce transplant shock and speed up establishment.

1 *Prepare* the soil by working the needed organic matter and amendments into the top 12 inches of soil. Sprinkle the area with water, or allow the soil to settle for several days before planting.

2 *Dig* a hole at last twice as wide and just as deep as the container. Hardy **Shrub Roses** are not grafted and should be planted at the same depth they are growing in the container.

3 Minimize damage to the root-ball—and you—by cutting the pot off the plant instead of trying to knock it out of the container. Move the rose near the planting hole, and cut off the bottom of the container.

4 *Place* the rose, pot and all, in the planting hole. Adjust the planting depth so the top of the pot is even with the surrounding soil surface.

5 *Slice* the side of the pot and peel it away. Slice through any girdling (circling) roots.

6 *Backfill* the planting hole with the amended soil. Water to eliminate air pockets and help settle the soil.

7 *Mulch* the soil with a 1- to 3-inch layer of cocoa bean shells, woodchips, or shredded bark.

Care

September is the time to enjoy the final show. Your management strategies should focus on encouraging the plants to start *hardening off* for winter. Avoid late-season fertilization and pruning that stimulate new growth.

Some gardeners move planters of **Miniature** and **Tree Roses** indoors for winter. Start *acclimatizing* any roses you plan on wintering indoors.

1 *Locate a cool sunny area to grow the plants over winter.*

2 Over the next few weeks, gradually *reduce* the amount of light the plants receive.

3 *Quarantine* (isolate) the roses for several weeks. Watch and control insects prior to introducing them into your indoor plant collection.

4 *Move* plants to their permanent indoor location. Keep soil slightly moist and continue to watch for insects and disease.

Watering

Cooler temperatures mean less frequent watering. Water when the top 2 to 4 inches start to dry.

Fertilizing

Do not fertilize. This is the time for rose growth to slow and for the plants to start preparing for winter.

Helpful Hints

Most **Grafted Roses**, including **Hybrid Teas**, **Climbing**, and **Tree Roses**, need protection to survive our harsh winters.

The Minnesota Tip Method requires work but yields consistently good results. This is the best method for overwintering **Climbers** and **Tree Roses** outdoors.

1 Start the process in mid-October in the northern part of the state and several weeks later in the southern part of the state. Loosely *tie* together the rose canes. Do not prune **Climbing Roses** and **Ramblers** in the fall. This eliminates the spring bloom.

2 *Dig* a trench from the base of the plant outward. It should be long enough and deep enough to accommodate the plant. Use a spade or garden fork to gently *loosen* the soil around the plant.

3 *Tip* the plant over and lay it in the trench. Be careful to bend the roots, not the stem. You don't want to break the graft that you are trying to protect. *Cover* the plant with soil.

4 Once the soil freezes, *mulch* with a thick layer of straw. Use chicken wire or hardware cloth to keep the mulch from blowing away. Start removing this protection in early April.

See October and November "Helpful Hints" for more ideas on winter protection.

Pruning

Stop *deadheading* after the final wave of flowers or in the latter part of the month. This allows rose hips to form and the plants to start hardening off for winter. Limit pruning to removal of dead, diseased, and damaged canes.

Pests

Continue to monitor and control pests. Maintaining a healthy, relatively pest-free plant throughout the season is the best start to winter protection. Prune off canes with sunken or discolored areas. Remove and rake away any diseased foliage. Continue fungicide treatments as needed.

Insect populations are still present. Monitor and treat only when damage occurs.

Weed control continues as long as they appear. Cleaning up weeds now reduces future weed and pest problems.

Planning

The roses have survived the first frost and continue to be beautiful. The **Hybrid Teas** are still blooming and rose hips provide additional interest. Start planning now for cold weather ahead.

Hybrid Teas and most other **Grafted Roses** benefit from winter protection. Most **Shrubs** and **Species Roses** will survive with little or no winter protection.

See September, October, and November "Helpful Hints" for detailed descriptions of several methods of winter protection.

Planting

Wait until next spring to plant **Hybrid Teas** and other nonhardy roses.

There may be time to finish planting hardy **Shrub** and **Landscape Roses**. Be sure to plant them as soon as possible. Make sure they get proper post-planting care. This will help reduce transplant shock and speed up establishment. See September "Planting" for detailed instructions.

Care

Plan and prepare for winter protection.

- Dig trenches for **Hybrid Teas**, **Climbers**, and **Tree Roses** that will be protected using the Minnesota Tip Method.

- Stockpile and cover soil or compost that you plan to use as winter mulch. Covering will help prevent it from freezing so that it will be workable when it is time to cover the roses.

- Gather and bag leaves if you plan on using the Leaf Mulch Method. (See October "Helpful Hints".)

- Fence in rose gardens being protected by the Leaf Mulch Method. Use a 4-foot-high hardware cloth to create a fence around the planting bed. Sink several inches of the hardware cloth fencing into the ground. This must be done before the ground freezes.

- Purchase and store rose cones (if using this type of winter protection) for later use. Do not start covering roses until after a week of freezing temperatures. This is usually mid-November in the northern part of the state and the end of November or early December in the southern part of the state.

Harvest a few roses now for winter enjoyment.

1 *Line* a solid cardboard box with a plastic bag. Use a 10-by-14-inch or other box of a convenient size.

2 *Move* the box to the basement, crawl space, or other location where it will stay cool, but above 40 degrees Fahrenheit.

3 *Fill* the box with wet sand once it is in its permanent location. It may be too heavy to move once filled.

4 *Pick* roses that are in full bud and show a little color.

5 *Remove* the leaves and submerge the stems (with the flowers above the water) in warm water for 45 to 60 minutes.

6 Make a hole in the sand for the rose stem. *Stand* roses in the sand so that the stems are covered and the buds are just above the sand.

7 *Remove* flowers when needed throughout winter. Recut the stem and place in hot water.

Watering

Continue watering the plants as needed. The cooler temperatures mean less watering. Supplement natural rainfall when the top 2 to 4 inches of soil start to dry.

Fertilizing

Do not fertilize. This is the time for rose growth to slow and for the plants to start preparing for winter.

Pruning

Stop *deadheading* roses. Allow rose hips to form and plants to harden off for winter.

Limit *pruning* to the removal of dead, broken, or diseased canes as soon as they are found.

Pests

Continue to pull or cultivate weeds. Removing weeds now will reduce the number of these invaders in next year's garden.

Helpful Hints

Most **Grafted Roses**, including **Hybrid Teas**, **Climbing**, and **Tree Roses** need protection to survive our harsh winters. There are many different ways to overwinter roses. Select a method that fits your location and gardening style. See September and November "Helpful Hints" for additional ideas.

I have seen good success with the Leaf Mulch Method demonstrated at several northern botanical and private gardens. Volume and dry leaves are critical to success. For this method:

1   *Surround* your rose bed with a 4-foot-high fence of hardware cloth before the ground freezes.

2   *Sink* the bottom few inches of fencing into the soil. This will help keep out **voles** and other unwanted guests.

3   *Prune* the roses back to 18 inches after a week of freezing temperatures.

4   *Cover* the roses with a 3-foot layer of tightly packed dry leaves. Use a leaf rake to gently compact the leaves around the roses. Some gardeners cover the leaves with a sheet of plastic to keep them dry.

5   *Remove* the leaves next spring when the temperatures begin to hover near freezing.

Watch for signs of animal damage. If deer have been nibbling on the garden all summer, they will continue dining throughout the winter. Repellents and winter protection will help minimize the damage.

Fall cleanup will help reduce future pest problems. Remove diseased leaves and insects prior to applying winter protection.

Planning

This is a busy month for rose care. As soon as the weather stays consistently cold, you will need to tuck your roses away for winter. In the meantime, work on your garden journal. This information will help you make future plant care decisions.

Planting

Wait until next spring. You have plenty to do getting roses ready for winter. You will need to protect any **Potted Roses** you purchased that did not get planted. Find an unused garden area in a protected location. Sink the pot in the soil. Once the ground lightly freezes, protect this rose just like all the others. Plant it in its permanent location once the ground is workable next spring.

Care

Timing is an important factor in successful winter protection of non-hardy roses. Wait until after a week of freezing temperatures to complete winter protection. Mulching and covering too early can lead to heat buildup, disease problems, and death of plants.

Care for indoor roses as you would your other houseplants. Grow them in a cool, sunny location. They will continue to drop leaves as they adjust to their new location. Keep the soil slightly moist and continue to watch for pests. Mites are a common problem on indoor roses.

Move all garden chemicals to a safe location for winter storage. Here are some storage tips:

- *Create* a lockable storage area to keep chemicals safely away from children.

- *Store* chemicals in a cool, dry location. Liquid pesticides will lose their effectiveness if exposed to freezing temperatures and sunlight. Granular chemicals will not perform well after they are wet.

- Always store chemicals in their original containers with the labels intact. Not only is it the law, but it is also much safer.

- Never store chemicals in containers that can be mistaken for food.

- *Dispose* of empty pesticide containers properly. Check the label for specific instructions.

Watering

Water as needed until the ground freezes. All plantings, including roses, benefit from a thorough watering prior to the ground freezing.

Fertilizing

This is a good time to take a soil test. You will have the information you need to improve your fertilization practices next season.

Pruning

Cut back roses only enough to apply winter protection. The major pruning will be done in spring. Do not prune **Climbers** and **Shrub Roses** since they bloom on old wood.

Pests

Fall cleanup will help minimize future problems. Rake and destroy fallen leaves. Remove any disease-infested leaves. One avid rose grower removes all the foliage from his 200-plus rose collection prior to winterizing them. I guess raking is not that big of a deal after all!

Helpful Hints

Most **Grafted Roses**, including **Hybrid Teas**, **Climbing**, and **Tree Roses** need protection to survive our harsh winters. There are many different ways to overwinter roses. Select a method that fits your location and gardening style. See September and October "Helpful Hints" for additional ideas.

Rose Cones are probably the most common and most misused method of winter protection. This method often fails because the graft is not adequately protected, heat builds up inside the cones, or the cones are put on too early and left on too late. Try improving your success by doing the following:

- Wait to *cover* your roses until after a week of freezing temperatures.
- Loosely *tie* and *prune* back canes just enough to cover them with the cones.
- *Cover* the base of the plant with 8 to 10 inches of soil to insulate the graft.
- Once this freezes, *cover* the plant with the rose cone. Adding a layer of straw between the plant and the cone will provide added insulation.
- *Cover* the edge of the cone with soil. Once this freezes, it will keep the cone in place and the animals out.
- *Vent* cones on warm, sunny days to prevent heat buildup that can damage the plants. Many cones come with removable vents. Add your own if needed by punching holes near the top on the side that faces away from the wind.
- Gradually *remove* the mulch in spring as temperatures begin to hover near freezing.

The Soil Mound Method is quite successful. For this method:

1 *Store* soil or compost in an area or manner to prevent freezing.

2 For additional protection, you can *encircle* the plant with a ring of hardware cloth. Sink the bottom few inches into the soil. This will help keep the animals out and the mulch in.

3 Start winterizing roses after a week of freezing temperatures.

4 Loosely *tie* canes together. Prune any extremely long canes to prevent wind whipping.

5 *Mound* 8 to 10 inches of soil around the base of the plant to help insulate the graft.

6 Wait for the soil to freeze. *Mulch* the remainder of the plant with straw or evergreen branches.

DECEMBER

Planning

The holidays and garden catalogs seem to arrive at the same time. Take this opportunity to add a few new roses to your gift list. See Roses "Helpful Hints" on page 362 for ways to keep enjoying roses throughout the year.

Continue to *record* the successes and failures of the past growing season. Once spring returns, it is often difficult to remember the details of past growing seasons.

Also, *record* any unusually warm weather that can delay dormancy or stimulate unwanted growth. These weather changes are hard on the plants, and the damage often doesn't show up until next spring. But since we can't change the weather, we might as well live with it and enjoy the surprises it brings. I remember several years when we had roses blooming in December!

Planting

Review next year's calendar and block out some time for planting and transplanting. Time seems to fly, and we often struggle to find the time to do the things we enjoy.

Care

Complete winter protection after a week of freezing temperatures. Check on winter protection already in place. Make sure rose cones and mulches are secure.

Check **Container Roses** in winter storage.

Watering

It is usually not necessary to water outdoor roses. In mild years, the ground may not freeze until late December. Wait to put the hose away so that you can water thoroughly before the ground does freeze.

Water **Container Roses** in winter storage anytime the soil is dry and not frozen.

Keep the soil slightly moist on indoor roses.

Fertilizing

Do not fertilize frozen soil. It can wash off the ground and into our waterways. Wait until spring to fertilize.

Indoor roses are still adjusting to their new location. Wait until growing conditions improve to fertilize.

Pruning

Prune only enough to apply winter protection. The canes need to be short enough to fit under the protective covering, but long enough to increase winter survival. Since rose canes die from the tip back, the longer canes have a better chance of surviving our tough winters.

Pests

Clean up roses before winter protection is applied. In mild years, gardeners in the southern part of the state may still be doing this in December.

Update your journal. Review pest problems, controls used, and your successes and failures. Then mark peak pest activity times on next year's calendar. These reminders can help you find and manage the pests before they become a large problem.

Shrubs

Shrubs have long been shoved up against home foundations or strung out along the lot line. Consider expanding the use of shrubs in your landscape. Look for opportunities and spaces that could use the facelift shrubs can provide.

- Mix both deciduous and evergreen shrubs with perennials to create year-round interest

- Use single plantings as specimens and focal points in the garden.

- Strategically plant large shrubs for screening a bad view.

- Add low-growing shrubs to areas around trees to create attractive and healthy planting beds.

- Increase the year-round interest in the landscape by including shrubs with colorful flowers, fruit, and bark.

- Attract birds and butterflies by planting shrubs that provide food and shelter.

Planning

Now that you see the possibilities, break out the landscape plan. Select the shrubs that are best suited to the growing conditions and your design goals. Proper planning will give you an attractive landscape with a lot less work.

- *Evaluate* the light, soil, wind, and other environmental factors that affect plant growth. Plant shrubs suited to the growing conditions. Use raised planting beds to improve drainage in poorly drained soils.

- *Measure* the area. Make sure the plants will still fit once they reach full size. Check the heights of windows, distance to structures, and mature size of nearby plants. Provide the space needed to minimize future pruning and frustration caused by trying to keep a 6-foot shrub in 3 feet of space.

- *Consider* the ornamental value of the shrubs selected. Include evergreens for year-round foliage, **Lilacs** and other flowering shrubs for an added splash of color, or plants such as **Red Twig Dogwoods** with decorative bark.

- *Match* your gardening style with the plant's maintenance requirements. Minimize your workload by planting drought-tolerant and pest-resistant shrubs. Avoid fast-growing shrubs that are too large for the location and will require frequent pruning.

Purchasing

Once the plan is complete, you are ready for the trip to the nursery or garden center.

Hook up the trailer or clear out the trunk to make room for your purchases. Throw a couple of tarps in the car. Use them to protect the seats and carpet in your vehicle or to cover leafed-out shrubs transported in the open air of a pickup truck or trailer.

Purchase healthy plants free of damaged stems, discolored or brown leaves, or other signs of pests and stress. Avoid unhealthy bargain plants that can end up costing you more money and time when they need replacing.

Planting

The planting process starts with a call to your utility-locating service. Call Gopher State One Call at 800-252-1166. Call at least three working days before planting. These free services mark the location of all

Shrubs

underground utilities. Working with utility-locating services can prevent costly damage to underground utilities and may save your life.

Most shrubs are sold in containers. The majority of these are grown in the container, but others are dug out of the field and placed in the container. We will call these potted plants. The remainder, mostly evergreens and a few select flowering shrubs, are sold as balled-and-burlapped plants.

All types of shrubs benefit from proper planting.

1 Adjust planting locations to avoid conflicts with both underground and overhead utilities.

2 Dig a hole that is the same as or slightly shallower than the depth of the rootball. Make it at least two times as wide as the roots. See shrub planting illustrations.

Hole Height

Hole Width

3 Roughen the sides of the planting hole to avoid glazing. Smooth-sided holes prevent roots from growing out of the planting hole and into the surrounding soil. Use your shovel or garden fork to nick or scratch the sides of the planting hole.

4 Remove the plant from container. Potted plants need special care since their root systems may not be well established in the container. Minimize root disturbance by using this technique: Cut off the bottom of the pot and place it in the planting hole. Slice the pot lengthwise and peel it away.

5 Loosen the roots of potbound container-grown shrubs. Use a sharp knife to slice through the rootball. Make several shallow slices (running top to bottom of the rootball) through the surface of the roots. This will encourage roots to grow out into the surrounding soil.

Use a similar technique with balled-and-burlapped plants.

1 Place the shrub in the hole. Remove the twine and peel back the burlap. Cut away the fabric.

2 Fill the hole with the existing soil. Use water, not your foot or a heavy tool, to settle the soil.

3 Water the planting hole and surrounding soil. Cover the soil surface with shredded bark or woodchips to conserve moisture, insulate roots, and reduce weeds.

To care for your new plantings:

- Check new plantings once or twice a week. Water shrubs in clay soil every seven to ten days. Those growing in sandy soils should be checked twice a week. Water when the top 6 inches begin to dry. Water thoroughly enough to moisten the top 12 inches of soil.

- Container plants grown in soilless mixes will need special attention. These potting mixes dry out faster than the surrounding soils. Keep the root system moist, but be careful not to overwater the surrounding soil.

- Wait until next year to fertilize new plantings. Fertilizer can damage the young tender roots and interfere with establishment.

- Remove only those branches that were damaged in the transport and planting process. The more branches left on the plant, the more leaves that will be formed and the more energy will be produced for the plant.

- Add the plant name to your landscape plan. Enter the planting information in your journal. Include the plant name, place of purchase, and planting date.

Pruning

No other gardening chore evokes such a wide range of emotions as pruning. Feelings range from pruning paranoia (fear of killing or maiming the plant) to visions of a chainsaw massacre. Before breaking out the tools, make sure there is a reason to prune. See Pruning Pointers on page 257 for more pruning tips.

Prune to maintain size, improve flowering and fruiting and bark color, or remove damaged or disease branches. When and how you prune are equally important.

- Prune spring-flowering shrubs, such as **Lilac** and **Forsythia**, in spring right after flowering. Spring bloomers flower on the previous season's growth. Pruning in late summer or winter removes the flower buds and eliminates the spring display.

- Trim summer-blooming plants during the dormant season. **Hills-of-Snow Hydrangeas, Potentilla**, and summer-blooming **Spireas** flower on the current season's growth.

- Remove dead, damaged, or disease-infected branches whenever they are found. Disinfect tools between cuts to prevent the spread of disease. Use rubbing alcohol or a solution of one part bleach to nine parts water as a disinfectant.

The "how" of pruning is a little trickier. Match the type of pruning to the plant and your landscape goals. Some plants, such as **Cotoneasters** and **Barberries**, need very little pruning, while **Forsythia** and common **Lilacs** need regular attention. Use thinning cuts and renewal pruning to contain plant size while maintaining the plant's natural appearance. Shearing transforms shrubs into rectangular hedges or spheres of green.

Where you make the pruning cut is equally important. Prune on a slight angle above a healthy bud, where a branch joins another branch, or where a branch joins the trunk. These cuts heal quickly and reduce the risk of insects and disease entering the plant. The location of the pruning cut also influences the plant's appearance and future growth.

- *Use thinning cuts* to open up the plant and reduce the size while maintaining its natural appearance. Prune off branches where they join the main stem or another branch. Thinning cuts allow air and light to penetrate the plant improving flowering, fruiting, and bark color. It also helps reduce some disease problems.

- *Use heading cuts* to reduce the height and spread of shrubs. Limit the number and vary the location of heading cuts to maintain the plant's natural appearance. Prune branches back to a shorter side shoot or above a healthy bud. Excessive heading can lead to a tuft of growth at the end of a long, bare stem.

- *Reserve shearing* for only the most formal settings. This technique is easy on the gardener but hard on the plant. Shearing makes indiscriminant cuts, leaving stubs that make perfect entryways for insects and disease. Prune so that the bottom of the plant is wider than the top. This allows light to reach all parts, top to the bottom, of the plant. See Shrubs on page 357 for tips on unshearing sheared shrubs.

- *Use renewal pruning* to manage overgrown shrubs, contain growth, and stimulate new, healthy, and more attractive stems. Start by removing one-third of the older (larger) canes to ground level. Reduce the height of the remaining stems by one-third if needed. Repeat the process the next two years for overgrown shrubs. By the end of the third year, the shrub will be smaller, more attractive, and healthier. Continue to remove older canes as needed throughout the life of the shrubs.

Shrubs

- *Use rejuvenation pruning* to manage the size of some fast-growing and overgrown shrubs. Make sure the plant will tolerate this severe pruning. Cut all stems back to 4 inches above the soil line during the dormant season. Late winter through early spring before growth begins is the best time. The plant will soon begin to grow and recover.

See March "Helpful Hints" for specific pruning recommendations.

Fertilizing

Shrubs receive most of their nutrients from fertilizers applied to nearby plantings and lawn areas. Organic mulches also add small amounts of nutrients as they decompose.

- *Start* with a soil test to determine if fertilizer is needed. The soil test report will indicate what type and how much fertilizer you will need. See "General Horticulural Practices" on page 10 for details on soil testing.

- *Apply* needed fertilizer in the spring for best results. Stop fertilization by midsummer. Late-season fertilization can stimulate late-season growth that may be winterkilled.

- *Use* a fertilizer higher in nitrogen, such as 21-0-0, at a rate of 1 to 2 pounds per 100 square feet of planting area. Two cups of synthetic inorganic fertilizer is equal to about 1 pound. Consider using a slow-release fertilizer to reduce the risk of burn and provide a more even fertilization over a longer period of time.

- *Spread* the fertilizer on the soil surface. Keep the fertilizer off the shrubs. Rake the fertilizer into the soil surface and water well. Fertilizer can be applied over organic mulch and raked into the soil below.

- Overfertilization can lead to rapid growth and increased pruning frequency. Young plants can be fertilized every few years to encourage rapid growth. Heavily mulched plantings benefit from additional nitrogen to keep the carbon (from wood products) and nitrogen in balance. Reduce or eliminate fertilizer applications on mature shrubs to limit plant growth.

Pests

Pest control starts by selecting the right plant for the growing conditions. Healthy plants are more resistant to insects and disease.

- Select plants hardy to your growing conditions. Plants that tolerate the temperature extremes of winter and summer will be less stressed and more able to withstand pest attacks.

- Purchase and plant healthy, high-quality shrubs. Bargain plants are often not suited for the climate, stressed from improper care, or come with pest problems.

Rejuvenating Shrub

Heading Back Shrub

Severe Heading Back Shrub

- Provide plants with proper care and check frequently for pest problems.

When problems occur, consult your local county University of Minnesota Extension Service for proper diagnosis and control options. See monthly "Pests" and July "Helpful Hints" for details on specific pest and their controls.

Pruning Pointers

Get the greatest ornamental value from your shrubs through proper pruning. Match the pruning method to the shrub for increased flowering, improved bark color, and maintenance of its natural form. See April "Helpful Hints" for details on pruning evergreen shrubs.

- **Barberry** (*Berberis* species) and **Cotoneaster** (*Cotoneaster* species) are generally slow growing. Remove only damaged and diseased stems to ground level in spring before growth begins.

- **Blue Mist Spirea** (*Caryopteris × clandonensis*) is marginally hardy and usually dies back to the ground over winter. Cut the plant back to several inches above the soil in late winter.

- **Burning Bush** (*Euonymus alatus*) needs minimal pruning, which can be done during the dormant season. Selectively remove vigorous growth to major side branches to maintain the desired size and shape. Do not use renewal or rejuvenation pruning on this single-stemmed shrub.

- **Butterfly Bush** (*Buddleja davidii*) usually dies back over winter. Prune back to 3 to 4 inches above the soil in late winter or early spring before growth begins.

- **Dogwoods** (*Cornus* species) can be pruned during the dormant season. Remove old and discolored stems of the suckering type to ground level. Wait for **Cornelian Cherry Dogwood** to blossom before pruning. Pruning will depend on the desired form.

- **Forsythia** (*Forsythia* species) flowers on the previous season's growth. Wait until after flowering to prune. Finish pruning by early June so that the plant has time to set flower buds for next spring's display. Remove three-year and older stems to ground level.

- The **Honeysuckles** (*Lonicera* species) are tough shrubs that can take severe pruning. Consider removing invasive species from the landscape. Renewal prune (remove one-third of the older stems to ground level) others to encourage new growth at the base of the plant. These tough shrubs will tolerate rejuvenation pruning back to several inches above ground level. Prune during the dormant season.

- The **Hydrangea** (*Hydrangea* species), **Hills-of-Snow**, **Annabelle**, and other snowball types of Hydrangea should be pruned back to ground level each winter. Wait until late winter if you want to enjoy the dried flowers in the winter landscape. **PeeGee Hydrangeas** are often trained into small trees or specimen plants. Regular pruning is not needed but can improve flowering. Prune the plant to the desired shape. Yearly pruning cuts can be made back to the first set of healthy buds above this framework.

- The **Juneberry** or **Serviceberry** (*Amelanchier* species) can be trained as multistemmed large shrubs or small trees. Do minimal pruning once the main stems are selected. Prune suckering types of Juneberries the same way you prune **Forsythia** and **Dogwoods**. Remove one-third of the older stems to ground level. Prune in late winter or just after spring bloom.

- **Lilacs** (*Syringa*) bloom on old wood and should be pruned after flowering. Remove old

Shrubs

flowers after bloom to increase next year's floral display. Prune one-third of the older canes back to ground level to encourage fuller growth at the base of the plant.

- **Potentillas** (*Potentilla fruticosa*) are summer-blooming shrubs that can be pruned anytime during the dormant season. Prune plants back halfway, then remove the older stems to ground level. Or prune the whole plant back to several inches above the soil line. The plants will recover but tend to be a little floppier with this technique.

- **Spireas** (*Spiraea* species) are divided into spring and summer blooming types. Spring-flowering **Bridal Wreath/Vanhoutte** types should be pruned right after spring bloom. Remove flowering tips to improve next year's bloom. Remove one-fourth of the older stems to ground level on established plants. Older, overgrown plants may be slow to respond to rejuvenation pruning. **Anthony Waterer**, **Japanese**, **Bumald**, and other summer-flowering **Spireas** can be pruned anytime during the dormant season. Wait until late winter if you want to enjoy the winter interest provided by the chestnut

brown stems and dried flowers. Prune these the same as **Potentilla**.

- **Viburnum** (*Viburnum* species) grow at different rates. Slow-growing species need very little pruning. Remove old, damaged, and unproductive branches to ground level.

Sharing Shrubs

Gardeners love to share special plants with friends and relatives. Tip cuttings, layering, and division can be used to pass along a piece of that special plant.

Try propagating **Lilacs, Forsythia, Weigela,** *and other shrubs by the tip cutting method now.*

1 Gather all the materials needed. This includes a sharp knife or hand pruners, small containers, well-drained potting mix, sand or vermiculite, and a rooting hormone for woody plants.

2 Remove several 6- to 8-inch pieces from the tips of the stems. Remove the lowest set of leaves. Dip the cut end in a rooting hormone for woody plants. Stick one or more cuttings into a pot filled with a well-drained potting mix, sand, or vermiculite.

3 Store the cuttings in a shaded location. Group it with other plants or place under trees or shrubs to increase humidity. Keep the rooting medium moist.

4 Transplant rooted cuttings as soon as the roots develop. Plant in a container filled with a well-drained soil. Check soil moisture daily and water as needed. These will be ready for planting next spring.

Try layering shrubs with long, pliable stems.

See May "Helpful Hints" in the Vines and Groundcovers chapter on page 331 for step-by-step directions.

Dig and divide rooted suckers to start new plants. **Dogwoods** and other suckering shrubs send out shoots.

1 Carefully remove the soil at the base of the sucker to see if it has roots.

2 Use a sharp spade to disconnect the sucker from the parents. Some gardeners prefer to leave it in place to develop a stronger root system. Others divide, dig, and transplant immediately. For greatest success, try this in early spring before growth begins.

Minnesota Shrubs

Common Name (Botanical Name)	Hardiness Zone	Light	Comments
Alpine Currant (*Ribes alpinum*)	3, 4	Full sun to shade	Small shrub that tolerates shearing through looks attractive in its natural form. Consider the native **Clove Currant** (*Ribes odoratum*) with fragrant yellow flowers.
Arborvitae (*Thuja occidentalis* cultivars)	3, 4	Full to part sun	Generally large upright evergreen shrubs. Select cultivars that hold their green color for winter, and fit the location and desired use. Prefers moist soil protection from snowloads.
Azalea (*Rhododendron* × 'Northern Lights')	3, 4	Part sun to shade	Small shrub with orange, yellow, pink, white, or orchid flowers in spring. Hardiest of the **Azaleas.** Protect from winter winds and sun.
Barberry (*Berberis thunbergii* species and cultivars)	4	Full sun to part shade	Small and medium shrubs that prefer well-drained to dry soils. Attractive red fruit and fall color. Spines make them good barrier plants.
Bird's Nest Spruce (*Picea abies* 'Nidiformis')	3, 4	Full sun	Slow-growing dwarf spreading spruce. Forms wide mound with dent in center.
Boxwood (*Buxus* species)	4	Part to full shade	Small shrubs that prefer shelter from winter sun and wind. Select 'Green Velvet', 'Wintergreen', and other hardier cultivars.
Burning Bush (*Euonymus alata*)	4	Full sun to part shade	Medium to large shrubs grown for attractive fall color. Avoid heavy shade and high nitrogen fertilizer for best fall display. Select hardier cultivars such as 'Nordine Strain' when looking for compact types.
Butterfly Bush (*Buddleja davidii*)	4b	Full sun	Medium shrub that dies back to ground level each winter. Attracts butterflies with its fragrant, long-lasting bloom.
Chokeberry (*Aronia melanocarpa*)	3, 4	Full sun to shade	Small shrub that tolerates moist to wet soils. White flowers in spring. Produces red or black fruit with red fall color.
Cotoneaster (*Cotoneaster* species)	3, 4	Full sun to part shade	Small to large shrubs with delicate white or pink spring flowers. Produces fruit and good fall color. Form varies from low-growing and mounded to spreading or upright.
Daphne (*Daphne* × *burkwoodii* 'Carol Mackie')	4	Full sun to part shade	Small shrub with variegated foliage and fragrant flowers. Often short lived.

Minnesota Shrubs

Common Name (Botanical Name)	Hardiness Zone	Light	Comments
Dogwood (*Cornus* species)	2-4	Full sun to shade	Medium to large shrubs. Many species and cultivars have decorative bark, bird-attracting fruit, and good fall color.
Forsythia (*Forsythia* species)	3, 4	Full sun	Small to large shrubs depending on the species. Select 'Meadowlark', 'Sunrise', or one of the other flowerbud-hardy cultivars. Plant hardiness varies with species and cultivar.
Fothergilla (*Fothergilla gardenii*)	4	Full sun to part shade	Small shrub with white fragrant flowers in early spring, and yellow, orange, and red fall color.
Fragrant Sumac (*Rhus aromatica*)	3, 4	Full to part sun	Use 'Gro-low' cultivar for a groundcover or small shrub. The straight species is a medium-sized and more upright shrub. Late to leaf out, glossy green leaves and orange-red fall color. **Staghorn Sumac** (*Rhus typhina*) should be saved for areas where it has room to spread or can be contained.
Hazelnut (*Corylus americana*)	3, 4	Sun to shade	Medium shrub that tolerates dry soils. Native plant with orange fall color.
Hydrangea (*Hydrangea arborescens*) (*Hydrangea paniculata*)	4	Part shade	Medium to tall, summer blooming shade-tolerant shrub. The white forms bloom on new growth while most of the pink and blue types (*Hydrangea macrophylla*) flower on the previous season's growth and need winter protection.
Juneberry/Serviceberry (*Amelanchier* species)	3, 4	Part shade	Large upright shrub, with four-season interest. White spring flowers, edible fruit in June, orange-red fall color and smooth gray bark in winter.
Juniper (*Juniper* species and cultivars)	2-4	Full sun	Low-growing, medium to large spreading or upright forms. Heat and drought-tolerant evergreen.
Lilac (*Syringa* species and cultivars)	3, 4	Full sun	Medium to large shrubs. Fragrant flowers in spring attract butterflies and hummingbirds. Select most mildew-resistant cultivars.
Mockorange (*Philadelphus*)	4	Full to part sun	Medium to small shrub grown for fragrant white flowers in spring. Select for plant and flower bud hardiness. Minnesota Snowflake (*Philadelphus* × *virginalis* 'Minnesota') is rated hardy zones 3-5 while the smaller summer double-blooming Glacier (*Philadelphus* × *virginalis* 'Glacier') is hardy in zone 4.
Mugo Pine (*Pinus mugo*)	3, 4	Full sun	Small to large mounded shrub. Select dwarf cultivars suitable to the landscape. Tolerates full sun and dry soil. Prune expanding growth in spring to control size.

Minnesota Shrubs

Common Name (Botanical Name)	Hardiness Zone	Light	Comments
Potentilla (*Potentilla fruticosa*)	3, 4	Full sun	Small shrub performs best in well-drained to dry soils. Covered with yellow or white flowers throughout the summer and fall. Red flowering types often fade in heat of summer.
Privet (*Ligustrum* species)	4	Full to part sun	Medium to large shrub usually sheared into a hedge. Select 'Cheyenne' or one of the other hardier cultivars for best results.
Rhododendron (*Rhododendron* × 'PJM Hybrid')	4	Sun to part shade	Small broadleaf evergreen turns purple in fall, flowers in spring. Protect from winter wind and sun.
Rose-of-Sharon (*Hibiscus syriacus*)	4b	Full to part sun	Medium to small upright shrub with white, blue, lavender, or red flowers in late summer. Can be killed in harsh winter. Treat like a herbaceous perennial.
Spirea (*Spiraea* species)	4	Full sun to light shade	Small to medium, mostly mounded in form. Spring and summer blooming, low maintenance plants.
Viburnum (*Viburnum* species and cultivars)	3, 4	Full to part sun	Small to large upright shrubs. Most provide flowers, fruit, and fall color for seasonal interest.
Weigela (*Weigela florida*)	4	Full sun	Small shrub with main flowering in spring followed by sporadic flowers throughout the summer. Compact forms available.
Winterberry (*Ilex verticillata*)	4	Full sun to part shade	Medium shrub that tolerates wet acid soils. Bright red fruit in fall and winter. Need male and female plants for fruit.
Witchhazel (*Hamamelis virginiana*)	4	Full sun to shade	Large shrub that tolerates city conditions. Yellow flowers and foliage in fall.
Yew (*Taxus* species and cultivars)	4	Sun or shade	Large upright and medium to small spreading evergreen plants. Protect from winter wind and salt to reduce winter browning.

JANUARY

Planning

Shake off the post-holiday blues and a few pounds with a walk around the block. Find out how friends and neighbors are using shrubs to add year-round interest to their landscape. Expand your search to include nearby botanical gardens and arboretums. Some may even sponsor winter walks with local experts.

- *Evaluate* the form, color, and fruit of individual plants. Consider how these can help improve your existing landscape.

- *Start* a list of plants you would like to add to your yard. Find out their ultimate size and desired growing conditions to see if they will fit in your landscape.

Now take a walk around your landscape. Look for areas that would benefit from some new shrub plantings. Make sure there is sufficient room for the shrubs you select.

- *Consider* the mature size as it relates to nearby buildings, existing plants, and overhead and underground utilities.

- *Investigate* dwarf varieties for smaller areas. Always check the ultimate size; dwarf just means they are smaller than the standard species but not necessarily as small as you might imagine.

- *Select* plants suitable for the growing conditions. Matching the shrub to the existing growing conditions will result in an attractive plant that requires very little maintenance.

Planting

Take advantage of this downtime to prepare your tools for the growing season. Clean and sharpen your spade. See November "Pruning" for tips on cleaning and sharpening tools. A sharp-edged shovel will slice through the soil with much less effort.

Care

Monitor the landscape for snow, deicing salt, and animal damage.

Do not shake or brush frozen snow off the plants. This can cause more damage than if the snow was left in place. Make a note on your calendar to prevent plant damage next season. Apply winter protection in late October or November before the heavy snows arrive.

Shovel walks and drives before applying deicing materials. This saves money and reduces plant dam-

age caused by these products. Consider using one of the more environmentally friendly deicing products such as magnesium chloride and calcium acetate.

Watering

No need to water plantings. The soil is either frozen or covered with snow. Check the soil moisture of all the aboveground planters you have stored in your unheated garage or porch. Water whenever the soil thaws and dries. Water thoroughly so that the excess runs out the bottom of the planter.

Fertilizing

Review soil test information and garden notes to decide whether you need to fertilize this season. Contact your local University Extension Office for soil test information. Test results will tell you if you need to fertilize and what you need to use.

Pests

This is a quiet time in the landscape, but a good time to spring a surprise attack on many garden pests. A little preventative pest management can help reduce plant damage, pesticide use, and your summer workload.

Check for signs of animals. Rabbits, voles, and deer will feed on stems and branches. Get busy if you find tracks, droppings, and feeding damage. Secure animal fencing and reapply repellents as needed.

Check **Ornamental Plums** and **Cherries** for Eastern tent caterpillar egg masses. The eggs look like a shiny glob of mud on the stem. Prune and destroy all that are found.

Watch for black knot cankers on **Plums** and **Cherries** at the same time. This fungal disease causes branches to swell, eventually turn black, and crack open, releasing infectious spores. Prune out infected branches below the swollen areas. Burn or bury cankered branches to reduce future infections.

Check the base of **Viburnum**, **Euonymus**, and **Spirea** stems for round, swollen growths called galls. These galls eventually girdle and kill the stem. Prune out infected stems below the gall, and discard. Disinfect your tools between cuts with rubbing alcohol or a solution of one part bleach to nine parts water.

Helpful Hints

Add a little flavor to your landscape. Include a few shrubs that produce edible fruit as well as add beauty to your yard. Many shrubs produce fruit that can be eaten fresh, sweetened and pureed into jelly, or baked in a pie. **Blueberries**, **Raspberries**, and **Currants** quickly come to mind. But you may be surprised to find some other ornamental shrubs that have edible parts.

- **American Cranberrybush Viburnum** (***Viburnum trilobum***) has long been used for preserves. Personally, I would need a lot of sugar to find this tasty. **'Andrews'**, **'Hahs'**, and **'Wentworth'** are selected for their larger fruit. If you are like me and do not like the flavor, the fruit is still attractive and provides good winter interest.
- **Cornelian Cherry Dogwood** (***Cornus mas***) produces bright red, cherrylike fruit. The elongated fruit is a little tart at first bite. Add a little sugar–or a lot–and make it into jelly or syrup. Don't worry, if you don't like the flavor the birds will take care of the fruit for you.
- **Rose** (***Rosa*** species) has both flowers and fruits, called hips, which add color and beauty to the landscape. Rose petals can be used fresh in salads or omelets, batter coated and fried, sugared, or made into jelly. The fruits are also edible and high in vitamin C. Most roses produce fruit but some, such as the **Rugosa Roses**, have a little better flavor. Rose hips have long been used for jelly, tea, and sauces.
- **American Hazelnut** or **Filbert** (***Corylus americana***). See Fruits.
- **Elderberry** (***Sambucus canadensis***). See Fruits.
- **Juneberry** or **Serviceberry** (***Amelanchier*** species). See Trees.

A word of caution—do not spray plants with pesticides if you plan to eat them. Instruct children never to eat plants or plant parts unless their parents or a trusted adult says it is okay.

Pruning

Prune winter-damaged branches as they are found. Wait until the snow melts and the worst of winter has passed to start major pruning. This way you can see what winter and the animals have left for you to work with.

Planning

Continue to update your landscape plan. Check out catalogs and visit home and garden shows to get some new ideas. The professionals at these shows can give you design and planting tips.

Planting

It is still too early to plant. Make note of any shrubs that need to be moved. Transplanting can begin as soon as the ground thaws.

Care

Nature still drops a few white reminders that winter is not yet over. See November "Helpful Hints" for minimizing winter damage.

- Monitor shrubs and other plants for winter damage. Do not shake ice or frozen snow off plants. Your good intentions can do more damage than nature. Make note of any damage that could have been prevented with winter protection.

- Use any breaks in the weather to start cleaning out shrub beds. Remove debris and broken branches.

Watering

No need to water shrub beds. Continue to check on aboveground planters. Water them whenever the soil thaws and dries.

Fertilizing

It is still too early to fertilize. Check your journal and review last year's gardening successes and challenges. Take a walk through the landscape and evaluate plant growth.

Pests

Keep monitoring for animal damage. Adjust protection as needed.

- Secure fencing and other animal guards. Make sure animals are not able to crawl under or over the barriers and reach the plants.

- Reapply repellents after severe weather as recommended on the label. Use a variety of repellents to help increase success. Animals often get used to the repellent and start feeding on treated plants.

- Scare tactics may provide additional relief. Noisemakers, coyote urine, and whirligigs may scare some animals. Vary the techniques to keep the animals wary of the area. Keep in mind that urban wildlife is used to the smell and noise of humans so scare tactics may not provide adequate control.

Insects:

- Check **Mugo Pines** for pine needle scale. Look for white flecks on the needles. A lime sulfur spray can be used now to kill the pest.

- Other scale insects (hard shells attached to stems) can be treated with lime sulfur while the plants are dormant. Check the label before treatment to make sure it can be used on your particular plant. Lime sulfur can stain walks and injure **Viburnums**.

- Check **Ornamental Plums** and **Cherries** for Eastern tent caterpillar egg masses. The eggs look like a shiny glob of mud on the stem. Prune and destroy all that are found.

Diseases:

- Also look for black knot cankers on **Plums** and **Cherries**. These appear as knots on the twigs. The knots start out the same color as the stem and eventually turn black, crack open, and release infectious spores. Prune out infected branches below the knots. Burn or bury cankered branches to reduce future infections.

- Check the bases of **Viburnum**, **Euonymus**, and **Spirea** stems for round, swollen growths called galls. These galls eventually girdle and kill the stem. Prune out infected stems below the gall and discard. Disinfect your tools between cuts with alcohol or a solution of one part bleach to nine parts water.

- Check **Dogwood** for signs of golden canker. This fungal disease is common on Dogwoods that have suffered heat and drought stress in summer. The twigs turn gold and die. Prune out infected stems. Disinfect tools between cuts.

Pruning

Continue to prune out damaged or hazardous branches as they are found. You may want to wait until the worst of winter has passed to start major pruning. Summer- and fall-blooming plants can be pruned now until growth begins in spring. Wait until after flowering to prune spring-blooming shrubs.

Try bringing a little spring indoors. Prune a few branches from spring flowering shrubs to force for indoor bloom. **Forsythia**, **Quince**, and

Helpful Hints

Wildlife can add color and motion to the winter and summer landscapes. Planting shrubs that provide food and shelter is a great way to bring birds into the landscape. Nature takes care of stocking the feeder, allowing you more time to sit back, relax, and watch the birds.

Shrubs That Attract Wildlife (Hardy in Zones 3 and 4)

Arborvitae (*Thuja occidentalis*): BS
Bayberry (*Myrica pennsylvanica*): BF
Chokeberry (*Aronia*): BF, BS
Coralberry (*Symphoricarpos orbiculatus*): BF, BS, HB
Dogwood (*Cornus* species): B, BF
Elderberry (*Sambucus canadensis*): B, BF, BS
Flowering Plums and Cherries: some species BF and BS, HB
Juneberry or Serviceberry (*Amelanchier*): BF
Lilac: B, HB
Rose (*Rosa* species): B, BF
Spirea (*Spiraea*): B
Viburnum (*Viburnum* species): B, BF, BS
Yew (*Taxus*): BS

Key:
B–Butterflies
BF–Food for birds
BS–Shelter for birds
HB–Hummingbird

Pussy Willows make nice additions to arrangements or in a vase on their own.

1 Use hand pruners to cut branches above a healthy bud or where they join another branch.

2 Place branches in cool water (60 degrees Fahrenheit) in a brightly lit location.

3 Mist as often as possible and keep the cut ends in water.

4 Move flowering stems to a cooler location at night to prolong bloom.

Planning

Complete your landscape plan and start shopping for those unusual plants. Contact nurseries and garden centers that specialize in unusual plants. You may have to make several calls to locate new and unusual varieties.

Build in preparation time for planting. Contact the utility-locating service three to ten days prior to digging. This free service locates and marks underground utilities. Having this information can help you avoid costly damage to utilities and possibly save your life. Minnesota gardeners should call Gopher State One Call at 800-252-1166.

Planting

Late winter through early spring is the best time to transplant shrubs. Moving large, established shrubs can be tricky and heavy work. Replacing overgrown or misplaced shrubs may be easier, cheaper, and more successful.

Start transplanting when the ground thaws and soil is moist. Complete this garden task before growth begins.

1 Loosely *tie* the branches to prevent damage and keep them out of your way.

2 *Dig* a trench around the shrub slightly larger and deeper than the desired rootball. (See "Helpful Hint.")

3 *Undercut* the rootball with your shovel. A sharp spade will make the job easier. Use hand pruners and loppers for larger or tougher roots.

4 *Slide* a piece of burlap or canvas under the rootball. Have several friends lend a hand. Extra hands and strong backs will make the job easier and reduce the risk of dropping the shrub and damaging the rootball.

5 *Set* the shrub in the prepared site. Carefully cut away or slide the tarp away from the shrub.

6 *Backfill* the hole with existing soil, water, and mulch.

Care

This month marks the start of the transition from winter to spring. Continue protecting plants from deicing salts, snow loads and animal damage. Start the repair work of leaching out salt-laden soils and pruning off broken branches.

Watering

Continue watering shrubs in aboveground planters. Water thoroughly whenever the ground thaws and dries.

Monitor soil moisture after the soil thaws. Melting snow and spring rains usually take care of the needed moisture.

Helpful Hints		
Recommended Rootball Size for Transplanting		
Shrub Size	**Rootball Size Minimum Diameter**	**Depth**
2 feet	12 inches	9 inches
3 feet	14 inches	11 inches
4 feet	16 inches	12 inches
5 feet	16 inches	12 inches
6 feet	16 inches	12 inches

Fertilizing

Use soil tests to get the most out of your gardening efforts. The test results will tell you about your soil and fertilizer needs. It can save you time and money spent adding unnecessary nutrients. It also helps you avoid damaging the plant and environment with misapplications of fertilizer. Contact your local University of Minnesota Extension Service for soil test information.

Take a soil sample as soon as the ground thaws. Take samples from several locations in the planting bed. Use a trowel or shovel to obtain samples 4 to 6 inches deep. Mix the samples together and allow them to dry. Send 1 cup of soil and the complete form to the University soil testing lab.

If soil test information is not available, use these guidelines for fertilization:

- Young shrubs can be fertilized every couple years to promote rapid growth.

- Shrubs growing in heavily mulched beds benefit from regular fertilization.

- Established shrubs need infrequent or no fertilizer.

- Use 1 to 2 pounds of a nitrogen fertilizer per 100 square feet. Two cups of an inorganic fertilizer is equal to 1 pound.

Pests

Insects:

- Continue to remove and destroy Eastern tent caterpillar egg masses on **Flowering Plums** and **Cherries**. The eggs are dark and shiny and appear to be cemented on the branch.

- Complete dormant sprays of lime sulfur on overwintering scale on **Mugo Pines** and deciduous shrubs before growth begins. Check the label before spraying. Make sure the pest and plant to be treated are listed on the label.

- Prune out and destroy brooms (fine twiggy growths) on **Honeysuckles**. Removing the brooms reduces the number of leaf-folding aphids that can re-infect these plants.

Diseases:

- Remove and destroy black knots from twigs of **Ornamental Plums** and **Cherries**. Destroying the knots now can reduce infection for this grow-ing season. Remove both the black and green knots for best results.

- Prune out gold-colored branches on **Dogwood**. These are infected by drought-induced golden canker fungus disease. Disinfect tools between cuts.

Pruning

Wait until after flowering to prune **Lilacs**, **Forsythia**, **Bridal Wreath Spirea**, and other spring-blooming shrubs. These shrubs have already set flower buds for this spring. Pruning at other times will not harm the plants but eliminates the bloom—the reason they are planted.

Prune summer- and fall-blooming shrubs now. Late winter pruning will not interfere with summer flowering and allows the plants to recover quickly.

Start by removing damaged, broken, and diseased stems. Disinfect tools between cuts to prevent the spread of disease. Rubbing alcohol or a solution of one part bleach to nine parts water will work. Clean your tools after pruning to minimize the adverse effects of bleach.

See the "Pruning" section in the chapter introduction for specific information on pruning.

APRIL

Planning

Continue to walk through your neighborhood, nearby botanical gardens, and your own landscape to gather ideas on shrubs for year-round interest. Make a list of spring-blooming shrubs you have or would like to add to the landscape. Keep in mind that the flowers may only provide a few weeks of interest while the shrubs will remain all year. Consider spring-flowering shrubs that have good fruit effect, fall color, interesting shape, or other ornamental features.

Record bloom times in your journal. It is fun and informative to see the bloom time variations from one year to the next.

Check local nurseries and garden centers for the more unusual and hard-to-find shrubs.

Plan ahead so that you will have enough preparation time for planting. Contact the utility-locating service three to ten days prior to digging. This free service locates and marks underground utilities. Having this information can help you avoid costly damage to utilities and possibly save your life. Call Gopher State One Call at 800-252-1166.

Planting

The growing and planting season has begun. As the soil thaws and temperatures warm, the nurseries are busy digging, transporting, and selling shrubs. You can get busy planting as well.

Finish transplanting shrubs before growth begins. See March "Planting" for details on moving shrubs.

A few catalogs and garden centers sell bare-root shrubs. These plants are cheaper, have a lower survival rate, and require your immediate attention for good results. Store bare-root plants in a cool, shaded location. Pack roots in peat moss and keep them moist. Soak overnight before planting. Place the shrubs in the planting hole at the same depth they were growing in the nursery.

Start planting balled-and-burlapped and container-grown shrubs. Plant them at the same depth they were growing at the nursery or in the container. Reduce root damage by cutting away containers, burlap, and twine. See "Planting" in the chapter introduction for more details.

Care

Move aboveground planters out of winter storage. Wait until temperatures hover around freezing if the leaves have begun to grow.

Remove and store winter protection. Continue applying wildlife repellents if animals continue to feed on shrubs. Make notes of any changes in winter protection that need to be made for next season.

Watering

New plantings should be watered often enough to keep the top 6 to 8 inches of the soil moist. Water thoroughly and wait for the soil to start to dry before watering again. Check clay soils weekly and sandy soils twice a week. Water as needed.

Established shrubs only need supplemental water in dry springs. Water thoroughly when the top 6 to 8 inches begin to dry.

Thoroughly water shrubs exposed to deicing materials. Heavy spring showers or a thorough watering will help wash these materials through the soil and away from the roots.

Fertilizing

Wait a year or two before fertilizing new plantings. Use your soil test as a guide to fertilizing existing plantings.

Apply fertilizer once in spring or early summer. Additional applications are not needed since most shrubs put out one flush of growth a year.

Apply 1 to 2 pounds of a nitrogen fertilizer per 100 square feet if soil test results are not available. Try a slow-release formulation to reduce risk and improve results.

Pests

Insects:

- Continue to locate and destroy egg masses of Eastern tent caterpillars. The eggs hatch and the caterpillars start building their webbed tents when the **Saucer Magnolias** (*Magnolia soulangeana*) are in the pink bud stage. Prune out and destroy tents as they are found.

- Do not apply dormant sprays once growth begins. These products can cause more damage to the expanding growth than the insects you are trying to control.

- Prune out and destroy the brooms on the tips of **Honeysuckles**. These contain hundreds of aphids that are waiting to feed on this season's growth.

- Watch for European pine sawflies on **Mugo Pine** when

the **Saucer Magnolias** begin dropping their petals. These wormlike insects feed in large groups, devouring pine needles a branch at a time. Smash them with a leather glove–clad hand or prune out and destroy the infested branch.

Diseases:

- Finish pruning out the green and black knots on **Flowering Cherries**, **Almonds**, and **Plums**. Removing these knots will reduce the source of future infection.

Helpful Hints

Prune evergreens to control size, remove damaged branches, and direct growth. Select the time and method of pruning that is best suited for the plants you are growing.

- **Pines** are terminal growers. They send out new growth from stem tips once a year. Control their size by removing one-half to two-thirds of the expanding buds (candles) in spring. More severe pruning on stems that lack terminal buds will kill the branch.
- **Spruce** can also be pruned in spring before growth begins. Prune stem tips back to a healthy bud. Make cuts at a slight angle just above the bud. Do not leave stubs that create an entryway for insects and disease.
- **Arborvitae** and **Yews** can be pruned in spring before growth begins or in early summer after new growth has expanded. Both plants form buds on older wood and tolerate more severe pruning than **Pines** and **Spruce**. Prune back to a bud or branch for best results. Keep the bottom of formal sheared hedges wider than the tops.
- **Junipers** require little pruning when the right size variety is selected for the location. Prune to control growth and keep the plant within the available space. Remove selected branches in spring or early summer. Cut the branches back to side shoots to cover cuts. Tip prune in summer for additional sizing.

Pruning

Finish dormant pruning of summer- and fall-blooming shrubs before growth begins. See "Pruning Pointers" on page 257 for more information.

Wait until after flowering to prune spring bloomers.

Planning

Refer to your landscape plan and planting list whenever you visit a nursery or garden center. All those beautiful plants, attractive tags, and promises of beauty can be tempting. It is too easy to succumb to temptation and end up with too many or the wrong type of plants for the available space.

Remember to call Gopher State One Call at 800-252-1166. Allow three business days between the call and planting. These free utility-locating services can prevent damage to underground utilities, save you money, and even save your life.

Planting

Keep planting. Balled-and-burlapped and container-grown shrubs can be planted all season long.

Amend planting beds in difficult planting locations. Create raised beds with existing or blended topsoil or add organic matter to the top 6 to 12 inches of the planting bed soil. Add organic matter to the whole planting bed, not just the planting hole, where shrub roots will grow.

To plant balled-and-burlapped and container shrubs:

- Dig a hole twice the diameter and the same depth or shallower than the rootball. Roughen the sides of the planting hole, using your shovel to nick or scratch the soil surface.

- Reduce root damage by cutting away the pots on container plants. Remove the bottom of the pot and set it inside the hole. Slice the side of the container and peel it away. Slice through potbound roots in several places around the rootball. Backfill with the existing soil and water.

- Set balled-and-burlapped shrubs in a properly dug hole. Remove the twine, cut away the burlap, and backfill with the existing soil. Water to help settle the soil.

- Mulch the soil around the base of the plant. Be careful not to bury the crown. A 2- to 3-inch layer of woodchips or bark will help conserve moisture, insulate roots, and reduce weeds.

Care

Gradually move shrubs outdoors that were wintered indoors. Those stored in heated garages, the basement, or other warm location need to gradually adapt to the cooler, harsher outdoor conditions.

Shrubs wintered in an unheated porch or garage should be moved outdoors before growth begins. Once growth begins, they need a little extra time for the tender new growth to adjust to the cooler outdoor conditions.

Watering

Give new plantings special attention. Water thoroughly whenever the top 6 to 8 inches of soil start to dry. Check clay soils once a week and sandy soils twice a week.

Established plantings only need to be watered during dry springs. Water thoroughly and wait for the top 6 to 8 inches to dry before watering again.

Water aboveground planters whenever the top few inches of soil begin to dry. Water thoroughly so that the excess drains out the bottom. Check planters every few days, daily during hot weather.

Fertilizing

Finish shrub fertilization. Only fertilize plants that are showing signs of deficiencies, those for which the soil test report indicates a need to fertilize, or young plants that you are trying to encourage to grow.

Apply 1 to 2 pounds of a nitrogen fertilizer per 100 square feet if soil test results are not available. Try a slow-release formulation to reduce risk and improve results. See the chapter introduction for fertilizer rates.

Wait a year or two before fertilizing new plantings.

Pests

Insects:

- Remove Eastern tent caterpillars as soon as they are found. Knock or prune out tents and destroy caterpillars.

- Continue checking **Mugo Pines** for European pine sawflies. Prune off infected branches or smash sawflies with a leather glove-clad hand.

- Treat **Mugo** and other **Pines** infested with pine needle scale. Apply insecticidal soap when the **Vanhoutte/Bridal Wreath Spirea** is in bloom and again seven to ten days later.

- Check and treat **Lilacs, Dogwood**, and other deciduous shrubs infested with oyster

Helpful Hints

A large expanse of shrubs neatly mulched in a planting bed can get a little boring. ***Brighten up shrub planting beds with the help of flowering bulbs and perennials.***

- Add some spring surprise to the shrub beds in your landscape. A mass planting of **Crocus, Grape Hyacinth**, and **Squills** can give you a carpet of color. Intersperse some **Daffodils, Tulips**, and **Hyacinths** for height and additional color.
- Consider using perennials to create seasonal interest. A mixture of spring-, summer-, and fall-blooming flowers can complement the seasonal interest the shrubs provide. See the **Perennials** chapter or the ***Minnesota Gardener's Guide*** for suitable plants.
- Try perennial groundcovers, such as **Deadnettle (*Lamium*), Bishop's Cap (*Epimedium*), Hosta**, and **Vinca** to mask the mulch and create a good growing environment. See the "Vines and Groundcovers" chapter for additional planting suggestions.

shell scale. These hard-shelled insects look like miniature oyster shells. Spray the stems and leaves with an ultrafine oil or insecticide labeled for use on shrubs with scale. Spray when the **Vanhoutte/Bridal Wreath Spirea** are in bloom and again when the **Hills-of-Snow Hydrangea** blossoms change from white to green.

Diseases:

- Watch for phomopsis blight on **Junipers**. Infected plants have cankered branches (sunken discolored areas) with brown and dead needles. Prune out infected branches 9 inches below the canker. Disinfect your tools between cuts.

Pruning

Prune spring-flowering shrubs as soon as they are done blooming. Finish pruning by early June so that the plants have enough time to set flower buds for next spring.

Renewal prune suckering shrubs, such as **Forsythia, Bridal Wreath Spirea**, and **Lilac**. Remove one-third of the older stems to ground level. See "Pruning Pointers" in the chapter introduction for details.

Remove faded flowers on **Lilacs** and **Rhododendrons** to encourage better flowering next year.

Planning

"The only constant in life is change." This is certainly true about gardening and landscaping. No matter how well you planned, something comes up and requires a change. The unexpected helps make gardening fun—or at least a bit challenging!

Keep adjusting your plans and make notes on the changes as they occur. You may find these changes actually improve the original plan.

Planting

Keep planting container and balled-and-burlapped shrubs. Both are available at nurseries and garden centers.

- *Call* the utility-locating services at least three days before planting. They will mark the location of underground utilities to prevent damage and injury. This is a free service that is just a phone call away. Call Gopher State One Call at 800-252-1166.

- *Select* healthy, well-shaped plants. Avoid shrubs with brown, speckled, or discolored leaves. These may have suffered drought stress or pest problems. Stressed trees take longer to establish and have a lower survival rate.

- *Cover* plants on the trip home from the nursery or garden center. Load them inside the car or cover those in the truck bed or trailer with a tarp. The windy trip home can dry out the new growth, increasing the stress on the plant.

- *Keep* roots of newly purchased shrubs moist until they can be planted. Cover balled-and-burlapped roots with woodchips if it will be a few days until planting.

- *Dig* a hole twice as wide and the same depth as the rootball. Remove the container, twine, and burlap from the shrub once it is placed in the planting hole. Loosen or slice through pot-bound roots. Backfill with existing soil and water.

Care

Consider removing grass and creating planting beds around shrubs. Grass is a big competitor with shrubs for water and nutrients. The weed whips and mowers used to cut the grass often damage the shrubs. Reduce maintenance and improve the health of your shrubs by mulching around shrubs. Kill or remove grass and cover with wood-chips or shredded bark. See August "Helpful Hints" for more details.

Replenish mulch around individual shrubs or planting beds. A 2- to 3-inch layer of woodchips and bark will help improve the growing conditions for the shrubs. Mulch insulates the soil, protecting the roots from temperature extremes. It also conserves moisture and reduces weed problems.

Watering

Temperature, soil type, and mulching influence the need for water. You need to check plants and water more frequently during hot spells and when growing in sandy soil. Reduce your workload by mulching planting beds. Woodchips and bark help to conserve moisture, reducing the need for water.

New plantings are still a watering priority. Keep the top 6 to 8 inches slightly moist. Check shrubs planted in clay soils once a week and those planted in sandy soils twice a week. Water thoroughly when the top 6 to 8 inches begin to dry.

Established shrubs only need supplemental water during dry periods. Water thoroughly when the top 6 to 8 inches of soil dry.

Fertilizing

Fertilize only those shrubs that are showing signs of nutrient deficiency or when recommended by soil test results. Apply needed fertilizer in one application in the spring. Finish fertilization that has not yet been done. See "Fertilizing" in the chapter introduction for more specific recommendations.

Pests

As the temperatures warm, the pest populations build. Healthy shrubs can tolerate most pest problems. When the numbers get too high, you may need to step in and lend nature a hand.

Insects:

- Check **Burning Bush** and other **Euonymus** for signs of the euonymus caterpillar. These worm-like insects build webbed nests and feed on the leaves. Use a stick to knock out the nests and remove the insects as soon as they are found. Large populations can be treated with *Bacillus thuringiensis* var. Kurstocki. This bacterial insecticide kills only true caterpillars and will not harm beneficial insects, wildlife, or people.

- Look for white, hard flecks on the leaves and stems of **Euonymus**. Treat these scale insects with insecticidal soap when the **Japanese Tree Lilacs** are in bloom. The bloom time and egg hatch coincide. Repeat applications two more times at 10- to 12-day intervals.

- Aphid and mite populations begin to build as the temperatures rise and the rains decline. Spray plants with a strong blast of water during extended droughts. The water dislodges many of the insects, helping to minimize their damage.

- Check all plantings for signs of Japanese beetles. These small, metallic-green insects emerge in late June and feed on a variety of plants. See July "Pests" for more recommendations.

Diseases:

- Continue to prune out phomopsis-blighted branches on **Juniper**. See May "Pests" for specific information. Cut out infected branches 9 inches below the canker. Disinfect tools between cuts. Use rubbing alcohol or a solution of 1 part bleach to 9 parts water solution.

- Watch other shrubs for twig blight. The fungal diseases causing twig dieback are most common in cool, wet weather. Remove blighted, brown, and dying branches as soon as they are found. Disinfect tools between cuts.

Pruning

Finish pruning spring-flowering shrubs early this month. This gives the plants plenty of time to develop flower buds for next spring's display.

Shear and shape hedges after new growth has emerged. Prune so that the top of the hedge is narrower than the bottom. This allows light to reach all parts of the shrub. Better light penetration means leaves from top to bottom. See Shrubs "Helpful Hints" on page 357 if you want to start "unshearing" sheared shrubs.

Remove damaged, dead, or insect-infested stems.

Planning

The middle of the growing season is usually peak pest time. The typical cool, wet weather of spring results in a variety of leaf spot, blight, and fungal diseases. The hot weather of July and August helps insect populations quickly multiply. Start monitoring your plantings for problems. Some plants seem to struggle every year no matter what you do. These may be good candidates for replacement. Make notes in your gardening journal on plants that should be replaced or the care provided to minimize future pest problems.

Planting

You can still plant container and balled-and-burlapped shrubs. Select plants with healthy green leaves. Avoid plants with brown leaf edges, indicating drought stress or pest problems.

Summer plantings need special attention. The warm temperatures slow down rooting and dry out soil. Mulch newly planted shrubs with a 2- to 3-inch layer of woodchips or bark. This will help keep roots cool and conserve moisture.

Care

Continue to replenish mulch as needed. Maintain a 2- to 3-inch layer of mulch around shrubs and throughout planting beds. Keep the mulch away from the crown of the plant. Burying the shrubs can lead to disease problems.

Watering

Check soil moisture around new plantings frequently. Shrubs planted in clay soils should be checked every five to seven days. Water when the top 6 to 8 inches just start to dry. Check shrubs in sandy soils twice a week. You will be watering more frequently in the hot, dry months of summer.

Established plants may need supplemental water during the dog days of summer. Water them thoroughly when the top 6 to 8 inches are slightly dry. Mulched plantings need less frequent watering.

Fertilizing

Do not fertilize. Summer fertilization is less effective and can even harm the roots in hot, dry weather.

Pests

Healthy shrubs can tolerate most pests in the landscape. When weather conditions favor the pests and not the plants, you may need to lend nature a hand. Always check with a local extension service, botanical garden, or garden center for help with diagnosis.

Insects:

Control large populations of aphids and mites with a strong blast of water from the garden hose. Treat shrubs with insecticidal soap if the populations grow and damage is severe.

Check shrubs for leucanium scale. This hard-shelled insect attacks a wide range of shrubs. Treat with an ultra-fine oil or insecticide labeled for use on this pest when the **Hills-of-Snow Hydrangea** are in full bloom and again in two weeks.

Continue monitoring and controlling Japanese beetles. Handpick and destroy small populations of these small, metallic green-brown beetles. Use an insecticide labeled for control of Japanese beetles on shrubs to control larger populations. Don't use traps to control this pest. Most entomologists believe the traps just bring more insects into your garden.

JULY

Check the base of wilted stems for signs of borers. Sawdust and holes indicate borers are present. Prune out and destroy borer-infested branches. Regular renewal pruning is usually sufficient control for these pests.

Diseases:

Look for swellings at the base of **Viburnum**, **Euonymus**, and **Spirea**. The disease-induced galls eventually girdle and kill the stem. Prune out infected stems below the gall. Disinfect tools between cuts.

Rake and destroy spotted leaves as they fall. This helps reduce the source of disease next season.

Monitor **Lilacs** and other shrubs for powdery mildew. Look for a white powdery substance on the leaves. Infected plants will survive, but their appearance declines as the season progresses. Reduce problems by increasing the light and air circulation. Thin overgrown plantings during the dormant season to increase light and air flow and to decrease disease.

Pruning

Prune **Arborvitae**, **Yews**, and **Junipers** once the new growth has expanded. Clip stems back to a healthy bud or side shoot to contain growth. See April "Helpful

Helpful Hints

Nature is the best pest manager. Weather, birds, and predacious insects help keep pest populations under control. Weather also increases or decreases the incidence of disease. Occasionally, we get involved when nature's controls are insufficient or the damage is more than we can tolerate.

Try these pest management tips:

- Patience is the first step in control. Give nature time to take care of the problem. Ladybugs will not move into an area if there is no food. So let the aphids graze and wait for the predators to move in.
- Sanitation is an environmentally friendly way to reduce pest problems. Remove weeds to reduce the source for insects and disease. Remove infected leaves and stems as soon as they are discovered. This provides immediate relief while reducing future problems.
- Handpick or trap insects as they are discovered. Have a bug hunt with your family or neighborhood children. Offer a prize or a treat for the best hunter in the group. Insects may give you the creeps, but they are a great way to get kids into the garden.
- Try using insecticidal soaps, **Bacillus thuringiensis**, neem, and other more environmentally friendly products. Always read and follow label directions. Make sure the product is labeled for controlling the pest and plant you are treating.
- Use insecticides as your last option. These products kill good insects as well as the pests. Read and follow all label directions before applying any chemicals. Minimize the impact by spot treating problems as they occur.
- Always evaluate the control method selected and record the results in your journal. This will help you manage future pest problems with great success.

Hints" for more details on pruning evergreens.

Touch up hedges and sheared shrubs when new growth expands. Prune so that the bottom of the plant is wider than the top. This allows light to reach all parts of the plant. Lightly shear summer-blooming **Spirea** to remove faded flowers and encourage rebloom. Repeat this after the second flush of flowers for a third colorful show.

AUGUST

Planning

Take a walk through the landscape. Look for those drab, lifeless spots found in every yard. Consider adding a summer-flowering shrub to brighten up those areas. Visit the library, garden center, or botanical gardens for ideas. Always select plants that are hardy to your area and tolerant of the existing growing conditions.

- **Butterfly Bush** (*Buddleja davidii*) is a sub-shrub that dies back to the ground in most winters. Fragrant flowers in white, pink, or lavender cover this plant from midsummer to fall.

- **Hydrangeas** (*Hydrangeas*) are good summer bloomers for sun and shade locations. **'Annabelle'** produces white snowball-like flowers in July. It flowers in July and August. The **PeeGee Hydrangeas** offer white flowers that fade to pink and brown from August through September.

- **Potentilla** (*Potentilla fruticosa*) is the summer bloomer that first comes to mind. Look for this shrub to be covered with yellow or white flowers from June through fall.

- **Spirea** (*Spirea japonica*) is a popular summer-blooming plant with white, pink, or lavender blooms.

- **Tamarisk** (*Tamarix ramosissima*) is a tall, light, airy shrub that produces light, airy pink flowers from late June through August.

Planting

Continue planting spring dug balled-and-burlapped and container-grown shrubs. Select plants with healthy leaves that have been watered and properly maintained throughout the season.

Mulch the soil around the shrubs to keep the roots cool and moist. This will improve establishment during the hot days of August.

Care

Replenish mulch in established plantings. Maintain a 2- to 3-inch layer of bark or woodchips around the plants. Do not bury the crowns. This leads to rot and disease.

Establish planting beds around trees and shrubs. See this month's "Helpful Hints" for details.

Watering

This is usually the hottest, driest month of summer. Check all plantings for moisture stress. You may need to prioritize watering needs if water bans are enacted.

New plantings are your highest priority. Make sure the top 6 to 8 inches remain moist, not wet. Check new plantings twice a week. Water thoroughly when the soil begins to dry. Improper watering is just as harmful as lack of water. Overwatered plants suffer from root rot and die. Shallow watering encourages shallow rooting that is more susceptible to drought.

Fertilizing

Do not fertilize now. Late-season fertilization can stimulate late-season growth that can be winterkilled.

Pests

Watch for aphids and mites. Summer thunderstorms often help keep these insects in check. You can create your own summer showers with the garden hose. Spray plants with a strong blast of water to help knock many of these pests off the plants. Try insecticidal soap when the populations start damaging the plants. Read and follow all label directions carefully.

Watch for the end of the Japanese beetles. They will soon return to the soil to lay their eggs for the next generation. Handpick and destroy small populations. Larger numbers can be controlled with an insecticide labeled for use on shrubs to control Japanese beetles.

Rake and destroy spotted and discolored leaves. This will reduce damage caused by the disease this season and next. Make notes regarding problem plants. Plan on making changes in the location or pruning practices to help relieve chronic disease problems.

Pull weeds as they appear. Deep-rooted perennial weeds can be spot treated with a total vegetation killer. These products kill the tops and roots of Quackgrass, Creeping Charlie, and Bindweed. They will kill anything green they touch, so keep these chemicals off the young stems and leaves of shrubs and other desirable plants.

Helpful Hints

Reduce maintenance and improve plant health by creating large planting beds around trees and shrubs. The larger bed eliminates competition from grass and damage caused by weed whips and mowers that get a little too close to the plants.

1 *Start by outlining* the bed. Select the size and shape that complements your design. You can always add more shrubs, perennials, and other plants to fill in the voids.

2 *Lay out* the garden hose to mark the area. Use a shovel or edger to create the outline of your new planting bed.

3 *Remove* the existing grass. Peel it off with a sod cutter and use this grass to repair problem areas. Or cut the grass short and cover with three layers of newspapers and several inches of woodchips. The grass and woodchips will eventually decompose. Or use a total vegetation killer to kill the existing grass and weeds. Keep these chemicals off desirable plants. Cover the dead turf with mulch.

4 *Mulch* the planting bed. A 2- to 3-inch layer of woodchips or bark will help reduce future weed problems. Do not put plastic or weed barriers under wood mulch. As the mulch decomposes, it creates the perfect environment for weeds. Weed seeds blow in, nearby turf spreads in, and soon the garden is full of grass and weeds that are growing through the weed barrier.

5 *Reserve* weed barriers for use under rock. The weed barrier helps keep the rock from working into the soil. This reduces the need to replenish the settled mulch and makes it easier for you to make changes to the area. Only use fabric weed barriers that allow air and water through. Do not use plastic that prevents water and nutrients from reaching the roots.

Pruning

Avoid late-season pruning that can stimulate late-season growth.

Finish touchup pruning on sheared plants as soon as possible. Remove only wayward branches. Save major pruning for the dormant season.

SEPTEMBER

Planning

Take a few minutes to record the highlights of the growing season. Make sure you have recorded all new landscape additions, place of purchase, and planting date. Evaluate and record the high and low points of the season. Good records help you repeat your successes, not failures.

Start watching for colorful signs of fall. The bright red **Sumac** growing along the freeway is a good wakeup call. Record the fall display in your landscape. Note any additions that should be made to improve the fall color. Visit local botanical gardens or take a walk in the woods to get ideas of the plants and combinations to include for a spectacular fall show.

Planting

Always start with a call to the utility-locating service. Call Gopher State One Call at 800-252-1166.

Start transplanting shrubs as the leaves begin to drop and the plants go dormant. Moving large established shrubs can be tricky and heavy work. Replacing overgrown or misplaced shrubs may be easier, cheaper, and more successful.

1 Loosely *tie* the branches to prevent damage and keep them out of your way.

2 *Dig* a trench around the shrub slightly larger and deeper than the desired rootball. (See March "Helpful Hint.")

3 *Undercut* the rootball with your shovel. A sharp spade will make the job easier. Use hand pruners and loppers for larger or tougher roots.

4 *Slide* a piece of burlap or canvas under the rootball. Have several friends lend a hand. Extra hands and strong backs will make the job easier and reduce the risk of dropping the shrub and damaging the rootball.

5 *Set* the shrub in the prepared site. Carefully cut away or slide the tarp away from the shrub.

6 *Backfill* the hole with existing soil, water, and mulch.

Continue planting balled-and-burlapped and container-grown shrubs. Planting can continue until the ground freezes. The sooner you get the plants in the ground, the more time the shrubs will have to adjust before winter. Complete evergreen planting this month.

Care

Fall cleanup begins.

Rake leaves out of shrub beds to eliminate unwanted animals' habitat and potential damage to surrounding plants.

Remove and destroy leaves from diseased shrubs. This will help reduce the source of disease next season.

Watering

Continue watering new plantings throughout the fall. The cooler temperatures mean less frequent watering. Check the top 6 inches of soil and water thoroughly as it begins to dry.

Established plants benefit from supplemental watering during a dry fall. Check the soil and water thoroughly when the top 6 inches are dry.

Check soil moisture in aboveground planters every day. Water thoroughly anytime the top few inches of the soil begin to dry. Continue to water planters until the soil in the planter freezes. Make sure all new plantings and evergreens receive a thorough watering before the ground freezes.

SEPTEMBER

Fertilizing

Wait until spring to fertilize shrubs. Fall is a great time to take a soil test. You will have time to read the report and plan your shrub fertilization program for next season.

Pests

Watch for the last few pests of the season. Cooler temperatures usually mean fewer aphids and mites. Make notes on this year's experiences to help guide you through next season.

Contact a plant care professional if your landscape suffered severe feeding damage from Japanese beetles and other pests. Professionals can use a soil-applied systemic insecticide in the fall for control next spring through fall.

Leaf spots and blotches are common problems in cool, wet seasons. Do not bother to spray the plants; it will not help. Remove small numbers of infected leaves as soon as they appear. Rake and destroy disease infected leaves. This reduces the source of infection next season.

Note plants covered with a white powdery substance. The powdery mildew fungus is a common problem on **Lilacs** and many other plants. Fortunately the plant will

Helpful Hints

Colorful autumn foliage is nature's curtain call for the season. Improve the seasonal show in your landscape by adding shrubs with good fall color. Add this to the list of features to consider when creating a beautiful garden.

Some shrubs with good, fall color to consider:

Red to orange
- American Cranberrybush Viburnum (*Viburnum trilobum*)
- Barberry (*Berberis*)
- Burning Bush (*Euonymus alatus* and many of its relatives)
- Chokeberries (*Aronia*)
- Cotoneasters (*Cotoneaster*)
- Fothergilla (*Fothergilla gardenii*) with tinge of maroon
- Running Serviceberry (*Amelanchier stolonifera*)
- Spireas (*Spiraea japonica*)
- Sumac (*Rhus* species)

Purple
- Dogwood (*Cornus*)

Yellow
- Arrow-wood (*Viburnum dentatum*) to red and purple
- Roses (*Rosa* species)
- Witchhazel (*Hamamelis virginiana*)

survive; it just looks bad. Thin out overgrown shrubs next spring to increase light and air circulation and to reduce disease problems.

Remove weeds from planting beds. Unwanted plants can compete with the shrubs and host unwanted diseases.

Pruning

Remove any damaged or pest-infested branches. Wait until late winter to do major pruning. This way you can take care of winter damage and regular pruning at the same time.

Planning

Enjoy the last few glimpses of color. Soon much of the landscape will be covered in snow.

Planting

Continue planting as long as shrubs are available and the ground is workable. The cool fall weather makes this a great time for planting. The good weather conditions mean less stress on the transplants and the planter. The planting process starts with a call to your utility-locating service. Call Gopher State One Call at 800-252-1166. Call at least three working days before planting. This free service marks the location of all underground utilities. Working with utility-locating services can prevent costly damage to underground utilities and may save your life.

Transplant shrubs as soon as they are dormant. See March "Planting" for more information. See September "Planting" for more specifics on moving dormant shrubs.

Finish planting evergreens early in the month. This gives the plants a little more time to put down roots before winter arrives.

Care

Rake and compost or *recycle* fallen leaves. Disease-free leaves can be shredded and left on the lawn, dug into annual gardens, or added to the compost pile. Bury or discard disease-infected leaves. These are a source of infection for the next growing season.

Prepare aboveground planters for winter. Find a sheltered location in an unheated garage or enclosed porch to store the planters for winter. Use bales of hay to insulate shrubs in planters left outside.

Watering

Water plants as needed until the ground freezes. New plantings, evergreens, and aboveground planters need the most attention. Water thoroughly when the top 6 inches of the soil dry.

Give all plants a thorough watering, especially new plantings and evergreens, before the ground freezes. Well-managed plants have a greater rate of winter survival.

Fertilizing

Wait until spring to fertilize. Evaluate the health and vigor of shrub plantings to determine what needs to be fertilized next year. Take a soil test to be sure nutrients are needed. Fall sampling ensures you have the fertilization information needed for spring.

Pests

Fall cleanup is the best way to reduce and even eliminate some future pest problems. Rake and bury or destroy diseased leaves. Prune out and destroy diseased branches. Disinfect tools between cuts.

Call in a professional to manage severe and ongoing insect problems. Professionals have a soil applied systemic insecticide that is applied in fall to control a variety of leaf feeding insects next summer.

Take a few minutes to review the year. Mark next year's calendar, based on this season's problems, for potential times of peak pest activity. This will remind you to monitor your landscape for problems. Catching the problems early makes control easier and more successful.

Start putting animal barriers in place. Surround new plantings with a 4-foot high fence buried several inches into the soil. This will help keep voles and rabbits away from the base of the plants.

Visit your favorite garden center and stock up on repellents if animals have been a problem in the past. Early applications, before feeding starts, appear to be more effective. Reapply repellents after harsh weather and as recommended on the label.

Pruning

You can begin dormant pruning, but I prefer to wait until late winter. The plants recover quicker from the pruning, and I like to leave the stems, fruits, and dried flowers intact for winter interest. As a low input (not lazy!) gardener, I like to do all my chores at one time. Late winter pruning allows me to repair winter and animal damage while shaping the shrubs. One time spent pruning versus two!

Wait until early spring to prune evergreens. Pruning now exposes the inner growth that has not been exposed to wind and sun. Fall pruning can increase winter injury.

Avoid pruning spring-blooming shrubs, such as **Lilac** and **Forsythia**. Dormant season pruning removes flower buds needed for next spring's display. Remove only dead, pest-

infected, or damaged branches at this time.

Helpful Hints

As you look through your landscape and nearby woods, you may see a few summer holdouts. These few shrubs are reluctant to give up their leaves. A closer look reveals the true identity of these plants— **Buckthorn** and **Honeysuckle**. These invasive plants have escaped cultivation and are now taking over our natural areas.

Buckthorn and **Honeysuckles** are tough plants once considered the answer for low-maintenance urban landscapes. Both tolerate a wide range of conditions and need little care. Sound too good to be true? It was. These tough plants are now crowding out our native plants and destroying food and habitat for wildlife.

Help control these invaders and preserve our woodlands with the following tips:

- Cut large plants (6 inches in diameter and larger) back to the ground and treat the stumps with a total vegetation killer such as Roundup® or Finale® or a brush killer such as Brush-B-Gon®. Use a low-pressure handheld sprayer, spray bottle, or sponge brush to apply the chemical. Treat the exposed vascular system located just inside the bark on the cut stem.
- Smaller plants can be treated using the basal bark method. No need to cut the trees. Apply the herbicide to the base of the plant. Cover the stem from the soil line up to 12 to 15 inches high.
- Always read and follow label directions carefully. Misapplications can damage the desirable plants and harm the applicator and the environment.

For help with identification and control of these invasive plants see:

- http://www.nps.gov/plants/alien
- http://www.dnr.state.wi.us/org/land/er/invasive/ factsheets/buckthorns.htm
- http://www.dnr.state.mn.us/fish_and_wildlife/exotics/ buck.html
- http://www.northerngardener.org

NOVEMBER

Planning

Pull out the journal and review problems encountered last winter. Check notes you made on winter protection needed to prevent plant damage this season. Locate and gather materials needed. Make a visit to the garden center to purchase needed supplies. Shop now before our thoughts and their shelves are overrun with the holidays.

Planting

Continue planting and transplanting as long as the ground is workable. Wait until spring to plant evergreens. This gives the plants a chance to put down roots and get established before the harsh winter weather arrives.

Late purchases can be protected until spring planting season arrives. Find a protected location away from wind and sun. Sink the pots into the ground to insulate the roots from temperature extremes. Enclose plants in a cylinder of hardware cloth 4 feet high and sunk several inches into the soil. This will help protect them from voles, rabbits, and possibly deer.

Care

Apply winter protection to shrubs exposed to deicing salts, snow loads, and winter wind and sun.

- Give special attention to **Rhododendrons** and other broadleaf evergreens. Use a screen of burlap to cut the winter winds and shade the plants from the drying winter sun. Or circle the plants with a cylinder of hardware cloth several feet tall and sunk several inches into the ground. Fill with straw or evergreen branches to protect the plants. I prefer evergreen boughs—much more festive.

- Loosely tie upright **Arborvitae**, **Junipers**, and **Yews** that are subject to splitting. Use strips of cotton cloth or old nylon stockings to tie the multiple stems together. This prevents snow from building up on the plant, causing it to split and bend.

- Do not use tree wraps on trees and shrubs. Research has found that they do not help and can, in fact, hurt the plants. If you feel you must use them, apply them in the fall and remove them in the spring.

Watering

Keep watering as needed until the ground freezes. Cool temperatures and fall rains often eliminate the need for supplemental watering.

Make sure new plantings and evergreens are thoroughly watered before the ground freezes. Once the ground is frozen, drain and store the hose until spring.

Fertilizing

No need to fertilize. Evaluate the health and vigor of the shrubs and the soil test results to determine if fertilizer is needed.

Store leftover fertilizers for winter. Granular fertilizers need to be kept in a cool, dry place. Keep liquid fertilizers in a dark location in above-freezing temperatures.

Pests

Make sure animal fences and barriers are in place.

- **Ornamental Plums**, **Euonymus**, fruit trees, and **Arborvitae** are a few wildlife favorites. Monitor these plantings for animal damage throughout the winter.

- Place snow fencing around desirable plants. A 5-foot fence around a small area will often keep out the deer. Make sure they cannot reach in and feed.

- Use a cylinder of hardware cloth, 4 feet tall and sunk into the ground, to protect plants from rabbits and deer.

- Start applying repellents to areas and plants that have suffered animal damage in the past. Preventative treatments often encourage animals to try feeding in another location.

Store pesticides in a secure area that is out of the reach of children and pets. Liquids need to be stored out of the light in a frost-free location. Granules need to be kept dry.

Pruning

Dormant pruning can be done now until growth begins in spring. Prune summer- and fall-blooming plants, such as **Hydrangea** and **Potentilla**. Or wait until late winter so that you can enjoy the winter interest these plants provide.

Wait until spring, after flowering, to prune **Lilacs**, **Forsythia**, and other spring-flowering shrubs. Remove damaged branches as needed.

Helpful Hints

Winter means ice and snow and the work that goes with managing both.

- Avoid dumping snow on shrubs. Heavy snow can break branches.
- Reduce the damage to your landscape plants and the environment by shoveling first and salting last. Use the snow blower or shovel to remove the majority of snow.
- Once the snow is removed, use sand or an environmentally friendly deicing product such as magnesium chloride and calcium acetate. This will minimize the damage to plants and our environment.
- Use burlap, decorative fencing, or other structures to protect plants from roadway salts. A physical barrier can keep the salt off the plants and reduce damage.
- Leach salt through the soil in the spring. Thoroughly water areas exposed to road and sidewalk salt. Heavy spring rains or a thorough watering will move the salt through the soil and away from plant roots.
- Use salt-tolerant shrubs in areas exposed to roadway and sidewalk salt. Some examples are: **Alpine Currant** (***Ribes alpinum***), **Fragrant** and **Staghorn Sumac** (***Rhus aromatica*** and ***Rhus typhina***), **Mockorange** (***Philadelphus***), **Pfitzer Juniper** (***Juniperus chinensis***, 'Pfitzerana'), **Rugosa Rose** (***Rosa rugosa***), **Siberian Pea Shrub** (***Caragana arborescens***), **Snowberry** (***Symphoricarpos albus***), and **Tamarisk** (***Tamarix ramosissima***).

Check, clean and sharpen hand pruners while waiting for the pruning season to begin. Replace the damaged or old blades that can no longer be sharpened. High-quality pruners have replacement blades, while cheaper pruners must be replaced when damaged. Replacement blades are available through garden supply catalogs and many garden centers. Replace nicked and damaged blades.

- Use a 3-cornered (tapered) metal file to sharpen the cutting edge of your hand pruner. Take the pruners apart for easier sharpening. Sharpen away from the blade for safety or toward the cutting edge for a sharpening edge—just be careful. Smooth off any burrs that form along the edge. Make a test cut to check for sharpness.

- Clean the blades with a lightweight oil. Spray to lubricate the working parts and prevent rust.

DECEMBER

Planning

Sit back, relax, and take a look out the window. Get out your gardening journal and record your thoughts on the past growing season. Make a few notes about what you want to do differently and what can stay the same. Now look out the window again. Is your landscape working for you now? Make a list of additions that should be considered in next year's plan. Consider adding some plants for winter interest, attracting wildlife, or feeding your family. See January, February, and September "Helpful Hints" for specific plant recommendations.

Planting

Clean and pack away the tools—another planting season is over. While storing your tools do a quick inventory. Remember the holidays are coming and gardening tools would make a great gift to give—or better yet, to receive! I will take a good pruning saw over a blender any day.

Care

Check winter protection and make sure it is securely in place—keeping out the animals or protecting the plants from harsh winter weather and deicing salt.

Carefully add holiday lights to the winter landscape. Do not wrap branches with strands of lights. Drape the lights over the branches or loosely secure the lights to the stems. Remove lights in spring. If left in place the ties can damage fast-growing shrubs. Plus, the wires will quickly dull your saw blades.

Watering

No need to water once the ground freezes. Check soil moisture in aboveground planters. Water planters anytime the soil thaws and dries. Drain and store the hose for winter.

Fertilizing

Store fertilizers for the winter. Keep granular fertilizers in a cool, dry place. Liquids should be stored in a cool (above freezing), dark location.

Pests

Secure fencing and animal barriers. Continue applying repellents to areas and plants frequently browsed by animals. Reapply after harsh weather and as recommended by the label directions.

Store pesticides in a secure location out of the reach of children and pets. Store granules and powders in a cool, dry location. Keep liquids in a cool (above freezing), dark location. Make a note of old products you no longer use. Watch for community clean-sweep programs next spring. These programs collect and dispose of old pesticides. Store the unwanted materials together and plan on disposing of them at the next community clean-sweep event.

Pruning

Continue dormant pruning on summer- and fall-blooming shrubs. Wait until after bloom to prune spring-flowering shrubs. Once the snow falls, limit your pruning to repair damage.

Prune off a few branches of **Red Twig Dogwood, Juniper, Winterberry, Arborvitae**, and **Yews**. Add these to your indoor or outdoor holiday dècor.

Trees

Trees create the framework of your landscape. They provide longevity and structure for the rest of your plantings. As they grow and mature, they also impact the growing environment for the surrounding plantings. Mature trees increase shade—and decrease the water available to their neighbors.

Trees can also impact your environment. Use them as windbreaks to block the cold winter winds blowing in from the northwest. Plant them on the east or west side of the house to keep your home cooler in the summer. Avoid planting shade trees on the south side of the house. These trees block the important winter sun that helps warm our homes and reduces heating costs in winter. Use trees to create beauty and function in the landscape. They can help block bad views or frame good vistas. Select trees that produce nectar for butterflies and bees, seeds and fruit for the birds, or shelter for wildlife.

Planning

Growing a tree into a healthy and attractive asset for the landscape starts with a plan.

- *Select* trees that are suited to the growing conditions. They should thrive in the light, winds, and existing soil.

- Make sure that the tree will still fit the space available once it reaches its mature size. Those little trees will grow big and often outgrow the small space we have allotted.

- *Grow* the most pest-resistant trees and cultivars available. Healthy trees will live longer with less care and cleanup from you.

- *Plant* for the future, not just immediate impact. Fast-growing trees are usually the first to break apart in storms, decline, or die from disease. Use a mix of fast- and slow-growing trees for immediate and long-term enjoyment. The slow growers will take over as the fast-growing trees begin to decline.

As you narrow down your selection, look for trees that provide year-round interest. Summer is short and memories of that beautiful summer landscape fade quickly during the long months of winter. Select trees with:

- Colorful bark or interesting growth habits for the winter landscape.

- Flowers and fruit for added color and for attracting birds and butterflies to your outdoor living space.

Planting

Start with a call to Gopher State One Call at 800-252-1166 at least three working days before planting. This free service marks the location of all underground utilities. Working with these utility-locating services can prevent costly damage to underground utilities and may save your life. Adjust planting locations to avoid conflicts with both underground and overhead utilities.

Visit your local nursery or garden center while waiting for the utility service. Decide what type of planting stock best serves your needs. *Trees are sold as bare-root, balled-and-burlapped, or container plants.*

- Bare-root trees are cheap and lightweight, but they have the poorest survival rate. They must be planted as soon as possible after digging. This makes them a less than ideal choice for most homeowners. They are frequently used by municipalities, parks, and other organizations for large-scale plantings. Bare-root plants are only available for you to buy from a few sources.

- Balled-and-burlapped trees are dug in early spring before growth begins or fall after leaf drop. The trees are dug with a small portion of the rootball intact. They are more expensive and heavier, but they have a greater rate of survival than bare-root trees.

- Container-grown trees are planted and grown in pots for several years. The smaller root system and pots make them easier to manage. They are moderately priced and can be planted spring through fall.

No matter what type of planting stock you select, make sure it is a healthy tree. Look for trees with straight trunks, a strong central leader (main stem), or appropriate growth habit. Avoid trees with damaged trunks, wilted or scorched leaves, and signs of insect and disease damage.

Give your healthy tree a safe ride home. Use a pickup, trailer, or large vehicle to move the plant. Loosely tie the branches to minimize breakage. Cover the canopy with plastic or fabric if the leaves have started to grow. Carefully lay the tree on its side. Wrap the trunk with carpet or fabric anywhere it comes in contact with the vehicle to prevent damage. Tie the tree in place, and do not forget the red flag for trees that extend 3 feet beyond the vehicle. Many nurseries will help.

Sound like a lot of work? You may want to spend a little extra money to have the experts deliver your tree. They have the staff and equipment to handle and move large trees. Many nurseries will even place the tree in a pre-dug planting hole for you. Consider the delivery charge as an insurance policy on your initial investment.

Once your tree is home, follow these planting tips:

- *Store* trees in a cool, shaded location until they can be planted. Cover the roots of bare-root and balled-and-burlapped trees with woodchips. Water all planting stock often enough to keep the roots moist.

- *Locate* the root flare on the tree by gently pulling the soil away from the trunk. The root flare is the area where the roots gradually flare away from the trunk. This area is often covered by soil.

- *Measure* the distance from the root flare to the bottom of the rootball. This is equal to the depth of your planting hole.

- *Dig* a hole the same depth as the rootball (flare to bottom) and at least two to three times wider than the root system.

- *Make* a wide, shallow, saucer-shaped planting hole. Research has shown that the roots will be better able to penetrate the surrounding soil.

For container-grown trees:

1 Roll the pot on its side or push on the container to loosen the roots.

2 Cut away the bottom of the container.

3 Place the tree in the planting hole so that the root flare is at or slightly above the soil surface.

4 Slice and peel away the container. Loosen the roots by hand or with a sharp knife.

Removing the Container

Trees

For balled-and-burlapped trees:

1 Place the tree in the planting hole so that the root flare is at or slightly above the soil surface.

2 Remove the twine and cut away the burlap and wire cages. These materials do not decompose in most soils and can interfere with root growth and eventually girdle parts of the tree.

For all trees:

1 Use your shovel to *roughen* the sides of the planting hole. This prevents glazing (smooth sides) in clay soils, which keeps the roots from growing into the surrounding soil.

2 *Fill* the planting hole with existing soil. Highly amended soils discourage root development into the surrounding soil. Water or gently tamp to help settle the soil and remove air pockets.

3 *Mulch* the soil with a 2- to 3-inch layer of woodchips or shredded bark. Keep the chips away from the trunk to avoid disease problems.

4 *Water* the planting hole and the surrounding soil thoroughly after planting. Water frequently enough to keep the top 12 inches of soil moist, but not wet. Most trees are killed with kindness from overwatering.

5 *Remove* only broken and damaged branches. Major pruning will be done in two to four years.

Fertilizing

Start with a soil test. A soil test will tell you how often and what type of fertilizer to apply. Contact your local county office of the University of Minnesota Extension Service for soil test information.

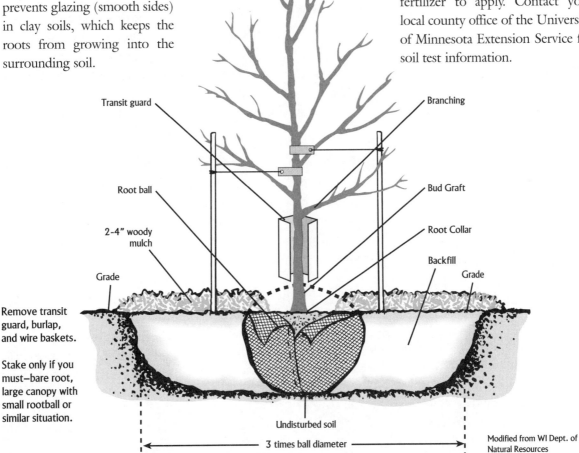

Transit guard

Root ball

2-4" woody mulch

Grade

· Remove transit guard, burlap, and wire baskets.

· Stake only if you must—bare root, large canopy with small rootball or similar situation.

Branching

Bud Graft

Root Collar

Backfill

Grade

Undisturbed soil

3 times ball diameter

Modified from WI Dept. of Natural Resources

Trees

Wait a year to fertilize newly planted trees. Use a slow-release fertilizer with the analysis and amount recommended by your soil test report.

Most established trees need infrequent fertilization. They get nutrients from decaying mulch or lawn fertilizer.

Increase natural fertilization by leaving grass clippings on the lawn. Shred fall leaves and leave them on the soil to decompose. Both add organic matter and nutrients to the soil without harming the lawn.

For more details on fertilization, see April and September "Fertilizing."

Watering

Proper watering is the key to successful planting and establishment. Excess water is the cause of many tree deaths. Water trees thoroughly, but only when needed.

- In clay soils, water the trees until the top 12 inches are moist. Check in a week. Water again when top 6 to 8 inches begin to dry. The soil will feel moist, but crumbly.

- Sandy soils need a thorough watering twice a week in hot, dry weather. Water thoroughly until the top 12 inches are moist. Check in four days. Water when the soil begins to dry.

Pruning

As trees grow and develop, they will need occasional pruning to maintain a strong, healthy, and attractive structure.

- *Remove* only broken and damaged branches on newly planted trees. The more branches mean more leaves and more energy produced to help the tree grow new roots.

- *Prune* young trees to establish one trunk and a strong framework of branches.

- *Prune* established trees to repair damage, remove hazards, and strengthen the tree.

- See January and February "Helpful Hints" for more details on pruning.

Pests

Minimize pest problems by planting the right tree for your location. Trees suited to their environments have fewer pest problems.

Check trees frequently for pest problems. Look for speckled and discolored leaves, holes, spots, and other signs of insects and disease. Early detection can make control easier and more effective. It may also save your tree.

Helpful Hints

Overzealous grass cutters often nick and injure tree trunks with the mower or weed whip, trying to get that last blade of grass. These small wounds create entryways for insects and diseases. Reduce damage to your trees and maintenance chores for you by creating large beds of mulch or groundcovers around your trees.

- Mulch the area under trees with woodchips or shredded bark. It improves the growing conditions, keeps mowers and weed whips away from the trunk, and means less work for you.

- Don't like mulch? Consider planting perennial groundcovers, such as **Vinca**, **Pachysandra**, and **Deadnettle**, around trees. See August "Helpful Hints" for details on adding flowers and groundcovers without killing the tree.

Contact a certified arborist or your local county University of Minnesota Extension Service for help in diagnosing pest problems. Consider hiring a professional for large jobs. They have the equipment and training to do the job safely.

Minnesota Trees

Tall Trees

Common Name (Botanical Name)	Hardiness Zone	Maximum Height/ Spread (In Feet)	Comment
Ash, White (*Fraxinus americana*)	3, 4	50+/50	Prefers moist soil; red to purple fall color; good shade tree.
Fir, White (*Abies concolor*)	4	70/30	Best fir for our state; good substitute for **Blue Spruce**; softer texture and fewer pests.
Ginkgo (*Ginkgo biloba*)	4	80/40 (great variability)	Slow-growing but tough plant with no pests; select male clone (fruit on female stinks).
Hemlock (*Tsuga canadensis*)	3, 4	75/25	Shade-tolerant evergreen; needs moist soils and a protected location.
Honeylocust (*Gleditsia triacanthos inermis*)	4	60/variable	Tough tree that is overused; casts only filtered shade so grass can grow beneath; select podless varieties for less mess.
Kentucky Coffeetree (*Gymnocladus dioicus*)	4	60/40	Possible substitute for **Honeylocust**; tough tree with bolder texture.
Linden (*Tilia* species)	3, 4	60+/40	Size and hardiness vary with species; Littleleaf, Redmond, and Silver are all suited to tough conditions; American prefers more yardlike setting; yellow fragrant flowers in summer.
Maple, Freeman (*Acer × fremannii*, 'Autumn Blaze')	3, 4	50/40	Cross between Red and Silver; good fall color; more tolerant of alkaline soils.
Maple, Norway (*Acer platanoides*)	3, 4	50/25	Tough tree that is overused and becoming invasive in our woodlands; dense canopy and surface roots.
Maple, Red (*Acer rubrum*)	3, 4	50/25+	Must have moist, acid soils; smooth gray bark with red fall color.
Maple, Sugar (*Acer saccharum*)	3, 4	75/50	Needs rich, moist soils; keep away from salt and heat; wonderful fall color.
Oak, Bur (*Quercus macrocarpa*)	3, 4	80/60+	Adaptable; dry to wet soil; bold addition to the landscape.
Oak, Red (*Quercus rubra*)	3, 4	75/60	Good Oak for urban situations; one of the faster growing Oaks; keep out of oak wilt–infested areas.

Minnesota Trees

Tall Trees

Common Name (Botanical Name)	Hardiness Zone	Maximum Height/ Spread (In Feet)	Comment
Pine, Austrian (*Pinus nigra*)	4	50/40	Full sun and dry soils; tough but overused tree; suffering from a wide range of insect and disease problems.
Pine, Scots (*Pinus sylvestris*)	3, 4	50/40	Orange bark and blue-green needles; full sun and well-drained soils.
Pine, White (*Pinus strobus*)	3, 4	50/40	Picturesque with age; does not tolerate urban conditions; full sun and moist soils.
Spruce, Blue (*Picea pungens*)	3, 4	60/20	Prefers sun; has stiff, formal habit; used extensively; suffers from insect and disease problems.
Spruce, Serbian (*Picea omorika*)	4b	50/20	Full sun; narrower than the **Blue Spruce** with pendulous branches.
Spruce, White (*Picea glauca*)	3, 4	50/20	Prefers full sun; 'Black Hills' variety is smaller, denser, and tolerates drier soils.

Medium Trees
(30–40 feet)

Common Name (Botanical Name)	Hardiness Zone	Maximum Height/ Spread (In Feet)	Comment
Alder (*Alnus glutinosa*)	4	40/20	Fast grower that tolerates moist to poorly drained soils.
Amur Chokecherry (*Prunus maackii*)	3, 4	35/35	Fast-growing tree with coppery bark.
Birch, Paper (*Betula papyrifera*)	3, 4	40/30	A favorite due to its white bark; needs cool, moist soils; subject to borer; grow *Betula platyphylla* 'Whitespire Senior' for a borer-resistant white bark Birch.
Birch, River (*Betula nigra*)	4b	40/50	Tolerates wet to dry soils; exfoliating brown, cream, and pink bark; borer resistant.
Ohio Buckeye (*Aesculus glabra*)	3, 4	30/30	Prefers rich, moist soils; fruit can be messy; orange to red fall color.

Minnesota Trees

Small Trees

Common Name (Botanical Name)	Hardiness Zone	Maximum Height/ Spread (In Feet)	Comment
Arborvitae (*Thuja occidentalis*)	3, 4	40/10	Prefers moist soils and full sun to part shade; columnar form makes it suitable as a screen.
Crabapple (*Malus* species and hybrids)	2–4	10–30/ variable widths	Select disease-resistant cultivars with small, persistent fruit. Many sizes and shapes are available with white, pink, or red flowers and yellow, orange, or red fruit.
Hawthorn (*Crataegus* species)	3, 4	20–30/25	Hardiness varies with species; white flowers; yellow to red fall color and fruit for wildlife; thorns.
Japanese Tree Lilac (*Syringa reticulata*)	3, 4	25/15	Prefers sun; large white flowers in mid- to late June; attractive bark.
Magnolia, Star (*Magnolia stellata*)	4b	15/10	Needs moist, rich soils; has white flowers before the leaves appear; smooth gray bark.
Maple, Amur (*Acer ginnala*)	3, 4	15/15	Full sun to part shade; orange to red fall color; starting to appear in native areas (invasive).
Pagoda Dogwood (*Cornus alternifolia*)	3, 4	15/20	Native tree with strong horizontal branching; needs moist soils and prefers part shade.
Redbud (*Cercis canadensis*)	4	40/12	Beautiful heart-shaped leaves. Early blooming with pink flowers. Plant in protected site. Select Minnesota strains.
Redcedar (*Juniperus virginiana*)	3b, 4	20/15	Full sun; well-drained to dry soils; do not plant with **Crabapples** and **Hawthorns** (alternate hosts for rust disease).
Serviceberry (*Amelanchier* species)	3, 4	25/variable	Four-season tree with white flowers, blueberry-like fruit, orange to red fall color, and smooth gray bark. Prefers full sun to part shade and moist soils.

Planning

January is a great time to update an existing landscape or start something new. Start with a tour of your landscape followed by a visit to the library and arboretum. A winter walk is a great way to plan changes and shed a few holiday pounds.

While touring your landscape:

- Look for areas that would benefit from the addition of trees. Trees can provide screening, seasonal interest, shade, and windbreaks.

- Select planting areas large enough to accommodate the trees when fully grown.

- Avoid planting too close to buildings, power lines, and other utilities.

While at the library, check out books on landscape design, trees, and plantings for your area. Landscape designs can be modified for our climate by substituting hardy trees for those not suited to our area. Check *Minnesota Gardener's Guide* and the University of Minnesota Extension Service publications for help selecting trees best suited for your landscape.

Your trips to botanical gardens, arboretums, and parks can help you select the best tree for your landscape.

- See which trees grow best in your climate.

- Look for trees with colorful bark, persistent fruit, or attractive form for winter interest. Add **Winter King Hawthorn** and **Crabapples** for their decorative fruit and bird attraction. Consider **Magnolias** and **Serviceberry** for their smooth gray bark that adds interest to the winter landscape.

- Evaluate trees based on their mature sizes and shapes.

Planting

It is winter, the ground is covered with snow, and the planting season is a mere thought. So sit back, relax, and rest up for spring planting. A few stretching exercises will help keep your gardening muscles limber. Use a little elbow grease to clean and sharpen your planting tools. A shovel with a sharp edge will make spring planting much easier.

Care

Monitor and adjust snow removal to minimize winter injury. You can take steps to reduce damage this season and reduce winter injury next year.

- Shovel snow before reaching for the deicing salt. Removing the snow by hand will reduce the need for plant-damaging salt.

- Check trees for snow and ice damage. Do not try to knock frozen snow and ice off trees. This can cause more damage than the snow and ice.

- Make notes on next year's calendar to adjust winter protection and prevent future problems. List all winter protection—such as tying evergreens, shielding plants from salt and wind, and watering in well before the ground freezes—that you want to complete before the snow flies.

Watering

The ground is usually frozen, and there is no need to water outside. Aboveground planters should be watered any time the soil is not frozen and dry.

Fertilizing

Wait until spring to fertilize. Fertilizing frozen soil does not help your trees and pollutes the groundwater.

Pests

Walk through the landscape and check for animal damage and overwintering insects. A little prevention now can save lots of headaches and extra work this season.

- Check and repair fencing and other animal barriers.

- Reapply repellents or alternate scare tactics to prevent and reduce animal damage.

- Remove egg masses of gypsy and tussock moths.

Pruning

Trees can be pruned during the dormant season. It is much easier to see the overall shape of the tree and what needs to be removed. Prune **Oaks** and **Honeylocusts** in winter to reduce disease problems. See February "Helpful Hints" for more pruning tips.

Save branches from flowering trees such as **Crabapples**, **Magnolias**, and **Pussy Willows** for indoor bloom.

- Recut the stems and place in a bucket of water in a cool (60 degrees Fahrenheit), brightly lit location.

Helpful Hints

Prune with a purpose in mind. Strive to maintain the plant's natural shape. Prune young trees to establish a strong framework. Use proper pruning to maintain a strong structure and healthy growth, as well as to improve flowering and fruiting on established trees.

- Wait two to four years after planting to start pruning for structure. The more top growth (branches and leaves), the faster the trees will recover from transplanting.
- Remove any branches that are crossed, sprouting from the same area on the trunk, or growing parallel to each other.
- Remove any branches that are growing straight up and competing with the main trunk.
- Remaining branches should be more horizontal (perpendicular to the trunk) than upright.
- Make sure branches are well spaced from top to bottom and around the tree trunk. See figure.
- Well-trained trees will need minimal pruning.
- Consider hiring a certified arborist (see November "Planning") for large jobs. They have the training and equipment to do the job safely and properly.

Tree After Thinning

- Start by removing dead and damaged branches.
- Next, prune out watersprouts (upright shoots on branches) and suckers (upright shoots at the base of the trunk) as close to their bases as possible.
- Remove any branches that are crossed, rubbing, or parallel.
- Only prune off lower branches for safety and clearance. The lower limbs are the tree's best defense against disease and old age.

- Mist the branches several times a day if possible until the stems start to bloom.

- Flowering stems can be used in arrangements with other flowers or by themselves.

- Prolong the blossoms by storing the blooming stems in a cooler spot (40 degrees Fahrenheit) at night.

Planning

Continue researching and planning additions to your landscapes. Visit area garden and home shows for landscape and planting ideas. Winter hikes through botanical gardens can be inspiring and a great way to beat the winter blues. Once you select the type of tree, you will need to consider the size and type of planting materials to purchase. Larger trees (over 3 inches in diameter) will give you bigger trees immediately, but they stay the same size for several years as they adjust to their new locations. Smaller trees adapt faster to transplanting and often outgrow their larger counterparts.

Planting

Patience is a virtue—especially for northern gardeners. Planting season is still a month or more away. Start contacting nurseries for information on plant availability and planting stock. *Trees can be purchased as bare-root, balled-and-burlapped, or container-grown stock.*

- Bare-root trees are the cheapest and lightweight, but they have the poorest survival rate. They must be planted as soon as possible after digging. This makes them a less than ideal choice for most gardeners. Bare-root plants are only available for you to buy from a few sources.

- Balled-and-burlapped trees are dug in early spring before growth begins or in fall after leaf drop. The trees are dug with a small portion of the roots intact. They are more expensive and heavier, but they have a greater rate of survival than bare-root trees.

- Container grown trees are planted and grown in pots for several years. The smaller root system and pots make them easier to manage. They are moderately priced and can be planted spring through fall.

Care

Shovel the snow before applying sand or deicing salt. This reduces the need for deicers that can be harmful to trees and other plants. Consider using some of the more plant friendly deicers, such as calcium chloride, calcium magnesium acetate, or sand. They are kinder to the plants and landscape.

Continue monitoring the landscape for animal and winter damage. Make notes of problems in your journal. Record problems with ice loads, snow damage, and poor drainage. Check November "Care" for maintenance strategies to reduce winter injury.

Watering

The ground is still frozen, so there is no need to water outside. Check soil moisture in tree planters overwintering in the garage or screened-in porch. Water the planters thoroughly whenever the soil is thawed and dry.

Fertilizing

No need to fertilize. Check your journal and any soil test information to start planning for spring fertilization. Fertilizing frozen soil will not help the trees, and it contributes to groundwater pollution.

Pests

Continue checking trees for overwintering insects. Egg masses of tent caterpillars look like small, shiny blobs of mud on stems. Gypsy and tussock moth egg masses are hairy masses found on tree trunks. Remove these whenever found.

Dormant oil sprays, such as Volck and All Seasons®, can be applied on warm days when temperatures are 40 degrees Fahrenheit or above for at least 12 hours. Dormant oil sprays are used to control many gall-causing insects (for aesthetic reasons only), some scales, aphids, and mites. Galls cause bumps on leaves while scale, aphids, and mites cause discolored and brown leaves. Make sure you have a problem before using this or any chemical.

Pruning

Trees can be pruned during the dormant season. It is much easier to see the overall shape of the tree and what needs to be removed. Prune **Oaks** and **Honeylocusts** in winter to reduce disease problems. See January "Helpful Hints" for more pruning tips.

- Remove damaged and hazardous branches as they appear. Consider hiring a certified arborist for large jobs. They have the tools, equipment, and training to do the job safely. See November "Planning" for information on hiring an arborist.

- Crossing, parallel, or rubbing branches can also be removed. See "Helpful Hints" for more details.

Helpful Hints

How you remove a branch is as important as deciding which branch to remove. Improper cuts create perfect entryways for insects and disease.

- Make the pruning cut flush with the branch bark collar. See the final cut of the three-step pruning cut illustration. Pruning cuts flush with the trunk are slow to close and make a great entryway for pests and decay. Stubs left behind look unsightly and also increase pest problems.
- Remove branches where they join the trunk or other branches. This will help maintain the tree's natural form and encourage balanced growth.
- Larger branches (2 inches in diameter or greater) should be double-cut to prevent branch splitting and bark tearing.
- Make the first cut on the bottom of the branch about 12 inches from the final cut. Cut about one-fourth of the way through the branch.
- Make the second cut on top of the branch within 1 inch of the first cut. Continuing cutting until the branch breaks off.
- The final cut should be flush with the branch bark collar. See the illustration.
- Do not apply pruning paints or wound dressings to pruning cuts. Recent research shows that these materials actually trap moisture and disease in rather than keeping them out.

Limb Removal

- **Birches**, **Walnuts**, and **Maples** can be pruned in late winter. The running sap does not hurt the tree; it just makes the job messy.

- Save branches from flowering trees such as **Crabapples**, **Magnolias**, and **Pussy Willows** for indoor bloom. See January "Pruning" for details on forcing these to bloom indoors.

Planning

Finalize your landscape plans. Stop by local nurseries and garden centers, or visit them at area home and garden shows. Ask them about additional ideas and plant availability. Some of the newer varieties or unusual plants may be difficult to find. Shop early to find potential sources.

Planting

Late winter and early spring are the best times to transplant trees. Moving trees can be tricky and heavy work. Save large, expensive, and special trees for professionals. They have the experience and equipment to move larger plants successfully. For more details, see September "Planting."

Care

As the snow melts, animal damage and winter injury will be more obvious.

- *Prune* or remove damaged branches. See February and this month's "Helpful Hints."

- *Check* the base of plants for girdling by rabbits and voles.

Damage appears as a lighter area on the trunk. You can often see the teeth marks. Vole and rabbit damage interrupts the flow of water and nutrients between the roots and leaves. Severe damage (feeding around most of the trunk) can kill trees. When in doubt, wait and see if the tree will survive.

Severely damaged trees will need to be removed and replaced. *Some gardeners try bridge grafting in a last attempt to save special plants.* Take a piece of branch from the damaged tree. Graft one end above and the other end below the damaged portion. You must line up the vascular system of the graft with the trunk of the tree. This difficult process requires lots of skill and a little luck.

Gardeners using tree wraps should remove them as temperatures warm. Research has shown wrapping tree trunks is not beneficial and can even be harmful to trees. If you use tree wraps, remove them in spring.

Watering

Wait for the ground to thaw, then check the soil moisture before watering. You may need to lend nature a hand in years with

limited snowmelt and dry springs. Thoroughly water trees subjected to deicing salt. This will help wash the chemicals through the soil and away from the tree roots.

Continue to water trees in above-ground planters. Water thoroughly whenever the soil is thawed and dry.

Fertilizing

Wait until the ground thaws. Fertilizing on snow and frozen soil will not help the trees and contributes to groundwater pollution. Contact your local county office of the University of Minnesota Extension Service for soil test information. Take a soil test as soon as the ground thaws so that you will know if you need to fertilize your trees.

Pests

Dormant oil sprays, such as Volck® and All Seasons®, can still be applied. Make sure the temperature is 40 degrees Fahrenheit or higher when you spray, and for the following 12 hours. Dormant oils are used to control some scale insects, galls (mainly an aesthetic concern), and other overwintering insects. Look for bumps caused by galls and discolored or brown leaves caused by mites, aphids, and scale feeding during the growing season. Only spray if a problem exists that requires this type of treatment.

Continue to monitor and destroy egg masses of Eastern tent caterpillar, gypsy moth, and tussock moth.

Cankerworms are voracious insects that eat the leaves of **Oaks**, **Elms**, **Apples**, **Crabapples**, and many other trees. These brown or green wormlike insects can be seen munching on tree leaves. Fortunately, birds and weather usually keep these pests under control. Severe infestations can be controlled. Apply sticky bands around the trunks of trees that were severely defoliated the previous season. Use a band of fabric treated with a sticky material, such as Tanglefoot®, to avoid injury to the tree. Put sticky traps in place in mid-March through mid-June and in mid-October through mid-December.

Prune out black knot cankers. The cankers start out as swollen areas on the branches of **Ornamental** and **Edible Plums**, **Cherries**, and **Flowering Almonds**. They eventually release disease-causing spores and turn into black knots on the tree. Removing the cankers now reduces the risk of future infection.

Helpful Hints

Snow, ice, and winter winds can often damage or destroy the main leader of **Spruce** and other evergreen trees. The loss of the central leader causes the tree to lose its nice pyramidal shape. As other branches compete for the lead position, the tree tends to flatten out. You can help restore the shape by giving nature a helping hand.

To create a new central leader:

1 Cut off the damaged leader, leaving a 1½-inch stub.

2 Select one of the shorter side shoots to serve as the new leader.

3 Tie the side shoot to the remaining stub. Over time, this branch will start to grow upright and become the new leader.

4 Remove the tie after one year.

5 Several side shoots may begin to grow upward. Prune out all but the leader trained to be an upright growing stem.

Stub

Pruning
Evergreen Trees

Pruning

Complete pruning before trees leaf out. Pruning during leaf expansion increases the risk of trunk and branch damage. See January and February "Helpful Hints" for details on proper pruning.

Complete pruning on **Oaks** and **Honeylocusts**. Dormant-season pruning helps reduce the risk of disease problems on these trees.

Birches, **Walnuts**, and **Maples** can be pruned in late winter. The running sap does not hurt the tree; it just makes the job messy.

Remove storm-damaged branches as they occur.

Planning

Plan a special Arbor Day event for your family, friends, neighborhood, or school group. Arbor Day is the last Friday in April. See Trees "Helpful Hints" on page 359 for ideas.

Planting

Start planting trees as soon as plants are available.

To plant your tree: Dig a wide, shallow hole. Make it at least two, preferably three or more times wider than the rootball. The depth should be equal to the distance from the root flare to the bottom of the rootball. See the "Planting" section in the chapter introduction for details.

Care

It is time to start preparing for spring:

- Remove screening, cloth strapping, and other winter protection. Hardware cloth fencing can stay in place. Make sure the material is not rubbing or girdling the plant.

- Remove winter insulation (bales of straw). Move trees growing in aboveground planters out of winter storage.

- Renew mulch around trees in lawn areas and planting beds. A 2- to 3-inch layer of shredded bark or woodchip mulch helps conserve moisture, reduce weeds, and add organic matter. Keep the mulch away from the trunk of the tree.

Keep lawn mowers and weed whips away from tree trunks. Mower blight (tree decline due to equipment damage) is the biggest killer of trees. Mulch, groundcovers, or planting beds reduce the need to hand trim and also protect trees from mowing equipment.

Watering

Water trees when the ground thaws and the soil is dry. Established trees will only need watering during dry periods. Thoroughly soak, with 1 to 2 inches of water, the area under the drip line when the top 6 to 10 inches of soil are moist and crumbly. This will be more frequent in sandy soils and during high temperatures.

Thoroughly water trees subjected to deicing salt. This will help wash the deicing chemicals through the soil and away from the tree roots.

Water new plantings often enough to keep the rootball and surrounding soil slightly moist. Provide 1 inch of water when the top 6 to 10 inches are moist and crumbly. This may be several times each week in sandy and gravelly soil, and as little as every two weeks in clay soils.

Continue to water trees in aboveground planters. Water until the excess drains out of the bottom of the pot. Check containers at least twice a week and water as needed.

Fertilizing

Spring—before growth begins—is a good time to fertilize established trees. Let the plant and a soil test be your guide. Trees often get nutrients from decomposing mulch, lawn fertilizers, and grass clippings left on the lawn.

Contact your local county office of the University of Minnesota Extension Service for soil test information.

Check tree for signs of nutrient deficiencies. Poor growth and off-color leaves may indicate the need to fertilize.

Wait a year to fertilize new tree plantings. They have been well tended in the nursery, and fertilizer may harm the newly developing roots.

If soil tests are not available, use a slow-release fertilizer containing just nitrogen or three times more nitrogen than phosphorus and potassium. Check the fertilizer analysis on the bag. The three numbers stand for the percentage of nitrogen, phosphorus, and potassium in the fertilizer, in that order. The first number should be three times larger than the other two.

Apply 2 to 4 pounds of actual nitrogen per 1000 square feet. This is equal to 20 to 40 pounds of a 10 percent nitrogen fertilizer and 10 to 20 pounds of a 20 percent nitrogen fertilizer.

Fertilizer can be sprinkled over and raked through mulch. Water to move the fertilizer into the soil.

Place fertilizer in the soil for trees growing in lawn areas. Remove small cores of soil 6 inches deep and 2 to 3 feet apart throughout the area around the tree. Holes should start several feet away from the trunk and continue several feet beyond the drip line of the tree. Divide needed fertilizer evenly between the holes. Water until the top 12 inches of soil are moist.

Pests

This is a great time to prevent or reduce pest problems that may develop later in the season.

Insects:

Reduce the spread of spruce gall on small trees. Prune out the small swollen sections (look like miniature cones or pineapples on the stem) while they are green and the insects are still nesting inside.

Start checking **Crabapples**, **Birches**, and other ornamental trees in late April for signs of Eastern tent caterpillars. These wormlike insects build webbed nests in the crotches of tree branches. Remove or destroy the tent (can be knocked down with a long stick) to control this pest.

Birch leaf miners are insects that feed between the upper and lower surface of the leaves. Their feeding causes the leaves to turn brown. They do not kill the tree but add to the stress, making the white-barked **Birches** more susceptible to borers. A soil systemic labeled for use on Birches to control leaf miner can be applied now to prevent infestations. Do not treat trees that were treated with a soil systemic in the fall.

Dead branch tips on your **Austrian Pine** may mean it has Zimmerman moth. Consult a certified arborist for advice and treatment. Spray applications should be made when the saucer magnolia is in the pink bud stage.

Diseases:

Apple scab is a common problem on **Crabapples** and **Apples**. This fungal disease causes black spots and eventual leaf drop. Badly infested trees may be leafless by July. Raking and destroying infected leaves will reduce the source of disease. Fungicides labeled to control apple scab on **Crabapples** will help reduce infection on susceptible trees. Make four to five applications of fungicides at ten-day intervals starting at bud break. Consider hiring an arborist with the training and equipment to do the job safely.

Dead branches on **Spruce** are often caused by cytospora canker. Remove infected branches and disinfect tools with rubbing alcohol or a solution of one part bleach to nine parts water. Mulch the soil under the tree and water during dry periods.

Pruning

Do not prune after the buds open and the leaves begin to grow. The tree is very susceptible to damage during this phase of growth. Resume pruning once the leaves are fully expanded.

Do not prune **Oaks** and **Honey-locusts** once growth begins. Wait until the dormant season to avoid disease problems.

Planning

The growing season is finally becoming a reality. Keep your landscape plan and garden journal handy. Record purchases and new additions to the garden. Check the growing conditions and your planting plans before purchasing new plants. All those beautiful plants are hard to resist after a long, cold winter. Make sure you have the space and proper growing conditions before purchasing additional trees.

Planting

Keep planting trees in the landscape. See the "Planting" section of the chapter introduction for details. Remove plant tags from the trunk and branches. Left in place, these can eventually girdle the stem.

Care

Evaluate the size and thickness of mulch rings around trees. Bigger is better in this case. A wide mulch ring, covering most of the area under the tree canopy, creates a good environment for the tree roots. Shredded bark and woodchips help conserve water, reduce weed growth, and add nutrients to the soil beneath.

Do not use weed barriers under bark, woodchips, and other organic mulches. They are only a temporary solution for weed growth and can create a maintenance headache in the long run. As the mulch on top of the weed barrier decomposes, it creates a perfect place for weeds and grass to grow. It also prevents the organic matter from improving the soil beneath the barrier.

Get the most benefits from mulch by:

- Mulching both new and established trees.

- Maintaining a 3-inch layer of mulch around trees.

- Keeping the mulch away from the tree trunk. Piling mulch around the trunk can lead to decay.

Watering

Spring often means lots of rain, but you may still need to lend a hand in dry years or with new plantings.

Keep the rootball and surrounding soil of newly planted trees slightly moist, but not wet. Water the area thoroughly so that the top 10 to 12 inches of soil are wet. Water again once this area begins to dry. New plantings usually need to be watered once every seven to ten days in clay soil and twice a week in sandy soil.

Established trees have a larger root system to retrieve water. Spring rains usually provide the needed moisture. Give established trees a thorough watering every two weeks during extended dry periods. **Paper Birches** and other moisture-loving trees should be watered regularly during dry weather. Check these plants once a week and water when the top 6 inches of soil start to dry.

Water aboveground planters thoroughly so that the excess water drains out the bottom. Check regularly and water as the top 6 inches of soil begin to dry.

Fertilizing

We often kill our plants with kindness. Trees receive many nutrients from grass clippings left on the lawn, decomposing mulch, and lawn fertilizers. Fertilize only when needed. Start with a soil test or consult a tree care professional if your trees do not look healthy.

Fertilize aboveground planters with any complete plant fertilizer, such as 10-10-10 or 12-12-12. Follow label directions for frequency and concentration.

Pests

Insects, like plants, are influenced by the weather. In cool seasons, insect problems develop one to two weeks later. In a warm spring, their populations are already starting to increase. Continue monitoring for the pests described in April "Pests."

Insects:

- Honeylocust plantbugs and leafhoppers begin feeding soon after buds break. This causes new growth to be distorted and sparse. Once the insects are done feeding, the trees will leaf out and be fine. Patience and proper care is the best control.

- Remove tent caterpillar nests from infested trees. Do not burn the nest while it is in the tree. This is more harmful to the plant than the insects.

- Watch for signs of gypsy moth larvae. These wormlike insects eventually grow to 2 inches long and have two rows of red and blue warts on their backs. Catch caterpillars as they crawl down the tree trunk looking for shade during the day. Wrap a 12- to 18-inch-wide strip of burlap around the tree trunk at chest height. Tie a string around the burlap 6 inches from the top. Let the top 6 inches of burlap flop over the string. Check under the burlap everyday between 2 and 6 P.M. Use gloves to remove caterpillars; drop them in soapy water to kill the insects.

- European pine sawflies are wormlike insects that feed in colonies. They will do a little dance for you when you get too close. Check **Mugo** and other common landscape **Pines** for feeding colonies of this insect. Even in large numbers, they are easy to control. Slide on a leather glove and smash the insects. Or prune out the infested branch and destroy the insects.

- Aphids and mites are common landscape pests. They suck out plant juices, causing leaf discoloration and distorted growth. Nature usually keeps them in check with rains and natural predators. In dry seasons, use the garden hose and a strong blast of water to dislodge the insects and reduce the damage. Lady beetles are a great aphid control.

Diseases:

- Phomopsis blight is a fungal disease that attacks **Junipers** and **Russian Olives**. It is most prevalent in cool, wet springs. The infected branches turn brown and die. Remove infected branches and disinfect tools between cuts.

- Fireblight is a bacterial disease that infects susceptible **Crabapples**. It causes the leaves to turn black and branch tips to curl. This disease spreads by splashing water, pollinating bees, and infected tools. Avoid pruning Crabapple trees during wet periods. Prune out infected branches 12 inches below the canker (sunken, discolored area) on the stem. Disinfect tools between cuts with rubbing alcohol or a solution of one part bleach to nine parts water.

Pruning

Give your saw a temporary break. *Limit pruning to disease control and repair.* Save major pruning for after the leaves have fully developed. This reduces the risk of damaging the bark.

Do not prune **Oaks**. Pruning cuts increase the risk of oak wilt. Save Oak pruning for the dormant season whenever possible.

Avoid pruning **Honeylocusts**. Pruning cuts make a great entryway for the life-threatening nectria canker.

Planning

Summer storms can leave you with broken branches and uprooted trees. Proper care and preventative pruning can help reduce storm damage to trees. Consider contacting a certified arborist (tree care professional) to evaluate the health and soundness of your trees. Together you can develop a long-term plan to maintain or improve your tree's storm resistance. If damage does occur, you will have a good working relationship with a professional who can help you manage storm damage. See November "Planning" for tips on hiring an arborist.

Planting

Nurseries and garden centers still have a good supply of balled-and-burlapped and container-grown trees. *Increase planting success by:*

- *Selecting* healthy trees with green leaves free of brown spots, dry edges, or other signs of pest damage and neglect.

- *Protecting* newly emerged leaves while transporting your tree home. Wrap the canopy with a blanket or plastic tarp. Many nurseries will wrap the tree canopy for you, but it is best to come prepared.

- *Storing* trees in a shaded location until you are ready for planting.

- *Checking* the trees daily. Water frequently enough to keep the roots and surrounding soil moist. Cover the rootball of balled-and-burlapped trees and containers with woodchips if the trees will be stored for a long period of time.

- See the "Planting" section of the chapter introduction for planting details.

Care

Continue mulching trees as needed. A 3-inch layer will help improve tree growth and reduce maintenance for you. Keep the mulch away from the trunk to avoid rot.

Consider replacing annual plantings under trees with perennial groundcovers. This means less root disturbance for the tree and less work for you in the long run.

Watering

Watering frequency is dependent upon the age of the tree, weather conditions, and soil.

- Most established trees need infrequent watering. Water established trees every two weeks during extended dry periods. Apply enough water to moisten the top 12 inches of soil.

- Moisture loving trees, such as **Paper Birch**, may need to be watered once a week during dry weather. Apply enough water to moisten the top 12 inches of soil. Water again when the top 4 to 6 inches begin to dry.

- Young trees should be checked once or twice a week and watered thoroughly as needed.

- Clay soils hold moisture longer and need less frequent watering. Thoroughly soak the top 10 to 12 inches of soil and wait until the top 6 inches begin to dry before watering again. Check the soil moisture every seven to ten days.

- Sandy soils dry out faster. Check the soil moisture every four to five days. Water thoroughly and wait until the top 6 inches of soil dry before watering again.

- Check the soil moisture in aboveground planters every day. Water trees when the top 6 inches of soil begin to dry.

Fertilizing

Yellow and off-color leaves may indicate a nutrient problem. Take a soil test before adding fertilizer. The soil test will tell you what type and how much of each nutrient you need to add. Adding nutrients your tree does not need can harm the plant and the environment, as well as waste your time and money.

Frequent watering of aboveground planters washes many nutrients out of the soil. Use a complete fertilizer, such as 10-10-10 or 12-12-12, to replace these. Follow manufacturer recommendations.

Pests

Continue monitoring for pests. Distorted, spotted, and discolored leaves may indicate you have an insect or disease problem.

Insects:

• See May "Pests" for tips on controlling gypsy moth, Eastern tent caterpillar, mites, and aphids.

• Continue proper care of **Honeylocusts** as they start to re-leaf and recover from leafhopper and plantbug damage.

• Start watching for Japanese beetles. The small, metallic green beetles feed on over 300 species of plants. The beetles skeletonize the leaves by eating the leaf tissue and leaving the veins intact. The Japanese beetle population is growing and additional outbreaks are appearing throughout the state. Stressed trees or those repeatedly defoliated by Japanese beetles would benefit from treatment. Use an insecticide labeled for use on trees to control this beetle. Consult a tree care professional for treatment of large trees.

Diseases:

• Complete scab treatments on **Crabapples** (see May "Pests" for details).

• Continue branch removal of cytospora-infected **Spruce** branches, fireblight-cankered **Crabapples**, and phomopsis-infested **Junipers** and **Russian Olives** (see May "Pests" for more details).

• Rake anthracnose-infected leaves as they drop from trees. This fungal disease causes brown spots on lower leaves of **Oak**, **Maple**, **Ash**, **Black Walnut**, and **Sycamore**. Though annoying, the disease is usually not life threatening. Sycamores may benefit from future preventative treatments.

Pruning

The old saying, "Prune when the saw is sharp" applies to June.

• Concentrate your efforts on repair rather than shaping. Remove crossing, broken, or diseased branches. Make cuts where branches join other branches or flush to the branch bark collar.

• Do not paint pruning cuts. Research shows that the tree will heal better without these products. Disinfect tools between cuts on sick trees with alcohol or a solution of one part bleach to nine parts water.

• Wait for the dormant season to prune **Oaks** and **Honeylocusts**.

Planning

The heat of the summer is a good time to evaluate your landscape. Make sure your shade trees are working for you. Check tree locations and their impact on your environment. Do you have trees located in areas where you want shade for outdoor leisure and activities? Are there trees on the east and west side of the home to keep your home cooler throughout the summer? Make a note on the landscape plan in your journal if you need some additional plantings.

Planning

Keep planting container-grown and spring-dug balled-and-burlapped trees. Check trees for signs of drought stress prior to purchase. Avoid buying trees with brown leaves and bare stems. Drought-stressed trees take longer to adapt to transplanting and have a lower survival rate.

Summer-planted trees will need extra attention during the hot part of summer. Check plants more often during extremely hot and dry weather.

Care

Monitor the landscape for opportunities to reduce maintenance and improve plant health.

- *Create* planting beds by joining several isolated trees together into one large garden. Fill the space with shrubs and perennials. Larger beds mean less mowing and eliminate the need for hand trimming around individual trees.

- *Remove* weeds and other unwanted plants from the bases of your trees.

- *Renew* mulch as needed. A 2- to 3-inch layer of woodchips will help conserve moisture and keep the roots cool throughout the heat of summer.

Watering

Summer often means hot, dry weather. You may need to lend nature a hand as the temperatures rise and the summer rains cease. *You may be forced to prioritize water use during extended periods of drought.*

- Trees in planters will need daily attention and frequent watering.

- New plantings will need the next most frequent watering.

Check new plantings in sandy soil twice a week. Water thoroughly when the top few inches start to dry. New trees growing in clay soil should be checked every five to seven days. Water as needed.

- Established and mulched trees can go the longest time between waterings. Even large established trees may need supplemental water during extended dry periods. Water thoroughly until the top 8 to 12 inches are moist.

Fertilizing

Wait until next spring to fertilize newly planted trees. Fertilizing now may damage newly forming roots.

Continue fertilizing trees growing in aboveground planters. Follow label directions.

Monitor established trees for signs of nutrient deficiencies. Small, pale leaves or stunted growth may indicate your tree needs to be fertilized. Root rot and flooded or droughty soils can also cause these symptoms. Take a soil test to determine the cause of the problem. Wait until fall to add any needed nutrients.

Pests

Monitor all trees for signs of insects and disease. Proper care and sanitation (the removal of infected plant parts) will help minimize damage and reduce future problems.

Insects:

- Aphid and mite populations can explode during hot, dry weather. These small insects suck out plant juices, causing speckled and discolored leaves. One or two summer thunderstorms or a strong blast of clear water from the garden hose will help contain the problem.

- Japanese beetles are out and feeding on a variety of trees, shrubs, and flowers. These small, metallic green beetles eat the foliage into a lacy mass of veins. Isolated populations have been found throughout the state. Healthy plants can tolerate the damage. Treat now with an insecticide or hire a professional to make a fall application of a soil systemic to prevent problems next summer on stressed trees.

- Check gypsy moth infested trees for pupal cases (cocoons). Look in bark crevices and protected areas of the tree trunk. Destroy any that are found.

Helpful Hints

Have you ever parked your car under a large tree and returned to find the windshield spotted with a clear, sticky substance? It is not tree sap, but honeydew. If you could see into the tree canopy, you would find it full of aphids. These small, teardrop-shaped insects can be green, black, white, or peach in color. As these insects suck out plant juices, they secrete the excess as honeydew.

Occasionally a black fungus, sooty mold, grows on the honeydew. The fungus does not infect the plant, but it does block sunlight, causing leaves to yellow and even drop. Lady beetles often move in and eat the aphids before this pest is even discovered. Other years, you may need to step in with a strong blast of water from the garden hose. Insecticidal soap will help control aphids and remove the sooty mold.

Diseases:

- Bare **Crabapples** are a common sight in summers following a cool, wet spring. The cause is probably apple scab. Rake and destroy leaves as they fall. This will reduce the source of disease next season. Consider replacing disease-susceptible **Crabapples** with newer scab-resistant cultivars. See April "Pests" for information on chemical control for apple scab.

- Anthracnose, a fungal disease, can cause spotting and eventually leaf drop on **Oaks**, **Maples**, **Ashes**, **Black Walnuts**, and **Sycamores**. Healthy trees will survive this damage. Sprays are not effective at this time. Rake and destroy fallen leaves to reduce the source of infection for next season.

- Continue to prune out dead and cankered branches. Disinfect tools with rubbing alcohol or a solution of one part bleach to nine parts water.

Pruning

Remove dead and damaged branches as they are found. Save large tree pruning for professionals. They have the equipment and training to do the job safely. It may be cheaper to hire an arborist than to pay the medical bills that could result from a pruning mishap!

Planning

Get out your garden journal, sit under the shade of one of your lovely trees, and make some notes on the growing season. Record details on your new plantings, the weather, pest problems, and plant care. This information will help you prepare for next season.

Planting

Late summer and fall are excellent times to plant trees. The hot weather will soon pass, and the trees will have the cool temperatures of fall for establishment. Many stores will have sales on plants at this time of the season. Good nurseries and garden centers have religiously watered and properly maintained their planting stock throughout the summer.

Some stores offer trees at reduced prices. Make sure you are really getting a bargain. Drought-stressed and poorly maintained trees are not a deal. These are very slow to establish and may never fully develop into healthy landscape specimens. After several years of struggling, you may end up replacing the tree. Not only have you spent money and time buying and planting two trees, but you have also lost valuable time—tree-growing time.

Care

A walk through the landscape will help you discover any maintenance practices that may be harming your trees.

- *Pull* mulch away from the trunks of the trees.

- *Check* new plantings and remove any labels, wires, twine, or other materials that can eventually girdle the trunks.

- *Inspect* all trees for trunk damage. Expand planting and mulch beds to protect trees from weed whips and lawn mowers.

- *Watch* for early signs of fall. Trees that color up early are letting you know they are in distress. Construction damage, girdling roots, root rot, and decline can cause all or part of your tree to turn fall color prematurely. Proper watering and care may help a stressed tree. Other problems need to be addressed by a certified arborist.

Watering

August is often a hot, dry month. You may need to break out the garden hose and give nature a hand.

- New plantings remain a high priority. Check soil moisture once or twice a week. Trees growing in sandy soil need a thorough watering every three to five days during drought. Those growing in clay soil should be checked every seven to ten days.

- Trees in aboveground planters should be checked daily. Water thoroughly when the top 6 inches begin to dry.

- Mulched and established trees need less frequent watering. Soak the top 8 to 12 inches of soil under the tree canopy every ten to fourteen days during extended droughts.

Fertilizing

Do not fertilize. Late-season fertilization can stimulate late-season growth that can be damaged or killed by cold winter temperatures.

Continue monitoring plant health. Stunted and discolored leaves can indicate nutrient deficiency, root rot, drought, or waterlogged soils. Take a soil test if you suspect nutrient problems.

Pests

Insects:

- Watch for aphids and mites that can continue to be a problem during the hot months of August. These small insects suck out plant juices, causing leaves to discolor and eventually turn brown. Let lady beetles and other predacious insects take care of these pests. High populations can be reduced with a strong blast of water from the garden hose.

- Inspect the landscape for Japanese beetles that are finishing their aboveground feeding. Heavy infestations may be treated in fall with a soil systemic, such as Merit, applied by a professional. (This product is not yet labeled for homeowner use.) This will kill the next year's beetle population as they feed on treated trees.

- Check tree trunks for female gypsy moths. The white, flightless moths crawl up the trunk to mate and lay eggs. Remove and destroy the female and egg masses as they are found.

Diseases:

- Continue to rake and destroy diseased leaves as they fall from the trees. This will reduce the source of infection for next season.

Helpful Hints

Surface roots are those roots that grow slightly above the soil and dull your mower blades as you cut the grass or interfere with the grass growing under your trees. Do not get out the axe. Those roots are important to the support and well being of your tree.

- Consider mulching under the tree canopy. A 2- to 3-inch layer of mulch provides a good environment for the tree and keeps those surface roots under cover.
- Do not build a raised bed around your tree. Burying tree roots can kill many species of trees. The roots of those that do not die will soon reach the surface again.
- Or plant perennial groundcovers under the tree. These plants help insulate the roots, but do not out-compete the trees for water and nutrients.
  - Do not rototill or add soil to the planting area.
  - Kill the grass by covering it with newspaper and mulch or with a total vegetation killer. Read and follow all directions carefully.
  - Select plants suited to the growing conditions. See the chapter on " Vines and Groundcovers" for suggestions.
  - Space the plants throughout the areas.
  - Dig a hole slightly larger than the root system of the groundcover.
  - Amend the small planting holes with peat, compost, or other organic matter. Plant, mulch, and water.
  - Weed control is critical for the first few years. Once the groundcovers fill in, your weeding chores will be minimal.

- Continue to remove cankered and diseased branches as they are found. Prune 9 to 12 inches below the cankered (sunken or discolored) areas of the branch. Disinfect tools with rubbing alcohol or a solution of one part bleach to nine parts water. Continue to give trees proper care to reduce the adverse effects of the disease.

Pruning

Save major pruning chores for fall. Late-season pruning can stimulate late-season growth that may be damaged in the winter.

Avoid pruning **Honeylocusts** and **Oaks** during the growing season. The open wounds increase the risk of disease.

Planning

Continue writing in your garden journal. Make sure planting records are complete. Record plant name, source, and planting location. Evaluate and record pest management strategies. This will help improve next year's success. Record fall color in your landscape. This may be a feature you want to improve in the future.

Planting

Fall is for planting. The cooler temperatures mean less watering for you and an easier time for the trees to get established. See October for a list of plants to avoid for fall planting. See the "Planting" section of the chapter introduction for planting details.

This is the second-best time to transplant trees. Wait until the leaves drop and the trees are dormant. Remember, moving trees can be tricky and heavy work. Save large, expensive, and special trees for professionals. They have the experience and equipment to move larger plants successfully.

- Start transplanting once the trees begin dropping their leaves.

- Loosely *tie* lower branches to prevent damage and keep them out of your way.

- *Dig* a trench around the tree slightly larger and deeper than the desired rootball. See "Helpful Hints" for recommendations on the size of rootball to make for the tree being moved.

- *Undercut* the rootball with your shovel. A sharp spade will make the job easier. Use hand pruners and loppers for larger or tougher roots.

- *Slide* a piece of burlap or canvas under the rootball. Have several friends lend a hand. Extra hands and strong backs will make the job easier and reduce the risk of dropping the tree and damaging the rootball.

- *Set* the tree in the prepared site. Carefully cut away or slide the tarp away from the tree.

- *Backfill* the hole with existing soil, water, and mulch.

Care

As the beautiful fall leaves start dropping to the ground, the cry for raking help can be heard throughout the neighborhood. Before you start to grumble, *consider recycling your leaves. It saves you work and improves the landscape.*

- *Shred* leaves with the mower and leave them on the lawn. As long as you can see the grass blades through the shredded leaves, the lawn will be fine. In fact, the leaves will quickly break down, adding nutrients and organic matter to the soil.

- *Rake* leaves, shred them with your mower, and dig them into annual vegetable and flower beds. The leaves break down over winter, improving the soil for next year's garden.

- *Bag* leaves and tuck them behind the plantings near your home. The bagged leaves add insulation to the house. In summer, use the leaves as a mulch in flower and vegetable gardens.

- *Shred* leaves with the mower and throw them in a heap to decompose. Composting really is that easy. The more work you do, the faster you make compost.

Watering

Cooler fall temperatures usually mean less watering. Continue to monitor soil moisture and water new plants as the top 6 inches of soil begin to dry.

Evergreens, new plantings, and transplants will all survive winter better when they receive sufficient moisture throughout the fall.

Fertilizing

Fall, after the trees are dormant, is a good time to fertilize established trees. Let the plant and a soil test be your guide. Trees often get sufficient nutrients from decomposing mulch, lawn fertilizers, and grass clippings left on the lawn.

Contact your local county office of the University of Minnesota Extension Service for soil test information.

Check trees for signs of nutrient deficiencies. Poor growth and off-color leaves may indicate the need to fertilize. Wait a year to fertilize new tree plantings. They have been well tended in the nursery and fertilizer may harm the new, developing roots.

If soil tests are not available, use a slow-release fertilizer containing just nitrogen or three times more nitrogen than phosphorus and potassium.

Apply 2 to 4 pounds of actual nitrogen per 1000 square feet. This is equal to 20 to 40 pounds of a 10 percent nitrogen fertilizer and 10 to 20 pounds of a 20 percent nitrogen fertilizer.

Fertilizer can be sprinkled over and raked through mulch. Water to move the fertilizer into the soil.

Place fertilizer in the soil for trees growing in lawn areas. Remove small cores of soil 6 inches deep and 2 to 3 feet apart throughout the area around the tree. Holes should start several feet away from the trunk and continue several feet beyond the drip line of the tree. Divide needed fertilizer evenly between the holes. Water until the top 12 inches of soil are moist.

Do not fertilize aboveground planters. Fall fertilization can stimulate growth and reduce winter survival.

Helpful Hints

Recommended Rootball Size for Transplanting

Tree Diameter at Chest Height	(Size in Inches) Rootball Diameter	Rootball Depth
1/2	14	11
3/4	16	12
1	18	14
1 1/4	20	14
1 1/2	22	15
1 3/4	24	16
2	28	19

Fall applications of soil systemic insecticides can be made by professionals (these products are not yet labeled for homeowner use) for spruce galls, birch leaf miners, Japanese beetles, gypsy moths, plantbugs, and several other pests.

Pests

Check tree trunks for gypsy moth egg masses. The eggs are covered with a yellow hairy substance. Each cluster can contain over 600 eggs. Remove and destroy any egg masses found.

Pruning

As the leaves drop, it is a good time to start pruning. The bare trees make it easy to see the plant's structure and determine which branches stay and which ones go. See January and February "Helpful Hints" for more pruning details.

Contact a certified arborist for professional help training young trees and pruning large trees. See November "Planning" for hiring tips.

Planning

As you finish your last few growing chores, it is time to start preparing for winter. Review last year's garden journal. Start making a list of plants that need winter protection from cold, snow, and animals. Start gathering materials now so that you won't need to scramble for materials as the first flakes of snow drop from the sky.

Planting

Small trees can be transplanted once the leaves color up and fall. See September "Planting" for details on transplanting trees.

Fall is a great time to plant most trees and shrubs. The soil is warm, air temperatures are cool (good for the plant and the person planting), and trees are in place and ready to start growing as soon as spring arrives.

- Purchase healthy balled-and-burlapped and container-grown plants from local nurseries and garden centers.

- Only buy healthy trees that are free from signs of pests and stress. Scorched (brown edges), tattered, and discolored leaves are clues that the plant is struggling. That bargain tree may not be such a deal if it needs replacing in several years.

- Plant evergreens by early October whenever possible. This will give their slow-growing roots time to establish before the ground freezes.

Avoid planting trees that are slow to root. Wait until next spring and summer to plant the following trees:

Acer rubrum	**Red Maple**
Betula species	**Birches**
Crataegus species	**Hawthorn**
Gleditsia triacanthos inermis	**Honeylocust**
Magnolia species	**Magnolia**
Malus species	**Crabapples** and **Apples**
Populus species	**Poplar**
Prunus species	**Ornamental** and **Edible Plums** and **Cherries**
Quercus species	**Oaks**
Salix species	**Willows**
Tilia species	**Lindens**

Care

Continue recycling leaves. Shred them and leave them on the lawn, or recycle them in the garden or compost pile. See September "Care" for more ideas.

Start gathering winter protection materials—burlap for windscreens and salt barriers, fencing for snow loads, and animal barriers.

Watering

Water as needed until the ground freezes.

Evergreens and new plantings need special attention. Water these plants thoroughly before the ground freezes. This will help minimize winter damage.

Fertilizing

Fall, after the trees are dormant, is a good time to fertilize established trees. Fertilize only if the soil test results or plant growth indicates a nutrient deficiency. Most trees get sufficient nutrients from decomposing mulch, lawn fertilizers, and grass clippings left on the lawn.

Wait a year to fertilize new tree plantings. They have been well tended in the nursery and fertilizer may harm the new developing roots.

Do not fertilize trees growing in aboveground containers. Late-season fertilization may reduce winter survival.

See September "Fertilizing" for fertilizer rates and method of application.

Pests

Start installing animal fencing around new plantings, fruit trees, **Euonymus**, and other animal favorites. Place a 4-foot tall cylinder of hardware cloth (reinforced wire screen) around these trees. Sink it several inches into the soil. This will keep voles and rabbits away from tree trunks.

Fall soil applications can still be made by professionals for preventing damage from spruce galls, birch leaf miners, Japanese beetles, gypsy moths, and several other pests. Only treat trees that have suffered problems in the past.

Install cankerworm traps if these voracious insects have caused repeated defoliation of **Oaks**, **Elms**, **Apples**, **Crabapples**, and many other trees. These small, green or brown, wormlike insects did their damage last spring. Apply sticky bands around the trunk of trees that were severely defoliated the previous season. Use a band of fabric treated with a sticky material, such as Tanglefoot®, to avoid injury to the tree. Place sticky traps in place in mid-October and remove in December.

Helpful Hints

Winter, snow, and ice are on the way. Deicing products can be hard on our landscape plants. Salts applied to walks and drives can wash into the soil and damage plants. Road salts can spray on nearby plants causing damage to twigs and needles. Salt damage causes stunted or distorted growth, leaf burn, poor flowering and fruiting, and premature fall color. Repeated exposure to deicing salts can kill plants.

- Shovel first and then apply only traction materials or melting compounds to walks and drives.
- Use sand or some of the newer more environmentally friendly deicing products, such as magnesium chloride or calcium magnesium acetate.
- Creating physical barriers between the plants and salt spray. Decorative fencing, burlap screens, or salt-tolerant plants can all protect salt-sensitive plants from injury.
- Thoroughly watering salt-laden soils in spring. Thorough and repeated watering will help wash the salt through the soil and away from the tree roots.

A few Salt-Tolerant (Soil and Spray) Trees:

Austrian Pine	Hackberry
Black Alder	Hedge Maple
Cockspur Hawthorn	Honeylocust
Eastern Redcedar	Kentucky Coffeetree
Ginkgo	Norway Maple
Green Ash	White Ash
Greenspire Littleleaf Linden	

Pruning

Keep pruning as needed.

- Start by removing crossed, broken, or diseased branches.
- Select healthy branches with wide crotch angles (the angle between the trunk and branch) that are evenly spaced around the trunk for the basic structure.
- Make cuts where a branch joins another branch, above a healthy bud, or flush with the branch bark collar. See January and February "Helpful Hints" for more pruning information.

Planning

Now is the time to finish your journal entries for this growing season. Once the snow flies and holidays arrive, it will be hard to remember the useful details of the past summer.

You can do a lot to maintain the health of your trees, but sometimes it may be necessary or better to call in a professional.

Ask friends and relatives for recommendations. Check the Yellow Pages or contact the Minnesota Arborist Association for a list of certified arborists. These are tree care professionals who have voluntarily participated in an international program that certifies a standard of tree care knowledge. Quality tree care companies participate in professional organizations, such as the International Society of Arboriculture and National Arborist Association. They also provide staff with training and educational opportunities.

Planting

Finish planting deciduous trees as soon as possible. This will give plants a little time to adjust to their new locations.

Consider having large tree additions made over winter. Some nurseries dig the rootball (leaving the tree in place) in fall. Once the rootball freezes, they move the tree to a pre-dug hole in its new location. The success rate has been good. It is expensive, but one way to get an instant tree.

Planning on having a living Christmas tree this holiday season? Dig the hole now before the ground freezes. Cover the hole with a board or fill it with mulch. Cover the soil to prevent freezing, making winter planting easier.

Care

Keep raking and mulching leaves as long as they keep falling. See September "Care" for tips on managing leaves in the landscape.

Install wind, sun, and salt screens. Burlap, weed barrier fabrics, or other barriers can protect new plantings and sensitive plants from winter damage.

Wrap **Arborvitae** and upright **Junipers** with strips of cotton or old nylon stockings. This will prevent the snow load damage that frequently occurs.

Do not use tree wraps for winter protection. Research has shown that they do not protect the plant and can cause damage if left on the tree too long. If you feel you must use tree wraps, apply them now and remove them in the spring.

Move containers to an unheated garage for the winter. Water the soil whenever it is dry. Or protect the roots of plants left outdoors by surrounding them with bales of hay.

Watering

Make sure your new plantings and evergreens are thoroughly watered before the ground freezes. Then, it is time to drain and store the garden hose for winter.

Fertilizing

There is still time to fertilize. Healthy trees need little if any supplemental fertilization. Consult your soil test results to see if your trees need any additional nutrients.

Pests

Finish installing animal protection. A 4-foot-high cylinder of hardware cloth around the trunk of new and thin-barked trees will reduce the risk of rabbit and vole damage. Sink the bottom few inches of the fencing into the ground before it freezes. This will keep out the voles.

Start applying repellents to plantings that are favored by deer and rabbits. All young trees as well as fruit trees, **Ornamental Plums**, and **Euonymus** are a few of their favorites. Start before feeding begins. This encourages them to go elsewhere for dinner. Reapply after heavy rains or as specified on label directions.

Leave cankerworm sticky traps in place until December.

Look for egg masses of gypsy moths and tent caterpillars. Remove and destroy as soon as they are discovered.

Store chemicals and fertilizers in a cool, dark location. It should be locked and free from light and freezing (for liquids) temperatures.

Helpful Hints

- Start looking for a local nursery or Christmas tree farm that sells living Christmas trees.
- Find out if it is balled and burlapped or container grown. Balled-and-burlapped trees will need a large container for indoor display.
- Dig a hole large enough to accommodate the tree. Roughen the sides of the planting hole with your shovel. Slice or scrape the surface to prevent glazing. Cover with a board or fill it with woodchips.
- Store soil under a tarp or in a location where it will not freeze.
- Purchase a tree that meets both your landscape and holiday needs. Make sure the tree will tolerate the growing conditions and fit in the planting location once it reaches its mature size.
- Store the tree in a cool, protected location outdoors. Water often enough to keep the roots moist.
- Move the tree inside to a cool location just prior to your holiday celebration. Place containers on a large saucer and balled-and-burlapped trees in a large tub. Keep the roots moist.
- Move the tree back outdoors after seven to ten days. Any longer in the warm indoors and the tree may break bud and begin growing. If the tree does start to grow, you will have an indoor evergreen tree to decorate for Valentine's Day, Easter, and May Day.
- After the holidays, move the tree to a screened-in porch or garage for several weeks. This allows the tree to gradually adjust to the cold outdoor temperatures.
- Plant, water, mulch, and shield from winter wind and sun. And keep your fingers crossed—it never hurts!

Pruning

Continue pruning as needed. Prune trees to repair damage or establish structure. Always prune with a goal in mind.

Consider waiting until late winter for major pruning jobs. This way you can remove winter damage at the same time you improve the tree's structure.

- Winter is a good time to prune **Oaks** and **Honeylocusts**.

- Wait one to two years before pruning newly planted trees. Then prune to establish a strong framework.

- Wait until spring to prune evergreens. Large branches removed in the fall can be used for holiday decorations.

Planning

Look out your windows and take a look at your trees in winter. Do they provide nice scenery as you look outside? Growth habit, bark color, and fruit can all add color and interest to the winter landscape. Note areas that are large enough to accommodate a tree and need a little winter interest. Visit www.northerngardener.org for information about classes on gardening and holiday decorations.

Planting

Live Christmas trees need to be planted as soon after the holidays as possible. Make sure you dig the planting hole before the ground freezes. See November "Helpful Hints" for more information.

Care

Keep the roots of living Christmas trees moist at all times. Minimize the time inside to maximize your chance of success. If the tree begins to grow, you are stuck with a big houseplant until next spring.

Be careful when hanging holiday lights on trees and shrubs.

- Always use lights made for outdoor use.

- Loosely attach the lights to the tree branches and trunks. Remove lights in spring before growth begins. Tightly wrapped lights can girdle a tree in one season.

- Use a sturdy ladder and work with a buddy. Or consider hiring a professional. Many landscape companies now install lights and other holiday dècor. They have the equipment and training to do the job safely.

Watering

Watering is usually not needed. Once the ground freezes, it is time to pack away the garden hose.

Fertilizing

Review your soil tests and make plans for next season. Record time, type, and amount of fertilizer used on trees. This will help keep track of future fertilization needs.

Make sure all liquid chemicals are stored in a cool, not freezing, dark location away from children. Store granular fertilizers in a cool, dry location away from pets and children.

Pests

Finish installing animal fencing. Apply repellents throughout the winter to new plantings and those favored by deer and rabbits.

Continue to scout and destroy egg masses of tent caterpillars, tussock moths, and gypsy moths.

Pruning

Prune trees in winter to repair damage and improve structure.

Wait until spring to do the majority of evergreen pruning. You can remove large branches that block walks and drives. These can be used for holiday decorations.

Vines and Groundcovers

Vines and groundcovers are the wall covering and carpet for your outdoor living space. They serve both functional and aesthetic purposes in the landscape. *Use vines and groundcovers to soften hard surfaces and structures, block bad views, and decrease maintenance.*

- Grow vines on trellises to create privacy, screen a bad view, or cover an ugly fence. Use them in both large areas and narrow spaces where most shrubs outgrow.

- Cover an arbor or trellis with vines to create shade. A decorative arbor covered with vines can create shade for outdoor patios and decks. Or create your own shade for shade-loving plants, such as **Hostas** and **Ferns**.

- Use groundcovers under trees and shrubs to improve growing conditions. A perennial groundcover will help keep tree and shrub roots cool and moist throughout the growing season. It also keeps harmful mowers and weed whips away from trunks, stems, and surface roots.

- Create groundcover beds around trees and shrubs to reduce mowing and hand trimming. Mow around one large bed of ground-cover, trees, and shrubs instead of individual plants.

- Add texture and seasonal interest to vertical and horizontal spaces. Vines and groundcovers allow you to expand planting options.

Planning

Select the right plant for your growing conditions. Select the plants that prefer the soil and light in the growing location. Matching a plant to the growing conditions will reduce pest problems, minimize maintenance, and give you the most attractive plant possible.

- Make sure the plant and its flower buds are hardy in your area. **Oriental Wisteria** plants will survive our cold climate but the flower buds will not. Select the **Kentucky Wisteria** that is both plant- and flower-hardy in northern climates.

- Avoid aggressive plants that can take over the landscape. These vines and groundcovers will require a lot of work to keep them inbounds. Several, such as **Crown Vetch** and **Oriental Bittersweet**, have become invasive and should not be planted.

- Select vines that are best suited to climb the wall, trellis, or support selected. Or select the support structure best suited to the vine you want to grow. Use twining type vines, such as **Honeysuckle**, **Clematis**, and **Bittersweet**, for chain-link fences, trellises, and arbors. Cover walls and stones with wires and netting to train vines over these types of structures.

- Consider using clinging vines, such as **Euonymus** and **Climbing Hydrangea**, on stone and brick structures. These vines use rootlike structures to hold them to the surfaces they climb. Do not train clinging vines directly on wooden buildings. Their roots can damage the wood and the excess foliage can trap moisture, causing the wood to deteriorate.

- Use groundcovers and vines in mass or mixed with other plants. Select companion plants that are equally aggressive and require the same growing conditions. Mix plants with plain, variegated, or colorful foliage and various flowering times to extend the season-long interest. Mix annual and perennial vines. The annuals will provide quick cover and flowers while the perennial vines are getting established.

Soil Preparation

Soil preparation varies with the location, existing conditions, and plants you are growing.

Do minimal digging around established trees and shrubs. Extensive, deep tilling can damage tree roots and kill the very plant that you are trying to enhance. Modifying the planting hole, but not the surrounding area, can limit plant root growth beyond the planting hole. Select the soil preparation method that best fits your growing conditions.

Start with a soil test. This will help you determine what if any fertilizer and amendments you will need. Add organic matter to new garden areas. Use organic matter as a mulch to slowly improve soil under established trees and shrubs.

For new beds (avoid the roots of young trees and shrubs):

1 Remove or kill the existing grass and weeds. Use a total vegetation killer, such as Roundup® or Finale®, to kill existing vegetation. Wait four to fourteen days (check the label for the product you elect) to till up and rake off the dead grass.

2 Add the recommended fertilizer and several inches of organic matter to the top 6 to 12 inches of soil. Follow soil test results, or use 2 to 4 pounds of a low-nitrogen (first of the three numbers on the bag) fertilizer per 100 square feet. Use fertilizers with little or no phosphorus (middle number on the bag) or potassium (last of the three numbers) since our soils tend to have excess amounts of these.

For plantings around established trees or where erosion is a concern:

- Kill the existing weeds and turf. Leave the dead layer intact to serve as mulch. Plant groundcovers through the dead layer. Cover the dead layer with woodchips, shredded bark, or other organic mulch. The double layer of mulch helps suppress weeds, prevent erosion on slopes, and adds organic matter to the soil.

- Or cut the existing grass and weeds very short. Cover with several layers of newspaper and woodchips. Plant the groundcovers through the mulch.

Planting

Start planting once the site is prepared.

1 *Dig* a hole at least two to three times wider but no deeper than the container.

2 Use the trowel or shovel to *roughen* up the sides of the planting hole. This eliminates a glazed surface that prevents roots from penetrating the surrounding soil.

3 Gently push on the container sides to loosen the roots. *Slide* the plant out of the pot. Do not pull it out by the stem. Place the plant in the hole so that the rootball is even or slightly higher than the soil surface.

- Or *cut away* the pot on delicate, poorly rooted, or potbound plants. Remove the bottom of the container. Place the plant in the hole (with rest of the container still attached) so that the rootball is even or slightly higher than the soil surface. Once in place, slice through the side of the pot and peel it away from the rootball.

Vines and Groundcovers

- Use special care when planting **Clematis**. Try to protect the plants from breakage. Leave the stakes attached that came with the plants. Use the cut-away pot method to minimize stress on the Clematis.

4 *Fill* the hole with the existing soil. Water to settle the soil and eliminate air pockets.

6 *Mulch* the plants with woodchips, shredded bark, or other organic matter.

Water

Check new plantings several times per week. Water whenever the top few inches just begin to dry. After several weeks, water thoroughly but less frequently. Wait until the top 3 inches just start to dry. Then water enough to moisten the top 6 to 8 inches. Water established plants on an as-needed rather than calendar basis. Thoroughly water, wetting the top 6 inches of soil. Water whenever the top 4 to 6 inches start to dry.

Fertilizing

Test your soil before adding fertilizer, sulfur, or lime. A soil test will tell you how much, if any, of these amendments you need to add. Contact your local county office of the University of Minnesota Extension Service for soil testing.

Or use 1 pound of actual nitrogen per 1000 square feet. This is equal to 3 pounds of ammonium nitrate (33-0-0), 4 pounds of ammonium sulfate (21-0-0), or 16 pounds of Milorganite® (6-2-0). One pound of synthetic inorganic fertilizer is equal to 2 cups, while 1 pound of Milorganite® equals 3 cups.

Select a fertilizer (such as those mentioned above) with little or no phosphorus, since our soils tend to be high to excessive in this nutrient.

Calculate the amount of fertilizer you need to add to your planting area.

1 Start with the fertilizer rate. Use this formula to convert actual nitrogen to actual pounds of fertilizer you will need.

2 Divide 100 by the percentage of nitrogen in the bag. Then multiply it by the amount of actual nitrogen recommended. This gives you the pounds of fertilizer needed per 1000 square feet.

3 Now calculate the square footage of your garden. Multiply the length by the width of the planting space. Divide this by 1000 since the fertilizer rate is usually given per 1000 square feet.

4 Lastly, multiply the amount of fertilizer needed per 1000 square feet by our area factor calculated above.

- For example: Our planting bed is 6 feet wide and 24 feet long. We want to use ammonium sulfate (21-0-0) for our fertilizer.

- Calculate the fertilize rate: $100 \div 21$ (percentage of nitrogen in the fertilizer) $\times$ 1 (the amount of actual nitrogen needed per 1000 square feet) = 4.8 pounds of 21-0-0 fertilizer per 1000 square feet.

Vines and Groundcovers

- Calculate the area: $6 \times 24 = 144$ square feet. Then divide by 1000 = 0.144.

- Now multiply 4.8 pounds of fertilizer per 1000 square feet $\times 0.144 = 0.7$ (a little less than $3/4$) pound of fertilizer for the planting area.

Don't let all the math get you down. See the "Fertilizer Needs" Chart on page 350.

Pruning

Prune vines and groundcovers with a purpose in mind. Cut back rampant growers to control their size, remove diseased or insect infested stems to reduce pest problems, and cut out wayward branches to direct growth.

- Remove diseased and damaged branches as soon as they appear. Disinfect tools between cuts with a solution of one part bleach to nine parts water.

- Time other pruning based on plant growth and flowering. Prune spring-flowering plants such as **Five-leaf Akebia** and **Barrenwort** after they bloom. Trim summer and fall bloomers such as **Sweet Autumn Clematis** and **Honeysuckle** anytime during the dormant season. I like late winter so that I can combine winter repair with routine pruning.

- Prune **Juniper** groundcovers in early spring (April) before growth begins or in mid-July when they are semi-dormant. Avoid fall pruning that opens up the plants to winter wind and sun damage.

- See April "Pruning" for pruning guidelines for selected vines and groundcovers.

Match the pruning technique to the desired results.

- Renewal prune established plants to encourage new basal growth. Remove one-third of the older stems to ground level.

- Control vigorous growing vines and groundcovers with rejuvenation pruning. Cut the entire plant back to 2, 4, or 6 inches above ground level.

- Use heading cuts to shape and control wayward growth. Cut the stems back to side branches or just above a healthy bud.

Pests

Avoid problems by placing the right plant in the most suitable location. Always select the most pest-resistant vines and groundcovers available.

Check plants throughout the growing season. Remove spotted leaves and small insect populations as soon as they appear. This is usually sufficient for controlling most insects and disease.

Properly identify any problem before reaching for a chemical control. It is important for the health of your plant, the safety of the environment, and the effectiveness of the control that you use the right product at the proper time and rate.

Some vines and groundcovers can be invasive and become a "pest" in the landscape. See Vines and Groundcovers "Helpful Hints" on page 356 for controls.

Minnesota Vines

Annual Vines

Common Name (Botanical Name)	Light	Height	Flower Color	Attachment	Comments
Black-Eyed Susan Vine (*Thunbergia alata*)	Full sun to light shade	up to 6 feet	cream, yellow, or gold with dark center	twining stems	Nice in hanging baskets or as a vertical accent in a container.
Canary Vine (*Tropaeolum peregrinum*)	Sun to part shade	up to 8 feet	yellow	twining stems	Avoid excess nitrogen that can prevent bloom.
Cardinal Climber (*Ipomoea × multifida*)	Full to part sun	up to 10 feet	crimson	twining stems	Unusual deeply lobed leaves. Attracts hummingbirds.
Cypress Vine (*Ipomoea quamoclit*)	Sun to part shade	up to 8 feet	red	twining stems	Light and airy foliage makes a nice backdrop for red flowers.
Firecracker Vine (*Ipomoea lobata*)	Sun to ligth shade	up to 10 feet	reddish-orange with a tinge of yellow and white	twining stems	Blooms as it grows throughout the season.
Hyacinth Bean (*Lablab pupureus*)	Sun	up to 12 feet	lilac, pink to purple, or white	twining stems	Provides fragrant flowers and attractive purple beans throughout the season. Edible fruit.
Mandevilla (*Madevillia* species)	Sun to light shade	up to 6 feet	pink	twining stems	Overwinter indoors or purchase large plants to obtain bigger sizes.
Morning Glory (*Ipomoea* species)	Sun to light shade	10 feet	blue, pink, lavender, or white	twining stems	Avoid excess water and fertilizer that can prevent flowering; reseeds readily.
Sweet Pea (*Lathyrus odoratus*)	Sun to part shade	4 to 6 feet	assorted	clinging tendrils	Prefers cool temperatures, so plant directly outdoors in early summer for fall display.

Perennial Vines

Common Name (Botanical Name)	Hardiness Zone	Light	Attachment	Comments
American Bittersweet (*Celastrus lutea*)	3 to 4	Sun to shade	twining	Rampant grower that tolerates drought; plant male and female for fruit.
Arctic Beauty Kiwi (*Actinidia kolomikta*, 'Arctic Beauty')	4	Sun	twining	Attractive foliage; green with pink and white blotch. Plant male and female for edible fruit.

Minnesota Vines

Perennial Vines (continued)

Common Name (Botanical Name)	Hardiness Zone	Light	Attachment	Comments
Boston Ivy (*Parthenocissus tricuspidata*)	4	Sun to shade	holdfasts	Fast growing with blue fruit and red fall color. Try 'Veitchii' for finer texture and a less aggressive plant.
Clematis (*Clematis* species and cultivars)	3 to 4	Sun	twining petioles	Mulch roots; see March "Helpful Hints" for pruning tips.
Climbing Hydrangea (*Hydrangea petiolaris*)	4	Shade	aerial rootlets	Large flowers in mid-June, with peeling orange bark. Marginally hardy for protected sites only.
Dutchman's Pipe (*Aristolochia macrophylla*)	4	Sun to shade	twining	Large leaves and unusual pipe-shaped flowers Tolerates a wide variety of soil.
Euonymus (*Euonymus fortunei* cultivars)	4	Shade	aerial rootlets	Plant in protected location; protect from winter wind and sun.
Five-leaf Akebia (*Akebia quinata*)	4	Shade	twining	Suffers some tip dieback in winter; rosy red flowers in early spring followed by purple fruit.
Grapes (*Vitis* species)	2 to 4	Sun	twining tendrils	See "Fruits" chapter for recommended cultivars.
Hops (*Humulus lupulus*)	4	Sun	twining	Fragrant flowers; used for making beer and grown for ornamental value.
Porcelain Berry Vine (*Ampelopsis brevipedunculata*)	4	Sun to part shade	clinging tendrils	Can be rampant grower or dies out over winter. Variegated foliage often reverts to green. Porcelain-blue fruit develops in late season.
Trumpet Vine (*Campsis radicans*)	4	Sun	aerial rootlets	Large orange or yellow flowers attract hummingbirds. Be patient and avoid over-fertilization to ensure flowers. See December "Helpful Hints" on page 344.
Virginia Creeper (*Parthenocissus quinquefolia*)	2 to 4	Sun to shade	holdfasts and tendrils	Rampant grower with blue fruit and red fall color.
Wisteria, Kentucky (*Wisteria macrostachya*)	4	Sun	twining	Large flowers bloom with leaves. Flower buds are hardy (unlike the oriental types).

Minnesota Groundcovers

Common Name (Botanical Name)	Hardiness Zone	Light	Comments
Ajuga (*Ajuga reptans*)	4	Sun to shade	Prefers moist soil. Evergreen foliage with spikes of red, white, or purple flowers.
Deadnettle (*Lamium maculatum*)	4	Shade	Tolerates dry shade. Variegated foliage with pink or white flowers; often used in containers and hanging baskets.
Epimedium (*Epimedium* species)	3 to 4	Shade	Prefers moist, organic soil; evergreen with red or yellow flowers.
Ferns (Various species)	2 to 4	Shade	Several species of Ferns make excellent groundcovers in moist shade. **Sensitive Fern** (*Onoclea sensibilis*) and **Bulblet Fern** (*Cystopteris fragilis*) are both fast spreading and low growing.
Ginger, Canadian (*Asarum canadense*)	2 to 4	Shade	Prefers rich soils; shade tolerant. Our hardiest ginger. Native. Produces concealed, bell-shaped brownish-purple flowers.
Ginger, European (*Asarum europaeum*)	4	Shade	Evergreen; provide winter protection. Prefers rich soils; slow to spread.
Hosta (*Hosta*)	3 to 4	Shade	Various sizes, leaf shapes, and foliage colors available.
Juniper (*Juniperus* species)	3 to 4	Sun	Select low-growing type and allow plenty of room for mature size.
Moneywort (*Lysmachia nummularia*)	4	Sun to shade	Rampant grower that weeds out easily; green leaves with yellow flowers. Do not use near natural wetlands (invasive).
Pachysandra (*Pachysandra termialis*)	4	Shade	Evergreen that needs protection in zone 4 and winter shade; white flowers in early spring. *P. procumbens* is a native semi-evergreen species.
Periwinkle (*Vinca minor*)	4	Shade	Evergreen foliage that needs winter shade; blue and white flowers with solid green or variegated foliage.
Russian Cypress (*Microbiota decussata*)	3 to 4	Sun to part shade	The look of an **Arborvitae** with the growth habit of **Juniper**; avoid waterlogged soils.
Variegated Yellow Archangel (*Lamiastrum galeobdolon*, 'Variegatum')	4	Part sun	Aggressive; variegated foliage with yellow flowers. Tolerant of dry shade. Good in shrub beds and containers.
Wintercreeper (*Euonymus fortunei*, 'Coloratus')	4	Shade	Evergreen with leaves that turn purple in winter. Plant in a protected area; shelter from winter wind and sun. Try **'Gaity'** for a hardier, variegated selection.

Planning

Take advantage of cabin fever and start planning new additions. Gather garden catalogs, last year's journal, and your most current landscape plan. Review any videotape and pictures of last season's garden.

- Look for areas that need a little vertical interest. Will a vine-covered arbor, trellis, or obelisk brighten up, shade, or screen problem areas in your landscape?

- Identify areas where groundcovers can be used to unify a planting bed, mask surface roots of large trees, or fill a bare area where grass will not grow.

- Visit home shows for ideas on how to incorporate these plants into the landscape. Many landscape companies build elaborate displays featuring vine-covered structures and beds filled with groundcovers.

Planting

It is winter in Minnesota, and it is way too early to plant. *Use this time to look for solutions to difficult planting situations. Consider a few of these and include some of your own creative solutions:*

- Minimize root disturbance when planting annuals under established trees. Sink old nursery pots in the soil so that the upper lip is even with the soil surface. Each year, set a smaller container filled with colorful annuals inside the buried pot. Replace them each season without disturbing the tree roots.

- Set aboveground containers in amongst groundcover. They add height, structure, and color without damaging the tree roots.

- Use annual vines in place of spike plants (**Dracaena**) for vertical interest in container gardens. Check out your favorite garden center for the smaller trellises and obelisks that fit inside containers.

- Grow perennial vines such as **Clematis**, **Porcelain Vine**, and **Climbing Hydrangea** in containers to add vertical interest to patios and decks. Overwinter tropical vines, such as **Mandevilla**, indoors like houseplants. Hardy vines can be wintered outdoors. Sink the pot in the ground to insulate the roots from cold winter temperatures. Or store the planters in an unheated garage, placed in a protected corner away from the door. Use packing peanuts or other material to help insulate the roots. As a last resort, try protecting the container out-doors in a protected location near your home. Insulate the roots by surrounding the pot with bales of straw or hay. Water whenever the soil is frost-free and dry.

Care

Take a walk through the landscape and see how the vines and groundcovers are surviving the winter. Note plants that are subject to snow loads and salt. Evaluate these plants in the spring. You may need to move sensitive plants or change snow management practices in the future.

- *Evaluate* the winter sun and winds. Both can be drying to evergreen groundcovers and vines. Use your old Christmas tree to create a windbreak and shade for **Pachysandra** and other sensitive plants. Make a note to move, shelter, or create a more permanent solution.

- *Check* vines, trellises, and arbors to make sure they are securely mounted. Secure them against strong winter winds that could dislodge the structure and damage the vines or nearby plantings.

Watering

No need to water outdoors. Monitor the landscape for ice buildup and flooding. Consider amending the area or moving the plants to reduce winter damage caused by these conditions.

Water tropical vines moved indoors for winter. Water thoroughly until the excess runs out the bottom. Wait until the top few inches dry before watering again. Check planters stored in the garage. Water the soil whenever the ground is thawed and dry. Apply enough water so that the excess runs out the bottom.

Fertilizing

Monitor the health and growth of tropical vines growing indoors. Use little to no fertilizer on these plants. The low light and low humidity is hard on these plants. Adding fertilizer can add to the stress. Only fertilize actively growing plants with pale or stunted growth. Use a diluted solution of any flowering houseplant fertilizer.

Pests

Check outdoor plants for animal damage. Look for tracks, drop-pings, and other signs of animal damage. **Euonymus, Junipers,** and other groundcovers make great winter housing and food for rabbits and voles. Apply commercial or homemade repellents to high-risk plantings. Repeat as recommended on the label.

Helpful Hints

Tired of a garden full of green? Select groundcovers that add seasonal interest to the landscape. Use groundcovers with variegated foliage to brighten shady locations, while flowering types can be used to add color throughout the season. Add some that have colorful leaves in the fall or evergreen foliage and attractive seedheads for winter.

- **Ajuga:** Select one of the bronze or variegated cultivars for added color.
- **Creeping Phlox:** Covered with white, rose, or purple flowers in spring. The evergreen foliage provides year-round cover.
- **Hostas:** Many cultivars of various sizes with green, chartreuse, or blue-green foliage are available. Some have white, cream, or yellow variegation. White and purple flowers in summer or fall are considered an added benefit by gardeners. Some have fragrant flowers.
- **Lamium:** Green leaves with various amounts of silvery white variegation. Mauve or white flowers in summer stand above the foliage.
- **Moneywort:** Bright yellow flowers cover the green leaves in summer. Use the less assertive, yellow-leafed variety for a colorful change.
- **Orange Stonecrop:** Covered with yellow-orange flowers in summer; the foliage turns yellowish orange in fall.
- **Pachysandra:** White flowers in April with glossy green evergreen foliage.
- **Variegated Yellow Archangel (***Lamium galeobdolon***, 'Variegatum'):** Variegated green and silver foliage with yellow flowers in summer; aggressive plant tolerates dry shade.
- **Wintercreeper:** Low-growing evergreen groundcover; the foliage turns purple in winter.

Pruning

Remove broken and damaged branches as they are discovered. Wait until the weather improves and snow clears to do routine pruning.

FEBRUARY

Planning

Attend garden lectures and workshops for ideas on landscaping with vines and groundcovers. Visit the library and check out landscape books and magazines for ideas and pictures of how to incorporate these plants.

Consider letting a few vines run wild. Use them as groundcovers or let them crawl over stones, onto shrubs, and up tree trunks. Use nonaggressive plants that will not suffocate their neighbors or strangle the stems and trunks. **Climbing Hydrangea** and **Euonymus** can be allowed to climb tree trunks for added interest. Do not use twining vines, such as **Bittersweet**, that can girdle the tree and potentially kill it.

Planting

Buy or build the support structure for new or existing vertical plantings. Install these structures prior to planting to avoid damaging tender roots and young stems. Select a structure that can adequately support the weight of the vine and provide a surface for the plant to cling around or attach to. See this month's "Helpful Hints" for one type of functional trellis.

Care

Monitor the health of tropical vines overwintering indoors. Increase the light and humidity around failing plants. Move them in front of an unobstructed south-facing window. Add artificial light if needed. Hang fluorescent lights above or aim spotlight-type fluorescent lights up into the foliage.

Increase the humidity around the plant by grouping it with other plants. As one plant loses moisture (transpires), those around it will benefit. Or place pebbles in the saucer. Place the pot on the pebbles. Keep water in the tray below the pot. As the water evaporates, it increases the humidity around the plant where it is needed.

Watering

Keep watering vines growing indoors for the winter. Water thoroughly so that the excess water runs out the drainage hole. Allow the water to collect in the gravel tray and increase the humidity around the plant.

Check container plants overwintering outdoors and in the garage. Water whenever the soil is frost-free and dry. Apply enough water so that the excess runs out the bottom.

Fertilizing

Fertilize nutrient-deficient vines growing indoors for the winter. Look for pale leaves and stunted growth. Use a diluted solution of any flowering houseplant fertilizer.

Do not fertilize plants that are showing signs of stress from low light and humidity. Stressed plants lose leaves and have little if any new growth. Correct the problem before fertilizing. Adding nutrients to stressed plants can injure the plants.

Pests

Check indoor plants for signs of whiteflies, aphids, and mites. All these insects suck out plant juices, causing leaves to yellow and brown.

- *Use* yellow sticky traps to trap whiteflies. They will not eliminate the problem, but usually reduce the populations to a tolerable level. Purchase traps from a garden center or make your own. Cover yellow cardboard with Tanglefoot® or other sticky substance. Mount on a stick and stand in the soil or hang from a branch in the plant.

- *Spray* aphid- and mite-infested plants with insecticidal soap. Be sure to cover the upper and lower leaf surfaces. Repeat once a week until these pests are under control.

Continue to check outdoor plantings for animal damage. Reapply repellents as needed throughout the winter. Try noisemakers and other scare tactics to increase the chance of success. Make note of additional fencing or animal barriers that need to be installed prior to next winter.

Pruning

Trim dead and damaged branches on outdoor plants. Wait until late March or April to do routine pruning.

Check vines growing indoors. Remove and discard dead leaves. Prune off wayward and dead branches. Cut them back above a healthy leaf or where it joins another branch.

Helpful Hints

Try adding a few trellises alongside your home. Vine-covered structures can brighten the outside of your house, soften the feel, and anchor your home in the landscape. Unfortunately, they also get in the way of painting and other routine chores.

Try constructing a hinged trellis to provide you with all the benefits of a vine covering, while still allowing easy access to your siding.

1 Select lattice or other attractive material suited for climbing vines. Cut it to the size needed for the plant and shape you prefer.

2 Cut 18- to 24-inch-long legs of pressure treated 2-by-2s, 2-by4s, or 4-by-4s, depending on the size of the trellis and mature size and weight of the vine. Mount the legs directly to the trellis using hinges. Or mount the legs to a pressure-treated 2-by-4 that is the same size as the bottom of the trellis. Attach this to the trellis using hinges. I have seen this constructed from PVC pipe as well.

3 Sink the legs into the soil so that the hinged portion is just above the soil surface. Attach eyebolts to the building and hooks to the trellis. Secure the trellis to the building using the hooks and eyebolts.

4 Grow your perennial vines next to the trellis. Tie the vines to the trellis until they attach by their own means.

5 Unhook and carefully bend the vine-laden trellis away from the wall whenever you need to paint, repair, or access that part of your home.

Hinged Trellis

Planning

Finalize your plans and start your planting list. Take advantage of the nice days and stake out new planting beds and measure existing gardens where groundcovers will be added. Calculate the square footage of your new and existing ground-cover beds. Multiply the length times the width to get the square footage of the planting beds. This information will be used to calculate needed plants and fertilizer.

Use the "Spacing Chart" to calculate the number of plants needed. Divide the square footage of the garden by the spacing factor. The answer is the number of plants you will need. For example, let's say your garden is 10 by 12 feet, and you want to grow **Moneywort** that needs to be spaced 15 inches apart. Multiply 10 feet times 12 feet to get 120 square feet. Looking at the spacing factor for 15-inch spacing; it is 1.56. Divide 120 (square feet of planting space) by 1.56 (spacing factor), which equals 77 plants.

Or do the math yourself:

1 Calculate the square footage of the garden by multiplying the length times the width of the planting bed.

2 Now look at the spacing requirements of the groundcovers you plan to use. Multiply the spacing needed by the same number to get the square inches needed per plant. Divide this by 144 to convert it to square feet, as the area of the garden.

3 Divide the square footage of the garden by the square footage of the groundcover you are trying to grow. The answer equals the number of plants needed to fill the planting bed.

Using the example above, your planting bed is 10 by 12 feet. You want to grow **Moneywort** that needs to be planted 15 inches apart.

Find the square footage of the garden: $10 \times 12 = 120$ square feet

Calculate the square footage needed per plant: $15 \times 15 \div 144 = 1.56$

Estimate the number of plants you need: $120 \div 1.56 = 77$ plants

Spacing (Inches)	Spacing Factor
4	0.11
6	0.25
8	0.44
10	0.70
12	1.00
15	1.56
18	2.25
24	4.00
30	6.25
36	9.00
48	16.00
60	26.00

Planting

Begin soil preparation as soon as the snow melts and the soil thaws and it is dry enough to work.

1 Start by removing or killing (with a total vegetation killer) the existing weeds and grass. Leave the dead grass intact under established trees or on hillsides where erosion is a concern.

2 Add the needed fertilizer and amendments to new planting areas. Wait for the soil to dry slightly before tilling. Grab a handful of soil and gently squeeze. Lightly tap the soil with your finger. If it breaks into smaller pieces, it is ready to work.

3 Work the needed fertilizer and 2 to 4 inches of organic matter into the top 6 to 12 inches of soil. See this month's "Fertilizing" and the chapter introduction for help on calculating needed fertilizer. Rake the bed smooth and wait for the soil to settle.

Care

Start spring-cleaning in your planting beds. Remove debris and leaves that have collected in groundcover beds and under vine plantings.

- Remove winter-damaged leaves and stems.

- Check shallow-rooted ground-covers for frost heaving. These plants are often pushed out of the soil after a winter of freezing and thawing. Gently press them back into the soil and water in place.

- Edge planting beds with a sharp spade or edging machine. This will help keep the ground-covers in and the surrounding grass out of the planting beds.

Helpful Hints

Prune **Clematis** to control growth, encourage branching near the base of the plant, and improve flowering. ***The type of Clematis you are growing will determine the time and type of pruning it requires.***

- **Spring-blooming Clematis** bloom on old wood. These are generally not hardy in Minnesota.
- **Repeat-blooming Clematis,** such as **'Nellie Moser', 'Henry', 'The President',** and **'Bees Jubilee'** bloom on old and new growth. Prune dead and weak stems back to a healthy stem or ground level in late winter or early spring before growth begins. Prune the remaining stems back to a pair of strong buds.
- The last group of **Clematis** blooms on new growth. Prune these in late winter or early spring before growth begins. Remove dead stems back to ground level. Cut the remaining stems back to 6 to 12 inches.

Watering

Water indoor vines when the top few inches of soil are dry. Apply enough water so that the excess runs out the bottom of the pot. Allow it to collect in the pebbles in the saucer.

Fertilizing

Take a soil test of new planting beds. Consider testing established plantings that are lacking vigor or have not been tested for several years. The soil test report will help you determine what type and how much fertilizer you need to add.

Fertilize before growth begins. Use the type and amount of fertilizer recommended by the soil test report. Or apply 1 pound of actual nitrogen per 1000 square feet. This is equal to 3 pounds of ammonium nitrate (33-0-0), 4 pounds of ammonium sulfate (21-0-0), or 16 pounds of Milorganite® (6-2-0). One pound of synthetic inorganic fertilizer is equal to 2 cups, while 1 pound of Milorganite® equals 3 cups. For more details, see "Fertilizing" in the chapter introduction.

Pests

Check **Euonymus** for scale. Mark your calendar so that you will remember to treat the scale when the **Japanese Tree Lilac** is in bloom (mid- to late June).

Continue monitoring animal damage. Apply repellents as long as animals are present and food supply is limited.

Pruning

Time to start pruning vines and groundcovers. Remove dead and damaged stems and branches. See specific directions for some common vines in this month's "Helpful Hints" and in April "Pruning."

Planning

The planting season is underway. Record the name, variety, and source for all the vines and groundcovers you add to your landscape. Note pruning and trimming done on new and established plants.

Planting

Prepare soil for planting. See March "Planting" for details on preparing the site.

Plant bare-root plants as soon as they arrive. Pack the roots in moist peat, and keep the plants in a cool, frost-free location until planted. Plant so that the crown (the point where stem joins the roots) is even with the soil.

Plant container-grown vines and groundcovers as described in the "Planting" section of the chapter introduction. Keep the soil moist until they can be planted.

Start annual vines from seeds indoors. Starting them indoors results in earlier flowering for a longer bloom period. See January and February "Planting" in the "Annuals" chapter for tips.

Care

Remove damaged leaves on groundcovers. To make spring flowers more visible, cut off old leaves on **Barrenwort** (*Epimedium*) before growth begins.

Watering

Continue to water as described in March and May "Watering." Keep the soil moist around new plants.

Fertilizing

Incorporate fertilizer into the soil prior to planting. Fertilize existing plants in spring before growth begins. See "Fertilizing" in the chapter introduction for additional information.

Pests

Pull weeds as soon as they appear.

Pruning

Remove damaged leaves and stems.

Prune following these guidelines:

- **Wintercreeper** (groundcover): Prune in early spring. Cut established plants back to 4 to 8 inches to encourage vigorous, dense growth. Use a hedge clipper or mower (on its highest setting) for large plantings.

- **Junipers**: Prune in early spring or early to mid-July. Remove dead branches and shape in spring. See July "Pruning" for details.

- **Bittersweet**: Prune in winter or early spring. After planting, prune to train young stems to climb the plant support. For established plants, trim to control size. Cut overly long shoots back to three to four buds from the main stem. Prune back large shoots to 12 to 16 inches above ground level. Do not overprune. This stimulates excess growth that will require additional pruning.

- **Boston Ivy** and **Virginia Creeper**: Prune during the dormant season. After planting, train young stems to their support. For established plants, prune to control growth and keep them inbounds. Remove or shorten any stems that are growing away from their support. Renovate overgrown plants by pruning them back to 3 feet of the base. Wear a leather glove to rub the remaining dried pads off the support.

- **Euonymus** (vines): Prune in mid- to late spring. For young plants, tip prune to encourage fuller growth. For established plants, remove old and dead wood. Train new growth to cover the support.

- **Five-leaf Akebia**: Prune after flowering. Follow the pruning guidelines for **Hardy Kiwi**.

- **Grapes**: Prune in late March or early April. See March "Helpful Hints" in the "Fruits" chapter for pruning information.

- **Hardy Kiwi**: Prune in late winter or early spring. After planting, cut back to strong buds about 12 to 16 inches above the ground. Train five to seven strong shoots on the support. Next spring, prune stout side shoots (laterals) by one-third and weak laterals back to one or two buds. For established plants, shorten growth by one-third to one-half to control its size. Occasionally remove an old stem to ground level. This

stimulates new growth at the base of the plant.

- **Honeysuckle**: Prune in early spring. After planting, cut back young plants by two-thirds. This encourages strong shoots to develop at the base of the plant. Next year, select strong shoots to form a framework. Remove other shoots. For established plants, prune out the tips of shoots that have reached the desired height. Cut off overly long shoots to healthy buds. Renovate overgrown plants by pruning stems back to 2 feet above the ground. Thin the new growth as needed.

- **Porcelain Vine**: Prune in late winter. After planting, train young shoots to cover support. For established plants, prune as you would **Grapes** to control growth. See March "Helpful Hints" in the "Fruits" chapter.

- **Trumpet Vine**: Prune in late winter or early spring. After planting, prune all stems back to 6 inches above ground level. Remove all but two or three of the strongest shoots. Train these stems to the support. Allow the framework to develop over the next two to three years, or until the plant fills the support. For established plants, prune yearly

to control growth. Remove weak and damaged stems to the main framework. Cut the side shoots back to two or three buds from the main stems forming the framework. Prune out dead main branches to the base. Train the strongest shoot to replace it. Renovate by cutting all growth back to 12 inches off the ground.

- **Wisteria**: At planting, cut back the main stem (leader) to a strong bud about 30 to 36 inches above ground level. Train two strong side shoots (laterals) over the fence, trellis, or arbor. Next spring, prune the leader back to 30 inches above the topmost lateral branch. Shorten the laterals by one-third of their total lengths. Select another pair of laterals to grow and help cover the trellis. Next winter, cut the leader back to 30 inches above the uppermost lateral. Then prune all the laterals back by one-third. Repeat each winter until the plant reaches full size. Prune established plants in early summer right after flowering. Cut offshoots (small branches) back to within five or six buds of a main branch.

Planning

Use one of the rainy spring days to catch up on your garden record. Update landscape plans to include new additions. Record the name, variety, source, and planting information for each added plant.

Planting

Kill or remove the grass and prepare the site for planting. Leave dead grass as mulch to control erosion on slopes and to minimize root disturbance under trees. Prepare the soil prior to planting according to the directions in March "Planting."

Harden off annual vines started indoors or in a greenhouse. Stop fertilizing and allow the soil to dry slightly before watering again. Place outdoors in a shaded location. Move into the sun for 1 or 2 hours the first day. Increase the amount of sun the plants receive each day. Move indoors or cover on cool nights. The plants will be ready to plant in two weeks.

Care

Move tropical vines outdoors at the end of May or in early June, once the danger of frost has passed.

Gradually introduce them to the outdoors. Follow the same procedures used for hardening off annuals (see "Planting" on page 19).

Dig and *divide* overcrowded, declining, and poorly flowering groundcovers. Use a shovel to lift plants. Remove dead centers and declining plants. Cut the remaining clump into several smaller pieces. Add organic matter and needed fertilizer to the top 6 to 12 inches of the soil. Plant the divisions at the recommended spacing for that species.

Watering

Check new plantings often. Keep the soil slightly moist. Water when the top 2 inches begin to dry. Water thoroughly enough to wet the rootball and surrounding soil. Water established plantings during dry weather. Soak the top 6 to 8 inches whenever the top 4 to 6 inches are dry. Apply needed water once every seven to ten days in clay soils and half the needed water twice a week in sandy and rocky soils. Water potted plants thoroughly as needed.

 ## Fertilizing

Fertilize existing plantings if this has not yet been done.

Follow soil test results or apply 1 pound of actual nitrogen per 1000 square feet. For more details, see the "Fertilizing" in the chapter introduction.

 ## Pests

Monitor **Wintercreeper** and **Euonymus** vines for euonymus caterpillar. These wormlike insects spin a webbed nest in the plants. Remove and destroy. Or treat with *Bacillus thuringiensis*. Spray the webbed nests and surrounding foliage. This bacterial insecticide will kill the caterpillars, but it will not harm people, pets, wildlife, or other types of insects.

Check **Junipers** for phomopsis blight. This fungal disease causes individual stems to turn brown and die. Prune dead branches back to a healthy stem or the main trunk. Disinfect tools between cuts with rubbing alcohol or a solution of one part bleach to nine parts water.

Pruning

Cut back **Creeping Phlox** after the flowers fade. Prune plants back halfway to encourage fresh, new growth.

Helpful Hints

Start new vines from existing plants. This is a great way to share special plants and family heirlooms with relatives and friends. Propagate groundcovers and vines by division, cuttings, and layering.

Dig and divide groundcovers whenever they are overcrowded, fail to bloom, the center dies, or you want to start new plants. Use a shovel or garden fork to dig a large plant. Use a sharp knife or two shovels to divide the clump into smaller pieces. Add organic matter to the original planting site and return one division to this space. Use the others to start new plants or share with friends.

Dividing Perennials

Experiment a little with cuttings of vines and groundcovers. Herbaceous plants (with soft stems) are easier to propagate this way than those with woody stems. Some root best from new growth in spring, while others root better from cuttings taken in winter.

1 Take short cuttings 3, 4, to 6 inches long from new growth. Dip the cut end in a rooting hormone and place in a container filled with moist vermiculite.

2 Keep the vermiculite moist and the plant in warm, bright (no direct sun) location. Wait several weeks for the plant to root.

3 Plant the rooted cutting in a container filled with well-drained potting mix. Plant it in its permanent location once the plant roots have filled the small pot and weather allows.

Layering is the most successful method of rooting woody vines.

1 Bend one of the long, flexible stems to the ground. Remove the leaves from the portion of the stem located between 6 and 12 inches from the tip. Cut halfway through the stem. Treat the cut with a rooting hormone.

2 Dig a shallow trench and bury this portion of the stem in moist soil. Leave the growing tip, with leaves attached, above the ground.

3 Keep the soil slightly moist throughout the season while the buried stem forms roots. It will continue to get water and nutrients from the parent plant through the attached stem.

4 Next spring, cut the long, flexible cane where it enters the soil. Dig and transplant the newly rooted vine.

Planning

Take a break from planting to evaluate your progress. I often find my paper plans do not always fit the space, look, or reality of my garden space. Adjust your plans as needed. Note any changes you made on your landscape plan.

Continue to record the name, variety, and sources of the plants you add. Write their locations on the landscape plan and in your journal.

Monitor for pest problems. Make a record of problems encountered throughout the season. List the plant affected, the pest problem, and the control methods used. Evaluate and record the results. This will help you avoid and control future problems.

Planting

Keep planting. Container-grown vines and groundcovers can be planted throughout the growing season.

Finish hardening off and transplanting annual vines into the garden. Anchor the trellis in place before or right after the planting. Gently tie vines to the trellis to get them started climbing on their new support.

Care

Apply a 2- to 3-inch layer of mulch around groundcovers and vines. Use this to conserve moisture, reduce weeds, and improve the soil.

*   Do not bury the crowns of the groundcovers or the base of the vines. This can lead to rot and decline.

*   Use shredded leaves, evergreen needles, cocoa bean shells, woodchips, or twice-shredded bark.

Renovate overgrown and weedy groundcovers. Dig out the healthy plants and remove them from the garden. Remove and compost or use a total vegetation killer to kill all the weeds and unwanted plants. Amend and fertilize the soil. Divide the healthy plants into smaller pieces. Plant the divisions at the proper spacing, water thoroughly, and mulch.

Watering

Check container plantings every day. Water whenever the top 2 inches begin to dry. Add enough water so that the excess runs out the bottom.

Water new plantings often enough to keep the soil around the roots slightly moist. Soak the top 6 to 8 inches of soil each time your water. Gradually decrease watering frequency. Water well-rooted plants when the top 2 to 3 inches of soil start to dry. Check plants growing in clay soils once a week and those in sandy or rocky soils twice a week.

Established and mulched plants need less frequent watering. Check during extended dry periods. Water when the top 3 or 4 inches are dry. Add enough water to wet the top 6 to 8 inches of soil.

Fertilizing

Do not overfertilize your plants. Avoid the temptation to give them just a little extra. Too much fertilizer can result in excess leaf growth, poor flowering, disease problems, and root damage. Follow soil test recommendations or limit fertilization to once a season.

Fertilize vines growing in containers. Use a diluted solution of any flowering plant fertilizer according to label directions. Or incorporate a slow-release fertilizer that will provide needed nutrients all season long.

Pests

Insects:

- Treat euonymus scale found on **Wintercreeper** and **Euonymus** vines. These hard-shelled insects can be found on the stems and leaves. Spray the plants with an insecticidal soap or ultrafine oil when the **Japanese Tree Lilacs** are in bloom. This is about mid- to late June. Repeat at 10- to 12-day intervals for a total of three applications.

- Check plants for mites and aphids. High populations will cause leaves to look speckled, yellow, and often become distorted. Spray plants with a strong blast of water. Follow up with insecticidal soap if necessary. Repeated applications may be needed.

Aphid

Diseases:

- Remove spotted leaves and stems on **Lily-of-the-Valley** and **Pachysandra**. These fungal leaf spot and blight diseases can usually be controlled with sanitation. Remove infected leaves and stems as soon as they appear. In fall, rake fallen leaves off the plantings to reduce the conditions that increase the risk of this disease.

- Check **Clematis** for wilt. Leaves wilt, and both the leaves and areas of the stem turn black. Prune infected stems back to healthy tissue or ground level. Disinfect tools between cuts. Use a solution of rubbing alcohol or one part bleach to nine parts water.

- Remove brown branches, possibly phomopsis blight, on **Junipers**. Cut brown stems back to a healthy side shoot or main stem. Disinfect tools between cuts.

- Monitor **Bugleweed** (*Ajuga*) for crown rot. Look for patches of dead and dying plants. Remove and discard sick plants. Improve soil drainage and avoid overhead watering to reduce future problems. Treat the infected area with a fungicide before replanting.

Pruning

Clip back or lightly mow **Bugleweed** after flowering. This improves the appearance and prevents unwanted seedlings from taking over the garden.

Cut back **Creeping Phlox** if this was not done earlier. Prune foliage back halfway. This encourages new, healthy, more attractive growth. You may even be rewarded with a few more flowers later in the season.

Prune **Climbing Hydrangea** after flowering in June. For young plants, limit pruning to broken and damaged branches. These slow-growing plants do not need formative training. For established plants, prune overly long shoots and outward facing stems. Very little pruning is needed. Severe die back is common in Minnesota. It should be considered only marginally hardy and used only in very protected areas in zone 4b only.

Planning

Visit botanical gardens and arboretums. See how they use vines and groundcovers in their gardens. Take a few pictures, sketch some ideas, and start making a list of additions and changes you want to make.

Participate in one of the many garden tours. Most are sponsored by beautification committees, master gardeners, and other not-for-profit groups. Support their efforts while gaining some insight from landscape designers, expert gardeners, and plant lovers like you. Visit www.northerngardener.org for a list of upcoming garden tours and classes.

Planting

Dig and *divide* overgrown and declining plants. Midsummer transplants need extra attention to help them through the summer heat. Mulch and water whenever the soil around the roots begins to dry. Reduce watering as the plants become established.

Keep planting. Always prepare the soil before adding groundcovers and vines. The goal is to grow a healthy plant in this location for many years to come. See "Planting" in the chapter introduction for guidelines.

Care

Mulch groundcovers and vines. Add a thin layer of woodchips, pine needles, or shredded leaves to the soil surface. Do not bury the crown of the plants or the base of the stems.

Watering

Water container plantings every day during hot, dry weather. Apply enough water so that the excess runs out the bottom of the pot.

Check new plantings several times a week. Keep the roots moist for the first several weeks after planting. Reduce frequency as the root system develops. Water when the top 2 to 3 inches start to dry. Add enough water to wet the top 6 to 8 inches of soil.

Water established plants during extended dry weather. Moisten the top 6 to 8 inches whenever it starts to dry. Check plants growing in sandy and gravelly soils twice a week and those in clay soils once a week.

Fertilizing

Only fertilize plants showing signs of nutrient deficiency. Look for stunted growth, poor flowering, and lack of vigor. Consider having a soil test before adding any fertilizer. Otherwise, supplement the spring fertilization with a small amount (3 to 4 pounds per 1000 square feet) of a low-nitrogen fertilizer. Apply the fertilizer beside the plants on the soil surface.

Fertilize vines growing in containers. Use a diluted solution of any flowering plant fertilizer. Read and follow label directions for the proper rate.

Pests

Pull weeds as soon as they appear. This is a big task when establishing a groundcover. Invest time now to eliminate the need to renovate a weed-infested planting. See this month's "Helpful Hints" for more ideas on controlling weeds.

Watch for scorch on groundcovers and vines growing in hot, sunny locations. Mulch the roots to reduce drought stress and scorch. Move plants that continually suffer from scorch to a shadier location.

Monitor plants for Japanese beetles. These insects have made it to Minnesota and are causing damage in several areas of the state. These metallic, green-brown beetles eat the leaves of hundreds of different plants. Pick beetles off the plants and drop in a bucket of soapy water.

Continue watching for mites and aphids. Look for speckled, yellow, and distorted leaves caused by their feeding. Spray infected plants with a strong blast of water. If that does not work, try several applications of insecticidal soap.

Pruning

Mow **Goutweed**, also known as **Snow-on-the-Mountain** and **Bishop's Weed**, back to 6 inches several times during the growing season. This will prevent flowers, reduce reseeding, and keep the foliage fresh. Or prune back once when foliage declines or scorches (brown edges). Cut the plants back to 6 inches and wait for new and improved growth.

Cut off wayward and overgrow stems on groundcovers and vines. Prune back to a healthy bud or side shoot. Make the cut within the out-line of the plant to mask the pruning job.

Helpful Hints

Consider groundcovers as an alternative for grass. They add interesting texture, colorful foliage, and often flowers to the landscape. They do not require frequent mowing, but they do require weed control. And it is a little more time consuming, especially during establishment, than lawns.

Try these tips for weed control:

- Pull weeds as soon as they are found. Remove them before they set seed and create more weeds—and work for you—in the future.
- Mulch new and established plants with cocoa bean shells, twice-shredded bark, shredded leaves, or other organic material. This reduces weeds while conserving moisture and improving the soil.
- Use a pre-emergent weedkiller to prevent annual weed seeds from germinating. Apply these early in the season and repeat as recommended on the label.
- Spot treat Quackgrass and other perennial weeds with a total vegetation killer, such as Roundup or Finale®. Be careful not to get any on the groundcover. These herbicides kill anything green they touch.
- Use a sponge-type brush and paint the weed leaves with the herbicide. Do not let the wet leaves or herbicide touch the groundcover. Cut the top and bottom out of a plastic milk jug. Cover the weeds with the milk jug and spray the weed inside the container. Once the herbicide dries, move the jug to the next weed and repeat.

Weed Control

Prune **Junipers** in mid-July. Remove dead and damaged branches back to a healthy stem deep in the plant to hide cuts. Disinfect tools with a solution of one part bleach to nine parts water. Remove overly long branches back to shorter side shoots to control size.

Deadhead the summer-blooming **Sedum**. It improves the appearance and can encourage repeat bloom.

Planning

Are there areas where you should consider adding more vines and groundcovers? Annual and perennial vines can provide quick shade, decorative windbreaks, and screening in the landscape. Consider them as an option for narrow spaces too small for trees and shrubs. This is a good alternative for **Columnar Buckthorn**, which has become an invasive weed in our landscape. Use groundcovers under trees where the surface roots make it hard to mow or the shade makes it impossible to grow grass. This will save work for you and create a better environment for the trees.

Planting

Keep planting groundcovers and vines. There is still time for the plants to establish roots before winter sets in.

Minimize the impact on established trees when planting groundcovers beneath their canopy.

1 Do not cover the roots with soil or till deeply. Cultivation damages the fine feeder roots located in the top 12 inches of soil.

2 Use an edger or sharp shovel to edge the new planting bed. Remove or kill the grass with a total vegetation killer, such as Roundup® or Finale®.

3 Leave the dead grass (if killed with an herbicide) intact to serve as your first layer of mulch. You will cover it with a decorative mulch after planting.

4 Dig a hole twice the width but the same depth as the groundcover. Remove the container and set the groundcover in the hole at the same depth as it was growing in the pot.

5 Fill with soil. Water to help remove air pockets and settle the soil.

6 Mulch the area with woodchips, evergreen needles, or shredded leaves.

Care

Mulch new and existing groundcovers. See July "Care" for more information.

Watch for brown leaf edges that can indicate scorch. Pay special attention to **Hostas** and other shade lovers grown in sun. Water is not always the solution. Often the plants are unable to take the water up fast enough to replace what they lose during extreme heat. Mulch the soil, water properly by moistening the top 6 inches whenever the top 3 to 4 inches start to dry, and consider moving plants to a more suitable location in the future.

Watering

Check container-grown vines daily. Water whenever the top 2 to 3 inches of soil begin to dry. Apply enough water so that the excess runs out the bottom.

Keep the soil moist around the roots of new plantings. Reduce watering frequency as plants become more established in a few weeks. Water whenever the top 3 to 4 inches of soil start to dry. Apply enough water to wet the top 6 to 8 inches of soil.

Water established plantings during extended dry periods. Wet the top 6 to 8 inches when they become dry.

Fertilizing

Do not fertilize in-ground plantings. Late-season fertilization can stimulate late-season growth that will not have time to harden off over winter.

Continue fertilizing annual and tropical vines grown in containers. Use a diluted solution of any flowering fertilizer according to label directions. Stop fertilizing perennial vines in containers that spend their winter outdoors.

Pests

Check **Honeysuckle** vines for aphids. A soil systemic insecticide applied to the soil may be easier to use than trying to cover the large plant with a spray.

Capture and destroy slugs eating holes in the leaves of **Hostas** and other shade lovers. Set out shallow tins, sunk into the ground, filled with beer. The slugs crawl inside and drown. Or place beer in an empty soda or beer bottle and lay on its side. This gives you a built-in cover to prevent the beer from being diluted by the rain. Tuck bottles under the plants for a tidier look.

Watch **Honeysuckle** and other plants for powdery mildew. This fungus causes a white film on the leaves. Severe infestations block the sunlight, causing leaves to yellow. Increase sunlight and air circulation to reduce this problem. Try some of the new soap- and neem-based fungicides to reduce further infection.

Helpful Hints

Renovate overgrown and weed-infested groundcover plantings. Starting over will be easier than trying to fix the existing planting.

1. ***Dig out*** the healthy plants. Heel in or place in pots for temporary storage. Dig a trench and set the groundcovers in an unplanted area of the landscape. Water often enough to keep the roots moist.

2. ***Edge*** the bed with a shovel or edger. Spray the area with a total vegetation killer, such as Roundup® or Finale®. Avoid contacting trees, shrubs, and other desirable plants.

3. ***Add*** 2 to 4 inches of organic matter. Include fertilizer if renovation is done early in the season. Otherwise wait until next spring to add needed nutrients. Apply 1 pound of actual nitrogen per 1000 square feet. This is equal to 3 pounds of ammonium nitrate (33-0-0), 4 pounds of ammonium sulfate (21-0-0), or 16 pounds of Milorganite® (6-2-0).

4. ***Till*** or ***spade*** the organic matter and fertilizer into the top 6 to 12 inches of soil. Rake smooth and allow to the soil to settle.

5. ***Divide*** healthy groundcover plants that were potted up or heeled in. Discard dead and less vigorous portions of the plant. Set plants at proper spacing with the crowns (the point where the stem joins the roots) even with the soil surface.

6. ***Water*** thoroughly, wetting the top 6 inches of soil. ***Mulch*** the soil with woodchips, shredded leaves, or other organic matter. Keep the roots moist for the first few weeks. Then water when the top 2 to 3 inches of soil start to dry.

Pruning

Remove badly scorched leaves.

Prune unsightly **Bishop's Weed** (**Goutweed**) back to 6 inches. This removes spent flowers and scorched leaves. Watch for better looking growth in a few weeks.

Planning

Time to start preparing for winter. Locate a sunny location or space under lights for tropical vines that will soon move indoors. Decide how to manage any perennial vines that will need some winter protection. These can be planted in ground, stored in an unheated garage, or given extra protection for the winter.

Keep evaluating the landscape. Take pictures, draw sketches, and update your landscape plans. This will help you when trying to make changes over the winter.

Planting

Keep planting. Fall is a great time to add new plants to the landscape. The soil is warm and the air is cool. These are perfect conditions for establishing new plants.

1 Start planting once the site is prepared. Dig a hole at least two to three times wider, but no deeper, than the container.

2 Gently push on the container sides to loosen the roots. Slide the plant out of the pot. Do not pull it out by the stem. Place the plant in the hole so that the rootball is even or slightly higher than the soil surface.

3 Fill the hole with the existing soil. Water to settle the soil and eliminate air pockets. See "Planting" in the chapter introduction for more details.

Plant **Autumn Crocus** in groundcover beds. These bulbs sprout leaves in spring. The leaves fade, and you will be surprised with pink or white leafless flowers in the fall.

Care

Move tropical vines indoors for winter as the temperatures cool, but before the first killing frost.

• *Prune* tropical vines back just enough to make them manageable for their indoor home.

• *Isolate* these plants from your other houseplants for several weeks. Monitor for insects, such as mites, aphids, and whiteflies. These insects cause the leaves to appear speckled, yellow, and often distorted.

• *Spray* infested plants with insecticidal soap to treat mites and aphids. Repeat weekly until the pests are under control. Use yellow sticky traps to reduce whitefly populations. Purchase them at a garden center or make your own. Apply Tanglefoot® or other sticky material to a piece of yellow cardboard. Place near the plants.

Whitefly Traps

Watering

Continue watering container plants thoroughly, until excess water runs out the bottom. Check outdoor container gardens daily. Water whenever the top 2 to 3 inches of soil begin to dry.

Water new plantings as needed. Keep soil moist around recently planted vines and groundcovers. Allow the top 3 to 4 inches of soil to start to dry before watering plants that have been in the ground for several weeks.

Check established plants during extended dry periods. Water when the top 4 inches of soil are dry.

Fertilizing

Keep fertilizing tropical and annual vines in containers. Use a diluted solution of a flowering fertilizer according to label directions.

Do not fertilize other vines and groundcovers. Late-season fertilization can stimulate late-season growth that is subject to winterkill.

Pests

Continue monitoring for insects and disease. Remove and discard spotted and discolored leaves as soon as they are discovered. This will reduce the source of disease next season.

Watch for insects. They should be less of a problem as the weather cools. Note scale insects that can be treated by professionals in the fall with a soil-applied insecticide. Or mark your calendar so that you remember to control them in winter with a dormant spray or next season with an insecticide.

Helpful Hints

Select vines and groundcovers for fall interest. Many provide fruit, flowers, and colorful foliage as a grand finale to the growing season.

- Smell the fragrance of sweet autumn **Clematis** as it climbs over an arbor or trellis. The delicate white flowers brighten the landscape, while the fragrance fills the air. Mine grows on a fence between my house and my neighbor's house. The vigorous vine often climbs onto the **Boston Ivy** on her home. We both enjoy the fragrance and attractive combination of white flowers and dark green leaves.
- Watch for fall color in the landscape. **Hostas** turn a brilliant yellow in the fall. This echoes the yellow of **Ginkgo** and other trees and shrubs in the landscape.
- **Boston Ivy** and **Virginia Creeper** are some of the first plants to show their fall color. They turn a beautiful red color that stands out against your home, trellis, or arbor providing support. Enjoy the blue fruit uncovered by falling leaves. But just look, do not eat!
- Check out *Sedum kamtschaticum* as the leaves turn a lovely bronze to gold in fall. This can add a little fall surprise at ground level in the landscape.
- Enjoy the fruit on **Bittersweet**. The orange and yellow fruit adds interest to the fall and winter landscape. Or harvest some to use in dried arrangements and wreaths. You may need to add a male pollinator or female fruit producer if your mature plants fail to bear fruit. Check the flowers next spring to find which one is missing. The female will have a swollen base, while the male has nothing but pinlike structures. Add the missing male or female plant for pollination and fruit formation. See illustration on page 133.

Pruning

Remove damaged and diseased leaves and stems. Wait until late winter or early spring for routine pruning.

Planning

Enjoy the change of season. Watch and evaluate the changing color of your landscape. Take pictures and videotape the colorful vines and groundcovers.

Take a few minutes to record the highlights and challenges of this growing season. Use this information, pictures, and garden reviews to plan future improvements and reduce pest problems.

Planting

Finish planting early in the month. This gives the plants time to start rooting into surrounding soil before the ground freezes.

Wait until next spring to plant tender and borderline hardy plants. Give them as much time as possible to become established before winter.

Plant bulbs throughout groundcover beds. Use them to spark up plantings and add another season of color. See this month's "Helpful Hints" for suggestions.

Store unplanted groundcovers and vines for winter.

- Find a vacant garden space in a protected area. Sink the pots into the ground. This insulates the roots from below-freezing temperatures. Do the same for hardy vines growing in containers. Mulch after the ground lightly freezes.

- Or move the potted vines into an unheated garage for winter. Place in a corner as far from the door as possible. Pack the pots with Styrofoam peanuts or other insulating material. Water whenever the ground thaws and is dry.

- Or move the planters to a sheltered location. Pack bales of straw around the pot for added root insulation.

Care

Blow or *rake* fallen leaves off plants. Large leaves trap moisture, block sunlight, and lead to crown rot and other disease problems on groundcovers.

Or try this technique. *Cover* plantings with netting to catch the falling leaves. Remove the leaf-covered netting. Drag it off or roll it up to keep the leaves on the netting until you clear the groundcover planting. Replace the netting and keep removing leaves until all of them have fallen to the ground.

Try overwintering tubers of **'Blackie'**, **'Marguerite'**, and **'Pink Frost' Sweet Potato Vines**. Dig plants after a light frost has killed the leaves. Discard any damaged or diseased tubers. Remove foliage and allow the tubers to dry overnight. Pack tubers in peat moss and store in a cool, dark location.

Watering

Water tropical vines growing indoors whenever the top few inches of soil begin to dry. Water thoroughly so that the excess runs out the bottom. Place a saucer filled with pebbles under the pot. Allow excess water to collect in the pebbles while the pot sits above the water. This increases the humidity around the plant, while eliminating the need to pour excess water out of saucer.

Check potted vines wintering outdoors. Water anytime the soil is thawed and dry. Water thoroughly so that the excess runs out the bottom.

Cooler temperatures mean less watering. Wait until the top 3 to 4 inches begin to dry before watering again. Apply enough water to moisten the top 6 inches of soil.

Water new and established plantings thoroughly before the ground freezes.

Fertilizing

Do not fertilize. Late-season fertilization can lead to late-season growth that can be winterkilled.

Take a soil test if this has not been done in the past. Start with new plantings or those showing signs of stress. Stunted plants with off-colored leaves may indicate a nutrient deficiency.

- Contact your local University of Minnesota Extension Service for soil test information. Take several 4- to 6-inch-long plugs of soil from scattered sites throughout the planting bed. Combine plugs, mix together, and measure out 1 cup of soil for testing.

- The soil test report will help you determine what type and how much fertilizer you need to add. Follow soil test recommendations to improve plant health and eliminate over-fertilization.

Stop fertilizing container plantings. Properly managed annual plants have plenty of nutrients to finish out the growing season. Perennial vines need to harden off for winter, and tropical vines need to adjust to the low light of the indoors.

Helpful Hints

Plant a little extra color in your groundcover beds. Add hardy bulbs to Vinca, Wintercreeper, Deadnettle, and other groundcovers.

- Select bulbs with flowers and foliage that complement, not compete with, the groundcover. Make sure the groundcover masks the fading bulb foliage rather than the bulb foliage detracting from the developing groundcover.
- Pick bulbs that flower with the groundcover for a nice combination. Or use bulbs with groundcovers that bloom in different seasons. This helps extend your flower display.
- Wait until October to start planting hardy bulbs. The cooler temperatures reduce the risk of early sprouting.
- Use a narrow trowel to dig a small hole for the bulb. This will minimize root disturbance. Plant the bulb at a depth that is two to three times its height. Cover with soil and water.
- Mix **Autumn Crocus** with **Vinca** vine. The Crocus leaves grow and die back in spring before the Vinca grows and flowers. Watch for the pink or white flowers that make a surprise appearance in the fall.
- Use **Siberian Squills** and **Glory-of-the-Snow** with **Deadnettle** or **Sweet Woodruff**. The bulbs' pretty blue flowers make a nice prelude to the groundcovers' decorative foliage and flowers.
- Mix **Daffodils** with **Virginia Bluebells** and **Hostas**. As the Daffodils and Bluebells fade, the Hosta leaves begin to emerge to hide their fading foliage.

Pests

Continue weeding. Fall is the time many weeds set seed for next season's crop. Removing them now will greatly reduce your weeding chores next season.

Rake and destroy fallen leaves. Remove diseased and dead leaves from groundcovers. These can harbor pests and serve as a source of disease in next year's garden.

Pruning

Prune out diseased stems and leaves. Disinfect tools between cuts with rubbing alcohol or a solution of one part bleach to nine parts water.

Planning

Start planning for next season. *Survey the landscape and look for alternatives to traditional planting techniques.*

• Consider adding a few vines to crawl through the perennial garden or up the trunk of a tree. Avoid fast-growing, twining vines that can strangle other plants.

• Use twining vines, such as **Clematis**, **Hardy Kiwi**, and **Akebia**, to disguise downspouts and mailboxes.

• Mix two different **Clematis** vines or an annual such as **Morning Glory** with a **Trumpet Vine** for added bloom and interesting foliage effect.

• Try the same with groundcovers. Mix several **Sedum** for color and texture variation. Use solid and variegated cultivars together. The lighter foliage contrasts nicely again the solid green leaves.

• Always select partners that are suited to the growing conditions and are equally aggressive. Otherwise, you will end up with only one—the stronger of the two—plant in the end.

Planting

It is too late to plant vines and groundcovers. Store unplanted vines and groundcovers for the winter. Sink the pots of these plants in the ground in a vacant garden space. This insulates the soil from cold winter temperatures. Mulch once the ground freezes.

Keep adding bulbs to groundcover plantings. Look for creative ways to brighten up your garden beds. See October "Helpful Hints" for a few ideas.

Care

Remove the last of the fall leaves. **Maple**, **Oak**, and other large leaves trap moisture and block sunlight from reaching groundcovers. This leads to crown rot and other fungal diseases. Gently rake or blow leaves off groundcover plantings.

Shred and compost or *recycle* the fallen leaves. Shredded leaves can be placed on the soil surface for mulch. They help insulate the roots, conserve moisture, reduce weeds, and add nutrients to the soil as they decompose.

Watering

Water all outdoor plants thoroughly before the ground freezes. Moisten the top 6 to 8 inches of soil.

Drain and store the garden hose for winter. It will last longer if properly stored.

Water container plants whenever the top 2 to 3 inches of soil begin to dry. Apply enough water so that the excess runs out the bottom. Water pots stored outdoors and in the garage whenever the soil is thawed and dry.

Check indoor plants several times a week. Water only when the top 2 to 3 inches begin to dry. Place the pot on a gravel-filled saucer. Allow the excess water to collect in the gravel. As the water evaporates, it increases the humidity around the plants. This also eliminates the need to empty the excess water from the saucer each time you water.

Fertilizing

Review plant growth and note areas that need soil tests. Use this as your first step in correcting problems. The soil test results will indicate if a lack of nutrients or incorrect fertilization is causing the problem.

Contact your local county University of Minnesota Extension Service for soil test information. They have information on how to take the test and bags for submitting samples.

Give tropical vines time to adjust to their indoor home. Yellow and falling leaves are due to low light and poor growing conditions. Once new growth begins, you can start fertilizing. Use a diluted solution of any flowering houseplant fertilizer. Apply to indoor vines with stunted growth.

Pests

Gather liquid fertilizers and pesticides from sheds and unheated garages. Inventory and store these and other pesticides in a secure location away from pets and children. Keep liquids out of direct sun and in a frost-free location. Move granules to a secure, dry space for storage.

Helpful Hints

Tired of watching grass die in the shade of your house and **Norway Maple**? Consider one of the shade-tolerant groundcovers for these areas. They provide an attractive solution to this problem.

- Consider plants with variegated leaves. They brighten up the shade and provide color all season long. **Deadnettle (*Lamium*)** grows well in the dry shade found under many large shade trees. Use one or more of the many colorful **Hostas** to brighten up the shade.
- Try **Canadian Ginger** under **Spruce** and **Pine** trees. They tolerate the heavy shade and grow right through the evergreen needle mulch. The attractive leaves provide texture throughout the season.
- Do not forget the flowers. **Vinca (Periwinkle)**, **Moneywort**, **Deadnettle**, and **Epimedium** will flower even in the shade. This seasonal flash of color is something your **Bluegrass** could not provide.
- Quit fighting the shade and give in to nature. Use woodchips or shredded mulch around trees where it is too shady for even these groundcovers grow. Or strategically place flagstone steppers in heavily shady areas. Allow the moss to grow and call it a moss garden.

Protect plantings from voles and rabbits. Place a cylinder of hardware cloth around **Euonymus** vines and other susceptible vines. Sink it several inches into the soil. Make sure it is at least 4 feet tall to discourage rabbits. Or spray susceptible vines and groundcovers, such as **Cranberry Cotoneaster**, with a homemade or commercial repellent. Repeat throughout the season.

Pruning

Remove dead and damaged branches whenever they are found. Disinfect tools between cuts on diseased plants. Use rubbing alcohol or a solution of one part bleach to nine parts water.

Planning

Winter has arrived, and it is time to relax, enjoy the holidays, and finish taking notes on the past growing season. Gather photos, plant tags, landscape plans, and your journal.

Planting

It is too late to plant outside and too early to plant inside. Look at the catalogs, landscape plans, and start a planting list.

Care

Check on vines stored in the garage or protected area for winter. Adjust location or winter mulch if needed. Use evergreen boughs to protect **European Ginger** and other tender plants from winter injury. Use your discarded holiday tree to create shade and windbreaks for tender vines. Evergreen vines, such as **Euonymus**, often suffer leaf burn from winter winds.

Watering

Water tropical vines growing indoors for the winter. Water thor-oughly whenever the top 2 to 3 inches begin to dry. Apply enough water so that the excess runs out the bottom of the container.

Check potted vines stored in the garage and sheltered locations out-doors. Water whenever the soil thaws and the top 2 to 3 inches are dry. Add enough water to moisten all the soil. Stop watering when the excess begins to run out the bottom of the pot.

Fertilizing

Do not fertilize outdoor plants. Fertilizing frozen soil can lead to groundwater pollution.

Helpful Hints

Another season ends and once again your Trumpet Vine did not bloom. All the books say "easy to grow, free flowering," but this is not the case for you and many others.

- Be patient. **Trumpet Vines** need to reach maturity to flower. Keep rampant growers under control. Prune them back to several buds beyond the main framework.
- Check the growing conditions. Make sure the plant is growing in full sun.
- Avoid high-nitrogen fertilizers that encourage leaf growth and discourage flowers. Keep fertilizers away from this luxury feeder. **Trumpet Vine** will seek out and use all the nutrients it can find, leading to a large plant with few flowers.
- Root prune as a last resort. Use a sharp shovel and slice through a few roots. Do this in one or two locations several feet from the trunk. Do not cut the roots all the way around the plant. This can injure the plant.

Pests

Take a walk outside before the snow gets too deep. Note any existing and potential problems to watch for in the future.

Pruning

Remove dead and damaged stems as they appear.

Arboretums and botanical gardens are the best places to find out which plants are hardy and suitable for your growing conditions. Pictures in books and catalogs often look very different from the actual plants that grow in Minnesota's challenging environment. I have a small yard, but I take home great ideas on plant combinations or unique plantings from botanical gardens. Visit often for landscaping ideas; plants change throughout the season.

August Schell Brewery
1860 Schell Rd.
New Ulm, MN 56073
Phone: (507) 354-5528
Fax: (507) 359-9119
www.schellsbrewery.com
Type: Display Garden
Dates: Year Round

Carleton College's Cowling Arboretum
Carleton College
One North College Street
Northfield, Minnesota, USA 55057
Phone: (507) 646-4000
Type: Japanese garden
Dates: Year Round

Como Conservatory
1325 Aida Place
St. Paul, MN 55103-1054
Phone: (651) 487-8201, (651) 487-8250
Fax: (651) 487-8255
Type: Conservatory
Dates: Year Round

Eastern Nature Center,
Elm Creek Park Reserve
13351 Elm Creek Rd.
Osseo, MN 55369-9344
www.hennepinparks.org
Phone: (763) 420-4300
Fax: (763) 420-4477
Type: Formal Garden
Dates: Year Round (no plants visible November - April)

Eloise Butler Wildflower Gardens
4125 E. Lake Harriot Parkway
Minneapolis, Minnesota
Phone: (612) 370-4900
Type: Wildflower, butterfly, and bog garden
Dates: Year Round

Enger Olson Observation Tower and Gardens
Sky Line Drive
Duluth, MN 55800
Phone: (218) 723-3300-Duluth City Hall
Type: Mature hosta clumps overlooking Lake Superior
Dates: Mid-April - Late October

Historic Mayowood Mansion Gardens
1195 W. Circle Dr. SW
Rochester, MN 55902
Phone: (507) 282-9447
Fax: (507) 282-9447
Type: 1910 home and garden, featuring teahouse, sculpture, container gardens, and perennial plantings
Dates: Open year round; call for reservations

The Japanese Garden at Normandale
9700 France Avenue South
Bloomington, MN 55431
Phone: (952) 487-8200
Toll free: (800) 657-3657
Fax: (952) 487-8101
Type: Japanese garden with many bridges
Dates: Year Round

Linnaeus Arboretum
Gustavus Adolphus College
St. Peter, MN 56082
www.gustavus.edu
Phone: (507) 933-7003, (507) 933-6181
Type: Arboretum
Dates: Year Round

Loring Park Garden of the Seasons
1382 Willow Street
Minneapolis, Minnesota
Phone: (612) 661-4800
Type: Woodland garden dominated by birch trees shading understory native wildflowers
Dates: Year Round

Minneapolis Sculpture Garden
726 Vineland Place
Minneapolis, Minnesota
Phone: (612) 370-3996
Type: Sculpture garden with 40 sculptures, and John and Sage Coweles Conservatory
Dates: Year Round

Minnesota Landscape Arboretum
PO Box 39
3675 Arboretum Dr.
Chanhassen, MN 55317-0039
www.arboretum.umn.edu
Phone: (952) 443-1400
Fax: (952) 443-2521
Type: 16 Display Gardens, 60 Plant Collections
Dates: Year Round

Munsinger Gardens & Clemens Gardens
1339 Killian Blvd.
St. Cloud, MN 56301
www.ci.stcloud.mn.us./web/departments/parks/parkindex.htm
Phone: (320) 650-1050
Fax: (320) 255-7250
Type: Natural, Formal Gardens
Dates: Mid April - Late October

Nokomis Naturescape Gardens
2401 E. Minnehaha Ave.
Minneapolis, Minnesota
Phone: (612) 370-4900
Type: Variety of native wildflowers and grasses
Dates: Year Round

Northland Arboretum
NW 7th St.
Brainerd, MN 56401
Phone: (218) 829-8770
Type: Arboretum
Dates: Year Round

Peace (Rock) and Rose Gardens
4125 E. Lake Harriet Parkway
Minneapolis, Minnesota
Phone: (612) 370-4900
Type: Rock garden with hardy perennials, dwarf conifers, alpines, and small flowering trees and shrubs
Dates: Year Round

Pergola Garden
4801 Minnehaha Ave. South
Minneapolis, Minnesota
Phone: (612) 661-4800
Type: Perennial garden featuring native wildflowers and grasses that border the new pergola overlook at the falls
Dates: Year Round

River Bend Nature Center Inc.
1000 Rustad Rd.
PO Box 186
Fairbault, MN 55021-0186
www.rbnc.org
Phone: (507) 332-8151
Fax: (507) 332-0656
Type: Arboretum/Nature Center
Dates: Year Round

The Rose Garden at Leif Erikson Park
13th Avenue East and London Road
Duluth, MN 55805
Phone: (218) 723-3300-Duluth City Hall
Type: Over 40,000 rose bushes, as well as many other floral delights
Dates: Year Round

Roseville Community Arboretum
Harriet Alexander Nature Center
2520 N. Dale St.
Roseville, MN 55113-1701
www.ci.roseville.mn.us
Phone: (651) 415-2161
Fax: (651) 765-1583
Type: Wildflower, Prairie, Butterfly, Begetable Gardens
Dates: Year Round

Generic Glossary

Acid soil: soil with a pH less than 7.0. Acid soil is sometimes called "sour soil" by gardeners. Most plants prefer a slightly acid soil between 6 and 7 where most essential nutrients are available.

Alkaline soil: soil with a pH greater than 7.0, usually formed from limestone bedrock. Alkaline soil is often referred to as *sweet soil*.

Annual: a plant that completes its entire life cycle in one season. It germinates, grows, flowers, sets seed, and dies within one year.

Balled and burlapped: describes a large tree whose roots have been wrapped tightly in protective burlap and twine after it is dug. It is wrapped in this manner to protect it for shipping, sales, and transplanting.

Bare root: trees, shrubs, and perennials that have been grown in soil, dug, and have had the soil removed prior to sales or shipping. Mail order plants are often shipped bare root with the roots packed in peat moss, sawdust, or similar material and wrapped in plastic.

Barrier plant: a plant that has thorns or impenetrable growth habit and is used to block foot traffic or other access to an area in the landscape.

Beneficial insects: insects or their larvae that prey on pest organisms and their eggs. They may be flying insects such as ladybugs, parasitic wasps, praying mantids, and soldier bugs; or soil dwellers such as predatory nematodes, spiders, and ants.

Berm: a low, artificial hill created in a landscape to elevate a portion of the landscape for functional and aesthetic reasons such as added interest, screening, and improved drainage.

Bract: a modified leaf resembling a flower petal, located just below the true flower. Often it is more colorful and visible than the actual flower, as in **Poinsettia.**

Bud union: the place where the top of a plant was grafted to the rootstock; a term frequently used with roses.

Canopy: the total overhead area of a tree including the branches and leaves.

Cold hardiness: the ability of a perennial plant (including trees, shrubs, and vines) to survive the minimum winter temperature in a particular area.

Complete fertilizer: powdered, liquid, or granular fertilizer with a balanced proportion of the three key nutrients—nitrogen (N), phosphorus (P), and potassium (K).

Composite: an inflorescence (cluster of flowers) also referred to as a head, containing petal-like and disk-like flowers. They are often daisylike with a flat (disk-like flowers) center and petal-like flowers surrounding the outside.

Compost: decomposed organic matter added to the soil to improve it's drainage and ability to retain moisture.

Corm: a modified bulblike stem. It is swollen, short, solid, and located underground. **Crocus** and **Gladiolus** are two such plants.

Crown: (**a**) *the point where the stems and roots meet. Located at, or just below the soil surface.* (**b**) the top part of the tree.

Cultivar: a CULTIvated VARiety. A unique form of a plant that has been identified as special or superior and has been selected for propagation and sale.

Deadhead: to remove faded flowers from plants to improve their appearance, prevent seed production, and stimulate further flowering.

Deciduous plants: trees and shrubs that lose their leaves in the fall.

Desiccation: drying out of foliage, usually due to drought or wind.

Generic Glossary

Division: splitting apart perennial plants to create several smaller rooted segments. The practice is useful for controlling the plant's size and for acquiring more plants.

Dormancy: the period, usually the winter, when perennial plants temporarily cease active growth and rest. **Dormant** is the verb form.

Established: the point at which a newly planted tree, shrub, or flower has recovered from transplant shock and begins to grow. Often indicated by the production of new leaves or stems.

Evergreen: perennial plants that do not lose their foliage annually with the onset of winter. Needled or broadleaf foliage will persist and continues to function on a plant through one or more winters, aging and dropping unnoticed in cycles of one, two, three, or more.

Foliar: of or about foliage—usually refers to the practice of spraying foliage with fertilizer or pesticide for absorption by the leaves.

Floret: a small individual flower, usually one of many forming an inflorescence considered the blossom.

Germinate: to sprout. Germination is a fertile seed's first stage of development.

Graft (union): the point on the stem of a woody plant where a stem or bud of a desirable plant is placed onto a hardier root system. Roses, apples, and some ornamental trees are commonly grafted.

Hardscape: the permanent, structural, nonplant part of a landscape; such as walls, sheds, pools, patios, arbors, and walkways.

Herbaceous: plants having fleshy or soft stems that die back with frost; the opposite of *woody*.

Hybrid: a plant produced by crossing two different varieties, species or genera. Usually indicated with a × in the name such as *Acer × fremanii.*

Inflorescence: a cluster of flowers occurring at the tip of a stem. This includes such arrangements as umbels (**'Queen Anne's Lace'**), composite or head (**Daisy**), spike (**Salvia**), raceme (**Snapdragon**) and panicle (**Coral Bells**).

Mulch: a layer of material used to cover bare soil to conserve moisture, discourage weeds, moderate soil temperature, and prevent erosion and soil compaction. It may be inorganic (gravel, fabric) or organic (wood chips, bark, pine needles, chopped leaves).

Naturalize: (*a*) *to plant seeds, bulbs, or plants in a random, informal pattern as they would appear in their natural habitat;* (**b**) to adapt to and spread throughout natural areas and appear as if native to that location (a tendency of some non-native plants).

Nectar: the sweet fluid produced by glands on flowers that attract pollinators such as hummingbirds and honeybees for whom it is a source of energy.

Organic material, organic matter: any material or debris that is derived from plants.

Peat moss: organic matter from peat sedges (United States) or sphagnum mosses (Canada), often used to improve soil drainage and water holding abilities.

Perennial: a flowering plant that lives over two or more seasons. Many die back with frost, but their roots survive the winter and generate new shoots in the spring.

pH: a measurement of the relative acidity (low pH) or alkalinity (high pH) of soil or water based on a scale of 1 to 14, with 7 being neutral. Individual plants require soil to be within a certain range so that nutrients can dissolve in moisture and be available to them.

Generic Glossary

Pinch: to remove tender stems and/or leaves by pressing them between thumb and forefinger. This pruning technique encourages branching, compactness, and flowering in plants.

Pollen: the yellow, powdery grains in the center of a flower. A plant's male sex cells, they are transferred to the female plant parts by means of wind, bees, or other animal pollinators to fertilize them and create seeds.

Raceme: an arrangement of single stalked flowers along an elongated, unbranched stem.

Rhizome: a swollen energy-storing stem structure, similar to a bulb, that lies horizontally in the soil. Roots emerge from its lower surface and stems emerge from a growing point at or near its tip, as in **Bearded Iris.**

Rootbound (or potbound): the condition of a plant that has been confined in a container too long, its roots are forced to wrap around themselves and even swell out of the container. Successful transplanting or repotting requires untangling and trimming away some of the matted roots.

Root flare: the transition at the base of a tree trunk where the bark tissue begins to differentiate and roots begin to form just before entering the soil. This area should not be covered with soil when planting a tree.

Self-seeding: the tendency of some plants to sow their seeds freely around the yard. It creates many seedlings the following season that may or may not be welcome.

Semievergreen: tending to be evergreen in a mild climate but deciduous in a harsher one.

Shearing: the pruning technique whereby plant stems and branches are cut uniformly with long-bladed pruning shears (hedge shears) or powered hedge trimmers. It is used when creating and maintaining hedges and topiary.

Slow-acting (slow-release) fertilizer: fertilizer that is water insoluble and releases its nutrients when acted on by soil temperature, moisture, and/or related microbial activity. Typically granular, it may be organic or synthetic.

Succulent growth: the sometimes undesirable production of fleshy, water-storing leaves or stems that results from overfertilization.

Sucker: a new growing shoot. Underground plant roots produce suckers to form new stems and spread by means of these suckering roots to form large plantings, or colonies. Some plants produce root suckers or branch suckers as a result of pruning or wounding.

Tuber: a thickened portion of underground stem used for energy storage and reproduction. **Irish Potato** is a tuber.

Tuberous root: a swollen root with one point of growth where stem joins the root. **Sweet Potatoes** and **Dahlias** grow from tuberous roots.

Variegated: having various colors or color patterns. The term usually refers to plant foliage that is streaked, edged, blotched, or mottled with a contrasting color, often green with yellow, cream, or white.

White grubs: fat, off-white, worm-like larvae of Japanese and other beetles. They live in the soil and feed on plant (especially grass) roots until summer when they emerge as beetles to feed on plant foliage.

Wings: (*a*) *the corky tissue that forms edges along the twigs of some woody plants such as* **Winged Euonymus;** (**b**) the flat, dried extension of tissue on some seeds, such as **Maple,** that catch the wind and help them disseminate.

Charts

Ordering Soils and Mulch

Garden Size in Square Feet	Cubic Yards of Material Needed to Cover Garden Space Depth of Desired Material			
	2	4	6	8
100	$1/2$	1+	2	$2^1/_2$
200	1+	$2^1/_2$	$3^1/_2$	5
300	2	$3^1/_2$	$5^1/_2$	$7^1/_2$
400	$2^1/_2$	5	$7^1/_2$	10
500	3+	6	9	12
600	$3^1/_2$	$7^1/_2$	11	15
700	4+	$8^1/_2$	13	17
800	5	10	15	20
900	$5^1/_2$	11	17	22
1000	6	12	$18^1/_2$	25

Peat Moss Bale Size	Area That Can Be Amended With:	
	1 inch	2 inches
1 cubic foot	24 square feet	12 square feet
2.2 cubic feet	50 square feet	25 square feet
3.8 cubic feet	90 square feet	45 square feet

Or calculate what you need:

Multiply the area (length times width) by the desired depth (in feet) of mulch or compost. Convert this volume from cubic feet to cubic yards by dividing by 27 (the number of cubic feet in a cubic yard). This is the amount of material you will need to order.

Fertilizer Needs
(Based on Nitrogen Recommendations)

Your soil test will tell you how much of what type of fertilizer you need to add to your garden. If this information is not available, you may have to adapt general fertilization recommendations for your garden. Use the chart or formulas here to calculate the amount of fertilizer needed to add the recommended amount of actual nitrogen (N) to the soil.

Fertilizer Analysis (N-P-K)*	Pounds of Fertilizer Needed to Apply:			
	1 lb. Actual N	1¼ lb. Actual N	1½ lb. Actual N	2 lb. Actual N
45-0-0 Urea	2.2	2.7	3.3	4.4
33-0-0 Ammonium nitrate	3.0	3.7	4.5	6.0
21-0-0 Ammonium sulfate	4.8	5.9	7.1	9.6
6-2-0 Milorganite	16.6	23.3	25	33.3
10-10-10	10	12.5	15.0	20
5-10-5	20	25	30	40

*Nitrogen-Phosphorus-Potassium

Or calculate the amount of fertilizer you need to add to your planting area. See the Fertilizing section in the "Vines and Groundcovers" chapter introduction.

Charts

Spacing Chart

Use this chart to calculate the number of plants needed. Divide the square footage of the garden by the spacing factor. The answer is the number of plants you need.

Spacing (Inches)	Spacing Factor	Plants Needed			
		25	50	75	100
4	0.11	227	454	682	909
6	0.25	100	200	300	400
8	0.44	57	114	170	227
10	0.70	36	72	107	143
12	1.00	12	50	75	100
15	1.56	16	32	48	64
18	2.25	11	22	33	44
24	4.00	6	13	19	25
30	6.25	4	8	12	16
36	9.00	3	6	8	11
48	16.00	2	3	5	6
60	26.00	1	2	3	4

The University of Minnesota Extension Service is a great resource for gardeners. They bring research-based information to you through classes, workshops, newspaper articles, and the master gardeners. Their printed publications are the best resource for gardeners and landscape professionals. The information and recommendations are based on the soils and climates of Minnesota. Contact your local county office, from the following list, for a list of publications and other resources available in your county.

Aitkin County
Aitkin County Courthouse
209 2nd Street NW
Aitkin, MN 56431-1257
Phone: (218) 927-7321
Fax: (218) 927-7372
e-mail: aitkin@extension.umn.edu

Anoka County
Anoka County Activities Center
550 Bunker Lake Boulevard NW
Andover, MN 55304-4199
Phone: (763) 755-1280
Fax: (763) 755-6950
e-mail: anoka@extension.umn.edu

Becker County
Ag Service Center, 809 8th Street SE
Detroit Lakes, MN 56501-2842
Phone: (218) 847-3141
Fax: (218) 847-6969
e-mail: becker@extension.umn.edu

Beltrami County
815 15th Street NW
Bemidji, MN 56601-2501
Phone: (218) 759-0038
Fax: (218) 759-0243
e-mail: beltrami@extension.umn.edu

Benton County
Courthouse, 531 Dewey St, P.O. Box 650
Foley, MN 56329-0650
Phone: (320) 968-5077
Fax: (320) 968-5319
e-mail: benton@extension.umn.edu

Big Stone County
Courthouse, 20 SE 2nd Street
Ortonville, MN 56278-1544
Phone: (320) 839-2518
Fax: (320) 839-3571
e-mail: bigstone@extension.umn.edu

The Blue Earth County Extension Service
P.O. Box 8608, 410 South 5th Street
Mankato, MN 56002-8608
Phone:(507) 389-8325
Fax: (507) 389-8812
e-mail:blueearth@extension.umn.edu

Brown County
300 2nd Avenue SW
Sleepy Eye, MN 56085-1402
Phone: (507) 794-7993
Fax: (507) 794-5290
e-mail: brown@extension.umn.edu

Carlton County
310 Chestnut Street
P.O. Box 307
Carlton, MN 55718-0307
Phone: (218) 384-3511
Fax: (218) 384-3512
e-mail: carlton@extension.umn.edu

Carver County
609 West First Street
Waconia, MN 55387-1204
Phone: (952) 442-4496
Fax: (952) 442-4497
e-mail: carver@extension.umn.edu

Cass County
Courthouse
P.O. Box 3000
Walker, MN 56484-3000
Phone: (218) 547-7392
Fax: (218) 547-7397
e-mail: cass@extension.umn.edu

Chippewa County
Courthouse
629 North 11th Street
Montevideo, MN 56265-1685
Phone: (320) 269-6521
Fax: (320) 269-5223
e-mail: chippewa@extension.umn.edu

Chisago County
38694 Tanger Drive
North Branch, MN 55056-9500
Phone: (651) 674-4417
Fax: (651) 674-0310
e-mail: chisago@extension.umn.edu

Clay County
919 8th Avenue North
P.O. Box 280
Moorhead, MN 56561-0280
Phone: (218) 299-5020
Fax: (218) 299-7533
e-mail: clay@extension.umn.edu

Clearwater County
Clearwater County Building
113 7th Street NE, Box B
Bagley, MN 56621-9103
Phone: (218) 694-6151
Fax: (218) 694-3875
e-mail: clearwater@extension.umn.edu

Cook County
Community Center Building
P.O. Box 1150
317 West 5th
Grand Marais, MN 55604-1150
Phone: (218) 387-3015
Fax: (218) 387-3016
e-mail: cook@extension.umn.edu

Cottonwood County
235 9th Street
Windom, MN 56101-1642
Phone: (507) 831-4022
Fax: (507) 831-4024
e-mail: cottonwood@extension.umn.edu

Crow Wing County
Courthouse, 326 Laurel Street
Brainerd, MN 56401-3578
Phone: (218) 824-1065
Fax: (218) 824-1066
e-mail: crowwing@extension.umn.edu

Dakota County Extension and Conservation
    Center
4100 220th Street West, Suite 101
Farmington, MN 55024-9539
Phone: (651) 480-7700
Fax: (651) 463-8002

Dodge County
42 East Main Street, P.O. Box 159
Dodge Center, MN 55927-0159
Phone: (507) 374-6435
Fax: (507) 374-2954
e-mail: dodge@extension.umn.edu

Douglas County
720 Filmore, Suite B090
Alexandria, MN 56308-1763
Phone: (320) 762-3890
Fax: (320) 762-3871
e-mail: douglas@extension.umn.edu

Fillmore County
902 Houston Street NW #3
Preston, MN 55965-1080
Phone: (507) 765-3896
Fax: (507) 765-4512
e-mail: fillmore@extension.umn.edu

Freeborn County
Courthouse Room 222, 411 South Broadway
Albert Lea, MN 56007-1147
Phone: (507) 377-5660
Fax: (507) 377-5272
e-mail: freeborn@extension.umn.edu

Goodhue County
Government Center Room 105
509 5th Street
West Red Wing, MN 55066
Phone: 651-385-3100 or 800-385-3101
Fax: 651-385-3089
e-mail: goodhue@extension.umn.edu

Grant County
411 First Street SE, P.O. Box 1099
Elbow Lake, MN 56531-1099
Phone: (218) 685-4820
Fax: (218) 685-4817
e-mail: grant@extension.umn.edu

Hennepin County
1525 Glenwood Avenue
Minneapolis, MN 55405-1264
Phone: (612) 374-8400
Fax: (612) 374-8417
e-mail: hennepin@extension.umn.edu

Houston County
620 North Highway 44/76, P.O. Box 228
Caledonia, MN 55921-0228
Phone: (507) 725-5807
Fax: (507) 724-2832
e-mail: houston@extension.umn.edu

Hubbard County
201 Fair Avenue
Park Rapids, MN 56470-1483
Phone: (218) 732-3391
Fax: (218) 732-8173
e-mail: hubbard@extension.umn.edu

Isanti County
555 18th Avenue SW
Cambridge, MN 55008-9386
Phone: (763) 689-1810 or (800) 621-7973
Fax: (763) 689-8257
e-mail: isanti@extension.umn.edu

Itasca County
1861 Highway 169 E
Grand Rapids, MN 55744-3396
Phone: (218) 327-4177
Fax: (218) 327-4219
e-mail: itasca@extension.umn.edu

Jackson County
419 Main St, P.O. Box 309
Lakefield, MN 56150-0309
Phone: (507) 662-5293
Fax: (507) 662-5016
e-mail: jackson@extension.umn.edu

Kanabec County
905 East Forest Avenue #140
Mora, MN 55051-1617
Phone: (320) 679-6340
Fax: (320) 679-6344
e-mail: kanabec@extension.umn.edu

Kandiyohi County
Health\Human Services Building
2200 23rd Street NE #2090
Willmar, MN 56201-9423
Phone: (320) 231-7890
Fax: (320) 231-6535
e-mail: kandiyohi@extension.umn.edu

Kittson County
Courthouse
410 South 5th Street, P.O. Box 369
Hallock, MN 56728-0369
Phone: (218) 843-3674
Fax: (218) 843-2580
e-mail: kittson@extension.umn.edu

Koochiching County
Courthouse Complex, 718 5th Street
Intl Falls, MN 56649-2486
Phone: (218) 283-1182
Fax: (218) 283-1183
e-mail: koochiching@extension.umn.edu

Lac Qui Parle County
Courthouse, 600 6th Street
Madison, MN 56256-1295
Phone: (320) 598-3325
Fax: (320) 598-3305
e-mail: lacquiparle@extension.umn.edu

Lake County
Courthouse, 601 3rd Avenue
Two Harbors, MN 55616-1517
Phone: (218) 834-8377
Fax: (218) 834-8365
e-mail: lake@extension.umn.edu

Lake of the Woods County Extension
Courthouse
206 SE Eighth Avenue, P.O. Box 598
Baudette, MN 56623-0598
Phone: (218)634-1511 or (800) 493-1511
Fax: (218)634-2509

Le Sueur County
88 South Park
LeCenter, MN 56057-1620
Phone: (507) 357-2251 or (800) 445-7543
Fax: (507) 357-6375
e-mail: lesueur@extension.umn.edu

Lincoln County
402 North Harold, P.O. Box 130
Ivanhoe, MN 56142-0130
Phone: (507) 694-1470
Fax: (507) 694-1290
e-mail: lincoln@extension.umn.edu

Lyon County
Courthousem 607 West Main
Marshall, MN 56258-3099
Phone: (507) 537-6702
Fax: (507) 537-6576
e-mail: lyon@extension.umn.edu

Mahnomen County
Courthouse, 311 Main , P.O. Box 477
Mahnomen, MN 56557-0477
Phone: (218) 935-2226
Fax: (218) 935-5412
e-mail: mahnomen@extension.umn.edu

Marshall County
Courthouse, 208 East Colvin Avenue
Warren, MN 56762-1698
Phone: (218) 745-5232
Fax: (218) 745-8801
e-mail: marshall@extension.umn.edu

Martin County
104 Courthouse, 201 Lake Avenue
Fairmont, MN 56031-1845
Phone: (507) 235-3341
Fax: (507) 235-5772
e-mail: martin@extension.umn.edu

McLeod County
840 Century Avenue, Suite B
Hutchinson, MN 55350-3754
Phone: (320) 587-0770 or (800) 587-0770
Fax: (320) 234-4310
e-mail: mcleod@extension.umn.edu

Meeker County
Family Services Center
114 North Holcombe Avenue #260
Litchfield, MN 55355-2274
Phone: (320) 693-5275
Fax: (320) 693-5289
e-mail: meeker@extension.umn.edu

Mille Lacs County
620 Central Avenue North
Milaca, MN 56353-1788
Phone: (320) 983-8317 or (888) 680-8317
Fax: (320) 983-8367
e-mail: millelacs@extension.umn.edu

Morrison County
Government Center, 213 First Avenue SE
Little Falls, MN 56345-3100
Phone: (320) 632-0161
Fax: (320) 632-0166
e-mail: morrison@extension.umn.edu

Mower County
Courthouse, 201 NE 1st Street
Austin, MN 55912-3475
Phone: (507) 437-9552
Fax: (507) 437-9471
e-mail: mower@extension.umn.edu

Murray County
2848 Broadway Avenue, P.O. Box 57
Slayton, MN 56172-0057
Phone: (507) 836-6927
Fax: (507) 836-6019
e-mail: murray@extension.umn.edu

Nicollet County
Courthouse
501 South Minnesota Avenue
St. Peter, MN 56082-2533
Phone: (507) 931-6800
Fax: (507) 931-9220
e-mail: nicollet@extension.umn.edu

Norman County
101 West Third Avenue
Ada, MN 56510-1200
Phone: (218) 784-7183
Fax: (218) 784-2473
e-mail: norman@extension.umn.edu

Olmsted County
1421 SE 3rd Avenue
Rochester, MN 55904-7947
Phone: (507) 285-8250
Fax: (507) 285-8401
e-mail: olmsted@extension.umn.edu

Otter Tail, East County
118 North Main, P.O. Box 250
New York Mills, MN 56567-0250
Phone: (218) 385-3000
Fax: (218) 385-3001
e-mail: eottertail@extension.umn.edu

Pennington County
Courthouse, P.O. Box 616
Thief River Falls, MN 56701-0616
Phone: (218) 683-7030
Fax: (218) 683-7033
e-mail: pennington@extension.umn.edu

Pine County
105 Fire Monument Road, P.O. Box 370
Hinckley, MN 55037-0370
Phone: (320) 384-6156 or (800) 657-3813
Fax: (320) 384-7299
e-mail: pine@extension.umn.edu

Pipestone County
Municipal Building
119 SW 2nd Avenue Suite 2
Pipestone, MN 56164-1684
Phone: (507) 825-6715
Fax: (507) 825-6719
e-mail: pipestone@extension.umn.edu

Polk, East County
Municipal Building
P.O. Box 69
McIntosh, MN 56556-0069
Phone: (218) 563-2465
Fax: (218) 563-4750
e-mail: epolk@extension.umn.edu

Polk, West County
University Teaching & Outreach Center
P.O. Box 556
Crookston, MN 56716-0556
Phone: (218) 281-8696
Fax: (218) 281-8694
e-mail: wpolk@extension.umn.edu

Pope County
Courthouse
130 Minnesota Avenue East
Glenwood, MN 56334-1628
Phone: (320) 634-5735
Fax: (320) 634-5736
e-mail: pope@extension.umn.edu

Ramsey County
Historic Ramsey County Barn
2020 White Bear Avenue
Saint Paul, MN 55109
Phone: (651) 704-2080
Fax: (651) 704-2081

Red Lake County
Courthouse, P.O. Box 279
Red Lake Falls, MN 56750-0279
Phone: (218) 253-2895
Fax: (218) 253-2656
e-mail: redlake@extension.umn.edu

Redwood County
Courthouse, P.O. Box 130
Redwood Falls, MN 56283-0130
Phone: (507) 637-4025 or (800) 310-8323
Fax: (507) 637-4017
e-mail: redwood@extension.umn.edu

Renville County
Renville County Office Building
410 East DePue Avenue, Room 320
Olivia, MN 56277-1483
Phone: (320) 523-3713 or (800) 450-2522
Fax: (320) 523-3755
e-mail: renville@extension.umn.edu

Rice County
Government Services Building
320 NW Third Street, Suite 7
Faribault, MN 55021-6143
Phone: (507) 332-6109
Fax: (507) 332-5999
e-mail: rice@extension.umn.edu

Rock County
311 West Gabrielson #2
P.O. Box 898
Luverne, MN 56156-0898
Phone: (507) 283-8685
Fax: (507) 283-5006
e-mail: rock@extension.umn.edu

Roseau County
606 5th Avenue SW, Room 130
Roseau, MN 56751-1477
Phone: (218) 463-1052
Fax: (218) 463-3252
e-mail: roseau@extension.umn.edu

Scott County
7151 190th Street West
Suite 100
Jordan, MN 55352-2104
Phone: (952) 492-5410
Fax: (952) 492-5405
e-mail: scott@extension.umn.edu

Sherburne County
Sherburne County Government Center
13880 Highway 10
Elk River, MN 55330-4601
Phone: (763) 241-2720 or (800) 433-5236
Fax: (763) 241-2727
e-mail: sherburne@extension.umn.edu

Sibley County
Courthouse
P.O. Box 207
Gaylord, MN 55334-0207
Phone: (507) 237-4100
Fax: (507) 237-4099
e-mail: sibley@extension.umn.edu

Stearns County
Midtown Office Buildings
3400 First Street North, Suite 400
Saint Cloud, MN 56303-4000
Phone: (320) 255-6169
Fax: (320) 255-6167
e-mail: stearns@extension.umn.edu

Steele County
635 Florence Avenue
P.O. Box 890
Owatonna, MN 55060-0890
Phone: (507) 444-7685
Fax: (507) 444-7682
e-mail: steele@extension.umn.edu

Stevens County
Colonial Square
208 Atlantic Avenue
Morris, MN 56267-1321
Phone: (320) 589-7423
Fax: (320) 589-7440
e-mail: stevens@extension.umn.edu

Swift County
Courthouse
301 14th Street North
P.O. Box 305
Benson, MN 56215-0305
Phone: (320) 843-3796
Fax: (320) 843-4850
e-mail: swift@extension.umn.edu

Todd County
Courthouse Annex, 119 3rd Street South
Long Prairie, MN 56347-1354
Phone: (320) 732-4435
Fax: (320) 732-6233
e-mail: todd@extension.umn.edu

Traverse County
Courthouse
702 2nd Avenue North , P.O. Box 457
Wheaton, MN 56296-0457
Phone: (320) 563-4515
Fax: (320) 563-4424
e-mail: traverse@extension.umn.edu

Wabasha County
611 Broadway Avenue #40
Wabasha, MN 55981-1613
Phone: (651) 565-2662
Fax: (651) 565-2664
e-mail: wabasha@extension.umn.edu

Wadena County
Courthouse, 415 South Jefferson Street
Wadena, MN 56482-1594
Phone: (218) 631-7623
Fax: (218) 631-7625
e-mail: wadena@extension.umn.edu

Waseca County
300 North State Street, Suite #1
Waseca, MN 56093-2933
Phone: 507-835-0600

Washington County
Suite 202, 1825 Curve Crest Boulevard
Stillwater, MN 55082-6054
Phone: (651) 430-6800
Fax: (651) 430-6801
e-mail: washington@extension.umn.edu

Watonwan County
Courthouse, P.O. Box 68
St. James, MN 56081-0068
Phone: (507) 375-1275 or (800) 204-1295
Fax: (507) 375-1260
e-mail: watonwan@extension.umn.edu

Wilkin County
P.O. Box 199
Breckenridge, MN 56520-0199
Phone: (218) 643-5481
Fax: (218) 643-1434
e-mail: wilkin@extension.umn.edu

Winona County
202 West 3rd Street
Winona, MN 55987-3115
Phone: (507) 457-6440
Fax: (507) 454-9362
e-mail: winona@extension.umn.edu

Wright County
Room 130, 10 2nd Street NW
Buffalo, MN 55313-1186
Phone: (763) 682-7394 or (800) 362-3667
Fax: (763) 682-6178
e-mail: wright@extension.umn.edu

Yellow Medicine County
1004 10th Avenue, P.O. Box 128
Clarkfield, MN 56223-0128
Phone: (320) 669-4471
Fax: (320) 669-7525
e-mail: yellowmedicine@extension.umn.edu

Yard and Garden Line

Call the Yard and Garden Line for directions on sending soil samples to the University of Minnesota's Soil Testing Laboratory.
Phone: (612) 624-4771 (Metro) or toll-free: 1-888-624-4771 (Greater Minnesota)

Plant Disease Diagnostics

University of Minnesota Extension On-line Publications and Information
http://www.extension.umn.edu

Utility Locating Service

Gopher State One Call is a FREE utility locating service. They will mark the location of any underground utilities in the planting area. Give them three working days to complete the task. This is important for your safety and pocket book. Digging into a utility line can be expensive and even deadly. Allow at least three working days before planting.
Phone: 1-800-252-1166 throughout Minnesota

Department of Natural Resources Urban and Community Forestry Program

The Minnesota Department of Natural Resources has helped communities build and care for their urban trees. They can provide tree care information to you and your community. Contact your regional office for more information.

DNR Information Center
500 Lafayette Road
St. Paul, MN 55155-4040
Phone: 651-296-6157

Metro Region Forestry Headquarters
DNR Urban Forestry
1200 Warner Road, St. Paul, MN 55106
Phone: (651) 772-7925

Bemidji Region Forestry Headquarters
DNR Urban Forestry
6603 Bemidji Avenue North, Bemidji, MN 56601-8669
Phone: (218) 755-2891

Brainerd Region Forestry Headquarters
DNR Urban Forestry
1601 Minnesota Drive, Suite 2
Brainerd, MN 56401-3971
Phone: (218) 828-2616

Grand Rapids Region Forestry Headquarters
DNR Urban Forestry
1201 East Highway 2
Grand Rapids, MN 55744-3296
Phone: (218) 327- 4418

Rochester Region Forestry Headquarters
DNR Urban Forestry
2300 Silver Creek Road
Northeast, Rochester, MN 55906
Phone: (507) 285-7428

Minnesota Garden Clubs and Plant Societies

The Minnesota State Horticultural Society is the place to go for information on Minnesota chapters of national plant societies and garden clubs. For those with access to the Internet, you may want to start at:
www.northerngardener.org

Garden clubs and plant societies are a great way to learn more about gardening and plants. Members trade knowledge, resources, and often plants. In many cases you will need to contact the national organization to find the club nearest you. For those with access to the Internet, you may want to start at:
www.globalgardens.com/gg/ societies-1.html

Institutions Offering Horticulture Programs

Anoka-Hennepin Technical College
Phone: (763) 427-1880

Central Lakes Community College
Phone: (218) 828-2525

Dakota County Technical College
Phone: (651) 423-8301

Hennepin Technical College
Phone: (763) 550-2115

North Dakota State University
Phone: (701) 237-8162

Rochester Community & Technical College
Phone: (507) 285-7219

South Dakota State University
Phone: (605) 688-5136

Southeast Technical Institute
Phone: (605) 367-7826

University of Minnesota at St. Paul
Phone: (612) 624-4242

University of Minnesota at Crookston
Phone: (218) 281-6510

University of Wisconsin at River Falls
Phone: (715) 425-3911

Helpful Hints

Fruits

Keep your Strawberry ***patch healthy and productive. Renovate matted row plantings right after harvest.***

- Start by removing weeds between the plants and rows. Pull or cultivate them with a hoe. This opens up space for the new runners to root and grow.
- Cut the foliage off diseased plants. Use your lawn mower. Set the mowing height low enough to cut off the leaves, but high enough to avoid injuring the crown (area where stems and leaves meet).
- Maintain aisles by removing plants that have spread into this area. Use a tiller or hoe to remove these plants. Work any summer or leftover winter mulch into the soil. Maintain planting rows 12 to 15 inches wide for maximum production.
- Add 6 pounds of a 10 percent nitrogen, 3 pounds (about 6 cups) of ammonium sulfate (21-0-0), or 2 pounds (about 4 cups) of ammonium nitrate (33-0-0) per 100 feet of row.
- Continue watering even after harvest. Make sure plants receive 1 inch of water each week. Supplement rainfall as needed.
- Fertilize again in mid-August to encourage flower bud formation. Use 3 pounds of a 10 percent nitrogen fertilizer, 1½ pounds of ammonium sulfate, or 1 pound of ammonium nitrate per 100 feet of row.
- Renovate **Everbearing** and **Day-neutral Strawberries** growing in the Hill System after the first harvest. Pull or cultivate weeds between plants. Remove the runners as soon as they form to increase fruit productivity. Replace plants every other year. Fertilize and water throughout the season.

Vines and Groundcovers

Any plant that sounds too good to be true probably is. **Crown Vetch** is one of those. The tough groundcover with the pretty, pinkish-lavender flowers that used to cover hillsides along the freeways has found its way into home landscapes and natural areas. It is taking over these areas and causing problems for gardeners, naturalists, and our environment. ***Control the spread of the invasive*** Crown Vetch ***with persistence.***

- Use a spade to create an edge around small plantings of **Crown Vetch**. Cover with black plastic for one season. The plastic blocks the sunlight robbing the plant of essential energy.
- Or mow plants in June and late August as they leaf out. Repeat for several years until you have effectively weakened and killed the plants.
- As a last resort, try chemical control. Treat plants with a total vegetation killer. Spot treat plants to avoid damaging nearby desirable plants. Apply in early spring, again in fall, and possibly once more the following spring.
- Herbicides containing Triclopyr, such as Weed-B-Gone® for difficult weeds, will not harm nearby grass. Treat **Crown Vetch** in early spring and fall as needed. Always read and follow label directions carefully when using this or any chemical.

Helpful Hints

Fruits

All your hard work and now you have beautiful plants, but no fruit! Sometimes it is the weather; other times it is the way we manage the plants.

- Take a look at the weather over the past year. Cold winter temperatures can damage flower buds on **Strawberries**. Make sure to apply a winter mulch to Strawberries if you do not have reliable snow cover throughout the winter.
- Late spring frosts often kill the early blossoms on **Peaches, Plums,** and other stone fruits. Cold temperatures can kill the swelling bud or flower. No flowers mean no fruit. Make sure future plantings are in areas that tend to be protected from late spring and early fall frosts. Look for higher spots and those facing southeast.
- Wet spring weather can interfere with bee activities. Bees are essential for transferring pollen from one plant to another. Without this pollen transfer, many plants will not develop fruit.

Now take a look at your management practices.

- Overgrown or overcrowded plantings can result in little or no fruit production. Thin overgrown fruit trees, **Raspberries,** and **Strawberries**.
- Remove weeds that compete with the plants for water and nutrients. Pull or cultivate weeds before they have a chance to produce seed and future offspring. Mulch to reduce weeds and conserve moisture.
- Avoid over-fertilizing fruit plants. Excess nitrogen can prevent flowering and fruiting. Take a soil test to determine how much and what type of fertilizer you need to use.
- Improper watering also interferes with fruit production. Drought stressed plants often fail to set flower buds for next year's harvest. Over-watering can lead to root rot and moisture stress. This, too, can prevent flower and fruit formation.

Shrubs

Tired of shearing your shrubs? Undo years of shearing and improve the plant's health over the next few seasons. The goal is to remove the tufts of green at the end of the branches, open up the center of the plant, and regain the plant's natural form.

- Start by removing the thickest cluster of twigs back to a side branch in the spring. Thin shoots and trim stubs that were left behind.
- Wait until the following spring for the next phase of pruning. Continue to cut out dense clusters of old growth back to side branches.
- Continue thinning and opening the shrub. You should start to see it regain its natural appearance.

Herbs and Vegetables

Use late additions to fill in empty spaces or replant rows that have already been harvested. Allow enough time for plants to grow and produce before the first killing frost. Check the back of the seed packet or the "Planting Chart" in the chapter introduction for average days to harvest. Then count the frost-free days left in the season. Compare the two and decide if you have time to grow and harvest this crop. Allow at least two weeks for harvest. Keep in mind that some plants, such as **Broccoli** and **Cabbage**, can tolerate a light frost. In fact, their flavor improves with the cooler temperatures of fall. Use this chart for quick reference.

Late Planting Chart

Vegetable	Days to First Harvest	Last Date to Plant with These Frost Dates 9/15	10/1
From Seeds			
Beets	50–60	7/15	8/1
Beans, Bush	50–60	7/15	8/1
Carrot	60–70	7/1	7/15
Chard	40–50	8/1	8/15
Chinese Cabbage	60–70	7/1	7/15
Cucumber	50–60	7/15	8/1
Kohlrabi	50–60	7/15	8/1
Leaf Lettuce	40–50	8/1	8/15
Mustard Greens	40–50	8/1	8/15
Peas	60–70	7/1	7/15
Radish	25–30	8/15	9/1
Spinach	40–50	8/1	8/15
Sweet Corn	65–70	7/1	7/15
Turnips	60–70	7/1	7/15
From Transplants			
Broccoli	60–70	7/1	7/15
Cabbage	60–70	7/1	7/15
Cauliflower	50–60	7/15	8/1
Chinese Cabbage	50–60	7/15	8/1
Collards	50–60	7/15	8/1
Kale	50–60	7/15	8/1
Kohlrabi	40–50	8/1	8/15
Onion Sets	40–50	8/1	8/15
Onion Plants	50–60	7/15	8/1

Helpful Hints

Herbs and Vegetables

Enjoy your herbs all season long by drying, freezing, and preserving them for later use. Gather herbs in the morning after the dew has dried. Discard any damaged or diseased leaves and stems. ***Choose an herb preservation method that best works for you.***

- ***Try gathering the short stems in small bundles.*** Secure with a rubber band and hang upside down in a warm, dark, and airy location. Use a spring-type clothespin to attach the bundle to a drying.
- ***Spread herbs on a cookie sheet and place in an oven on its lowest setting.*** Prop the door open to increase the air circulation. Stir occasionally. Remove when the leaves are thoroughly dried. They will crumble when pinched and rubbed.

Clip or Clothespin

Rope or Twine

Drying Herbs and Flowers

Rubber band

- ***Use your microwave to speed things up.*** Spread a cup of herbs on a single layer of paper towel in the microwave. Set on high for about 3 minutes. Experiment to find the best time for your machine. Heat an additional 20 seconds if the herbs are not yet dry. Stop the process when the herbs feel brittle and the leaves easily pull off the stem.
- ***Try freezing herbs.*** Spread the herbs on a cookie sheet in the freezer for several hours. Once frozen, place them in freezer bags and containers for later use. Blanch (pour boiling water over) **Basil** prior to freezing. Most other herbs do not need to be blanched to maintain flavor and quality.

Trees

Celebrate Arbor Day

The last Friday in April is Arbor Day. It is a good day to celebrate with family, friends, and your favorite tree.

- Plant trees in your yard, nearby school, or park (check with the property owner first).
- Take a walk or hike to find the oldest or largest tree in the neighborhood or nearby park.
- Perform mulching, weeding, or other needed maintenance of existing trees (always talk to the property owners first).
- Plan activities with school children and youth groups for an Arbor Day program filled with plays, songs, and performances related to trees, tree planting, and care.
- Enjoy a family picnic under your favorite tree.

Helpful Hints

Houseplants

If your **Dieffenbachia** has reached the ceiling or your **Rubber Plant** is nothing but bare stems with a cluster of leaves at the top, try air-layering. This low-risk propagation technique is a great way to start new plants and reduce the size of the parent plant. *To air-layer:*

Figure 1

Figure 2

1. Select a healthy stem. *Make* a slanting cut several inches below the leaf cluster. The cut should be 1 to 2 inches long, cutting halfway through the stem (see Figure 1).

2. *Wedge* the cut open with a wooden toothpick. Apply a rooting hormone over the cut surface (see Figure 2).

3. *Wrap* a plastic bag around the stem. Secure it at the bottom with a twist tie, string, or masking tape (see Figure 3).

Figure 3

Figure 4

4. *Moisten* a handful or sphagnum moss. Squeeze out the excess water and pack the moss around the cut and inside the plastic bag (see Figure 4).

5. *Secure* the bag above the cut with a twist tie, string, or masking tape. Add water if you see the moss is beginning to dry.

Figure 5

Figure 6

6. Finish the process as soon roots appear through the moss. *Cut* the stem beneath the plastic. Remove the wrap and *plant* in a suitable potting mix (see Figures 5 and 6).

7. *Cut back* the stem on the parent plant to the desired height. It will sprout new leaves and start growing.

Helpful Hints

Perennials

Tired of watering? Try mulching the garden and growing drought-tolerant perennials. Consider the sun-loving **Ornamental Grasses** or some of the perennials from the following list in the drier areas of your landscape. *These perennials will tolerate dry soils once established.*

Artemisia	*Artemisia*	Poppy Mallow	*Callirhoe involucrate*
Black-Eyed Susan	*Rudbeckia*	Potentilla	*Potentilla*
Blanket Flower	*Gaillardia × grandiflora*	Prickly Pear Cactus	*Opuntia humifusa*
		Purple Coneflower	*Echinaceae purpurea*
Boltonia	*Boltonia asteroids*	Rockcress	*Arabis caucasica*
Butterfly Weed	*Asclepias tuberosa*	Russian Sage	*Perovskia atriplicifolia*
Cushion Spurge	*Euphorbia polychroma*	Sea Lavender	*Limonium*
		Sea Thrift	*Armeria maritime*
Daylily	*Hemerocallis*	Sea Holly	*Eryngium*
Dropwort Meadowsweet	*Filipendula vulgaris*	Sedum	*Sedum*
Evening Primrose	*Oenothera*	Snow-in-Summer	*Cerastium tomentosum*
Gayfeather	*Liatris*		
Globe Thistle	*Echinops ritro*	Threadleaf Coreopsis	*Coreopsis verticillata*
Goldenrod	*Solidago*	Thyme	*Thymus*
Lamb's Ear	*Stachys byzantina*	Yarrow	*Achillea*
Moss/Creeping Phlox	*Phlox subulata*	Yucca	*Yucca*

Tired of deadheading? *Include* Ornamental Grasses *and some of the perennial plants from the following list. These either do not require deadheading or have a long season of bloom even without deadheading.* You may still want to clip off faded flowers of some of these for aesthetics or allow the seedpods to develop for added interest.

Astilbe	*Astilbe*	Joe-pye Weed	*Eupatorium fistulosum*, 'Gateway'
Bugbane	*Cimicifuga*		
Butterfly Bush	*Buddleja davidii*	Oriental Poppy	*Papaver orientale*
Corydalis	*Corydalis lutea*	Peony	*Paeonia*
Cranesbill Geranium	*Geranium sanguineum*	Perennial Verbena	*Verbena canadensis*
		Siberian Iris	*Iris siberica*
Fringed Bleeding Heart	*Dicentra eximia*	Threadleaf Coreopsis	*Coreopsis verticillata*
Goat's Beard	*Aruncus dioicus*		
Heliopsis	*Heliopsis helianthoides*, 'Summer Sun'		

Helpful Hints

Herbs and Vegetables

Do not throw away those leftover seeds. Leave them in their original packet and store them safely for next season. Place the packets (or a labeled envelope) in an airtight jar in the refrigerator. Keeping seeds at a consistent, cool temperature increases their longevity. You can expect seeds to last from one to five or more years.

Or use old seeds to make crafts with the kids. Seed art is a traditional craft and a fun activity for children. Create pictures, make ornaments, or decorate bland items with colorful seeds. Use a clear, drying glue or hot glue (watch those little fingers) for this project. Do NOT use seeds treated with fungicides.

Seed Longevity	Seeds
1 year	**Onions, Parsley, Parsnips,** and **Salsify**
2 years	**Corn, Okra,** and **Pepper**
3 years	**Beans** and **Peas**
4 years	**Beets, Fennel, Rutabagas, Squash, Chard, Tomatoes, Turnips,** and **Watermelon**
5 years	**Brussels Sprouts, Cabbage, Cauliflower, Eggplant, Muskmelon, Radishes,** and **Spinach**

Seeds You Save	
Self-pollinating	**Beans, Peas,** and **Tomatoes**
Insect-pollinated	**Cucumber, Melon, Squash,** and **Pumpkins**
Wind	**Beets, Sweet Corn, Spinach,** and **Chard** hybrid

Roses

Here are some tips for enjoying your roses throughout the winter:

- Harvest rose hips and include them in holiday and winter arrangements. The colorful fruit looks good mixed with fresh evergreens or dried materials. This is a great way to enjoy your roses all winter long.
- Enlarge and frame pictures of your favorite garden roses. These make great gifts and greeting cards as well.
- Remove one of the rose buds you stored in sand last October (see October "Pruning"). Place it in a vase of hot water and watch the bud expand.
- Purchase one of the small tabletop roses that are often found at garden centers and floral shops.
- Help a friend plan a rose garden.

Minnesota Annual Precipitation in Inches

Total Precipitation in Inches

January 1 to December 31

Averaged from 1961 to 1990

under 25   25   30   35   40

Minnesota Average First Frost

Kittson · Roseau · Lake of the Woods · Koochiching · Cook · Marshall · Pennington · Red Lake · Beltrami · Itasca · Lake · Polk · Clearwater · St. Louis · Norman · Mahnomen · Hubbard · Cass · Clay · Becker · Wilkin · Wadena · Crow Wing · Aitkin · Carlton · Otter Tail · Todd · Morrison · Pine · Traverse · Grant · Douglas · Mille Lacs · Kanabec · Stevens · Pope · Stearns · Benton · Big Stone · Swift · Sherburne · Isanti · Chisago · Kandiyohi · Meeker · Wright · Anoka · Lac qui Parle · Chippewa · McLeod · Hennepin · Washington · Yellow Medicine · Renville · Carver · Ramsey · Lincoln · Lyon · Redwood · Sibley · Scott · Dakota · Nicollet · Le Sueur · Rice · Goodhue · Brown · Wabasha · Pipestone · Murray · Cottonwood · Watonwan · Blue Earth · Waseca · Steele · Dodge · Olmsted · Winona · Rock · Nobles · Jackson · Martin · Faribault · Freeborn · Mower · Fillmore · Houston

Median Dates

Aug. 27 – 31	Sep. 21 – 25
Sep. 1 – 5	Sep. 26 – 30
Sep. 6 – 10	Oct. 1 – 5
Sep. 11 – 15	Oct. 6 – 10
Sep. 16 – 20	Oct. 11 – 15

Minnesota Average Last Frost

Kittson, Roseau, Lake of the Woods, Marshall, Pennington, Red Lake, Beltrami, Koochiching, Itasca, Cook, Polk, Clearwater, Lake, St. Louis, Norman, Mahnomen, Hubbard, Clay, Becker, Cass, Wilkin, Wadena, Crow Wing, Aitkin, Carlton, Otter Tail, Todd, Morrison, Pine, Traverse, Grant, Douglas, Mille Lacs, Kanabec, Stevens, Pope, Stearns, Benton, Isanti, Chisago, Big Stone, Swift, Sherburne, Anoka, Washington, Ramsey, Chippewa, Kandiyohi, Meeker, Wright, Hennepin, Lac qui Parle, Yellow Medicine, Renville, McLeod, Carver, Scott, Dakota, Lincoln, Lyon, Redwood, Sibley, Nicollet, Le Sueur, Rice, Goodhue, Wabasha, Brown, Pipestone, Murray, Cottonwood, Watonwan, Blue Earth, Waseca, Steele, Dodge, Olmsted, Winona, Rock, Nobles, Jackson, Martin, Faribault, Freeborn, Mower, Fillmore, Houston

Median Dates

- Jun. 11 - 7
- Jun. 6 - 2
- Jun. 1 - May 28
- May 27 - 23
- May 22 - 18

Median Dates

- May 17 - 13
- May 12 - 8
- May 7 - 3
- May 6 - 2

Bibliography

American Horticultural Society, The, Christopher Brickell and Judith Zuk, ed. *A-Z Encyclopedia of Garden Plants.* New York, NY: DK Publishing, Inc., 1997.

American Horticultural Society, The, Christopher Brickell and David Joyce. *Pruning and Training.* New York, NY: DK Publishing, Inc., 1996.

Dirr, Michael. *Manual of Woody Landscape Plants.* 4th edition. Urbana, IL: Stipes Publishing, 1990.

DiSabato-Aust, Tracy. *The Well-Tended Perennial Garden:Planting and Pruning Techniques.* Portland, OR: Timber Press, 1998.

Fizzell, James. *Month-By-Month Gardening in Illinois.* Franklin, TN: Cool Springs Press, 1999.

Harris, Richard, et al. *Arboriculture: Integrated Management of Landscape Trees, Shrubs and Vines.* Upper Saddles River, NJ: Prentice Hall, 1999.

Johnson, Warren T. and Howard H. Lyon. *Diseases of Trees and Shrubs.* Ithaca, NY: Cornell University Press, 1987.

Johnson, Warren T. and Howard H. Lyon. *Insects that Feed on Trees and Shrubs.* Ithaca, NY: Cornell University Press, 1991.

Morrow, Baker H. *A Dictionary of Landscape Architecture.* Albuquerque, NM: University of New Mexico Press, 1987.

Ortho® Books. *Ortho's All About Annuals.* San Francisco, CA: Chevron Chemical Company, 1981.

Ortho® Books. *Ortho's All About Roses.* San Francisco, CA: Chevron Chemical Company, 1983.

Polomski, Bob. *Month-By-Month Gardening in the Carolinas.* Franklin, TN: Cool Springs Press, 2000.

Reilly, Ann. *Park's Success with Seeds.* Greenwood, SC: Geo. W. Park Seed Co., Inc., 1978.

Rodale's Illustrated Encyclopedia of Herbs. Emmaus, PA: Rodale Press, 1987.

Roses for the North. University of MN: Minnesota Agricultural Experiment Station, 1995.

Rose Gardening. Compiled by Jim Browne, William Radler, and Nelson Sterner. New York, NY: Pantheon Books, 1995.

Schneider, Donald. *Park's Success with Bulbs.* Greenwood, SC: Geo. W. Park Seed Co., Inc., 1981.

Still, Steven M. *Manual of Herbaceous Plants.* 4th edition. Urbana, IL: Stipes Publishing, 1994.

University of Minnesota Extension Publications. Please call 1-800-876-8636 for a list of publications.

University of Wisconsin Extension Publications. Please call 1-877-947-7827 for a list of publications.

Voigt, TB, et al. *Ground Covers for the Midwest.* Champaign, IL: University of Illinois Printing Division, 1991.

Wyman, Donald. *Shrubs and Vines for American Gardens.* New York, NY: McMillan Publishing, 1969.

Wyman, Donald. *Wyman's Gardening Encyclopedia.* New York, NY: McMillan Publishing, 1977.

Index

Index

Index

Index

Index

Index

Melinda Myers

Melinda Myers, best known for her common-sense and practical approach to gardening, has over twenty years of horticultural experience in both hands-on and instructional settings. She is a Certified Arborist and Horticultural Instructor at Milwaukee Area Technical College, where she teaches students preparing to work in the field of landscape horticulture. Outside the classroom, Myers shares her expertise through a variety of media. She has hosted the "Plant Doctor Radio Show" on WTMJ since 1982. She hosted Wisconsin Lawn and Garden, a weekly show on PBS, from 1996 to 1999. She hosted "Yardworks," a nationally syndicated yard care and garden show, and has scripted and hosted various other cable gardening programs.

Myers is also an accomplished garden writer. She has written a bi-monthly column, "Gardeners' Questions," for the *Milwaukee Journal* since 1986, and has been a contributing editor and columnist for *Birds & Blooms Magazine,* a publication with 2 million subscribers throughout the United States and Canada, since 1996. Myers has written several books, including *The Garden Book for Wisconsin, My Wisconsin Garden: A Gardener's Journal, Month-By-Month Gardening in Wisconsin,* and *Minnesota Horticultural Society's Minnesota Gardener's Guide*.

Her thirteen years experience at the University of Wisconsin Extension service allowed her to work with backyard, community, and master gardeners throughout Wisconsin. As Milwaukee's Assistant City Forester, Myers helped manage the street tree, boulevards, and green spaces for the city. She has worked with the Young Adult Conservation Corps supervising crews that maintain University of Wisconsin urban test gardens and provide trail repair and other conservation work. Myers has been a member of the Wisconsin Arborist Association since 1979, has chaired the Arbor Day Committee Chair since 1987, and is a past president. Since 1985 she has been a member of the International Society of Arboriculture, and serves as the Arbor Day Committee Liaison to Wisconsin. Currently she heads her local committee for the "Harvest for the Hungry" program, a part of the GWAA Plant-A-Row for the Hungry initiative. A horticultural consultant to numerous community and beautification groups, Melinda began the Master Garden Program in Milwaukee County.

For her work and media presence Myers has received recognition and numerous awards including the 1998 Garden Communicator's Award from the American Nursery and Landscape Association and the 1998 Quill and Trowel Award from the Garden Writers Association of America.

Chuck Levine

Chuck Levine is a professional horticulturist and a teacher of horticulture and botany for the Minnesota State Horticultural Society, Intermediate School District #287, and Hennepin Technical College. Chuck's personal garden is an acre of urban paradise and has been featured in the *Minneapolis Star Tribune* and on several garden tours. He is a member of The Garden Writer's Association of America, the American Vocational Association, and the City of Roseville Community Arboretum Advisory Council. He serves on the Minnesota State Horticultural Society's Board of Directors and Executive Committee. Chuck has developed and implemented a curriculum on vocational plant production for the Hennepin County Corrections Facility in Plymouth, Minnesota. He has worked as a horticulture specialist for the Chicago Botanic Garden and the Minnesota Extension Service. Chuck has appeared as a garden expert on radio and television and has been published in the *Northern Gardener, Chicago Tribune, Garden Magazine,* and *Tropical Fish Hobbyist*.